CAMBRIDGE COLLEGE
GARDENS

Brimming with creative inspiration, how-to projects and useful information to enrich your everyday life, Quarto Knows is a favourite destination for those pursuing their interests and passions. Visit our site and dig deeper with our books into your area of interest: Quarto Creates, Quarto Cooks, Quarto Homes, Quarto Lives, Quarto Drives, Quarto Explores, Quarto Gifts, or Quarto Kids.

First published in 2019 by White Lion Publishing, an imprint of The Quarto Group.
The Old Brewery, 6 Blundell Street
London, N7 9BH,
United Kingdom
T (0)20 7700 6700
www.QuartoKnows.com

This page: A gnarled pine specimen in Cambridge Botanic Garden.
Page 4: Roses adorning one of the Tudor-Gothic windows in the screen (1828) along the frontage to King's College.

CAMBRIDGE COLLEGE
GARDENS

TIM RICHARDSON

PHOTOGRAPHS BY CLIVE BOURSNELL AND MARCUS HARPUR

WHITE
LION
PUBLISHING

CONTENTS

Introduction 7

Christ's College 19

Churchill College 31

Clare College 43

Corpus Christi College 57

Darwin College 65

Downing College 75

Emmanuel College 87

Fitzwilliam College 99

Girton College 107

Gonville & Caius College 121

Homerton College 129

Jesus College 139

King's College 151

Lucy Cavendish College 165

Magdalene College 169

Murray Edwards College 181

Newnham College 189

Pembroke College 197

Peterhouse 209

Queens' College 217

Robinson College 227

Selwyn College 233

Sidney Sussex College 241

St John's College 251

Trinity College 271

Trinity Hall 287

Wolfson College 303

The Gardeners 312

Index 316

Acknowledgements 320

INTRODUCTION

CAMBRIDGE IS RENOWNED INTERNATIONALLY AS a centre of learning, with a special historical bias towards the sciences and mathematics. But it is also the most beautiful university city in the world. ('Arguably', of course – because argue is what universities do.) That beauty derives largely from the visual appearance and palpable atmosphere of the 31 colleges which constitute the university today – a beauty arising from the architecture of their courts, chapels, halls and libraries, certainly, but also by dint of the various gardens and landscape settings in which they sit. The area of meadows and gardens 'behind' or to the west of the colleges on the River Cam is known as the Backs, and is perhaps the most outstanding aesthetic feature of the university, especially if one includes great buildings such as King's College Chapel in the scenographic whole. A walk along the Backs was eulogised by an American visitor, William Everett, writing in his *On the Cam* in 1865:

> There is nothing of the kind lovelier in England. The velvet turf, – the ancestral elms and hoary lindens, – the long vistas of the ancient avenues, – the quiet river, – its shelving banks filled with loiterers, its waters studded with a scene of gay boats, and crossed by light, graceful stone bridges; the old halls of grey or red or yellow rising here and there, – the windows peeping out from among the trees, and the openings into old court-yards, with their presage of monastic ease and learning, – the lofty pinnacles of King's Chapel o'ertopping all…

The beauty of the Backs as a landscape feature has been appreciated since the early 18th century, while the garden areas of the Cambridge colleges have perhaps received rather less notice. Yet as we shall see, gardens have been an extremely important element in the life of the university. Walking through the colleges, it rapidly becomes apparent that buildings and gardens are almost indivisible if one is open to appreciating the setting as a whole.

Since the medieval period the college gardens have incorporated spaces for leisure, food production and scholarly meditation, all in the safely cocooned atmosphere of a sociable community. And they still do – with kitchen gardens and allotment areas once again coming to the fore at a number of colleges, and prospective students citing the attractiveness of the gardens and grounds as a major reason for selecting a college. The lucrative out-of-term conference business, which currently keeps many of the colleges financially afloat, is another impetus for investment in the quality of the surroundings. And there is now a timely sense of environmental responsibility, including the conservation of plants, insects and animals, as well as the benefits to people's physical and mental well-being that a garden provides. Gone are the days when a college's front court might well have been a muddy quagmire surrounded by a gravel path, with thick forests of ivy festooning the crumbling walls. Today, every college in Cambridge presents a smart appearance to the world, and in several cases the garden teams are cherished and well-resourced.

Cambridge is haunted by the spectre of another university. It was founded just a few years earlier – but established itself with far more alacrity and remained dominant until the 16th century. As a result, Cambridge has developed a habit of comparing itself with Oxford. It is true that the colleges of both universities appear similar. But there are a number of salient differences in their layout and visual tone.

It is well attested that Cambridge University came into being because a group of scholars left Oxford in 1209 following a series of violent altercations with the townspeople, and the execution of two Oxford scholars. The story goes that a woman – possibly a prostitute – was shot and killed with an arrow by an Oxford scholar. Quite how and in what circumstances an Oxford student might shoot a prostitute with a bow and arrow is unclear (it is possible he stabbed her at close range, since arrows were sometimes used as hand-weapons). A vigilante band of townsmen hanged not the perpetrator but two (possibly three) of his fellow students, by way of revenge. This summary justice

outraged ecclesiastical law, since the students were de facto clerics and not subject to civil authorities. If the story is true – and it came largely from Roger of Wendover, who is not a particularly reliable source – it is not altogether surprising that a number of Oxford students wanted to leave the city at this point.

One group decamped to Paris, which had a greater scholarly reputation than Oxford at that time, while others went to Reading and Northampton, the latter already established as a centre of learning. (Most of those scholars returned to Oxford between five and ten years later when the pope had intervened and the troubles died down.)

Cambridge was not perhaps an obvious choice as an alternative safe haven for scholarly refugees. It had no existing culture of scholarship, bar a few 'grammarians' who offered a basic education to the wealthier sons of the town. It had long been a strategic staging-post, with its Norman castle on the site of an Iron Age fort, and also offered a riverine trading link with the Hanseatic port of King's Lynn to the north (it was the invading Danes who had established Cambridge as an 'inland port'). Several monastic orders had founded priories in the town, institutions which also undertook the training of young clergymen; the oldest, Barnwell Priory, was constructed north-east of the city in 1112, while the Benedictine nunnery which later became Jesus College was founded in 1133. But despite its situation as a 'gateway' to the east

of England and the Midlands, Cambridge had not grown into a large town, and its strategic importance had faded somewhat by the 13th century. Natural obstacles, including the thick forests of Essex, meant that there was no direct link by road with London. The river trade remained important right up until the mid 19th century, but essentially Cambridge was for many centuries a small market town – it did not even have a bank branch until 1780 – overtopped by a ruined castle.

It is now thought likely that Cambridge was chosen by this group of fleeing Oxford scholars chiefly because a number of them originally hailed from that part of the country. John Grim, a Cambridge man, had been the master of the 'schools' in the centre of Oxford (in the area where the Radcliffe Camera stands today), which was the most senior position in the university prior to the creation of the chancellorship in about 1214. It is believed that Grim led his colleagues to his home town, where – due to his local connections – they would have had a better chance of obtaining favourable rates for the rent of the townhouses used as hostels for students, which the masters rented and then sublet out to their charges. (The collegiate situation which prevails today is only a somewhat more developed version of this system.) Grim was not the

ABOVE The old Cambridge tradition of vine-growing is continued in Trinity Hall's Avery Court.

only man in this group to be associated with the east of England: his confederates in the migration included at least three masters known by town names of the eastern counties – one of them, for example, was Adam of Horningsea (a village in Cambridgeshire).

These self-exiled scholars initially settled around Great St Mary's Church in the very centre of Cambridge, which was, in terms of the urban plan of the town, the direct equivalent of the area in Oxford occupied by the schools which they had just vacated. When the troubles in Oxford had blown over, the scholars opted to stay on in Cambridge, where an organised system of education was gradually established during the 13th century. There were still no colleges in Cambridge at this early period (the first college, Peterhouse, would be founded in 1280); the several hundred students in the town were dispersed across it in small groups in the various hostels where they received their education and board and lodging (according to Thomas Fuller, historian of the early university, there were 34 hostels in Cambridge by 1280). Additionally, young monks who were lodged in the priories were also being educated at this time and must be accounted part of the university system. The Franciscans or grey friars came to Cambridge in 1226, then the Dominicans or black friars in the 1230s. The Carmelites and Augustinians also had a presence, as well as forgotten orders such as the Friars of the Sack on Trumpington Street. In most cases these priories were the precursors of future Cambridge colleges that were overlaid on the same sites, notably Jesus, Magdalene, Emmanuel and Sidney Sussex. Additionally St John's Hospital was established in the north of the city centre in 1135 for the healing of the sick; it was later used as the nucleus of St John's College and was also the place where the handful of scholars who later constituted Peterhouse were initially based. (The term 'college' refers to the scholars, not the buildings.)

The subjects taught in early Cambridge were theology, civil law and what we would now call liberal arts (chiefly classical literature), with medicine and specialisms such as grammar and rhetoric following a little later. But other subjects, notably those necessary to the management of the Church, such as ecclesiastical law, were also taught and studied. By 1377 there were between 400 and 700 young men, most of them aged 15 to 25, studying in Cambridge, of whom a third were friars in the priories (the monks tended to start younger, some arriving at the age of 12). All of the students in the colleges were in minor holy orders and destined to become priests, a status which pertained – in theory – until the mid 19th century.

ABOVE The lime avenue at Trinity College in autumn, with flanking cherry trees.

THE EARLY COLLEGE GARDENS

The early hostels of Cambridge were townhouses of various sizes which in some cases had plots of land attached that were used as gardens or orchards. The priories tended to have much larger estates, with stew ponds containing the freshwater fish which were essential for the table on Fridays and holy days. There are few references to the gardens of the hostels at this period, and early maps do not show a great deal of detail, but it appears that these gardens were essentially productive, with vegetable plots, fruit bushes and possibly orchard trees. They would also have been used for leisure purposes – as places for walking under trees and sitting, possibly on a covered seat or within a bower. The gradual encroachment of leisure activities into the garden – hitherto seen as a productive space – characterised the general trajectory of garden-making in the medieval period, and there is no reason to suppose the situation was any different in Cambridge.

As the colleges came into being in the 14th, 15th and 16th centuries, their gardens evolved in this manner. The enclosed or semi-enclosed courts, which are the first thing visitors see on entering a college, tended to be relatively unadorned, even into the mid 19th century. The centre of the court was often laid to grass by the mid 18th century, but before that date it was in some cases left as compacted mud or hoggin (sand mixed with gravel). Unlike at Oxford, trees were a common adornment, especially in first courts, with the walnut a favourite. These were usually planted singly, though they could be in pairs or even quartets (as at Gonville Hall, now part of Gonville and Caius College). There are still a few specimen trees in Cambridge courts – in Gisborne Court at Peterhouse and in New Court at Trinity, for example – but the tradition has generally subsided. A peculiarly 'Cambridge' horticultural custom still found in the courts of a number of colleges is the practice of training and tightly clipping shrubs and climbers up the walls like buttresses.

With regard to the gardens away from the courts, most colleges began with a kitchen garden, perhaps augmented by an orchard and in some cases a meadow or 'close', often later renamed a 'paddock'. Dovecotes, providing both eggs and pigeon meat, were a feature common to almost all colleges, and a couple even had a vineyard – not for the production of wine, but verjuice for cooking. There was usually an area delineated as the master's garden, and there would also be a fellows' garden (the fellows being the tutors), though there were many variations on this structure, with the master and fellows sharing a garden in some cases, while at certain colleges the fellows enjoyed two or even three separate garden areas. The younger scholars – whom we would now call undergraduates – were allowed access to these gardens at certain times. Those who paid higher fees, named fellow-commoners, were given free access to the fellows' garden, which was often kept under lock and key. In many cases the college fellows were responsible for the upkeep of their garden and paid an annual subscription to allow for this; apples, pears and soft fruit from the garden were an important addition to their fare

in the dining hall, where a dessert of fruit (sometimes taken in their 'combination' or combining room at one end of hall) was the most important course, accompanied by white wine.

At Christ's College, there is a record of the fellows paying kitchen staff individually for preparing their fruit for the hall table, for there are bills 'To Greene for dressing Squashes and Colyflowers' and also codlings (cooking apples). The 'garden book' at Christ's is indeed our best source of information with regard to daily life in a fellows' garden (see pages 21–24 for more detail). A 'black walke' is another feature mentioned in it, where coal dust was used instead of gravel to create a particularly black effect. This feature also appears at Peterhouse and Queens' and may have been peculiar to Cambridge.

The style of the fellows' gardens reflected the fashions of the period in which they were made, though in many cases they signally failed to keep up with fashion subsequently. The late-17th-century college gardens depicted in our best source for illustrations, David Loggan's *Cantabrigia Illustrata* (1690) – which is more reliable than his earlier book on Oxford – show walled gardens laid out in 'knots' or small parterres: hedge-enclosed areas with plants and gravel within, or else a bolder feature such as a sundial with a gnomon. Those colleges with a little land planted avenues of trees (usually elms or limes) as walks with gravelled paths, where the fellows would be sheltered from rain and sun; the pleasure of walking under files of trees, including young trees, was an important aspect of garden-making in the 17th and 18th centuries which has been rather forgotten, though it can be rekindled if one walks in the avenues at Trinity, King's and St John's today.

The Backs began to be developed for their picturesque appeal after the construction of the Gibbs Building at King's College in 1732. By the end of that century, Richard Bankes Harraden could report:

> These walks [at Trinity] which together with those of St John's, Clare-Hall, and King's colleges, skirt the whole west side of the town, afford the most advantageous view of the principal buildings. There are few places in Europe, where so many elegant edifices may be taken into the eye at once, on one side, and a rural landscape of native simplicity on the other.

This contrast between the picturesque nobility of the eastern, college side of the Backs and the agricultural vistas unfolding to the west was often commented upon – though it has been largely lost today.

Capability Brown's celebrated attempt to redesign the Backs as a single landscape entity, in the late 18th century, may have failed – and happily so – but there is a virtue in considering aspects such as avenues of trees and drainage from a communal point of view. The Backs as a whole — which is generally taken to be the area west of the colleges down to Queen's Road — is now overseen by an inter-collegiate panel, with the addition of experts such as landscape architect Robert Myers, who work to a landscape survey and plan made in 2007.

From the 1820s (a decade in which a great deal was done in Cambridge), most fellows' gardens were 'naturalised', taking the form of lawns with specimen trees and amorphously shaped flower beds. In the 19th century the emphasis was mainly on ornamental matters, but a college's ability to grow fruit remained important. Orchards were particularly valued, and appear to be the part of the garden to which the fellows became most sentimentally attached. Indeed, in many cases fellows' gardens had originally gone by the name of 'the orchard' or 'fellows' orchard'. At a number of colleges – such as Christ's, with its mulberry jam and honey – the produce of the garden is still treasured. Some colleges made an effort at self-sufficiency, but only Queens' boasted a walled garden of the kind one might find at a country house.

Mulberries are a noted feature at several colleges. We know from the archives that Christ's, Jesus, Corpus Christi and Emmanuel planted mulberry trees as a result of James I's celebrated (failed) attempt to start a silk industry in England after 1608. (Pembroke may also have joined in at this time.) Colleges purchased up to 300 mulberry saplings from the king's (French) representative to create plantations, but there is no evidence that more than a handful of trees were ever in fact planted out. It appears that the colleges were humouring the king in his latest little obsession. It is said that the 'wrong' mulberry – the black mulberry or *Morus nigra* – had been selected, but this is not true. Black as well

as white mulberry leaves can be consumed by silk worms, and in fact formed the basis of the ancient silk industries of China, India and Persia. The problem is more likely bound up with a lack of expertise and – crucially – a lack of enthusiasm for the enterprise. Nevertheless the mulberries that have survived are treasured by the colleges.

Fellows' gardens were not places reserved for food production and peaceful perambulation alone. They were also recreation areas, sanctuaries where the younger fellows might let off steam within the safety of the college precincts. Archery butts, for example, were often set up in the orchard, and the pastime remained popular right up until the end of the 17th century. This was one of several recreations enjoyed by the fellows in the college environment, where dice, cards, swimming, unsanctioned ball games and the keeping of falcons and dogs were all expressly banned by the university authorities at various points.

Perhaps the most important of these amenities was the college bowling green. Bowls became something of a national obsession from the early 17th until the late 18th century, and a great deal of the budget set aside for a fellows' garden tended to be spent on titivating the grass and on the construction of arbours and summer houses where the

ABOVE A Cambridge tradition: shrubs trained as buttresses, here in Trinity College's Great Court.

fellows and their guests could sit. There was a sense of competitiveness between the colleges about their bowling greens. The garden was the resort of fellows after dinner in hall, the main meal of the day, which was in earlier times taken in the morning and then gradually moved later and later in the day.

The life of a fellow in the 16th century could be rather spartan and difficult – at least to judge by a sermon preached in London in 1550 by Thomas Lever, fellow of St John's. He said that he and his colleagues had a 'dinner' at 10a.m., as their main meal, a kind of beef broth supplemented with oatmeal, and then

> After thys slender dinner they be either teachynge or learnynge untyll v. of the clocke [5p.m.] in the evening, when as they have a supper not much better than theyr dyner. Immedyatelye after the whyche, they go eyther to reasonyng in problemes or unto some other studye, untyll it be nyne or tenne of the clocke, and there beyng wythout fyre are fayne to walk or runne up and downe halfe an houre, to gette a heate on their feete whan they go to bed.

It appears Lever was exaggerating the hardships in college for his audience, for St John's was busily developing at this point in time,

with the master's garden already stretching down to the Cam. By the mid 17th century, fellows would typically congregate at the bowling green after dinner, at least in the warmer months, to continue their conversations (and in some cases their drinking). There would have been light gambling on the bowling matches and – certainly by the mid 18th century – card games. A bowling green could become quite a rowdy place, as it was a resort where the fellows could relax, away from the eyes of others, behind high hedges or in a far corner of the garden.

Tennis or handball (later fives) courts, either open or enclosed by a roof, were another amenity enjoyed by both fellows and junior members of college, and from a much earlier date (the earliest record of a handball court appears in 1487, at Corpus Christi College). Like the bowling green, these courts also became venues for general sociability; there are several references to students being fined for raucous behaviour in them. Football – the rough, early version of the game – was also tolerated within colleges, but only if played by members of that college alone, to prevent inter-collegiate fights breaking out. There were football areas at Sidney Sussex (where Oliver Cromwell played) and at Trinity, probably by the river, where the Wren Library stands today.

ABOVE LEFT An open-cornered court at Pembroke College.
ABOVE CENTRE The view from Trinity Bridge towards St John's.

Another amenity provided by a handful of Cambridge colleges was a cold bath. These became fashionable in the 1730s and around that time Peterhouse, Christ's and Emmanuel colleges all installed them. (Peterhouse lost its bath while the other two were subsequently remade in their current form as swimming pools. There was also possibly another bath at Caius, and both Pembroke and Clare had indoor plunge pools for a time.) Immersion in natural spring waters, usually cold – though hot at Bath – had been a popular practice in England for centuries, with the various types of mineral-rich waters curing different ailments. In the early 18th-century it became commercialised, with more spas and bathing houses being established. At private houses, small circular plunge pools became fashionable, usually sited outdoors. Gentlemen (and sometimes also ladies) would fully immerse themselves several times in the water for a bracing, health-giving shock. The leading book on the topic, first published by Dr Floyer in 1702, attested: 'I have observed some of the best Cures, done by the Cold Baths, is from a sudden Plunge over Head, and so immediately go out, and repeat it two or three times in a Day…'

Such an activity would have been viewed as downright dangerous in earlier times, especially as Cambridge had developed a reputation as an unhealthy place. Its proximity to the damp Fens – even today, Coe Fen is just over the wall from Peterhouse – has meant that the town has

been perceived as unusually susceptible to disease. There is some truth in this: Cambridge was subject to several visitations of the plague; for example in the summer of 1349, 16 out of 40 scholars at King's Hall (later part of Trinity College) died during the Black Death, and there was another outbreak of plague in 1665–66. In February 1792, soon after his arrival in Cambridge, Coleridge wrote home: 'Cambridge is a damp place — the very palace of winds.' And D. H. Lawrence was similarly offended when he stayed in 1915: 'I cannot bear its smell of rottenness, marsh-stagnancy. I get a melancholic malaria.' The situation was not improved by the fact that mains drainage only came to the town in 1895.

For the population of Cambridge up until that point, the chief virtue of the river in Cambridge was its convenience. As in, it was used as a public convenience. Both the river and the King's Ditch, which ran across the middle of town, functioned as open sewers, sources of excruciating odours in summer and at random moments. In earlier times it would have been distinctly inadvisable to have ventured in an open boat along the 'backsides' (as the Backs were formerly called). The stretch farthest downriver, at Magdalene, contained everything

put into the Cam by the town and tended to be the most noxious of all. The vicinity of Magdalene Bridge was also an industrial zone, an area of loading and unloading of smaller barges which could navigate the river through Cambridge, before being transferred to or taken off larger boats at the wharves by Silver Street Bridge and Queens' College, another noisy hive of activity. The river remained a trading route into the late 19th century – William Everett in the 1860s evokes 'the heavy black silent barges forcing their way slowly up'. It was always busy with traffic of one sort or another, including swimming cows near Lammas Land, in the south. Swimming humans could be found at Coe Fen, in the south of the town, where on his daily walk in 1859 the Trinity fellow and diarist Joseph Romilly found to his consternation 'a shoal of naked bathers' (all male of course).

Two more Cambridge watercourses ought to be mentioned, one natural and one constructed. The natural one is the modestly named Bin Brook, a tributary of the Cam which runs east to west across Cambridge before joining the Cam at St John's. It plays a role in the landscapes of Robinson, Trinity and St John's colleges. The artificial watercourse is Hobson's Conduit, created in 1610–14 by Thomas Hobson to bring fresh water into the town (and also to flush out the noxious King's Ditch). The two runnels against the edges of Trumpington Street are known as Pem (after Pembroke College) and

Pot (after Peterhouse College). The fountain in Trinity's Great Court is still fed by this source, which is now controlled by the city council, running from April to September.

The river itself was not always viewed as a picturesque adornment. A particularly revealing, if not entirely complimentary picture of Cambridge emerges in a letter written home by Alexander Chisholm Gooden, a freshman at Trinity in 1836:

> If I had been asked my opinion on the first night after my arrival, I should have described Cambridge as a dull and shabby town. The colleges which present on the side of the street very much the appearance that our own Inns of Court do (especially the Temple) are of all colours sizes and styles of architecture.

His description continues:

> After entering the gate of a college you generally find a quadrangle (at Trinity a very fine one) from which you pass on to one or more, and so to the college walks which are commonly behind the buildings. This takes from the beauty of the colleges because the gardens are not seen until you actually enter them. The trees are very fine, the gravel walks very well kept, and the grass-plots very well rolled.

> The river Cam both in colour and width strongly resembles a ditch…and where it *flows* (I should rather say creeps) through the college grounds the banks are grassy and sloping and lined with elms and other large trees.

A feeling of openness is key to understanding the landscape and garden appeal of Cambridge. That aesthetic is encapsulated by the Backs, as the city's jewel, but it also refers to the area west of the Cam, where the colleges began to extend their landholdings farther in the 19th century. Medieval Cambridge was wedged between its two 'great fields' to east and west, used as agricultural and unenclosed common land well into the 19th century, when new colleges began to encroach upon the western part. The continuing importance to Cambridge of these two agricultural areas is shown by their inclusion as engravings in Loggan's *Cantabrigia Illustrata* (1690), alongside the grand colleges. The existence of these large expanses of open land, together with the tradition of common land extending right into the city centre – Parker's Piece, Midsummer Common, Christ's Pieces, Coldham's Common, Sheep's Green, Lammas Land, Jesus Green, Coe Fen – serve to give Cambridge its unique atmosphere, where public open spaces directly abut the busy urban scene. This can still be felt in Cambridge city centre today, where Parker's Piece suddenly and incongruously appears

TOP LEFT Vegetable-growing at Darwin – an old horticultural tradition at one of the newer colleges.

halfway along busy Regent Street, and Christ's Pieces pops up at the end of King Street. This sense of openness has arguably been translated into the design of the courts in the colleges.

CAMBRIDGE AND OXFORD GARDENS COMPARED

The most obvious visual difference between the two university cities is the building material used for their construction: Oxford relies on honeyed Cotswold stone, while Cambridge, with no source of good stone nearby, turned to locally made brick, the Cambridgeshire clays producing a rich carmine red or a soft yellow-grey. Certain notable buildings, such as King's College Chapel, were built of stone from Midlands quarries such as Ketton, and in the late 18th and 19th centuries many colleges underwent a process called ashlaring, which is facing, with smooth-cut stone, walls made of brick or rough-textured 'clunch' (a soft, rubbly local limestone).

Perhaps the spatial differences between Cambridge and Oxford are even more noticeable. There has always been more room in Cambridge for colleges to build and expand, and concomitantly the area available for garden development tends to be more generous.

With more space in which to move, there is often a rather more rational layout to the structure of the courts in Cambridge, which extend in axial directions, mostly east-west and sometimes north-south,

and are sized proportionately. (As ever, there are exceptions – Christ's College, for example, is not in the least bit rational in its layout.)

In Oxford, by contrast, colleges had to squeeze themselves around a well-established medieval town centre, meaning that the quadrangles (not courts) of Oxford can be all kinds of rectangular shapes and sizes. The very term quadrangle implies 'four-sided' and the Oxford colleges are indeed made up of wholly enclosed spaces, in the main.

In Cambridge a different aesthetic emerged, in which the edges of the courts were often left open, so that views beyond are visible and there is less of a sense of containment. Indeed, a court might be described as a quadrangle with a window left wide open (and pleasantly so). There are fine examples of this at Emmanuel, Jesus and Pembroke. The three-sided court also became a feature of Cambridge colleges, after Dr Keys in the 1560s had created the exemplar at the college that bears his name (see pages 120–127). The more modern colleges also followed this general rationale – Fitzwilliam contains three-sided, open-ended or open-cornered courts, as does Wolfson. This can be related to Cambridge's unique semi-urban atmosphere, where views of the 'pieces' suddenly open up at unexpected moments within the city.

ABOVE Informal borders at Hughes Hall, which was founded in 1885 and gained full collegiate status in 2006.

Meanwhile the river itself plays a different role in Cambridge, defining the set-piece effects of the Backs as it runs northwards through the city, whereas the river in Oxford is more of a meandering sideshow, popping up at opportune moments.

The larger amount of space available in Cambridge has led to a different emphasis in the college gardens, compared with Oxford. In Cambridge, more colleges have been able to create tree-lined walks and avenues, and orchards, meadows and paddocks are more commonly seen. A paddock could be used for livestock and was also a place where the master and sometimes the fellows could graze their carriage horses or hacking ponies. It is also more common in Cambridge to find fellows' gardens at a considerable remove from the college (as at King's and St John's), and it was sometimes possible for the fellows to have multiple gardens (at one time, Queens' had three). On the topic of grass, it appears that front and other courts were grassed over at an earlier date in Cambridge than in Oxford, where the process did not begin until the late 18th century. At Cambridge there was often a strong sense that the college's land was physically connected with adjacent common land and agriculture. This visual link with the surrounding landscape was important at certain places, such as Clare, Trinity and St John's, where an effort was made to engineer straight vistas through the courts and beyond (almost unheard of in Oxford).

Horticulturally speaking, there are some features found in Cambridge and not Oxford. This includes the tradition of trees in the middle of courts already mentioned, and the way plants are trained up formally as buttresses on ranges and in chapel bays (Trinity Hall provides one of the best examples of this). Another general point is that Cambridge has been rather more bold when it comes to commissioning striking – as opposed to polite or recessive – modern architecture. It has also been more active in the realm of contemporary garden sculpture (Jesus College leading the way). One slightly curious phenomenon is the way noise is taken rather more seriously in Cambridge, where it is felt that the gardeners and visitors to college alike are a potential distraction for students. Oxford is much more gung-ho about this – perhaps simply because Cambridge has traditionally been a quieter environment. In Cambridge, garden teams are often commanded not to mow the grass, or else they resort to silenced lawnmowers (they use these at King's), during and before the summer examination period. For those colleges with gardens and accommodation near the river, the clanging of metal punt poles and the near constant stream of commentary from the riverine tour guides represents serious noise pollution.

ABOVE One of architect Ralph Erskine's distinctive glass-walled courts at Clare Hall, a striking modernist design.

The relationship of Cantabrigian gardeners to their colleges is similar to the system in Oxford, where in some places a garden fellow or garden steward is the point of liaison with the head gardener, while at other colleges a garden committee might convene to make decisions and advise. The garden budget is usually overseen as part of this process. The larger amount of garden space in Cambridge results in bigger garden teams, and more interest overall from the fellows in horticultural maintenance. Some Cambridge colleges have garden committees which are too large to be effective. At one, a committee numbering more than a dozen took several years to decide on some new garden furniture, having ordered in multiple samples on whose merits they could not agree (in the end, the head gardener simply took the initiative and ordered the furniture). At another college a valued tree was damaged in a May Ball (always a bane of the gardeners' lives). A decision was made to replace it and the students were canvassed as to their choice between four different types of tree. Votes were counted and two were finally chosen and ordered in. Then the garden committee decided not to replace the tree after all. The whole process had taken three years. Perhaps the colleges might heed the advice of the respected landscape architect Peter Youngman, who was asked to consult on a Cambridge college garden in 1948 and commented in a letter preserved in the archive: 'A garden is a work of art, and a committee can no more design the details of a garden than it can compose a sonata or a sonnet.' A note written on the reverse of the letter records that all of Youngman's recommendations had been summarily rejected. As a rule, and for reasons one can only speculate about, the colleges feel they instinctively know what is best for their domain. The evidence of this book is that they may sometimes be correct in this assumption.

Finally, not every college in Cambridge has been given its own chapter in this book, for reasons of space rather than perceived horticultural quality. Interspersed in the pages of this introduction are photographs of four colleges: St Catharine's, Clare Hall, Hughes Hall and St Edmund's. The university's garden portfolio also includes the botanic garden and 16th-century Madingley Hall, headquarters of the university's continuing education programme, 6.5 kilometres/4 miles from the city. At Madingley there is a garden of clipped yew hedges, a walled garden and a historic wildflower meadow, all maintained to a high standard, complemented by parkland where Capability Brown advised in 1756.

But it is the gardens of the colleges themselves which must be accounted the glory of the university. *Floreant Horti Cantabrigienses.*

ABOVE The orchard at St Edmund's College, which began life in the 1890s as a lodging house for Roman Catholic students.

CHRIST'S COLLEGE

CHRIST'S IS EXCEPTIONAL. INTELLECTUALLY, THIS college has long pursued a freethinking agenda. The Christ of Christ's College is not the figurehead of established religion, but the revolutionary who overturned the tables of the money changers in the temple. Its most famous sons – John Milton and Charles Darwin – found that the originality of their thinking placed them in opposition to Establishment opinion at various times, and Christ's still cherishes its reputation as a haven for intellectual iconoclasts. Yet even these celebrated alumni hardly had a conventional relationship with their college – that is not the Christ's way. Dr Johnson relates how Milton was one of the last undergraduates to be whipped by his masters, while Darwin held aloof during his time there, commenting that he was on cordial terms with only 15 other undergraduates.

Physically, too, it has a different feel to the other older Cambridge colleges. Its appearance potentially reflects its individualistic attitude in that its very shape is decidedly unorthodox – a fat, 2.5-hectare/6-acre triangle into which the college has expanded over the centuries, defined only by Hobson Street to the west and the open space of Christ's Pieces to the east. The ground plan does not follow the geometric pattern favoured by most old Cambridge colleges: Second Court is a truncated transitional space, Third Court is situated at an awkward diagonal, while New Court, which occupies the northern part of the college estate, is not really a court at all but a gigantic modernist ziggurat.

The college was founded in 1505 by Margaret Beaufort, who took over an existing institution, uncompromisingly named Godshouse, which had been established in 1437 for the training of priests. (Godshouse was originally situated near Clare College but it was moved to the Christ's site in 1448 to make way for King's College and its chapel.) More land was rapidly acquired during

LEFT A portrait roundel of alumnus Charles Darwin greets visitors at the entrance lodge. An olive tree has been planted in the far corner of First Court.

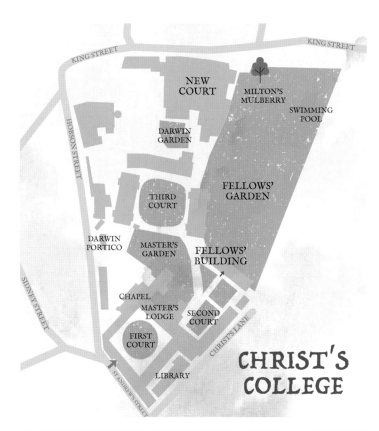

New Court

Milton's Mulberry

Swimming Pool

Darwin Garden

King Street

King Street

Hobson Street

Fellows' Garden

Third Court

Darwin Portico

Master's Garden

Fellows' Building

Sidney Street

Chapel

Master's Lodge

Second Court

First Court

Christ's Lane

St Andrew's Street

Library

CHRIST'S COLLEGE

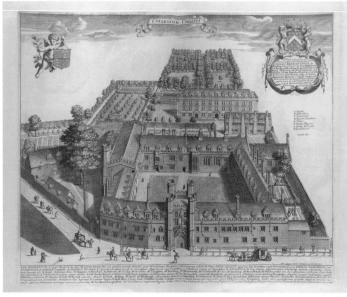

ABOVE David Loggan's engraving of 1690 shows there was once a garden (far right) where the library stands today and a tree plantation on the site of Third Court (top left).

FAR RIGHT *Hydrangea macrophylla* cultivars form an elegant frontage to the Fellows' Building.

the next century including the 'grett orchard', initially leased from Jesus College in 1507, which would become the fellows' garden, and a large parcel of land which began life as part of the master's garden and would later be utilised as the site of Third Court. Building began at the new college almost as soon as it was founded, and the purchase of the orchard is an indication that a garden was a vital element from an early date. One could perhaps guess this anyway from the college's ornately decorated gatehouse. It was one of the first structures completed and features the yales (mythical beasts with revolving horns) associated with Margaret Beaufort, as well as the red rose of the House of Lancaster and the marguerites, or daisies, which are a pun on her name.

There are certainly no daisies in the lawn of First Court, but it is an awkward shape. The space superficially looks square but it is not equal-sided, with the south-west (entrance) side on to St Andrew's Street somewhat skew-whiff. The turf in the centre of the court is laid in a perfect roundel (a good way of disguising its imperfect dimensions, perhaps) and is the only example of a circular lawn in the entrance court of a Cambridge college. The lawn is first shown in this form on Custance's city map of 1798. There is a notable collection of mature shrubs on the walls of this suntrap court which is, it is said, on average two degrees warmer than anywhere else in Cambridge. Most striking is a magnificent wisteria against the entrance to the master's lodge on the north-east range, a venerable specimen which looks almost as impressive when bare in winter, so extensive and complex is its branch structure. A chunky *Hydrangea petiolaris* decorates the south-eastern wall while the north-west range sports a variety of shrubs including *Clematis cirrhosa* (winter clematis), ceanothus, rosemary, plumbago and trachelospermum, several of the larger plants trained up to form geometric buttress shapes, in the Cambridge fashion. A bulky *Salvia guaranitica* thrives in the western corner, heralding the presence of this genus across college; head gardener Sergio Ballarin inherited *Salvia* as an interest from his time on the garden staff at Murray Edwards College.

In the northern corner of First Court is the first indication of the slightly wayward horticultural style which has characterised Christ's in the past half-century or so, during which time a succession of garden stewards (fellows in charge of garden matters) have commandeered parts of the garden. Formerly a huge *Magnolia grandiflora* occupied this space, and when it was removed a decision was taken to install in its place a gnarled old olive tree surrounded by a clump of box plants – a grouping that is tonally at odds with everything else in the court.

The college extends northwards into Second Court, which is not really a court at all but a semi-open space cut in half by the curving wall of the master's garden on its western side, with two unequal panels of lawn prefacing the broad and tall Fellows' Building at the court's north-eastern end. This building, completed in 1642, is a free-standing range – another unusual sight in a Cambridge court – and is one of the most celebrated early essays in architectural neoclassicism in Britain. Despite this, the college has no idea who designed it, though it did keep a record of the names of the college members who paid for it by subscription.

Second Court is essentially a transitional space where there is little cause to linger, but it has been much improved recently by the wholesale herbaceous revamp of an overgrown shrub border against the wall to the master's garden. This now features salvias, nepeta, aquilegia, irises and various daisy-flowered subjects such as heleniums and asters, planted in clumps in classic fashion, as opposed to drifts and mingled groups. A ginkgo and silver birch add height. Interventions such as this raise the tone of the college and improve the daily lives of its members, even if they are not always conscious of the effect.

The fellows' garden unfolds behind the Fellows' Building, reached in somewhat dramatic fashion via an ornamental gateway and a short passageway that penetrates beneath the centre of the building. Today the fellows' garden is laid to lawn with mature trees and mixed borders at the fringes, an informal layout introduced in the first half of the 19th century, when most fellows' gardens

in Cambridge were given this form. Before that, Christ's fellows' garden featured a bowling green in its south-western corner, with an enclosed but open-to-the-sky tennis court adjacent to the Fellows' Building. The tennis court lasted from 1564 until 1711 and the bowling green is first mentioned in 1586 – a notably early date for this particular amenity (most colleges made their bowling greens after 1620). David Loggan's engraving of the college of 1690 also shows two summer houses of singular design: the first is a two-storied, glazed hexagonal structure on the eastern side; the second is at the far, north end of the garden, beyond a central avenue of trees, with pedimented doorways on all four of its sides. Otherwise the fellows' garden appears to have been quite thickly wooded at this time, perhaps the inheritance of its earlier 'orchard' identity; there are records of ash and elm trees being planted in 1614–15, as well as the college's celebrated mulberry in 1609.

The archives and muniments (treasure) rooms of several Cambridge colleges preserve account books which contain details of expenditure on the gardens, as well as the names and payment rates of the people who worked in them. These references are typically embedded within the general accounts – payments for clock maintenance, carpenters' bills and so on. No other college

in either Cambridge or Oxford has preserved a dedicated 'garden book' like the one kept at Christ's College. Spanning the years 1645 to 1714, this tall, pamphlet-like notebook bound in vellum is an extraordinarily detailed record of all expenditure on the fellows' garden at this time. It was clearly kept up assiduously and is therefore a reliable guide to exactly what was going on in the garden on an almost daily basis. While this garden book is a unique survival, there is no reason to suppose that other colleges did not keep similar records which have now been lost. A fellows' garden might require its own accounts book because it was one part of the college estate which was under the direct management of the fellows as a group of individuals, as opposed to the master or governing body. The fellows oversaw and paid for the construction of summer houses, bowling greens, plunge pools and other accoutrements in their own private domain.

At Christ's College, an annual subscription was paid by each fellow for the upkeep of their garden, and this rate is itemised at the beginning of each year's accounts. In addition, it was decreed in 1681 that every new fellow should pay £1 towards the fellows' garden, and also invest in their own pair of bowls (traditionally these were monogrammed with the fellow's initials). This rule regarding fellows' bowls was observed until the mid 19th century. Away from the fellows' garden, from 1686 there was a quarterly payment levied on every college member for keeping the turf in the courts.

The opening two pages alone of the Christ's garden book, relating to the year 1645–46, are a treasure trove of information about the fellows' garden, or 'orchard' as it is usually termed at this date. (Traditionally, the fruit from the orchard trees, vines and soft-fruit bushes in a fellows' garden belonged to the fellows themselves, who could enjoy their bounty at mealtimes in hall.) The inventory begins with a list of 21 names of the men who laboured in the garden across the year – Messrs Harrison, Ball, Field, Marshall, Barnes… — and their rate of pay, which was a shilling per day across the board. We can gain a sense of the relative costs of different plants from the bills itemised: 'Flowers in ye Orchard. 300' cost 9s 6d, while 'A hundred of Rose-Trees' is just 2 shillings. 'Roots of Rosemary 57' are 4s 4d while an unspecified amount of 'Straw-berry roots' appear to have been considerably more expensive, at 12 shillings. 'Seeds for ye kitchen garden' are not particularly cheap, at 4s 6d, and 'boxe in ye new border' is 6s 6d. Garden equipment was expensive, with a 'Watering pott' bought on 28 August costing 4 shillings; later in the accounts there are various bills for the repair of such pots and for mending other items including wheelbarrows and a lawn-roller whose frame was broken.

In Cambridge fellows' gardens during the 17th and early 18th centuries, the bowling green tends to be one of the most expensive features to maintain, with the quality of the turf and the spruceness of the seats and summer houses adjacent a source of competitive pride among colleges. The accounts for 1646 include a very large bill, of £1 19s 3d, 'For ye Seat at ye upper-end of ye Bowling Green' and an additional payment of 14 shillings 'For painting ye Seat'. There is also a 2s 6d bill for 'ye bowlz-boxe', which was not a bill for a special box to contain the fellows' bowls (the accounts for the following year mention 'a baskett for ye bowls' at just 8d) but must refer to box plants around the green. We can gain a sense of the feelings aroused by bowling greens from the diary of Samuel Ward, who spent seven years as a student and fellow at Christ's. His journal entries for 1595 mainly relate to his own perceived sinfulness, including 'my pride in walking in the middest of the orchard when St John's men were there' and 'my over-myrth at bowling after supper…how I had almost hurt Mr Pott' (a fellow).

The next year, 1646–47, contains the garden book's first reference to mending the lock to the door of the orchard, something which demands at least twice-yearly attention. There is a bill of 11 shillings for 'Rebuilding the Butts', which refers to the archery butts that remained a common feature in college orchards and fellows' gardens even at this date. These butts were not made of compacted straw but of cut turf or 'sod', and were generally much larger than modern archery targets – typically 2.75 metres/9 feet wide, 2 metres/7 feet high and 1.25 metres/4 feet thick, though they could be larger. A pair of butts would be set up to face each other, sometimes with adjacent platforms also made of turf, so that the archers could shoot from one end and then collect their arrows and shoot again in the other direction.

In the same year there are various bills for herbs and seeds in the kitchen garden, as well as payments for 'gilly flower rootes' (3s 8d) and for 50 tulip bulbs – at 3 shillings, not quite as expensive as one might have thought. There is also a large bill of £1 'For 20 load of Gravell for ye Orchard-Walk', the first of numerous payments for gravel across ensuing years. Clearly it was seen as vital that the walks were regularly refreshed, thus creating a neat and well-maintained appearance. Like several other colleges at this time, Christ's was using coal-dust as an alternative to gravel as a path surface, partly for reasons of economy; this is probably what is being referred to in 1650 with a bill of 5 shillings 'for labouring about the blacke walke'. The accounts for 1647 also contain the first of numerous references to 'the braking of Wallnuts', confirming that the appeal of these trees in Cambridge colleges was as much culinary as it was ornamental. By the time of the Loggan engraving in 1690, the trees in the fellows' garden had grown tall, and in 1702 there is reference to fees paid to 'poor men' for pulling down rooks' nests from the top branches.

Titivations to Christ's fellows' garden continued apace in the year 1650, which sees payments 'for labouring 7 dayes dressing ye…great Knot' (7 shillings) and 'for 12 dayes worke in heightning and digging the great knot' (12 shillings). It is not clear where this 'great knot' was or precisely what form it took, but it was most likely a substantial figure in clipped evergreen, probably box, with fine gravel or sand lain between.

Potentially of interest with regard to the history of the college are hitherto overlooked payments to 'Mr Grumbold'. This can only be the mason Robert Grumbold, who worked as an assistant to Christopher Wren. The garden book entry for 1689–90 has the following item: 'May 24. paid Mr Grumbold for…stone work in ye Orchard as p[er] Bill' (£4 3s). Nine years later in 1698–99 there is a payment of 16 shillings to 'Mr Grumbold for More work before ye orchard door', which must refer to the Fellows' Building. None of the summer houses and other structures in the fellows' garden were made of stone, so it is at least possible that Grumbold's initial bill of £4 3s relates to decorative carving around the doorcases and above the window frames of the Fellows' Building. It has always been a source of surprise for architectural historians that a building of 1642 should contain these decorative elements, which seem so advanced for the date,

especially when no named architect is associated with the work. (Inigo Jones has been suggested in the past, on the basis of no real evidence.) Perhaps the 1642 building was left relatively plain, though neoclassical in form, and Grumbold was engaged half a century later, in 1689, to ornament it in fashionable style?

The fellows' garden today is much more open in feel than it has been in recent years, thanks to the head gardener's policy of lifting the crowns of the grand old yews, box and other trees which encircle the space, and which formerly gave the appearance of impermeable green walls at the edges of the lawn. More trunks are now exposed and some tempting cross-vistas have been revealed. In addition, a new curving path has been made along an established 'desire line' used by students taking a short cut through the garden from New Court towards Second Court. This path is defined by an arc of a border made up of

ABOVE LEFT A new border has been made in Second Court where the path curves around the edge of the master's garden.

ABOVE CENTRE Foliage of ginkgo (top) and *Mahonia japonica*, with the dining hall windows beyond.

drifts of grasses and other semi-translucent plants like fennel and *Verbena bonariensis*, as well as certain prairie-style perennials such as rudbeckia. The new border complements *A Pattern of Life* (2001) by Tim Harrisson, a sculpture resembling limestone pavement which is embedded in the lawn. There are numerous mature and specimen trees ranged about the garden, including a gigantic London plane on the east side, growing through the wall that gives on to Christ's Pieces, a trio of tulip trees with the yellow horse chestnut *Aesculus × neglecta* 'Erythroblastos' behind (scarlet autumn colour), a blue cedar, and on the west side a *Davidia involucrata*, a ginkgo, a tall *Pinus nigra* and a *Metasequoia glyptostroboides*. The main border is situated in front of a clump of trees in the northern section of the garden and is gardened in a classical manner with geraniums and asters backed by thalictrum, aconites and aruncus, with acanthus, salvias and *Achillea filipendulina* 'Gold Plate' lending body. At the northern end of the lawn is an area of variegated shrubs and bamboos which creates a frisson of the east, and there are plans to grow peonies there.

The north-west corner of the garden is also the site of the most celebrated feature of Christ's gardens: Milton's Mulberry. It is unlikely Milton himself had any connection with this tree,

since he was at Christ's from 1625 to 1632 and there is a record of the mulberry first being planted in 1609, as part of James I's attempts to create a British silk industry. The king's envoy had been despatched to various parts of Britain where he was tasked with persuading patriotic landowners to buy young trees and establish plantations.

The Christ's mulberry (which is probably an offshoot from the original tree) has a chequered history, and bears the scars to prove it. It was blown over on the night of 14 November 1795, and then set up again. It was only at this time that it began to be referred to as Milton's tree. It was repaired in around 1805 in a rather curious manner, with sheets of lead placed across damaged areas (some of this lead can still be found about its crown). Its drooping branches began to be propped up by poles in the early 19th century, adding to the decrepit look, and finally in 1856 the whole tree was 'mounded' up – that is, the exposed roots above ground, which had been showing since it had been blown over, were covered with soil so that the tree now appears to be growing out of a hillock. It is likely to have been at this point that the old

ABOVE RIGHT The college swimming pool is first mentioned in 1748, though it would not have taken this form.

tree sent up the shoot from which its beleaguered bole which grew up to become the tree we see today. The Christ's mulberry is not the most beautiful specimen but the garden team are all too aware that its upkeep must remain at the top of their agenda. It became something of a cult tree in the early 19th century, when the 17-year-old Alfred Tennyson wrote a paean to it when he first came up to Cambridge, satirising its treatment at the hands of the college fellows.

The mulberry produces a fine crop of berries each year (as does a second mulberry tree nearby) and the college makes batches of mulberry jam, which are the preserve of the fellows. Another long-standing college obsession is with bees and beekeeping – three hives are shown on the Loggan engraving, in a service area west of the master's lodge. Today the college's hives can be found among the trees near the mulberry, where they are looked after by the gardeners. Jars of the college honey are strictly portioned out to the fellowship – three jars each in a good year.

Behind the mulberry tree is a fine specimen of the cinnamon-barked *Arbutus × andrachnoides*, while against the old north wall of the garden is an interesting collection of plants including an *Azara microphylla*, *Albizia julibrissin*, trumpet-flowered *Eccremocarpus* and a pomegranate. In addition there is a fernery of *Dicksonia* and other 'prehistoric' foliage plants on the western side of the garden, near a door to Third Court.

There is another curiosity in the fellows' garden – this time in its north-eastern corner. This is the outdoor swimming pool or 'cold bath' which is first mentioned in Thomas Salmon's 1748 guide to the university, where he describes the bath as 'surrounded with a little Wilderness'. Edmund Carter's guide, published five years later, also mentions a 'very good Cold-Bath'. This feature would not originally have taken the form it has today, which is a conventional rectangular bathing pool, but would have been much smaller, regarded more as a plunge pool for sudden life-enhancing immersions. It is not clear when the pool was altered and enlarged, nor even when the triple-arched pavilion was erected at its south end, though it is conjectured this dates from the mid 18th century. The north end of the pool is dignified by an exedra of three portrait busts and a memorial urn on tapering pedestals, the most prominent one honouring Milton. The only place for students to sunbathe in this constricted space is directly beneath the gaze of these dignitaries. The pool is shaded by a large cut-leaf beech and is famously chilly; its maintenance eats up a lot of the garden team's time.

The western part of the college consists of a series of extremely large 20th-century accommodation blocks in a variety of styles, none of which are aesthetically successful in context. In the 1930s Christ's nearly commissioned the most radical building ever conceived for Cambridge: a range by Walter Gropius, founder of the Bauhaus school in Dessau, Germany. But instead the governing body plumped for a series of stylistically timid yet oversized buildings, in the process creating Third Court, an extremely difficult space to deal with horticulturally. It was made into an iris garden in the 1950s and is now in the process of being redesigned by the head gardener. The plan is to add salvias to the iris collection, to lend more height, and to allow cloud-pruned yew hedging to define the space more surely, with gravel of a more suitable colour and straight steel edges to the borders. It is hoped that a planting of crab apples (*Malus trilobata*) will create more of a glade feeling. Cloud-pruned osmanthus and pomegranates have been planted against the north range.

In 1966 Christ's decided to 'go modern' after all and employed the architect Denys Lasdun, designer of the National Theatre, to create the monumentally zigguratic New Court, north of Third Court. This development, too, proved disastrous in terms of its architectural presence, which is wholly alien to everything around it, while any potential garden component was rendered impossible because the flat concrete terraces freely leaked water. It was scheduled to be three times as large as it is now, and it is a mercy the plan was never realised. As it is, the only horticultural ornament to the bleak terraces is

a collection of clipped Portuguese laurels in concrete versions of Versailles tubs, which do little to relieve the monotony of badly stained concrete. There was an attempt in the 1980s to replant the terraces of New Court to create a 'cascade' effect, and Lasdun corresponded with the college regarding plant choice. But it seems that this came to nothing, and in 2002 the terraces with their failed lawns were simply paved over. It would nevertheless still be possible for New Court to be rescued from this purgatory if the college invested in the services of a visionary and practical-minded landscape architect.

Like so much else at Christ's, the master's garden is unique in its proportions and decor: an unconventional n-shape, wrapped around the unorthodox agglomeration of buildings which make up the master's lodge. There is a long, south-facing border along one wall (kniphofia, *Verbena rigida*, alliums, rudbeckia, sedum, agapanthus) but its principal feature is a highly unusual decorative rill or canal realised in dark red brick which runs the breadth of the garden, east to west, and is now ornamented, slightly strangely, with topiary balls and pyramids that do not look quite in scale. The rill, which is actually part of the historic Hobson's Conduit water supply, appears to have been home-designed by the master in around 1920, in the Christ's spirit of keeping everything 'in

college'. The feature itself has been treated rather eccentrically, being abruptly cut off three-quarters along its length by a brick wall which bounds the master's garden, where it is flanked by a pair of strawberry trees (*Arbutus unedo*). The rill continues outside the master's domain and terminates in a sort of shrine to Darwin in the form of a loggia or summer house (1920) with informational boards inside – yet another slightly bizarre feature that is like nothing else in a Cambridge college. A large *Magnolia × soulangeana* shades the rill in this unregarded part of college, and a fine specimen of Caucasian wingnut (*Pterocarya × rehderiana*) can be seen over the wall where it shades the college car park.

Darwin was celebrated again in 2009 with the creation of the Darwin Garden at the foot of the steps up to the New Court ziggurat. This is yet another singular feature in this college of garden curiosities, where several such literal-minded celebration gardens have been made over the years, including a failed planting based on species mentioned in Milton's *Lycidas*. The idea behind the Darwin Garden was to celebrate the voyage of the *Beagle* (1831–36) by packing the garden with plants from Australia, New Zealand and the Galapagos Islands. These included a monkey puzzle tree, several kniphofias, *Podocarpus salignus* and *Dianella tasmanica*, though much of the detail has now been lost and the garden is dominated by its structural planting of *Berberis darwinii*, *Escallonia resinosa* and *Acacia pravissima*. No attempt has been made to integrate the garden with its surroundings, and it feels under-sized. This miniature jungle is centred on a life-size bronze statue of the young Charles Darwin sitting on a bench, a figurative work of startling conventionality in the context of a Cambridge college. (The original plan was simpler – a bust of the great man on a pedestal – which would have avoided the kitsch effect of the current tribute.) Secreted about Darwin's person on this statue is a beetle, reflecting his passion for collecting insects in the surrounding countryside during his time at Cambridge. Rather less respectable was Darwin's membership of a college dining society called the Glutton Club, which delighted in trying unusual foods. It is reported that the club was disbanded soon after its members had attempted to eat an owl.

CHURCHILL COLLEGE

THE GROUNDS OF THE COLLEGE founded in 1960 in honour of Sir Winston Churchill occupy a 17-hectare/42-acre site. They do not so much constitute 'gardens' as areas of landscape set around a collection of striking buildings which form the most coherent modernist statement extended across an entire Cambridge college. The notable garden elements here are the open spaces inside a series of 11 accommodation courts arranged in clusters at the eastern end of the demesne, each one focused on a tree or pair of trees. In addition, there are gardens associated with the student accommodation in some of the more distant, western parts, while monumental abstract sculpture plays an exceptionally dynamic role at the heart of the ensemble. Austere and uncompromising, Churchill may not be to everyone's taste, but it expresses its character in the most direct manner imaginable. 'Take it or leave it', it seems to say.

A modest landscape scheme was envisaged with some clarity during the college's construction (which was completed in 1968). But the planting was only partially implemented and then lost much of its detail and finesse over the decades. It is only now being put back in good order, thanks to a dynamic head gardener supported by a college archivist who is committed to a successful landscape design.

Sir Winston himself had the germ of an idea for a college focused on science, maths and technology following a visit to the Massachusetts Institute of Technology (MIT) in 1949. (Today, 70 per cent of Churchill College students take these subjects.) This idea eventually led to a public appeal for funds for the new college in Cambridge, and then in 1959 to an architectural competition described as the most important to have been held in post-war Britain. The competition was extraordinary for two reasons. First, the 20 invited architectural firms were all modernist in outlook, marking a clear departure from the neo-Georgian style favoured by the Establishment in the immediate post-war period. Secondly, a number of the unsuccessful firms went

LEFT The view north from West Court (left) towards Barbara Hepworth's bronze sculpture *Four-Square (Walk Through)* (1966). In the foreground a narrow-leaved ash tree (*Fraxinus angustifolia*) displays its early-autumn foliage.

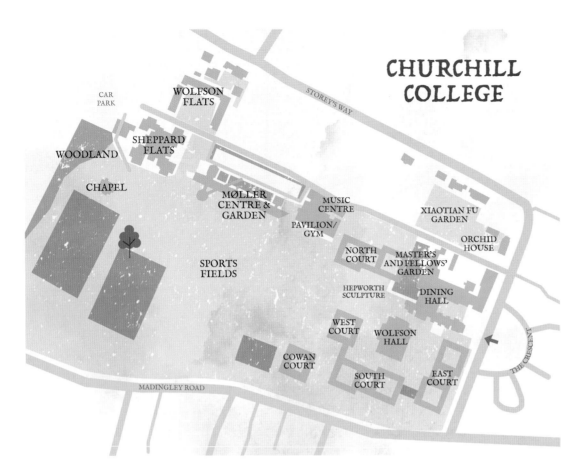

CHURCHILL
COLLEGE

WOLFSON FLATS

CAR PARK

STOREY'S WAY

SHEPPARD FLATS

WOODLAND

CHAPEL

MØLLER CENTRE & GARDEN

MUSIC CENTRE

XIAOTIAN FU GARDEN

PAVILION/ GYM

ORCHID HOUSE

NORTH COURT

MASTER'S AND FELLOWS' GARDEN

SPORTS FIELDS

HEPWORTH SCULPTURE

DINING HALL

WEST COURT

THE CRESCENT

WOLFSON HALL

COWAN COURT

SOUTH COURT

EAST COURT

MADINGLEY ROAD

on to design the new campus universities of the 1960s and early 70s, in several cases reprising themes they had first essayed in their submissions to Churchill. For better or worse, the competition heralded the beginning of a new architectural era in British higher education.

As the (then) tyro garden designer John Brookes noted in a review of the competition entries in the *Journal of the Institute of Landscape Architects*: 'Very few [of the proposals] seemed to produce shapes or ideas comparable with 20th-century British architecture.' The inability of most modernist architects to conceive of complementary modernist landscape designs is a recurring theme in 20th-century design history. Several entrants imagined amorphously shaped lakes so large that the college would have appeared stranded in flooded fields. The only participant to produce a coherent and detailed landscape plan was Sir Frederick Gibberd, the creator of Harlow New Town and an architect who was also – unusually – committed to the idea of gardens and landscape. Curiously, while several other competition entries showed a resemblance to new-town design, with 'zones' of accommodation ranged like suburbs around a college centre, Gibberd's proposal did not echo the typology he had helped to define. His loosely cellular system had more in common with Edwardian Arts and Crafts, comprising a variety of modernist garden rooms, each focused on a specimen tree. That idea was to be key to Churchill's landscape plans – but in someone

else's hands, because Gibberd's 'garden rooms' were gathered around accommodation blocks which rose to seven storeys. Such monolithic buildings were not what the competition judges were looking for, and his proposal was rejected at the first stage. The winning entry, by Sheppard Robson & Partners, was a low-rise solution based on the concept of a central 'spine' of college buildings surrounded by satellite clusters of accommodation blocks – perhaps influenced by Richard Sheppard's previous experience in designing schools. This campus plan had the same orientation as the great colleges on the Backs – that is, a facade and gatehouse facing east towards town, giving way to college courts to the west and then a great lawn or meadow, in this case utilised as playing fields. But there the easy comparisons end.

The college's austere facade, consisting of two massive flanking blocks of light-coloured brick divided by horizontal concrete beams, may not appeal to traditionalists, but it must be accounted one of the most impressive gatehouses in Cambridge. Its drama is only increased by the vivid colour of rampant Virginia creeper on the adjacent squash courts. The college describes itself as a 'memorial', and there is something Cenotaph-like about this entrance. In fact it bears a strong resemblance to Edwin Lutyens' India Gate memorial in New Delhi. If so, this was a clever nod from the architects towards both the concept of memorialisation and Sir Winston's role in 20th-century history.

A short run of moat at the entrance is all that remains of Sheppard Robson's original plan for a large lake in the south-east corner of the site. But it adds further distinction to Churchill's opening salvo. Observant visitors may also spot the native bee orchid (*Ophrys apifera*) growing in the vicinity.

Behind this monumental entrance, the architects specified a two-storey 'concourse' running dead straight, east to west, with entrances to the porter's lodge, buttery, 'club room' and dining hall, with the senior combination room (SCR) and master's lodge adjoining. A separate building just to the south contains a large lecture hall (the first to be purpose-built in an Oxbridge college), the library, an exhibition, and the archive where Churchill's papers are deposited. The buildings themselves are mostly realised in brick, with horizontal concrete banding formed by the load-bearing beams. This brick-and-concrete treatment, pioneered by Le Corbusier at the Maisons Jaoul 'double house' (1952–55) in Neuilly, was a modernist idiom thought to be suitable for residential developments (it was later used at the Barbican in London). The larger collegiate structures, such as the library and dining hall, feature either precast or 'shuttered' (textured like wood) sections of concrete as part of the composition. This is perhaps most successful in the case of the library's elegant vertical 'ribs' of concrete. The striking, triple barrel-vaulted roof of the dining hall, which is

today the architectural feature most associated with the college, was not part of Sheppard Robson's original design. It is redolent of a very 1950s style of English modernism exemplified by the Festival Hall on London's South Bank.

Grouped around these central buildings were the ten flat-roofed accommodation courts in three clusters of three (two large courts separated by a smaller court), plus one stand-alone large court. The larger courts were grassed, the smaller ones paved, with the division between the 'cloistered' walkways around the court and the open space marked by an elegant band of light grey granite gravel that is still regularly refreshed today. The playing fields stretch out to the west, on the far side of which were placed accommodation blocks for graduates and families.

Despite its radical architecture, and unlike most other colleges founded in the 20th century, Churchill College was in many ways positively retrogressive in outlook at the outset. It was to be an all-male college. The lifestyles envisaged for the master, fellows and students seem anachronistically aristocratic today, with servants' bells provided in the master's lodgings (a new-build house of the 1960s, remember) and careful planning of a wine cellar demarcated into areas for fellows' and students' bottles. Some of the architects' modern ideas slipped under the wire, however, such as the necessity for car parking – indeed, a road bisects the campus – and also the enforced mingling of students and fellows by the placement of the buttery (the students' domain) on the route from the SCR to the dining hall. This was supposed to encourage the fraternisation of the entire college body, but proved predictably unpopular and was soon got around. The all-male ethos was dropped in 1972, when Churchill became one of the first three traditionally male colleges in Cambridge to admit women.

The ground plan we see today at Churchill is not quite what the architects had envisaged, either. Sheppard Robson's original idea had been for a series of 20 courts that would loosely encircle the main buildings and create the impression of one large enclosed court. But budgetary constraints led to a reduction in the number of courts and an enlargement and rearrangement of those remaining. This entailed the loss of a sense of enclosure around the heart of the college, since a large 'hole' now opened up to the west of the lecture hall, revealing vistas out to the playing fields. The meaningful landscape element of the original plan was thus eliminated, because without some sense of enclosure, the grassy areas between the buildings become 'dead space', having lost their identity as a constituent element of a great court. (One can compare this with St Catherine's College in Oxford, the greatest modernist statement of either university, where the Danish designer Arne Jacobsen made every inch of the college site – architecture and exterior space alike – expressive of a coherent overall vision. He even produced a planting plan.)

It was perhaps difficult for the architects to anticipate the psychological impact of what may have seemed at the time a minor change to their ground plan. Their focus would have been almost entirely on the buildings. Yet the result is that a walk from the accommodation blocks to the main buildings of college has become a chilly commute across open space, rather than an immersion in the college community as described physically by a structure of connecting courts. With their inherent sociability and prevailing atmosphere of cocooned privilege, traditional enclosed courts and quadrangles act as a metaphor for collegiate life, a 'function' which some modernist architects seem to miss. There are very few places for students simply to lounge about at Churchill.

A related issue is the division in this scheme – and to be judicious, in the schemes proposed by all the other architectural practices – between 'public' areas of college such as the hall and library, and the residential areas or staircases. In line with the modernist credo, it was assumed that a 'rational' plan, informed above all by the functionality of different buildings, is an inherent good. But one of the keys to the success of traditional collegiate structure is the way in which these functions are jumbled up together in a positively irrational manner, with student accommodation cheek-by-jowl with chapel, hall and master's lodge. It is a structure which undoubtedly contributes to a college's sense of community, and since it is missing at Churchill, the college has had to work harder at creating an atmosphere of sociability and communal endeavour.

A major compensation for the undesirable sense of open-endedness west of the principal college buildings is the role now played by Barbara Hepworth's bronze sculpture *Four-Square (Walk Through)* (1966). This monumental work is the jumping-off point for views out across the playing fields, up to the extraordinary postmodern tower associated with the Møller Centre, and on to the copse beyond. The sculpture lends the scene a certain grandeur appropriate to a Cambridge college and is arguably the most expressively dynamic artwork placed in any Oxbridge college garden. The great bronze is held in affectionate regard by the students, who naturally gravitate towards 'the Hepworth' on warm, sunny evenings.

The site for the new college was to be a large, open area of agricultural land off Madingley Road, sloping slightly upwards to the west. There were a few existing trees, including a line of elms at the eastern end, but aerial shots of the period show it to be an almost blank canvas. An often waterlogged canvas, alas – as the construction team discovered. Attempts to create the playing fields were hindered by a series of particularly wet and cold winters and the heavy Gault clay. Early on there had been talk of an outdoor ice rink for the college; it was certainly cold enough, but at this point the priority was simply creating a usable area of turf where hockey, rugby and perhaps even cricket could one day be played.

At the outset, in 1959, Sheppard Robson had the foresight to engage the landscape architect Sheila Haywood as a consultant; she was to stay on as an advisor until 1974. Haywood had initially trained as an architect but then spent ten years in the office of Sir Geoffrey Jellicoe, Britain's leading post-war landscape architect. Less well-known than other pioneering female landscape architects of her generation, notably Sylvia Crowe and Brenda Colvin, Haywood was a modest and retiring person who did not promote her practice through books and articles, or by public appearances. Nevertheless she was a quietly effective member of that group of post-war landscape architects involved with large-scale schemes at power stations, reservoirs and factories. Haywood's own speciality in this regard was the rehabilitation of gravel pits, a characteristically unheralded genre.

Crowe, Colvin and Haywood had all designed domestic gardens, especially earlier in their careers, but later on, as landscape architects, they tended to favour trees and shrubs over what may have been considered the 'frippery' of herbaceous planting design in the immediate post-war era. Haywood did not publish anything specifically about her work at Churchill, but in an article of 1954 she observed how 'The shaping of trees is a subject which has always interested me: I would sooner see an exciting and stimulating shape in a commonplace tree or shrub than a horticultural rarity which lacked

form.' Accordingly, Haywood's ideas for the Churchill site were based around a framework of trees – principally evergreen oaks – with shrub plantings near the buildings, their rounded lines complementing the angularity of the architecture. The chief shrub was to be yellow-flowered *Mahonia aquifolium*, bolstered by clipped box hedging. There was to be more detail within the enclosed courts, but in the wider landscape the basic shrub and tree palette was kept deliberately limited. At this time serviceable shrubs such as *Viburnum tinus*, cotoneaster and pyracantha were not quite the clichés they would later become – but to modern eyes the approach might be described as 'austerity planting'.

Haywood's first plan, entitled 'Outline Landscaping Proposals' (1959) consists of a single sheet of paper and a sketch. A tonal distinction is made between the planting around the buildings (mainly specimen trees, and some shrubs) and the planting inside the courts (more decorative and thematic). The following year Haywood elaborated upon this theme with a second proposal, suggesting 224 specific trees for the landscape, including 'large trees to reduce bleakness' on the playing fields (cut-leaf beech is one recommendation). She also specified 'decorative trees' around buildings, notably *Acer griseum* and *A. pensylvanicum* (there is a fine example in the Master's and Fellows' Garden). Of the courts, she stated: 'The grass courtyards in particular need in my view a certain amount of both lightening and

modelling to give them more interest. I have made some suggestions on each one, and you will see that in general I have suggested the introduction of either paving patterns or some vertical emphasis such as statuary.' Haywood did indeed come up with planting plans for each of the enclosed courts, as well as for the plots around the Sheppard flats to the west, and these are now lodged in the college archive. The signature style across the piece is bold contrast in colour and form, chiefly realised through tough shrubs such as hypericum, potentilla and cotoneaster, with splashes of floribunda rose (the old shrub roses were only beginning to be 'rediscovered' at this date). Choisya, cornus and fatsia were also freely deployed, but there is little herbaceous detailing. Among the trees suggested as focal points in the larger courts are *Magnolia kobus*, *Acer davidii* and *Rhus typhina*, and some of these survive today, or have been replaced with the same species. The smaller, paved courts would feature lavender and thyme, while Haywood's plantings in the borders against the buildings comprised hard-wearing cotoneaster, viburnum, skimmia, aucuba, mahonia and crataegus.

ABOVE LEFT A grove of *Prunus* 'Tai-haku' by the Wolfson Flats.
ABOVE CENTRE *Gemini* (1973) by Denis Mitchell, with the autumn foliage of liquidambar beyond.

Trees were planted – indeed, Sir Winston himself came and planted a black mulberry and an oak as 'foundation trees' in October 1959 – but the framework was never fully implemented. The result is an impression of individual specimen trees dotted about the college site, with some avenues associated with new buildings. The playing fields were left as open spaces, creating the rather bleak aspect Haywood had warned against. The shrub plantings, predictably, lasted far longer than any herbaceous material and for years dominated the college's garden appearance. The problem with Haywood's chosen shrubs, if not kept in check, is that they soon become great lumpen shapes which occupy planting space but do not result in lively horticulture. Accordingly, the planting at Churchill gradually lost its detail over the decades. When the present head gardener, John Moore, arrived in 1996, he recalled 'a monoculture of mahonias, *Viburnum tinus*, *V. rhytidophyllum*, garrya and cotoneaster'. (As it happens *V. rhytidophyllum* is rather fashionable at the moment – but perhaps one can have too much of a good thing.)

The gardens have been enriched and enlivened over the past decade through a plant palette which reconfigures the horticultural identity not just of the enclosed courts but of other parts of the college site, too. In the courts themselves, the concept of the focal tree has been energetically reintroduced, so one might come across the 'banana courtyard' (as the gardeners call it), with huge *Musa basjoo* specimens and *Dicksonia* tree ferns surrounded by grasses, or a courtyard with two contrasting trees, such as *Magnolia kobus* and *Robinia pseudoacacia*. Others are focused on a ginkgo, or a paulownia, while one or two are rich in the foliage of, for example, *Sambucus nigra*. Churchill's mulberry 'fell over' in 1994 and now needs propping, but it remains untouchable and still forms the heart of one court. Haywood had suggested topiary forms originally, though this was never achieved in her time. The idea has recently been introduced in South Court.

A recent addition is Cowan Court, unveiled in 2016. Designed by architects 6a, it has been realised in a wood-shingled 'modernist shack' style which fits well with the college aesthetic. The open centre of the court has been planted up with a grid of silver birch trees on wood chippings. Not only is this the biggest cliché of modernist garden design, it also falls headlong into the trap of overplanting, a mistake one sees frequently in Oxbridge colleges. Unless it is thinned in due course, this court will inevitably become dark and over-burdened by foliage.

ABOVE RIGHT A number of courts are focused on a specimen tree – here in North Court a white mulberry, *Morus alba*.

OVERLEAF The view west towards the Møller Centre, with the far end of the herbaceous border and an avenue of young fastigiate limes, which will grow up to obscure an uninspiring facade.

There is one set-piece herbaceous border, against the southern wall of North Court, with irises, kniphofia, aruncus, alchemilla, knautias, dahlias, cephalaria, grasses, lychnis, asters, rudbeckia, and the giant sculptural forms of cardoons and macleaya looming at the back. This area is almost bare in winter, of course – so a little further on one finds a winter border with cornus, hellebores, sarcococca, viburnum, hamamelis, hebe, mahonia and wintersweet. Close by is the Master's and Fellows' Garden, mainly laid to lawn, with a lovely maple, a dawn redwood and a massive *Magnolia grandiflora*, as well as 'Iceberg' roses on supports, pink penstemons, lysimachia, rheum and ligularia. A small gap in a fence leads to an effective trio of hornbeams for shade. It is also the site of the Sir Winston Churchill plant collection, which displays about a dozen of the 21 varieties named after the great man, including two roses, a conifer, a dahlia, an iris, a dianthus, a fuchsia, a peony, four orchids, three saxifrages and an eating apple. There is a small garden associated with the master's lodge itself, an intriguing little space with a Japanese-inspired front garden on two levels with a pond.

The main spinal route of the college continues west along the edge of the playing fields, past North Court and up to the glass-fronted music pavilion and gym, which has a small courtyard featuring seating and the serviceable grass *Calamagrostis* 'Karl Foerster', phormiums and cistus. This part of the college begins to take on the character of a business park, an impression reinforced by the presence of the massive Møller Centre, a residential management-training facility designed by Henning Larsen and opened in 1992. This is not an attractive building, but a double avenue of fastigiate limes breaks up its facade.

Behind these buildings and running east-to-west in parallel with the college's spine is the original service road, now known as Churchill Road. Thousands of narcissus are planted among the silver birches lining it, and the entrance to the Møller Centre is also here. This is an impressive box parterre laid out in the shape of the Maersk shipping line logo, the company that paid for the building, with lavender, nepeta, echinaceas and grasses colouring it up. Beyond are the Wolfson and Sheppard flats, postgraduate and married quarters which were part of Sheppard Robson's original design. The swastika form of the Sheppard Flats would have been a sick joke at this of all colleges if it had been intentional (it is not clear if it was), but it does create some attractive garden possibilities. Associated with the Wolfson Flats and the so-called 'pepperpot' graduate buildings is a grove of *Prunus* 'Tai-haku', with fine shows of spring blossom. The Wolfson Flats, made

ABOVE The long border against the south side of North Court, with asters, sedums, dahlias and cosmos planted in clumps and drifts in the contemporary way.

for families, incorporate an original 1970s playground which is now of some historic interest, though the children who use it may disagree.

The far western part of the site, on gently rising land, is now taken up by what the garden team refers to as a 'mini arboretum', with ash, copper beech, horse chestnut and hawthorn combined with purple acers, clerodendrum, *Magnolia* 'Leonard Messel', cornus and + *Laburnocytisus* 'Adamii'. There is an aspiration to create a perimeter walk around the entire college, which is ringed mainly by native British trees – there are now around 700 trees on the site in total. The college chapel stands alone at the western end of college – it is only 'affiliated' with this rational, empiricist, scientific institution – surrounded by some 20,000 daffodils in spring. The playing fields at Churchill are a venue for rocket and balloon launches by Cambridge University Spaceflight, a student society founded in 2006.

There are a few more secret areas to be discovered. At the eastern end of Churchill Road, near the entrance, are a number of early-20th-century houses acquired by the college on Storey's Way. The large rear garden of one of these, No. 72, and part of No. 70, is the site of the new Xiaotian Fu Garden, created in 2016 using funds donated by the eponymous college alumna and designed by the head gardener on a cruciform plan, with brick benches and four small square pergolas entwined with Chinese wisteria. The central sculptural focus of

the garden is a magnificent limestone rock from the Three Gorges region of the Yangtze River, while another gnarled rock stands at the entrance. Next door is No. 76, which harbours what is possibly an even greater surprise: a serious orchid collection in an immaculately kept greenhouse. The collection was the gift of alumnus Dr Frank Maine, who grew orchids while a student at Churchill. It now numbers more than 250 varieties, including *Paphiopedilum* 'Winston Churchill' (of course). Behind this are the middle common room (MCR) greenhouse and vegetable plot, and an attractive old remnant orchard.

The gardens at Churchill College have effectively been resurrected in recent years and now boast some fine moments, notably in the enclosed courts with their signature plantings. Yet the site as a whole still cries out for a coherent overall landscape plan. It is to be hoped that in due course the college will engage a first-rate firm of landscape architects capable of imposing a rigorous landscape scheme to complement, finally, the uncompromising nature of the architecture. In the meantime, college members and visitors can enjoy a rich variety of garden spaces, many of which come as a surprise.

ABOVE *The Now* (1999) by Nigel Hall sits on the college's front lawn as part of a permanent curated collection of sculpture. A short run of moat is visible in the foreground.

CLARE COLLEGE

SOME OF US ARE SEEN to best effect from behind. Clare College falls into this category. The college buildings are viewed to advantage from across the Cam and the vantage point of the fellows' garden – which is perhaps the most romantic in Cambridge and is certainly the most fabled. The palatially elegant west range of Old Court, completed in 1688, is much closer here to the viewer than are the college buildings in other celebrated vistas along the Backs. Three storeys of tall sash windows (altered to suit the fashion in the Regency period) and then a balustrade, attic dormers with dignified pediments and lofty chimneys, only add to the feeling that the visitor has been elevated, somehow, to a higher plane of existence, in intimate conversation with the 'country house' across the water. Superlative horticulture helps. And a beautiful bridge across the river. Old Court admires the fellows' garden while the fellows' garden admires Old Court. The mirroring water between them brings to mind the story of Narcissus.

The college is set upon a plot of land that is squeezed between King's, Trinity and the Old University buildings – with Trinity Hall squashed up against its northern edge. On maps it looks like a planning error: King's College Chapel, that great medieval edifice, is just 11 metres/36 feet away from the south-east corner of Clare's Old Court. But Clare slots in like a slim debutante shimmying past a crowd of noisy matrons. There is a serenity about this college, settled inside its own self-admiring little capsule, sanguine and content. Aware of its own beauty, it does not take much mind of its neighbours. Beauty can afford to be generous, too, and Clare lends its gorgeous profile – the south range of Old Court – to a scene that belongs to King's and to all of Cambridge, complementing and balancing King's chapel and the facade of the Gibbs Building in the composed view across Scholars' Piece.

LEFT The view along the Avenue towards Clare Bridge and Old Court's west range. Clipped yews in the Scholars' Garden loom to the right.

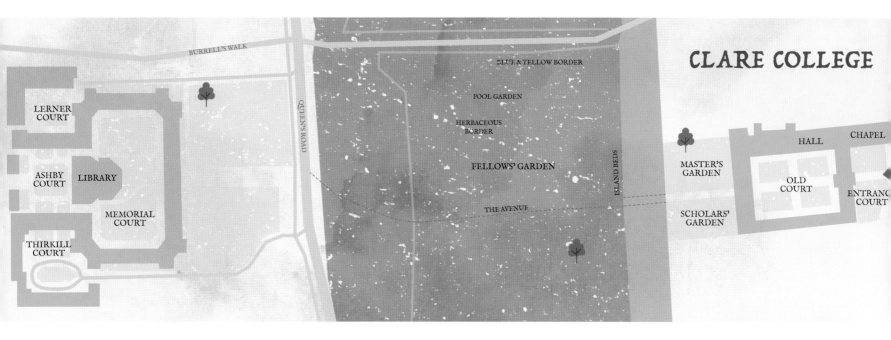

Labels on map: BURRELL'S WALK; QUEEN'S ROAD; LERNER COURT; ASHBY COURT; LIBRARY; MEMORIAL COURT; THIRKILL COURT; BLUE & YELLOW BORDER; POOL GARDEN; HERBACEOUS BORDER; FELLOWS' GARDEN; THE AVENUE; ISLAND BEDS; MASTER'S GARDEN; SCHOLARS' GARDEN; HALL; CHAPEL; OLD COURT; ENTRANCE COURT

Clare is unusual in that the heart of the old college consists only of one court, constructed over a continuous period from 1638 to 1715. But what a court it is. A felicitously scaled exercise in 17th-century neoclassicism, it displays a remarkable homogeneity of style among the Cambridge colleges, even allowing for the variations in its facades, with a continuous balustrade and a run of dormer windows to top it off and unify. The names of the several architects or 'surveyors' responsible for Old Court are not known, but it is thought they were among those working under the young Christopher Wren at Pembroke and Emmanuel, where his chapel designs introduced a fashion for the neoclassical to the university, most clearly reflected in the west range of Old Court.

Clare's own chapel (1769) was tacked on to the eastern side of college, and overlooks the small entrance court giving on to Trinity Lane which has wrought-iron gates and railings and a fine monumental gateway of 1675 topped by swagged urns. This entrance court, tucked away at the end of the lane, is like a slightly quaint 'front garden' to the college. It is laid to lawn with a double lavender hedge lining the central path, a few shrubs along the north (chapel) wall such as hebe and holly, and an old prunus in the lawn which is about to be replaced.

Inside college, Old Court is simply four plats of perfect grass kept up by one of the six gardeners here, who is designated the lawn specialist. At one time each plat featured a single tree; they are shown on Loggan's 1690 engraving of the college, where they appear to be elms or oaks. Head gardener Steve Elstub says he would have liked to reinstate these trees but the requirement for a marquee to be erected here has made it impossible. It would probably prove too controversial a move, anyhow, as Clare is proud of its architecture and does not wish to see it obscured. An interesting feature, which one comes across occasionally in the Cambridge colleges (never in Oxford), is a row of clipped bay laurels on the north range which

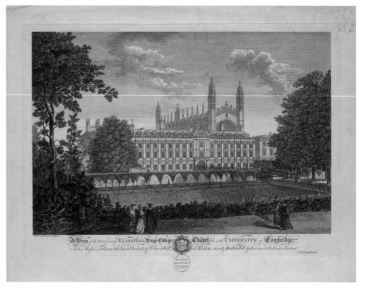

ABOVE By the mid 18th century, the fellows' garden at Clare had become a fashionable place for both town and gown to perambulate. At this time there was an elegant pleached lime hedge along the river's edges, as shown in this engraving from the 1760s by Peter Spendelowe Lamborn.

TOP RIGHT Subtropical planting in the fellows' garden, with a view across the river to the master's lodgings.

appear to be growing up as a green foundation for the pilasters of the hall. It is an effective device made even more attractive by the addition of creeping rosemary, lavender and santolina.

A passageway takes the visitor west out of Old Court and into a short avenue that is in fact the beginning of a causeway leading to Clare Bridge and out into what were once fields. The avenue is raised up and bounded by low walls and a large clipped beech hedge on the north side. This obscures the master's garden beyond, which is largely laid to lawn, with a gravel path to the riverside down the middle. There is a huge copper beech here and a traditional herbaceous border (evergreen clematis an interesting addition) on the northern, south-facing side. An attractive double flight of steps leads up to a doorway in the west range of Old Court; this is the garden entrance to the master's lodging, one of the most salubrious such situations in Cambridge. In the early 19th century *New Cambridge Guide*, the Clare master's garden was described as 'pleasant and tasteful, with a large green-house and a terrace walk'.

The Scholars' Garden is almost a mirror image on the other side of the avenue, reached via a gate and steps down which squeeze between two huge clipped yews shaped like sugar loaves. Students have nicknamed them Tweedledum and Tweedledee. The garden features a central gravel path and a long, blowsy, south-facing

herbaceous border with geraniums, inulas, cardoons, thalictrum, daylilies, aconitum, hostas and delphiniums. In the shadier border against the south wall are shrubs such as big lilacs, viburnums and lavender, with abundant *Clematis montana* behind. A clipped yew bastion hedge at the eastern end of the path marks a sort of full stop against the college building, contrasting oddly with a huge misshapen yew in the south-eastern corner. In the basement of the west range here there was once a cold bath or plunge pool, much in vogue in the early-to-mid 18th century, which was removed only in the late 19th century. The river end of this garden is raised up to form a viewing terrace over the water. This was the site of the old college privies. It is sometimes forgotten that conveniences or 'necessary houses' were very much a part of life in gardens, even at institutions such as Cambridge colleges.

The landscape architect Robert Myers has been a consultant to the college for several years, and plans have been afoot for a complete redesign of the Scholars' Garden, including the replacement of the path with a rill – but nothing has come of this as yet. Mr Myers has also been engaged recently on redesigning the horticultural aspect of Clare College's Memorial Court, designed in the 1920s by Giles Gilbert Scott as a massive extension to the college across the river and just beyond the Queen's Road to the west. 'Mem Court' was

subsequently extended by the addition of several more courts, and the creation of a new college library in dubious postmodern style in the middle of the original court in 1986. The position of this development was dictated by the presence of two old Scots pines retained as features inside the court, now complemented by other specimen trees and sculptures, notably Henry Moore's *Falling Warrior* (1957) and a metal sculpture representing the DNA double helix, by Charles Jencks. Myers has greatly enhanced the constituent parts of Mem Court with stylishly understated plantings of grasses, hydrangeas, pittosporums and viburnum, along with small groups of birches underplanted with acanthus and ferns.

Clare was founded as Clare House (soon renamed Hall) in 1338, having begun 12 years before as University Hall. This makes it the second oldest college in Cambridge, after Peterhouse. It was renamed Clare College in 1856, and confusion sometimes arises because the Clare Hall that exists today is a separate institution, established in 1966. Cambridge University has been the recipient of the generosity of a number of female benefactors, and in this case it was Lady Elizabeth de Clare, a granddaughter of Edward I, who stepped in to save the new University Hall after it was almost burned down and in financial difficulties. Lady Clare is honoured by the college's use of her surname, not her Christian name, yet Clare is certainly a pretty name for a college, and many prospective students have admitted that they were attracted by it. Perhaps it is fitting, therefore, that Clare was among the first three all-male colleges to admit undergraduate women, in 1972.

The early form of the college, before the rebuilding programme had begun in 1638, was also based around a single court – but it was considerably smaller, leaving more space for gardens between the west range and the river. The old master's garden occupied a long rectangle immediately west of Old Court, with a bowling green tucked in to the south. Beyond this, against the river, was the *Hortus Sociorum*, or communal college garden, in three sections, comprising a productive area to the south, then a pair of lawns with a little covered seat against the river wall, and a more informal area with trees and another covered seat to the north. All of this is shown on a drawing of the college at this period by Edmund Prideaux, and all of it has gone.

The ambitious scheme to completely rebuild the by now dilapidated Clare was prompted by the college's bitterly disputed acquisition in 1638, from its neighbour King's, of a piece of land

---

ABOVE LEFT Two large beds at the eastern end of the fellows' garden frame views out of and into the space.

over the river named Butt Close, which would later become the fellows' garden. (As a matter of fact, and despite the claims to the contrary, Barnabas Oley – an influential fellow and benefactor of college – secured only an extendable lease; Clare was finally able to buy the land outright in 1823.) Butt Close was so named because archery had been practiced there in earlier times. A water meadow, it frequently flooded, and it is not unknown for the river to burst its banks even today; the most dramatic occasion in living memory was in 1978, when the fellows' garden was under 1.25 metres/4 feet of water.

The Clare Bridge, designed by Thomas Grumbold in 1639, was one of Oley's first building projects, along with the causeway raised on sturdy brick walls which allowed traffic to cross the fields beyond to the west without getting bogged down. This was to be the principal access route for materials for the new college buildings. Clare Bridge is the oldest and also one of the prettiest bridges in Cambridge, a three-arched stone structure with a balustrade surmounted by ball finials. (One of these balls has a segment taken out of it – for reasons no one can remember or divine. The most plausible explanation is that it was the work of a disgruntled stonemason – the job would have taken some skill.) Lime trees were planted along the new causeway at this time, and as they matured

Clare's walk westwards towards the fields became known for its beauty, as Thomas Salmon's guidebook *The Foreigner's Companion through the Universities* (1748) attests: 'The whole University almost resort to Clare-Hall to walk in Summer Evenings, where, on the one hand, they are entertained with the View of elegant Buildings, Gardens, Groves, and a River; and, on the other, Fields of Corn which are equally beautiful at all Seasons of the Year almost, even in the Depths of Winter.' It is possible that Salmon was referencing Joseph Addison's famous essay concerning landscape gardening in the *Spectator* of 1712, when he suggests 'Fields of Corn make a pleasant Prospect, and if the Walks were a little taken care of that lie between them…a Man might make a pretty Landskip of his own Possessions.'

The Butt Close paddock was not developed as a garden at this point but we know from King's College's 1647 deposition (explaining why it should keep hold of the land) that 'This little piece of ground…is all we have both for the walkes and exercise of at least an hundred persons, and allso for the feeding of Tenne horses.' One cannot help imagining that Clare also wanted this land – 1 hectare/2½ acres – because of the potential for building a new court across the river in future. It certainly fought extremely hard in the early 19th century to win the legal right to do this. The Loggan engraving made in the 1680s shows it as an unadorned open space bounded by trees. Loggan's city map of the same date labels it 'Clare Hall Meadow' and more clearly shows a double avenue of trees against the river, as well as a double row along the northern edge of the causeway (the southern side belonging to King's). The riverside avenue is also shown on 18th century engravings, along with a hedge beyond that ran parallel to it, north-south, bisecting the paddock. By the time of Peter Spendlowe Lamborn's engraving of the college made in the 1760s, the riverside limes had been elaborately pleached into arches which echo the rhythm of the pediments of the college's west facade beyond; the hedge is also clearly depicted, cutting across the lawn (it remained *in situ* until the 1920s).

In Harraden's *Descriptive Guide* to the university, a pamphlet compiled in the 1780s, it is remarked that Clare possesses 'a handsome Bridge leading into the fields', with no 'garden' mentioned. So it appears that the recreational use of the space between the late 17th and early 19th centuries was as a 'walk' along the riverside – college members could process under an avenue of trees while sheltered from rain and sun, also avoiding the boggy meadow itself. (Wet or cold feet were a very real danger to health and to be avoided at all costs – hence the emphasis on dry-shod formal walkways.) The Lamborn engraving shows a few other details of note. The brick supporting walls of the causeway avenue are clearly visible (these disappeared only in the 1920s when builder's spoil from the creation of Memorial Court was used to 'naturalise' them). And just visible through the trees are several brick structures against the river in the Scholars' Garden – probably the aforementioned privies. By the time of John Le Keux's engraving of 'The Garden, Clare Hall' in about 1840, the pleached limes of the riverside avenue have gone – but a single gowned fellow is still perambulating the banks of the Cam, with small shrubs and trees irregularly arrayed around, and sheep grazing on the grass. By the 19th century Clare's garden was renowned,

BELOW The sunken Pool Garden is a horticultural inner sanctum for the dons. An impression of greater length is created by the two pairs of sentinel Irish yews.

with one guidebook describing how it is 'the favourite promenade of the university and town; and, on a fine summer's evening, is filled with an assemblage of well-dressed company'.

In the later 19th century the western half of Butt Close paddock – which by then was known as the River Garden – was given over to an orchard (where a large summer house was added in the 1920s), while the eastern half was further subdivided by a diagonal hedge. Behind this hedge, to the north and west, was a productive area, backed by a low wall for fruit-growing (part of it still stands), while in front, facing the river, was a large triangular lawned area with a perimeter path. This is the same lawn we see today. Specimen trees including a swamp cypress by the river and Judas tree were also planted around this time (they survive today), and there was a line of elms against the northern boundary, with yews beneath. Most of this can be seen on a prospect of the college drawn by Harold Tomlinson in 1926. Lacking the space for a separate kitchen garden within reasonable distance of the college, Clare secreted its orchard and vegetable garden behind the large hedge, while it appears that the gravelled walk around the lawn was essentially an extension of the old riverside walk. The presence of the specimen trees indicate an attempt at the informal 'gardenesque' style which was very much in vogue in Oxbridge college fellows' gardens by the mid 19th century.

There is, however, evidence of another college garden at Clare, created in the mid 19th century on the site where Memorial Court stands today. The official college history published in 1899 states that 40 years earlier 'the fields at the back of the College across the turnpike road were laid out as a garden, in accordance with plans prepared by Mr Stretton.' (It is not known who this Stretton was.) This area also appears on late-19th-century Ordnance Survey maps labelled as a Clare College garden, though it does not appear to have loomed large in the life of the college and may have been neglected or curtailed. It is possible this area was earmarked as a kitchen garden, but the project was abandoned.

The River Garden itself was in decline and overgrown by the 1930s, when a nickname for Clare College was 'the palace in the jungle'. It could not be said that the college is 'in' the fellows' garden, exactly, so it is likely that this moniker was inspired, too, by the state of the scholars' and master's gardens. These had also devolved into the gardenesque style by the early 19th century, with serpentine paths around sinuous beds and specimen trees, and may well have become just as unkempt as the area over the river. Nevertheless, despite its apparently semi-dilapidated state, some fellows still enjoyed the River Garden; one liked to sleep in the open there, bowls continued to be played on the lawn and an autumn border was kept up throughout the war. It is always the case that those who revivify gardens tend to exaggerate how run-down they were when they arrived; head gardeners are especially prone to be scathing about their predecessors' work. It seems to be a natural impulse.

At the end of hostilities in 1945 the college fellowship met and a decision was taken to transform this orchard-cum-vegetable-garden-with-lawn-attached into a new fellows' garden. Nevill Willmer, a microanatomist who had conducted research into optics, was invited to take charge of the project, as he was known to have an interest in such matters. Describing himself as 'a keen Sunday painter', Prof Willmer devised a number of what he called 'viewpoints' in his mind's eye, and planned various horticultural effects dependent on colour intensity and optical length. The Arts and Crafts movement and specifically Hidcote were his inspiration; the plan was for a garden of 'rooms' or episodes which would make for a succession of delightful surprises. As Willmer put it in one of his detailed accounts of the garden's development: 'The plan was to provide a variety of "scenes" and develop a series of vistas, making use of trees as dominant points of interest, as background for herbaceous borders or shrubs, or as frames to enclose a vista and direct the eye along it.' The garden was meticulously thought-out by its designer, who strove to increase one's impression of the size of the garden by means of optical illusions and changes in the level and direction of paths. The garden Willmer designed and saw realised in 1947 almost in its totality is very close to what we see and enjoy at Clare today.

There are two entrances into the fellows' garden. The first is via a gate and set of steps immediately north of the bridge; the second is two-thirds of the way along the lime avenue of the causeway. This second gate (2007) was designed by Wendy Ramshaw and features a fish-eye lens in an oculus, ostensibly so that visitors barred entry might be able to get a glimpse inside by this means (not that much of a consolation, in actuality). The visitor emerges from this gate through a layer of shrubs chosen for autumn colour and the decrepit trees of the old lime avenue, and out on to the expansive apron of lawn, which on this southern side has been left uncut at the fringes, to create wildlife habitat. The lawn prefaces a majestic view across to the west range of Old Court, peeping out enticingly from behind the copper beech in the master's garden. A great herbaceous border runs along the northern edge of the fellows' lawn and traces a sinuous curve almost its entire length, following the rough outline of the old diagonal hedge which formerly subdivided the garden, and which today takes the form of a great bubbling line of clipped yew. A giant dawn redwood, behind the border and the hedge and almost at the centre of the garden, towers over the scene. It was planted in 1947. The herbaceous border is some 7.5 metres/25 feet deep in places and is absolutely packed with flowers in summer. These have been planted out in seemingly random abandon, with explosions of purple, white, red and yellow along the entire length, created by peonies, daylilies, delphiniums, bearded irises, anchusa, stachys, anemone, geraniums, rudbeckia, solidago, sedums, crocosmia, achillea, aquilegias, heleniums, roses and much else. The result is a multicoloured border of big effects, suited to the scale. There is not a discernible theme, as such, but an exotic and structural note runs through the plantings, with red-leaved bananas taking centre

garden and the sunken Pool Garden lying at the heart of Prof Willmer's design. This rectangular space is bounded by yew hedges on three sides, with the old fruit wall forming its northern boundary. There was already a pool garden on this site, occupying a smaller space, and Prof Willmer continued the idea of a hedged 'inner sanctum' for fellows. (One of the roles of a fellows' garden has always been as a space where academics can let their hair down without fear of being spied upon by students.) The 1920s summer house in the centre of the garden was removed and the existing pool garden was redesigned and replanted, with the exception of two gnarled apple trees which are remnants of the old orchard and add character to the enclosure. The result is a feature indebted to 1920s Arts and Crafts style, with a central waterlily and iris pool set in an apron of lawn, bordered by a low terrace wall overflowing with cottage plants. This sunken centre is surrounded by another area of lawn, flowing up to the yew hedge. The overall impression is of a dinky and delicate feature, low-slung and appealingly small in scale. Prof Willmer stated that his inspiration had been a visit to Pompeii, where he had seen a similar pool, but there are countless examples of sunken 'Italian' pool gardens of this genre to be found in southern England. Perhaps the Pompeii reference was made to please the classicists, often a powerful lobby within colleges. The planting around the pool has a decidedly alpine theme, with thrift, saxifrages, species tulips, ophiopogons and small sisyrinchiums planted in the grit on top of the low walls. At the north end of the Pool Garden is a bed of stachys and geraniums with grasses, and roses 'Constance Spry' and 'Mermaid' on the boundary wall, mingling with *Clematis* 'Perle d'Azur'. Two pairs of sentinel Irish yews, also at the northern end of the space, are deliberately of unequal size, to enhance the impression of length. Overall, however, this formal feature lacks something (a central ornament, perhaps?).

The eastern exit from the Pool Garden, through another gap in the hedge, leads out to a double border of great elegance and intensity, realised almost entirely in flower tones of blue, mauve and yellow. The delphiniums, one of the main features here, were apparently planted to mimic the silhouette of King's College Chapel, visible above the roofline of Clare's Old Court. Other plants in the border include geraniums, aconitum, anchusa, yellow bearded iris, achillea, verbascum, cistus and yellow roses. There is a lollipop laburnum in one corner, while at the east end a

stage, while glaucous cardoons create a backdrop against the yew behind and the zingy tones of euphorbia offset the rest. The ground plan of this garden was carefully devised by Prof Willmer; the herbaceous border is designed to be viewed down its entire length both from its western end and from a more distant viewpoint, from the top of the steps of the master's lodgings. This latter vista is framed between two island beds on the eastern side of the garden, by the river, which contain 'hot' late-summer plantings designed not to upstage the main border earlier in the season. At the far western end of the lawn are three smaller beds specifically intended to form a distant 'full stop' to the border when seen from the master's lodge. The rationale of the planting in these beds is slightly mysterious, but the principal note is a 'hot corner' with a jungly feel, with abutilons, cannas, bananas, yellow wallflowers and phormiums. Adjacent is an area planted up with the pastel tones of phlox in white and pink, a curious juxtaposition.

A gap in the yew hedge opposite the oculus gate takes the visitor into the 'garden rooms' of the fellows'

ABOVE *DNA Double Helix* (2005) by Charles Jencks was installed in Memorial Court to honour the discovery of the chemical structure of DNA in 1953.
LEFT A long border hidden behind the Pool Garden, with a palette of purples, blues, and yellows.

specimen of *Aesculus glabra* (Ohio buckeye) droops decorously. This tree was a sapling when it was about to be removed in 1947 – but its strong autumn coloration was noticed by a young gardener and it was retained. It is one of a small number of trees that survive from the garden's earlier incarnation. Every fourth year the herbaceous plants in the fellows' borders are lifted and divided – which is one reason why they are always packed to the gills. And there are always plenty of flowers left over for cutting for displays in the college chapel and for feasts, which the head gardener arranges himself, as is traditional and correct. South of the blue-and-yellow border, in the shade of the dawn redwood, is a small bog garden with hostas, ferns, aquilegia, meconopsis and candelabra primulas. A large collection of astrantias can also be enjoyed here in early summer.

The north exit from the sunken garden, through an iron gate in the old wall, takes the visitor into a shady, kinking west-east walk edged by a low clipped box hedge. This feature was formerly known as the Dean's Walk, supposedly because the college dean in Willmer's time liked to pace here while composing his Sunday sermon. It was previously overshadowed by an avenue of elms, removed in 1947 and replaced by a yew hedge in Willmer's plan. This walk has been realised as a narrow garden, almost a border, of white-flowered subjects including forms of aquilegia, iris, spiraea, osteospermum

and buddleia, together with a *Davidia involucrata* (handkerchief tree) and cornus to vary the height. It runs adjacent to the blue-and-yellow border, immediately south, and some white-flowered plants such as choisya and philadelphus overflow pleasingly into that area.

These two features terminate at the eastern, river end of the garden, where the pleached lime avenue once was. A rose pergola running along the riverbank in 1945 was removed by Prof Willmer. In its place are the two substantial island beds which frame views in and out of the garden, planted up with hot-coloured plants such as dahlias, cannas, heleniums and crocosmia, supplemented by all kinds of annuals. The southern bed is more orange in theme while the northern one is red and crimson. The plants are arranged in height order in the old-fashioned way, with small plants at the front, giving these globular beds almost a Regency feel – quite in keeping with the architectural style of the college. With the pergola gone, Willmer noticed an oriental quality in the riverside scene, with Clare Bridge seen through the fronds of a willow, so he enhanced this theme by planting a pair of pink weeping cherry trees on the bank, underplanted with *Anemone blanda*.

ABOVE Clare Bridge vies with Trinity Bridge for the accolade of 'prettiest bridge across the Cam'. It was designed by Thomas Grumbold in 1639.

At the other end of the garden, running along the western perimeter next to one of the dikes that mark three of its sides, a narrowing yew walk has been given the unappetising name, 'the tunnel of gloom'. It leads past an immaculate little nursery and gardeners' buildings (Mr Elstub heads an extremely well-organised outfit) and into a small scented garden overhung by weeping silver lime (*Tilia tomentosa* 'Petiolaris') and the remnants of various shrubs planted here under Willmer's direction, such as viburnum, philadelphus, wintersweet, skimmia, roses and honeysuckle. This area has lately been altered to become more of a subtropical garden, with bananas, cannas, ricinus and other exciting foliage plants.

Much has been made of the impact of Prof Willmer's scientific interests on the fellows' garden – the way his knowledge led to experiments with different colours at different light levels and distances, together with the use of optical illusion. It is suggested that from his research flowed an understanding that in low light blue flowers become lighter and red flowers darker, that blues fade in the distance while reds hold their colour, and that the use of yellow in the foreground and pastel colours beyond increases the impression of distance. In fact the type of colour theory Willmer pursued was already well-established, having been developed in considerable detail by Gertrude Jekyll and her followers in the Edwardian era, who

were themselves applying the findings of Chevreul and the French mid-19th-century textile manufacturers. The garden's layout was not notably innovative, either, in that it remained dependent on the old 19th-century structure and inherited its major aesthetic shortcoming: the rather strange diagonal division of the garden into a section of lawn and a veg garden which was then developed into 'garden rooms'.

The Clare College fellows' garden nevertheless rightly remains one of the high points among Cambridge's college gardens. Its sustained renown can be attributed to Willmer's vision and also to the skills of the resident gardeners in whom Clare has been singularly fortunate over the course of the past 70 years, beginning with Walter Barlow in Willmer's time, and continuing with Mr Elstub today. As for Clare College, it is impressive that the master and fellows continue to allocate resources to the garden. They clearly appreciate what they have.

ABOVE LEFT Strappy subtropical foliage is a relatively recent addition to the fellows' garden.
ABOVE RIGHT The view west from college across Clare Bridge.
OVERLEAF Narcissi light up the scene by Clare Bridge in spring. The weeping cherry beyond is just beginning to blossom.

CORPUS CHRISTI COLLEGE

WHAT A CHANGE SUDDENLY CAME over little Corpus in the 1820s! Almost overnight it transformed itself from a slightly shabby medieval college of modest means and proportions, into a grand if not grandiose institution with a new frontage towering over Trumpington Street. No other college has altered its physical form so completely since the time of David Loggan's celebrated series of Cambridge engravings, published in 1690. The college was completely redesigned and reoriented by the architect William Wilkins in a sturdy and uncomplicated Gothic manner, more than doubling in size at a stroke with the addition of spacious New Court, which destroyed a large portion of the old college in the process. Up until then Corpus Christi, founded by two town guilds in 1352, had not even had the confidence to use its real name (which at times had had a slightly dangerous whiff of 'popery' about it). It had generally been known instead as Bene't College, after the church adjacent that had served as its chapel for several centuries.

As for a garden in this new Jerusalem – there was not much room. Corpus has always been squeezed into its city-centre site, fixed as it is between the two immovables of St Bene't and St Botolph churches. The new master's lodge and its garden were generously appointed, but the old fellows' and master's garden had been sacrificed to make way. The fellows now found themselves in brand new accommodation in the east range of New Court, and perhaps that was seen as adequate compensation. But it seems a shame for the college to have lost its garden at this time. Surely every college in the centre of town needs a garden, to take the edge off the pressures of urban existence and provide some perspective. It must be acknowledged, though, that the current garden team at Corpus have been extremely successful in carving out little garden areas in nooks of the college – there are flowers everywhere, while

LEFT New Court at Corpus Christi forms the centrepiece of the college as it was reimagined in the 1820s. It was almost a complete rebuild, with a grand new entrance on Trumpington Street.

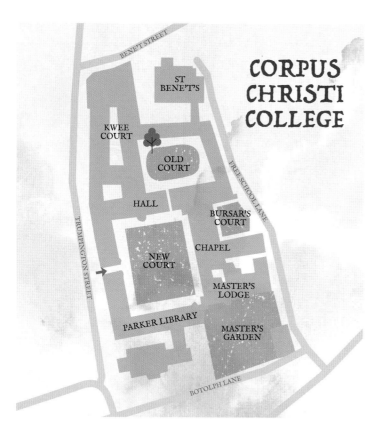

CORPUS CHRISTI COLLEGE

TOP RIGHT Bicycles outside some of the medieval buildings in charming Botolph Court. These ancient houses were converted into student accommodation in 1983.

BOTTOM RIGHT Bursar's Court, perhaps the most romantic of several little gardens hidden away within college, with an exuberant border backed by cardoons encircling a lawn.

shadier parts that might be overlooked in colleges with more space, have here been filled with hostas, ferns and other foliage plants.

The college's original, extremely modest entrance was on the north side, via Bene't Passage off Bene't Street, passing the church's old graveyard. One emerged into the single court, Old Court, which was railed around with wooden-post fencing by the time of Loggan's engraving. The southern section of the site – the part later demolished – gradually evolved, as different tracts of land were acquired, into a jumble of buildings with various functions, plus the master's and fellows' gardens and other amenities including a tennis court and bowling green. One 18th-century visitor described the fellows' garden as 'snug' but also 'well provided with conveniences'.

Through most of its existence this garden space was divided into different walled sections. The master's garden was at the northern end, directly behind the master's lodge facing into Old Court. Against the southern boundary of the college estate, and entirely separate, was a walled area containing an orchard. We know that this was laid out and planted in 1542 under the direction of Andrew Pierson, fellow, following the demolition of several outbuildings. Richard Lyne's view of Cambridge of 1574 shows three enclosures, one containing the densely planted orchard, then another garden adjacent with what look like larger trees, and then the master's garden, with just two large trees shown. The schematic renditions of the trees cannot be taken as an accurate indication of the appearance of these gardens, but it does show an attempt at differentiation – it is clear these three spaces each had their own character. In addition it seems that there was another garden at Corpus at this early date; Hamond's map of 1592 shows a square garden of beds laid out in a cruciform pattern, just west of Old Court towards Trumpington Street, which was still divided from the college by a row of small houses and gardens.

There is a record of the orchard just a few years later (1577) in the college archives in the form of a lease of part of it from the master and fellows to one of their number, Richard Willoughby. He was granted a 40-year lease on a triangular section of the orchard, measuring 36 metres/118 feet broad, east to west, by 22 metres/71 feet at one end and 15 metres/48 feet at the other. The master and fellows undertook to build a wall to section it off, at the college's expense, and were to ask no rent from their colleague, save a donation of a dish of apples (at least 12) each year for the hall table. It seems, on the face of it, a good deal for Willoughby, though we don't know the exact circumstances of the arrangement. He had fallen out with the previous master over his (the master's) puritanical leanings, while the current master was a thoroughgoing royalist, so perhaps that had something to do with it.

More pertinent than this speculation is the way the orchard document makes a few matters plain about the 16th-century garden at Corpus. First, the orchard is described as belonging to the fellows specifically at this point, so it is clear that – as at

Pembroke – Corpus's fellows' garden began life as an orchard. Second, the document mentions the existence of both the tennis court and 'the Masters gallery', the latter being perhaps the most remarkable appurtenance in the Corpus garden at this time. It had been erected between 1544 and 1553 during the mastership of Matthew Parker, an exceptional college principal who later became Archbishop of Canterbury. It was Parker who assembled the extraordinarily rich library of Anglo-Saxon and other ancient books that still bears his name and is the college's most treasured possession. The two-storey gallery extended some 21 metres/70 feet south out of the lodge at a right angle, the upper level carrying the master and his guests across the western end of the private master's garden and providing views down into it. Parker's gallery was cherished for several centuries; in his 1753 history of the university, Edmund Carter records that the master's lodge 'is not very spacious, yet hath many good Apartments (especially the long Gallery), with a pretty flower Garden'. It was Parker who first put up a wall between the master's garden and the rest of college; he also built the dovecote (1547).

As if not to be outdone by the principal, the fellows erected their own rather grand summer house in the early 17th century. The first version must have been a little flimsy, as it was blown away in a gale in 1648, but it was then rebuilt at a cost of £50. This building is shown on Loggan's engraving: a two-storey structure with an elegant open arcade or loggia below and a gallery above. It was pulled down in 1756, when the rubble was used to create a terrace at one end of the college bowling green, which had been laid out just north of the fellows' garden some time in the early 17th century (perhaps on the orchard land earlier leased to Willoughby). Some of this rubble was used to create an alcove seat next to the bowling green, which was in all likelihood a replacement for the little alcove made of branches visible on Loggan's engraving.

By the late 17th century the fellows of Corpus had made themselves a miniaturised version of the kind of garden enjoyed by those in colleges blessed with more spacious surroundings. One visitor in the mid 18th century described how the Corpus fellows 'would stroll in their pleasant orchard, or sit in their gallery summer house, or if it were wet, walk in the arcade underneath; or perhaps they would watch the scholars busy in the tennis-court, or would themselves play on their bowling green'. This all cost money to maintain, and in the college records for 1699, fellow-commoners

(wealthy students who were allowed to dine with the fellows) are charged a levy of ten shillings per year to help pay for the upkeep of the garden.

The tennis court at Corpus was the first one on record at the university. It had been made out of an unfinished bakehouse, possibly as early as the 1480s and certainly by 1515. At this time it was not tennis but a form of fives or handball which was played, and the roofless court was open to the elements. Parker had this building finished and fitted up in 1569 as the Pensionary, providing accommodation for six students. A replacement tennis court was housed in a building constructed for the purpose, at the far end of the fellows' garden; its roof can be seen on the Loggan engraving and its foundations were rediscovered in 1999. The game played here would have been 'real tennis', in which the walls can be used for rebounds. As for the bowling green, it was retained at this college for quite some time, as Carter records in 1753: 'The Fellows Gardens are very Pleasant, having a grand Bowling-green, a beautiful Summer-house, with variety of Wall and other Fruit, all which are kept in excellent order.' Bowling fell from fashion soon afterwards and by the time of William Custance's map of Cambridge in 1798, it is not clear whether the bowling green exists any longer. And of course within 30 years it was all swept away to make way for New Court.

The visitor to Corpus Christi College today steps trepidatiously into New Court, which bursts with self-confidence: hall to the left, old library to the right, pinnacled chapel straight ahead. Wilkins's monumental gatehouse – with castellated turrets at each corner – seems to be making up for five centuries of condescension, the old 'Bennet College' now just a bad dream. The perfect striped lawn here is sometimes mown twice a day in summer, and there are 'Keep Off the Grass' signs translated to both Chinese and Japanese.

The planting in New Court also expresses confidence, with bright tulips in reds and yellows in the beds against the master's lodge (south-east corner) in spring, huge borders of purple and pink petunias, and window boxes overflowing with annuals all summer – geraniums and petunias supported by ivy and plectranthus. A ceanothus in the north-eastern corner has been trained up the wall in a rectangular

RIGHT Old Court, with its distinctive buttresses, is horticulturally adorned by climbers such as *Campsis radicans* and a range of shrubs and annuals in pots.

shape, in the Cambridge manner. In the south-facing border on the north side of the court, against the hall, is a bright mix including *Salvia* 'Amistad' and *Azara microphylla*, with lavender at the base. The beds surrounding this court are relatively large, and in places edged with grass panels; those against the west (entrance) range can cope with *Cornus* 'Midwinter Fire', *Fatsia japonica*, the grass *Stipa gigantea* above alliums and *Rosa* 'Munstead Wood', with additions for winter interest such as the scented *Daphne odora*, sarcococca, pulmonaria and ferns, and pots of lilies in one corner. (The college crest features three lilies and head gardener Dave Barton likes to make the connection in the horticulture.) In the north-west corner of the court is a little gathering of *Musa basjoo* (banana plants) in pots. The shady south side, against the library, is just as well-stocked as the rest, with hostas, brunnera, heuchera, pittosporum and more fatsia. The paving at this college is particularly smart, with pristine panels of pebbles flanking the flagstones.

Old Court, with steeply pitched roofs and big buttresses on the walls, is much smaller and is blessed with a pleasingly rickety feel. The oval lawn was encircled by iron railings in photographs dating from around 1900, but is now open. There is a fine specimen of the climber *Campsis radicans* on the north wall, and pyracantha and *Hydrangea petiolaris* against the hall to the south, but the floral and foliage effects in this court are achieved mainly by means of container plants. There are maples, weeping standard wisteria and purple *Rhododendron impeditum*, all in pots, as well as huge wooden tubs containing bulbs and annuals in season.

From here it is possible to pass west into narrow Kwee Court, previously a service yard and now the entrance area for the new library. As ever at this college, the most has been made of the horticultural possibilities, which would have looked doubtful to many. In the small triangular beds here are the expected lilies, both regale and crinum, as well as delicate pale yellow *Rosa* 'Claire Austin' growing on supports, with sky-blue delphiniums, salvias, ferns, hostas, heucheras and the little pink-and-white dahlia, 'Rebecca's World'. Four pots of the black bamboo, *Phyllostachys nigra*, provide a fanfare at the doorway into the library.

North of Old Court is a rectangular garden space in the shadow of St Bene't Church, on the site of its former graveyard. Corpus used the church as its chapel until it built its own in 1578, and one curiosity is that the eastern range of this court, dating from about 1500, was made as a connecting passage between the Saxon church and college. The beds surrounding the grassed centre are generously planted with sweet peas and standard roses in various colours, bolstered by a shrub mix including myrtle, spiraea, *Viburnum* × *bodnantense*, photinia and wisteria. There are ferns on the shady south side.

Corpus, it transpires, is a college filled with superabundant little pocket gardens, and perhaps the finest is the romantic space east of New Court, on the north side of the chapel, called Bursar's Court.

An old mulberry grows on the south side against the dignified backdrop of the chapel windows, with cyclamen below it in spring, while on the western side a pergola is festooned with grapevine and *Rosa* 'Teasing Georgia', and underplanted with asplenium ferns and hostas. The circular lawn is surrounded by delightful herbaceous plantings – a hottish border against the north wall with lilies, sunflowers, dahlias, rudbeckias, white lychnis, the deep crimson sweet William 'Sooty' and that fiery stalwart *Crocosmia* 'Lucifer'. There are cardoons for height and structure, and cordoned apples at the back. The shady south side features a nicely balanced mix of pulmonaria, hostas, alchemilla and viburnum, while in the corners are crab apples 'Golden Hornet' and 'Red Sentinel'. There is a secret doorway out of college here, surrounded by the pink climbing rose 'The Generous Gardener'.

The present master's garden occupies the space that had been reserved in the 16th century for the fellows' orchard and garden. It's surprisingly spacious, with a wide lawn, an evergreen oak in one corner, a *Parrotia persica* tree, a tulip tree (*Liriodendron tulipifera*)

ABOVE The planting beds around New Court are smartly edged with cobblestone panels and narrow strips of lawn. Hostas and *Fatsia japonica* are among a wide range of plants chosen for foliage effects.

and an extremely old mulberry. There are three big bays on the master's lodge, with *Clematis montana*, wisteria and a Banksian rose climbing up the facade, along with a *Magnolia grandiflora* which flowers gratifyingly low. The landscape architect Todd Longstaffe-Gowan was recently engaged to alter the garden so that it is more suitable for events, and the master and his wife hope to implement the plan imminently, which will result in a larger terrace area, the removal of the existing greenhouse and the creation of a small new rose garden on the east side.

The master's garden is often used as an entertaining space, but is not freely available to college members (partly because until now the only way in to it has been via the master's study). For a period the 19th-century fellows did have their own garden, a little way from college on spare land east of the Corpus cricket pitch on Sidgwick Avenue. When it was laid out in 1883, there was a dispute between the fellows as to the design of the garden, with some arguing for a mount at one end and a 'valley' effect beyond it. The fellow leading the faction in favour of a flat site lost the battle and never set foot in the garden again. It is said that he was taking tea one day with the Mistress of Newnham, when he looked out of her drawing room and exclaimed at how pleasant the view was. 'Why, it is your own college garden,' came the reply, at which the unfortunate man retreated to a distant corner of the room and changed the subject. In 1948 the college decided to sell the cricket pitch and fellows' garden to the university and the land was built upon.

There are some compensations for members of college who are garden-lovers, because Corpus's graduate hostel one mile (1.6 kilometres) away at Leckhampton (known as 'Leckers' in college) has 3.8 hectares/9.5 acres of grounds as well as an open-air swimming pool. The house is an attractive essay in Victorian red-brick Arts and Crafts, with four large gables, a balustraded balcony and a ground-floor loggia giving on to the garden. Around it are spacious lawns (with a Henry Moore sculpture), mature trees, a croquet lawn, a wildflower meadow blessed (unusually) with self-seeding *Lupinus polyphyllus*, and several herbaceous borders, while the two modern blocks which have been added to the site, in 1964 and 2012, are of good quality and relatively unobtrusive.

For a college to lose one fellows' garden may be regarded as a misfortune; to lose two looks like carelessness. But the Corpus Christi garden team work hard to create an atmosphere in the gem-like spaces of the 'Old House', and in this they have been notably successful.

ABOVE A burst of tulips is a springtime feature in the beds and window boxes in front of the master's lodge in New Court.

DARWIN COLLEGE

Q UIRKY LITTLE DARWIN IS A happy sort of place, a haven for graduate students who mix on (almost) equal terms with their down-to-earth tutors. That happiness is certainly increased by the characterful college garden, an L-shaped strip of land made up of the back gardens of a run of houses along Silver Street and – around the corner – Newnham Terrace. Then there is the river, or at least a diverted tributary of it, and also, wonder of wonders, two private islands reserved for college use, connected to the 'mainland' by a charming wooden bridge – not quite mathematical like the one just downriver at Queens', but certainly anagogical, in that it carries the visitor up and over the water and into the metaphysical realm that is Darwin's archipelago.

The college was founded in 1964 as the first graduates-only institution in Cambridge on the initiative of Trinity, St John's, and Gonville and Caius colleges, and began with just 14 students in its first year. The heart of the college was and remains Newnham Grange, a late-18th-century house altered in the 1880s, with a large converted granary building adjacent. The property had been in the Darwin family for around 80 years and was donated on condition that the new college's name should honour the whole family – not just Charles Darwin, who never saw the house; it was his son Sir George Darwin who had bought Newnham Grange in 1885. In addition to these two properties (the Grange and the Old Granary), in 1966 the college acquired the Hermitage, a mid-19th-century building in Regency style a little way west along Silver Street. And in more recent times it has expanded around the corner into the row of Victorian houses in Newnham Terrace. Today's Darwin College effectively spans the entire distance between the Granta pub on Newnham Road, all the way along to the Silver Street Bridge, presenting an orderly and business-like facade to the world which reveals nothing of the riverine never-never land that lies behind.

LEFT The college punts moored against the river frontage, with the burgeoning garden behind. The magnificent copper beech tree has been a feature in the garden since the 19th century.

The domestic atmosphere of the garden at Darwin is often commented upon, which might seem inevitable, given that it is composed almost entirely of the remnants of back gardens. The spreading lawn and mature trees make it a pleasant enough spot, but it is the architecture which contributes most to this impression of domesticity – the modest verandah of the Grange, and the elegant bow-window effect of the Hermitage's rear elevation, clad in purple wisteria. There is a quirkiness, too, to lift the scene above the norm, reassuring us that we are in a special place. This is expressed in the unrestrained late-1960s modernism of the octagonal dining hall, raised up on its external spiralling staircase like a spaceship come down to land, and in the insistently regular brick facade of the Rayne Building, which now connects the Grange and the Hermitage. Both buildings were the work of the notable modernist architectural practice Howell Killick Partridge & Amis. Then there is the Old Granary at the site's eastern end, a characterful ex-industrial building made considerably more curious by the addition of tall windows and a long balcony punched through the brickwork, poised directly above the water, like the *piano nobile* of some palazzo along the Grand Canal. The picturesque 'spectator's gallery', fashioned behind a portion of its long facade, comes as a fine surprise, with views over what was once a pristine croquet lawn but is now – as of 2019 – the new John Bradfield Court, largely occupied by a 'multi-purpose' building designed by architects Allies & Morrison. The final, triumphant transcendent note comes when the visitor decides to cross the bridge to Little Island, instilling a sense of escape from reality which only an island – even a very small island – can produce.

The main lawn occupies the north-west corner of the college estate, a space chiefly defined by the dining hall and the Hermitage. It features an armillary sphere – that favoured 'intellectual' garden accoutrement of Oxbridge colleges, commonplace enough to have become a cliché. The lawn narrows at the eastern, Newnham Grange end, until it becomes a paved pathway forming a terrace above the river. The college's punt fleet is moored here, next to a narrow river's-edge path planted with acanthus and a large fig tree. The small verandah outside what was Sir George Darwin's study in the Grange is draped in the vine 'Black Prince', which produces small black grapes.

Students and tutors are often found lying or sitting on the gently sloping lawns at Darwin, the scene somewhat reminiscent of Georges Seurat's celebrated painting *Sunday on La Grande Jatte*. Several large trees dominate the area around the lawn in a somewhat random manner, notably a stark paperbark birch, an extremely tall pear tree, a liquidambar, an oak, a huge old copper beech which has been chopped about by necessary tree surgery in recent years, and a pair of slender but venerable London planes over on Big Island. The beech is presumably the same tree mentioned by Maud Darwin, Sir George's wife, in a letter written just before they moved in to the Grange: 'The fruit trees are all in blossom, the lilac and wistaria out and the river so nice. There is a lovely beech tree with iron steps down to the river, it is the most romantic place possible.' The basis for that vision was laid down in the early 19th

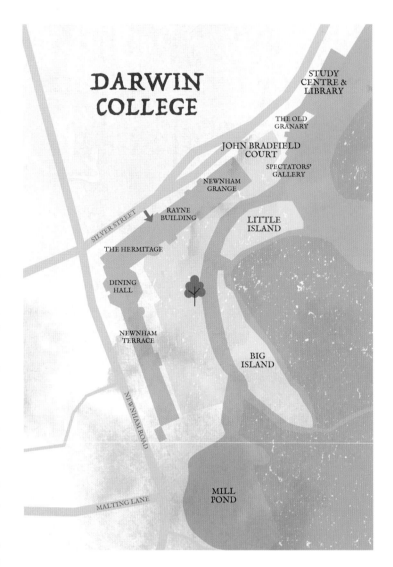

RIGHT Wisteria festoons the rear of Newnham Grange, the late-18th-century house which forms the heart of the college.

century, to judge by the sale particulars for the Grange when it was purchased by the previous owner in 1851: 'Green-House, Shrubberies, Lawn, and Ornamental Garden, extending to the beautiful meandering Stream forming a branch of the River Cam, across which are two Islands, presenting altogether a most delightful Residence, suitable for a Genteel family.' Some of that garden would have been lost when the Hermitage was constructed a few years later. But it still feels genteel enough for the family (genteel or otherwise) which is Darwin College.

Next to the dining hall is a curious little garden space known as Jurassic Park containing various 'prehistoric' plants such as Wollemi pine, Dicksonia tree ferns, pseudopanax and *Trachycarpus fortunei*, as well as hostas and ferns. Perhaps a boulder representing an asteroid would be an apt addition, as some of these plants look a trifle addled. This marks the beginning of a series of gardens occupying what were formerly the back gardens of the Victorian houses along Newnham Terrace. Their dividing walls have been shortened to facilitate access but not removed altogether, allowing for a sense that these remain discrete areas. As such, each one has its own theme. There is a rose garden, an allotment garden tended by students, a woodland garden and a garden with classic herbaceous borders – yellow roses, fuchsias, penstemons, kniphofias. There are several old apple trees, including the variety 'Blenheim Orange', and the college has acquired, perhaps over-ambitiously, a cider press. The last

garden in the row is a delightfully secluded space with a little summer house converted from a Victorian potting shed, and a plantation of *Camellia sinensis* at its boundary. There is a limit to what the college can achieve, horticulturally, as Darwin no longer employs a head gardener but uses a contract garden service that visits once a week.

On the eastern side of the college estate is the Old Granary, a remnant of the industrial character of this part of Cambridge, where numerous warehouses, wharves, mills and a brewery were associated with the two-way river traffic. Goods coming up from King's Lynn joined the Granta here (as the Cam is usually called south of Silver Street); while for goods heading north, it was the last navigable stretch of the river before barges took over along the Backs. Big boats unloaded and narrow barges took on new cargoes in this frenetic commercial zone. The Beales family, first owners of Newnham Grange, made their money from the river trade in coal and corn, and originally there were three granaries on this site. The Old Granary itself is an intriguing building in its present form, especially when seen from Lammas Land, the area of common land across the water from Darwin College. The architect employed by Sir George Darwin to internally reorganise Newnham Grange and convert the granary into accommodation was John J. Stevenson, a Scottish architect of scholastic inclinations who operated at the cusp between the elegant red-brick formalism of the Queen Anne style and

the nascent idealism of Arts and Crafts. In his writings he attacked the concept of restoration and what he saw as the desecration of medieval churches by many of his contemporaries, including his old master George Gilbert Scott. He favoured complex, asymmetrical fenestration on facades and the addition of white-painted balconies, verandahs and exterior staircases. That look, which sails dangerously close to quaintness, is certainly evident on the river frontage of the Old Granary, with its famously 'rickety' balcony.

Stevenson's masterstroke here was the 'spectator's gallery', on the north side of the Old Granary facade, overlooking what was originally a tennis court and later, by the mid 20th century, a croquet lawn. This beamed gallery is highly romantic in the Arts and Crafts spirit and evidently fulfilled a similar function to the kind of corner loggia that became popular in the Edwardian period in sunken Italian or courtyard gardens. Its great point of difference is the way it is raised up by one storey, giving it a frisson of an Elizabethan belvedere or decorative lookout tower. It remains to be seen whether this gallery will still have a meaningful function when John Bradfield Court is completed, since the new building is covering over the old croquet lawn and thereby completely altering the character of the space. One cannot help feeling doubtful about the way Darwin has destroyed its most distinguished

exterior space in order to build one fairly small room – 'big enough to host a lecture for 65 people'. At least the landscape designers involved are first-class: Christopher Bradley-Hole and Brita von Schoenaich. Historically there was one other garden in this part of college – a long sliver of land east of the granary up towards Silver Street Bridge was made by Sir George Darwin into a walled kitchen garden with fruit trees. This was destroyed in 1994 to make way for the college's new study centre (a fancy term for 'library'), which looks better inside than out.

On the way back down towards the bridge over to Little Island, the visitor passes a 'dry garden' with cardoons, cacti, succulents and black ophiopogon grass. The wooden fretwork bridge was completely rebuilt in 2004 after the old one was almost washed away in floods two years before. This part of Cambridge has always been a place of bridges. In the medieval period the whole area was known as Small Bridges because of its complex network of islands, dikes and tributaries, and the various bridges which connected and crossed them. The most important of these

---

TOP LEFT A pair of London planes on Big Island tower over the lawns of the college garden, which has a pleasantly informal feel.
BOTTOM LEFT A memorial armillary sphere and the flaming foliage of a *Rhus typhina* 'Tiger Eyes' specimen, outside the college dining hall.
BELOW Apple trees in a quiet glade on Big Island.

was looked after by a priest, or hermit, who was charged with its upkeep and would possibly have taken a toll. Bridges have long been associated with priests. There was a tradition of small chapels on medieval bridges; the chantry chapel on the old Wakefield Bridge is the most notable survival. The first mention of the Cambridge hermit is in the 1390s, when he is named as one John Jaye. In 1428 reference is made to both a hermitage and a hermitage garden, which survived for more than a century after that before being demolished. Darwin College's 19th-century Hermitage was named in honour of this history.

The point about islands is their apartness and, in theory, their inaccessibility. The harsh truth is that the idea of the island is often considerably more attractive than the reality. Islands, particularly those on English rivers, can be a disappointment. Maud Darwin was nevertheless enchanted by the islands across the water from the Newnham Grange garden when she arrived in 1885: 'We found both islands lovely, the one just opposite the house simply a mass of blossom and nettles. Peonies, laburnum, lilacs, cherries, currant and gooseberries. It was much larger than I thought too and so pretty.' Initially the Darwins would have crossed the water by boat but Sir George soon applied for permission to build a bridge to Little Island and from there another bridge to Big Island (at this point both islands were being leased from Cambridge Corporation). These bridges have been continually repaired and rebuilt

to this day. Little Island is a favoured spot for student barbecues and simply 'chilling', on simple wooden plank benches beneath a venerable old plane tree (one of the oldest in Cambridge, for sure), or on the grass near the willows which dip their fronds into the water. There is autumn colour from a *Parrotia persica* tree but otherwise the island herbage is simply self-sown sycamores and the kind of native scrub which is a haven for insects and birds. Big Island feels even more cut off. It is a well-known trysting place, with an open glade at its centre. For students who decide to use their time even more profitably, the college has some salient advice: 'Those wishing to spend the afternoon quietly working on their dissertation with a laptop can retire to the Big Island, as wi-fi covers the whole garden.'

ABOVE The bridge that leads across the water to Little Island has been rebuilt several times since it was first constructed by Sir George Darwin, who lived at Newnham Grange in the late 19th century.

TOP RIGHT The autumn scene in the college garden, with the modernist Rayne Building in the background.

BOTTOM RIGHT Tulips and Solomon's seal are among the spring delights in one of the old back gardens of the terrace of Victorian houses along Newnham Road, which the college now owns.

OVERLEAF A tranquil spot on Little Island, shaded by a yew and a fine old plane tree whose trunk can be seen (left).

DOWNING COLLEGE

DOWNING IS A DREAM. THE impression is of walking into an idealised field, an Elysium where gods and heroes might disport themselves. At the perimeter of this pasture, pristine neoclassical buildings seem to be floating, like galleons moored in some great ancient seaport reimagined by Claude, or as the perfected revelation of Plato's doctrine of ideal forms.

Nowhere else in either Cambridge or Oxford is quite like Downing, which was conceived in deliberate divergence from the norm of successive quadrangles and courts, in favour of an arrangement where each building can stand independently while lending balance to the whole. The pasture-like space in front of the buildings was not imagined as a garden, exactly, although horticultural elements have developed over time, but rather as a limpid green suspension in which the buildings, framed by their honeyed Ketton-stone facings, appear like golden diadems set in lucent aspic. The result is an environment that can seem stark, grandiose and alienating, or else delightfully surreal and fittingly impressive – depending on one's disposition… and the weather.

The tortuous process of Downing's century-long gestation has been told and retold, so the following is only the most potted of histories. In the year 1700 George Downing, later 3rd Baronet of Gamlingay Park, was obliged to marry his cousin, Mary, in secret, when he was 15 and she was only 13. Since they were deemed too young to live together, George set off on travels around the continent, instructing his teenage bride to remain with her family in Shropshire until he returned. But it was not to be. When Mary was 15 and already a notable beauty, she accepted an invitation to become a 'maid of honour' at the court of Queen Anne (keeping her marriage secret). On hearing of this, George wrote to her in plaintive terms, begging her to retire to country obscurity, but both she and her parents defended their decision. That was, effectively, the end of the marriage as far as the unbending George

LEFT The view across the Quadrangle towards the dining hall from the portico of the master's lodge.

BELOW RIGHT The scale and ambition of the Downing scheme can be appreciated from the plan of 1822 drawn by its architect, William Wilkins.

FAR RIGHT Despite the relative simplicity of its layout, the landscape at Downing is possessed of many moods, its character changing with the weather.

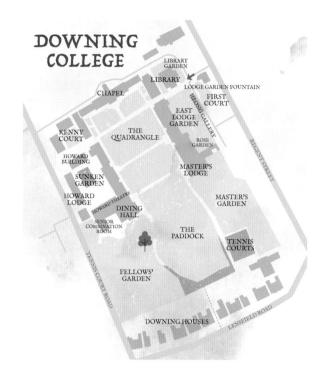

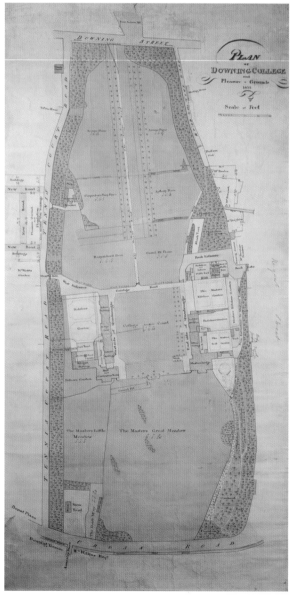

was concerned. The couple were officially estranged, and when he inherited the baronetcy in 1711 Sir George retired to a new-built house on his estate at Gamlingay Park in Cambridgeshire, where he embarked upon a long affair with his housekeeper.

Sir George was a rich man and his landholdings produced a healthy annual income of more than £4,000. He had a daughter by the housekeeper but no legitimate heir – so who would inherit? Sir George's will stipulated that his estate would first pass to a cousin, Jacob Garrard Downing (later 4th baronet), and thence to his issue. If Sir Jacob had no children, however, the estate would go to one of three more cousins, each named by Sir George in clear order of succession, and then their heirs. In the unlikely event that all four cousins died childless, provision would be made instead to establish a 'Downings Colledge' in Cambridge.

Sir George died in 1749 and his cousin Sir Jacob duly inherited. When it became apparent that his wife, Margaret – later styled Lady Downing – would bear no children, and as all the other cousins died childless one by one, the couple began a concerted effort to hold on to Sir George's land and money, and in so doing prevent the establishment of the college. It is even claimed that they had new farm buildings placed on wheels so they could be removed easily from contested estates. After Sir Jacob's death in 1764, Lady Downing energetically continued these machinations in the Court of Chancery, further delaying the college's foundation and depleting the endowment. Just before her death in 1778 she tore down the mansion at Gamlingay and sold off the contents, while her will took several more decades to unpick. No wonder Lady Downing is something of a bogeywoman in the college's history: her portrait now hangs in the senior combination room (SCR), having been removed from college hall where it was prone to being pelted with food on high days.

If Lady Downing is the villainess, then the college's hero is the MP Francis Annesley, a descendant of the first Sir George Downing. He spearheaded the ultimately successful attempts to prise the Downing inheritance away from Lady Downing's heirs-at-law, and then became the college's first master at its foundation in 1800, exactly 100 years after the loveless marriage that began the story.

Building started six years later, on a piece of land known as Pembroke Leys, to the plans of William Wilkins, who was a 24-year-old fellow of Caius when he designed it. An amateur architect, he had travelled widely in Europe, soaking up scenes of the classical world as he went. Wilkins's Downing College was conceived in an austere, intellectual and 'pure' Greek Revival style which set it apart from the exuberant, worldly neo-Palladianism of the previous century. It was self-consciously at the cutting edge: a superior, slightly uptight and 'very Cambridge' form of neoclassicism.

The landscape setting imagined by Wilkins was to be as important as the architectural style. He planned a college of discrete, separate buildings in four ranges gazing at each other across a vast open space at the centre known simply as College Court, divided into four grass plats by two wide pathways forming a cross, appropriate to the monumental scale. The original Downing site was almost double the size it is today (the northernmost portion was sold off in around 1900 and is now the location of the university laboratories), and Wilkins's plan involved thick shelter belts of trees at the perimeter giving on to large areas of grassy sward (these trees survived until the 1970s and the onset of Dutch elm disease). The idea was that the college buildings would appear to be set majestically on a green plain, gradually hoving into view as one approached from the north, down a dead-straight drive lined with lime trees, culminating in a grand entrance portico, or propylea.

Wilkins's experience of ancient Greek and Roman ruins rising up from the landscape must have stimulated his vision for Downing, as well as paintings of cult Italian scenes from the Grand Tour – the Temple of the Tiburtine Sibyl, for example – by artists such as Claude, Poussin, Rosa and Dughet. The idea of a long, narrow avenue of tall trees leading directly to a grand entrance comes from the Italian Renaissance, though in the Mediterranean the trees would have been cypresses, not limes. Closer to home, the classic views of Cambridge from the Backs will surely also have been an irresistible inspiration, notably the tableau of King's College chapel and the Gibbs Building, with the college meadow and Scholar's Piece in the foreground. And then there is the domestic context, which has not been commented upon: the Downing layout perhaps also picks up on the relationship in Cambridge town between dwelling houses and a central open area, or 'piece'. It is true that sometimes the college feels like a strange little model town – Poundbury *avant la lettre*. Ultimately, Downing is an other-worldly amalgamation of all these various but complementary visions. Little wonder it has a slightly surreal quality.

In the event, and as so often happens with Oxbridge colleges, the money ran out before the vision could be fully realised. By 1820 the east and west ranges had almost been completed, including the college hall at the south end of the west range, but nothing was to be seen of the north range and its entrance lodge or the great south range, intended as the site of the library and chapel, connected by a vaunting central portico. The lime trees of the north-south avenue

had been planted, but they simply led straight into the open green space of College Court. The six buildings of the east and west ranges stood as separate entities, albeit linked by screen walls. (Later, the spaces between them were filled in to create continuous ranges, which is usually described as a fundamental misunderstanding of Wilkins's original plan, when in fact the screen walls would have had a similar visual effect – it appears the architect lost this battle early on.) The intention was that each of these buildings should house a professor and his faculty, an idea reprised a few years later by Thomas Jefferson at the University of Virginia – though there is no evidence he knew of the nascent Cambridge college. The Downing layout specified separate enclosed gardens behind several of these faculty buildings, but it seems that only two were realised. Another – hitherto unremarked – example of an innovative scholastic layout at this period was the Royal Military Academy at Sandhurst, where Old College and related buildings were completed in 1812, including a row of houses with gardens for the 'professors' who taught the officer cadets, very much along the lines envisaged at Downing. It is perhaps no coincidence that Sandhurst was the work of James Wyatt, who had come up with early plans for Downing in 1804 but was then dismissed.

The master's lodge was the first building to go up, but Wilkins soon clashed with the second master, William Frere, and his wife, Mary, over her desire to keep livestock on the land abutting Lensfield Road and the area designated for the fellows' garden, and even to erect sheds for them in the space allotted as the master's garden. One must have some sympathy with the architect, having to deal with the apparent determination of his employer's wife to utilise a portion of the college's acreage as a working farm, though pursuing agricultural interests on college land was not unheard of. In his diary for June, 1846, the Trinity fellow Joseph Romilly recorded going for a walk in Downing with his sisters: 'saw in the meadow there the white goat & her 2 kids, but we were kept from them by an iron fence'. In the 1820s Mrs Frere began a series of musical entertainments and 'public breakfasts' in the master's lodgings which became notable events in Cambridge's social calendar. For his part, the master was engaged in planting trees on the estate, especially oaks, commenting in a letter: 'I mean whatever else comes of my memory to be famous for introducing the oak to Cambridge.' The first college gardener was appointed in 1812 and remained for 47 years.

Wilkins's own coloured plan of the college in 1822 is our best guide to what had probably been achieved in the landscape by that date. Wilkins had been frustrated by the demands on space of the master, and the plan seems to bear this out, since much of the land in the eastern part of the college, around the master's lodge, appears to have been commandeered by the principal as his own domain. There is an enclosed 'flower garden' adjacent to the master's lodge; this is the only garden area depicted in any detail, so one might assume it was laid out in this fashion and would have functioned as the master's garden. It is bordered to the east by a curious strip labelled 'entrance to meadow', a rather awkward thoroughfare which was most likely an afterthought. The meadow itself, occupying the entire southern part of the estate (or 'domus', as they like to call it at Downing, with instinctive aureation), is labelled as 'The Master's Great Meadow' (known as the Paddock today), with 'The Master's Little Meadow' to the west, occupying the site later given over to the current fellows' garden. On this plan, a small area next to the kitchens is labelled 'Fellows Garden'. Downing's fellows did not do well out of Wilkins's design at this early date: as well as this piffling garden, which the master's wife was trying to use for grazing anyway, their common room was merely a screened-off area at the far end of the hall.

Back on the eastern portion of the domus, there are two distinct areas labelled 'Master's Kitchen Garden' and a separate 'Master's Fruit Garden', with a hothouse whose foundations were recently rediscovered in precisely the spot marked on the map. A single 'Professor's Garden' is squeezed in among this array of master's appurtenances, and there is ample evidence that it was indeed in existence. In 1809 the first master wrote to the professor of medicine, stating: 'I trust your garden has profited from these late incessant rains here, and that you was in time to put your trees into the ground in the spring…I wish you had more ample space to put your taste into execution.' In 1814 'the garden of the Professor of Medicine' is mentioned in the college accounts, designating James Webb as the man to look after it. (He was previously charged with 'carrying and bringing the college letters'.) Wilkins proposed at least one more 'professor's garden', behind the west range. There is evidence of it being associated with the professor of law. The college accounts of 1822 mention a wall being built around this garden, two years after completion of the west range itself.

RIGHT The area around the north end of the east range has been planted up with shade-loving shrubs, bulbs and perennials to help create a sense of entrance to college.

On a larger landscape scale, the 1822 plan shows the eastern range prefaced by a double line of young trees. The southern (open) end of College Court is partly closed off by a clump of 11 trees and the northern end (also open) is lined with wooden railings against the carriage road which linked the west entrance with the 'back gate' on the eastern side (today the college's main entrance). A fountain is marked at the centre of College Court, though there is no evidence one was ever installed. The college doggedly stuck to the plan of using the north approach as its main entrance into the early 20th century, when visitors would progress down the avenue of limes, which were flanked by tennis courts. This ended when the college sold off the northern part of the estate to the university between 1896 and 1902, though some of the old lime trees survived into the 1950s as a reminder of the original arrangement. Perhaps it was a blessing, anyhow, that Wilkins's idea for a grand processional avenue up to a classical gateway at the college entrance was never realised: it may well have been deemed absurdly pretentious by the sharper tongues of the university. Was it really necessary for a Cambridge college to have quite such a grandiose prelude?

Downing's basic ground plan remained unchanged for the next 111 years, until finally in 1931 Herbert Baker created the north range. A centrally positioned chapel, with portico, was added to it by Baker's partner Alex Scott in 1953. This later neoclassical work is not in the same Greek Revival style as the Wilkins buildings, and is rather bland in context, but most visitors will not immediately register the difference. The new north range emphasised the east-west main axis of the college, which had been adopted after the abandonment of Wilkins's original north-south plan, establishing the east gate, giving on to Regent Street, as the main entrance. Entering the college today, visitors pop out into one corner of College Court (now known as the Quadrangle), which would have seemed hopelessly anti-climactic to Wilkins, perhaps. But one compensation is the element of surprise: Regent Street is among the busiest and most ordinary commercial thoroughfares in central Cambridge, so the visitor now moves in short order from a humdrum mercantile melee into this expansive, uncompromising vision of antiquity.

Various other 20th-century buildings in the college have garden areas associated with them, and several of these have recently been rejuvenated to pleasing effect by consultant landscape architect Alice Foxley. She has been commissioned to produce a revised masterplan for the whole 8 hectares/20 acres of the domus, with a special

ABOVE Snowdrops in the master's garden, a generously appointed space with mature trees and well-stocked borders.

emphasis on the entrance area and routes around college. The first garden space visitors come across is First Court, immediately behind the (air-conditioned) porter's lodge. It is announced by a sandstone vertical cascade feature, underplanted with asplenium ferns, irises and martagon lilies. First Court itself is a small paved area made in conjunction with the Heong Gallery of 2016 (converted from an original building of 1903), featuring a stylised grove of five *Alnus glutinosa* (mixed 'Laciniata' and 'Imperialis'). An inscribed slate plaque on the wall celebrates the first Sir George Downing's status as one of the inaugural graduates of Harvard College in 1642; he went on to be the first tutor there. The link is further cemented by the second verse of the (Latin) 'Harvard Hymn', inscribed in red lettering on stone, like an extremely elegant ticker-tape message.

On the western side of the new gallery is East Lodge Garden, which feels like a miniature arboretum, setting the tone for much of the rest of the college. A huge Indian bean tree (*Catalpa bignonioides*) stands out among the specimens of yellow birch (*Betula alleghaniensis*) and Tibetan cherry (*Prunus serrula*), with its shiny red bark, though several of these trees are to be removed or relocated as part of Foxley's plans (a good idea, to solve overcrowding). At the far end of the space is a magnificent cedar of Lebanon, while clipped yew hedges impart structure. A new acquisition in 2018 for this area is Barbara

Hepworth's sculpture *Two Forms (Divided Circle)* (1969), which makes for an extremely dignified addition, visible also from First Court through the windows of the Heong Gallery. This sculpture formerly stood in Clare College's fellows' garden. There are plans to sow grass here as meadow.

The southern end of East Lodge Garden gives on to a formal rose garden, announced by a fine stone statue of a griffin. Inspired by the rose garden at Warwick Castle and created in 1988, it has never really been fit for purpose. Roses were trained on trellis and arches, with the addition of iris and clematis, to create a quiet, contemplative haven. The plan is to remove the roses from the centre of the space, leaving only the pergola around a simple lawn with pool.

Opposite East Lodge Garden to the north is the Maitland Robinson Library (1993), designed by Quinlan Terry in a festive postmodern manner, with two unusual painted blue urns on pedestals fronting it and containing a changing display of flowers with clipped evergreens (such as yew pyramids). The Library Garden, the third of a trio of 'study

---

ABOVE The East Lodge Garden has been transformed into a woodland garden to complement the planting around the library, visible beyond.
OVERLEAF Crocuses in the fellows' garden, a private space which is nevertheless easily visible from the dining hall's massive portico.

gardens' envisaged in rejuvenated form by Alice Foxley (in addition to the rose garden and East Lodge Garden), has been planted with evergreens and shade-loving ferns, hydrangeas, sarcococca, brunnera and *Geranium phaeum*, in a mainly green-and-white scheme with pink and blue notes. It is exuberant, detailed and highly effective. Opposite it, against the north end of the east range, a wide mixed border lends a sense of continuity to this revivified route into the heart of the college; it includes characterful shrubs such as *Viburnum × bodnantense* 'Dawn' and *Philadelphus* 'Manteau d'Hermine' along with various cornus (for winter colour), escallonia, fuchsia, penstemons, astrantias, astilbes and hellebores. It is remembered in college that much of this area at the eastern edge of the estate was unmanaged scrub and self-seeded trees until built upon. As of 2018 these new gardens constitute the start of a processional landscape design at Downing which will continue as a 'park loop' around the domus.

The visitor progresses westwards towards the main event – the Quadrangle. The imposing portico of the chapel hoves into view on one's right, with a trio of fine old plane trees on the lawns in front. The main Quadrangle area to the left is laid to grass, as it always has been, adorned now by a double avenue of limes and hornbeams running east to west in front of the northern range. The presence of these mature trees, planted in 1968 on the advice of landscape architect Sylvia Crowe, has become contentious because they effectively obscure several key vistas, even though a break in the avenue allows for views to and from the chapel. Crowe's thinking at the time was to lend a better sense of proportion to the Quadrangle by defining its northern boundary more surely and thus 're-establish a sense of the Wilkins square'. This has been the thorniest issue during the recent landscape reappraisal at Downing; it appears the trees are safe for the time being. Among Crowe's other suggestions was the addition of a 'slightly raised' rectangular pool in a paved area in front of the chapel – which would have been a good idea, since the one thing the Quadrangle space signally lacks is the enlivening presence of water.

If the visitor moves farther into the Quadrangle, Wilkins's buildings, notably the hall and master's lodge, appear sturdy and serene, their massive porticoes facing each other across the greensward, with their fluted Ionic columns and starkly unadorned triangular pediments. As ever with neoclassical buildings, the best vistas are always from a diagonal. There is no hint of humour or levity in Wilkins's version of Greek Revival, but on sunny days the college seems to warm up, in every sense. As for the tree plantings here, a Capability Brown or a Repton might have dramatised the Quadrangle and its buildings by means of carefully disposed clumps and single specimens, but the arrangement today appears somewhat random; this is something that is also being addressed by the new landscape plan. Three large plane trees near the dining hall were removed in 2018 to open up the vistas somewhat, part of Foxley's aim to define the 'interplay between garden and grove' in what is conceived as a 'loosely picturesque' landscape.

The Quadrangle extends southwards until it meets the large expanse of the Paddock, used as a cricket pitch in summer. Various interesting trees can be found dotted about, including a black walnut, several maples, a dawn redwood, a 'Raywood' ash and a young *Quercus palustris* among horse and sweet chestnuts. Wild flowers are encouraged under the trees and in a hazel spinney. The far, southern end of the Paddock backs on to Lensfield Road, where Downing owns a row of 19 houses used as student accommodation, each with its own garden maintained by the college team. The vista past the eastern front of the master's lodge and on to the tall spire of the Church of Our Lady and the English Martyrs beyond is one of the quiet beauties of Cambridge, somewhat reminiscent of Constable's view of Salisbury Cathedral.

The garden of the master's lodge is not open to the public, or even to members of college, but it is one of the best green spaces at Downing. This is quite unusual in Oxbridge colleges, where generally the best parts can be seen by all visitors. At 0.3 hectare/¾ acre, it consists of a lawn edged with fine trees, including a handkerchief tree (*Davidia involucrata*), Judas tree and various limes, maples and sorbus, as well as huge specimens of walnut and English oak. A big border at the far, southern end boasts a muscular mix of pampas grass, acanthus, eryngium, lychnis, crocosmia, sedum and verbascums, while the southern facade and portico of the lodge itself lend considerable dignity to the scene. Crocuses and other bulbs drift under the trees in season.

On the other side of the Paddock, mirroring the master's garden, is the fellows' garden, also officially off-limits to the public and students, though certainly more permeable. It sits immediately to the south of the dining hall and the SCR, and is screened off from the Paddock to the east by a pleached lime avenue. The SCR building was constructed in 1966–69 to the plans of architects Howell Killick Partridge & Amis as a modernist interpretation of classical form. This modernist hiccough in the middle of Downing's protracted digestion and regurgitation of neoclassical tropes can be adjudged a partial success. The exacting quality of the architecture is akin to Wilkins's style in that the building is an idealised if not abstracted form, acutely aware of its place in history: an other-worldly pavilion or *fabrique*, it points up the kinship between modernism and neoclassicism. Yet the broken roofline and its dark grey colouring give it a slightly shed-like appearance that undermines its dignity. The reference is Vitruvius's primitive hut, an architectural in-joke that will please some but pass others by. The simple, natural garden around the building is greatly to its benefit. The fellows' garden is certainly an improvement on what was on offer in 1822: an expansive lawned area provides a foil for numerous good trees, including a group of incense cedars, a copper beech, a walnut, a catalpa, a *Magnolia × soulangeana*, a pair of London planes and several evergreen oaks, while a crab apple stands in the centre.

Two more garden spaces associated with recent architectural developments currently represent missed opportunities at Downing College, though the new head gardener has them in his sights. Kenny Court, in the north-west corner, consists of two undistinguished buildings set at right angles to each other across a grassy court with

various clipped shrubs and small trees, centred on a *Paulownia tomentosa* (foxglove tree). It is at present a rather nondescript and interstitial place. The courtyard known as West Lodge Garden occupies a large sunken rectangle in front of a trio of buildings, including the college's very own theatre, designed in the 1980s in extrovert neoclassical style by Quinlan Terry. Relatively narrow rectangular beds line the edges of the sunken space, their light weighting struggling to compete with the powerful presence of the Howard buildings. The restrained naturalistic planting here was designed in 1992 by Sarah Clayton, who also instigated the fine plantings at Trinity Hall's Wychfield extension in Storey's Way – but much of the original detail appears to have been lost. Large grasses such as *Stipa gigantea* conspire with *Verbena bonariensis*, euphorbia species and epimediums in a rhythmic, naturalistic manner, but at this scale they simply cannot hold their own in the architectural context, and the result is that this part of the college has a slightly done-over, hotel-like appearance. The Howard buildings created something of a stir when they were completed, particularly in the largely modernist-dominated architectural profession. For a time in the 1990s Downing, traditionally known as 'Cambridge's neoclassical college', became 'the postmodern college'.

Finally, mention must be made of Downing's 'backstage' area, a narrow strip at the northernmost edge of the domus currently given over to car parking and the college bar and buttery. Some rather good if commonplace tree specimens can be sought out here by the inquisitive visitor, including mature limes, sycamores, chestnuts, oaks, beech, yew and birch. One can also glimpse the ghost of Wilkins's original plan for the site; there is the wistful presence of the lonely western gate and a sense of sudden curtailment at the college's northern edge.

The question periodically arises of 'finishing' Downing by making it as much like Wilkins's original plan as possible. There are dreams, for example, of a south range to semi-enclose the Quadrangle in line with the original plan. But is this necessary? Perhaps now is the time to stop thinking of this college as incomplete. Downing has developed its own character out of this fabric and in most respects has made the very best of what it has. There are a number of other examples of 'unfinished' quadrangles in Oxbridge colleges (the New Buildings at Magdalen, Oxford, being only the most dramatic) but nowhere else does it seem to rankle as much as here. In fact, this is the only place where it appears to rankle at all. It seems strange, when what Downing has to offer today, in the context of all the Oxbridge colleges, is quite extraordinary.

ABOVE The master's lodge as seen from its garden, with the yellow autumn leaves of *Ginkgo biloba* and the scarlet foliage of a smokebush, *Cotinus coggygria*.

EMMANUEL COLLEGE

'A LITTLE PARADICE'. THAT IS HOW Emmanuel's fellows' garden was described by Edmund Carter in his 1753 *History of the University of Cambridge.* The fellows' garden at 'Emma' remains a little paradise, and remains open to fellows only, though it is possible for visitors to gain glimpses of it. It has long been among the most famous of the fellows' gardens in the university because of what is arguably the greatest tree in Cambridge: a massive, ancient and extraordinarily characterful oriental plane (*Platanus orientalis*). Planted early in the 19th century – no one knows the exact date – it exhibits an unusual 'weeping' habit. Its boughs sink right to the ground and in some places even burrow beneath it, sending down roots, before emerging again. Other branches entwine like lovers, while some seem to be making a break for it, over the wall into Parker Street. This living monument even inspired a poem entitled 'El Árbol' ('The Tree') by the Spanish poet and literary critic Luis Cernuda, written while he was based at Emmanuel in the Second World War.

There are some 2 hectares/5 acres of garden at Emmanuel, land originally inherited from the 13th-century Dominican priory which previously flourished on the site. Like Jesus College, another institution created over the top of an existing monastic complex, Emmanuel initially deployed the term 'close' to describe the large area of pasture next to it; the name 'paddock' was adopted only in the late 19th century, presumably because it was then being used primarily for grazing the master's and fellows' carriage horses and hacks, and for haymaking. Familiar from cathedral terminology, a close denotes a piece of land that is mainly open but with some trees or avenues, and is generally associated with a venerable religious house. Emmanuel's paddock contains a long pond which is the modern incarnation of the priory's old stew pond (supplying fish for the table on Fridays and other meatless days), while the open character of the ground is still very much apparent. Given its change of usage across the centuries,

LEFT A view across the Paddock, showing two of three large fastigiate yews at the edge of what was originally a monastic fish pond.

perhaps inevitably some confusion has grown up as to the essential identity of the space. Is it a garden, or is it a paddock? Can it be both?

The Priory of the Holy Trinity was founded in 1238 and by the end of the century the friars' land extended to around 4 hectares/10 acres. It was highly successful as an institution, being one of 18 monastic houses established by the Dominicans in English towns during the first 20 years after their arrival in 1221. The 'black friars' played an important role in the early university and the priory became a centre of learning, attracting scholarly young monks from across Europe. However, the priory met its demise at the dissolution in 1538 and was half-ruined by the time the college took over the neglected site nearly 50 years later, in 1584. The existing gardens would probably have been in equally poor condition. In any case the express intention of Emmanuel's founder, Sir Walter Mildmay, was to eradicate any physical sign of the former Roman Catholic priory, so that the Protestant priests educated at the college would be emancipated from the old papal regime, as he saw it. The name of the college is derived from a Hebrew word meaning 'God is with us', which in this context might be glossed as 'God is with *Us*'. From the mid 17th century Emmanuel would become known as the 'most puritanical' of the Cambridge colleges, though this reputation has perhaps been rather over-egged. In fact, during the English Civil War, the master of every Cambridge college bar one (Trinity Hall) pledged allegiance to the king, while university fellows and students were predominantly royalist, too (it was the town that took the side of parliament). Evidence of the Dominicans' legacy does pop up around college, despite Mildmay's intentions: it is believed Front Court was built on the site of the old cloister, while parts of the priory's fabric, including its church, were incorporated into the college hall.

Emmanuel is one of those colleges – Corpus Christi is another – which has switched around its entrance front. The original way into college was from what is now Emmanuel Street, where a path led up to an east-west building range with stubby wings protruding northwards from each end (not due north – all the compass directions in this chapter have been simplified). On either side of this pathway were long rectangular grass panels, making this a 'garden entrance', as shown by early city maps. There was an impressive gateway against the street, but this was not a court, exactly; more an example of what was known in Oxford as an 'angle' – a building range shaped like a square bracket ( ]). Only in 1824 was this entrance court finally 'completed' on the Emmanuel Street side to create what is now New Court, a deliciously inappropriate name, considering its antiquity, since it incorporates elements of the 13th-century priory.

Vying with the magnificent plane tree as the college's greatest visual adornment is Christoper Wren's chapel, completed in 1677 in deceptively simple neoclassical form with pleasing baroque flourishes. In the college's original orientation, the new chapel could only be discovered lurking behind the old front range. In the late 18th century, however, the entrance was moved over to St Andrew's

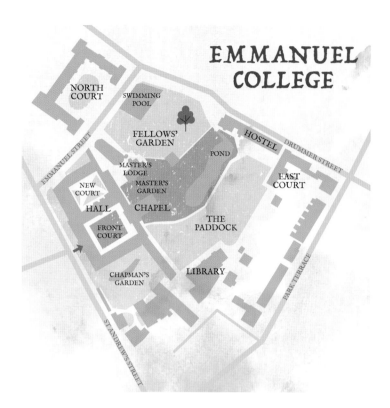

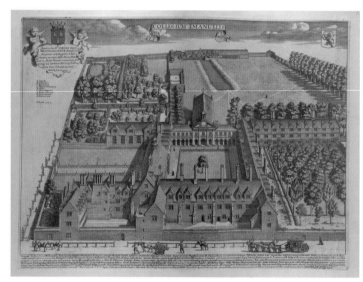

ABOVE David Loggan's 1690 engraving shows the original, straight-sided form of the pond in the Paddock. The college's old entrance, to the north, can be seen (left) and above it the master's and then the fellows' gardens.

TOP RIGHT Looking across Front Court towards Christopher Wren's chapel. On the right, at the corner of the lawn, is one of the stone scrolling brackets the college has retained.

Street, to the west, so that the chapel became the first thing anyone sees on arrival. This was an astute move. Wren's chapel creates a truly memorable opening salvo in Front Court, an explosion of architectural innovation which still 'blows away' first-time visitors to Emmanuel. The repeating arches of the cloister seem to give the building a weightless appearance while also conspiring with the strong horizontal force of the fenestration on the upper storey to create an intimation of the infinite. The horizontal dynamism of the facade is decisively interrupted by the vertical movement of the four columns of the portico; these are narrower and more delicate than the columns of the cloister over which they are laid, creating a certain tension at the core of the building that never ceases to intrigue. Front Court was over time remodelled in neoclassical fashion to complement Wren's chapel, which did initially look somewhat incongruous next to the college's older buildings. One unusual feature is the retention of scrolling brackets at the corners of the grass plat in the centre of the court; such details were formerly commonplace in the colleges, when conveyances such as handcarts – which might cut corners in a court – were a regular sight.

The chapel is all the more extraordinary to behold in the context of the college's entrance front on St Andrew's Street, which was smartened up and regularised in the 1770s by the Cambridge architect James Essex. Its general proportions and the four columns of the portico are in hock to Wren's chapel, just visible through the entrance lodge, but there the similarities end, for as a design this facade is almost risibly conventional, lending the college the appearance of a slightly too-grandiose bank branch in a provincial high street. The impression Emmanuel presents to the world is, however, enhanced considerably by a series of small front-garden spaces ranged behind black railings along the street frontage. The two beds on either side of the gravel path in front of the porter's lodge are intensively planted with a mix of colourful flowers and foliage plants, including strappy phormiums, rich red dahlias, cistus and eryngium, giving way to tightly clipped panels of yew which create the impression of a labyrinth or Greek key pattern. Set within these yew panels are specimen trees blessed with good flowers, fruit and foliage: bird cherries (*Prunus padus* 'Watereri') and *Malus hupehensis* (Chinese crab apple). A line of pleached limes forms a fine backdrop at all seasons. These front gardens may be somewhat curious, stretched along the street in this way, but they are a highly effective elaboration, reassuring visitors and passers-by that this is a characterful and cherished place.

There is a strong sense of forward movement through Front Court towards the Paddock, via its open south-east corner. That dynamism is reinforced by the policy of mowing the lawn stripes in an east-west

direction, so the visitor feels propelled forward. In addition, Wren's chapel effectively functions as a garden building. Its ground floor is called a cloister but its effect is that of a classical loggia, since the large arches are all open to the court at ground level and they do not turn a right angle. Instead the 'cloister' mediates a transcendent transitional moment as the visitor steps over towards the Paddock; the half-light and inside-outside character interrupts the flow and creates a sense of formal division between visual episodes. David Loggan illustrated this most deliberately in his 1690 engraving of Front Court, by placing the trunk of the first tree of the avenue in the Paddock so that it is visible between the cloister arches, thus emphasising the permeability of the spaces. Even before the chapel was built, the east side of Front Court appears to have had some kind of pierced screen; John Hamond's map of Cambridge, made in 1592 (just eight years after the college's foundation), shows a line of wooden posts here, which would have provided a sense of mediation between the court and garden.

The word 'garden' is being used, but as we have ascertained, that may not be quite the right descriptor for Emmanuel's Paddock, a roughly square-shaped expanse of grass of about 1.25 hectares/3 acres largely enclosed by undistinguished college buildings. It is currently studded with a variety of trees, some of them mature, including a fine weeping silver lime, oriental planes, cherries, *Aesculus × carnea* and a *Catalpa bignonioides*. Emmanuel's trees have always been its chief horticultural interest.

Hamond's map shows the rectangular stew pond in an otherwise unadorned paddock. The area is labelled 'Emanuel college walkes', indicating that it was valued very early on as a place for pleasurable perambulation. Hamond shows no trees, but 90 years later they are very evident as mature specimens on the western and southern side on David Loggan's detailed engraving of the college and on his accompanying city map. (Perhaps the man who supervised the planting was the wonderfully named Blasé Hopwood, whom we know was the college gardener in 1631.) There is also an undated drawn plan in the college archive which, as it does not feature the chapel, begun in 1670, therefore almost certainly predates it; this shows three perimeter avenues of trees semi-enclosing the space against the north, south and west sides, the northern one specified as limes and the western one as 'high trees' (probably elms). One attractive aspect of Emmanuel at this period, which the Loggan engraving makes plain, is the sense of a continuous walkway from the master's lodge in the north-east corner of Front Court, along Wren's cloister by the chapel, then out into the Paddock by a quick dog-leg turn, and into the 'natural cloister' created by the avenues running south and then east. The variety of light effects provided by the different tree species and the special contrasting shade of the cloister would have been intensely

pleasing to the late-17th and early-18th-century aesthetic sensibility, for 'variety' in such things was valued above all.

The Paddock remained in basically the same form until the mid 19th century, when circular planting beds were added, after the fashion, near the pond. Letters in the college archive indicate that the trees in the Paddock at the end of the 19th century were mainly elms. One curiosity regarding the wall of the Paddock against the fellows' garden is that it has a distinctive V-shaped top – because at one time it was thatched. (This may sound unlikely but a few examples of this ancient practice do remain – there is a double thatched wall flanking a public footpath at Blewbury in Oxfordshire, for example.)

The pond itself retained its straight sides and utilitarian air until 1963, when it was given serpentine edges – and the island with swamp cypress added – so as to create the impression of a meandering river, an illusion bolstered by the waterfowl which are such a popular presence today. This alteration was achieved by re-using bricks and other debris from the demolition of the old master's lodging. (One of Emmanuel's current fellows recalls seeing the bricks being wheelbarrowed down to the pond for this purpose.) Shrubs and small trees were planted around the pond at this time. The garden designer John Codrington had been consulted by the college on the matter, the bursar having first written to Vita Sackville-West in 1960, who had recommended him in her stead ('PS Codrington knows my Kent garden well'). Codrington's ideas for the planting around the pond, which were acted upon with the support of college fellow Ronald Gray, are stored in the college archive – they are illustrated by attractive before-and-after views with foldable flaps, modelled after Humphry Repton's celebrated Red Books.

From the 1960s into the 1990s, a number of trees have been planted in the Paddock, especially on the perimeter edges and around the pond. The trio of fastigiate Irish yews at the college end of the pond, for example, are unmistakably an example of 1960s landscape design, while the two 'chimerical' trees – a + *Laburnocytisus* 'Adamii' and + *Crataegomespilus* 'Dardarii' planted around the point of transition between Front Court and the Paddock – were donated in 1991 by the professor of genetics. On the route to the library are a series of trees planted as trios: *Koelreuteria paniculata*, *Cupressus arizonica* 'Conica' and *Calocedrus decurrens*, with a walnut by the library entrance.

In recent decades the main path running along the south side of the pond has been resurfaced with concrete pavers, and Victorian-style street lamps added. These institutional accoutrements have somewhat confused the aesthetic even if they are a practical necessity. Yet another identity for this space has been as a 'cut-through' used by members of the public. There is also a sports component to the Paddock: in early summer a large section is close-mown to create two informal grass tennis courts. All of this results in a confusion of tone. The main jolt is caused by the area around the pond, which currently looks like an ornamental garden set in what should properly

be a small field with an unadorned if not naturalistic flavour. What to do about this? There is a case for reinstating something of the 'field in the city' atmosphere by means of a new mowing regime (leaving the grass to grow longer), a careful look at the municipal-style street lamps, benches and other furniture, and a concerted attempt to screen off parked cars in the key views. This might entail removing some of the trees that create a manicured feel, such as the purple-leaved plum near the 19th-century red-brick hostel visible beyond the pond, and increasing the tree population with more straightforward deciduous species such as limes, planes and oaks. Finally, it might be an idea to revert to the venerable name of Emmanuel Close.

The fellows' garden, enclosed by walls, is situated north of the Paddock. Hamond's 1592 map shows what looks like an orchard occupying the site. The priory had been leased to William Shirwood of Cambridge for 21 years in 1539, immediately after the dissolution, at which point we know it included orchards, gardens and dovecotes; these are all listed again in documents at the time of the college's foundation. We know that the first master, Laurence Chaderton, was an enthusiast for trees, and planted many in the grounds. One of his contemporaries, William Bedell, was an Emmanuel man who became Bishop of Kilmore; he wrote to a Cambridge friend with the request: 'Remember me to Mr Chaderton…I would entreat you also to get me some grafts out of Emmanuel college orchard of the timely cherries.' The orchard shown on the Hamond map was presumably a survivor from the priory days, perhaps augmented by the pomologically aware master. The college accounts mention the planting of mulberry trees in 1608 and again in 1612 (when 40 were purchased, in line with James I's desire for an English silk industry). And there are references to walls being built around the (pre-existing) master's and fellows' orchards in the 1630s. The first mention of the bowling green is in 1638, a sure sign that the garden was in regular use for leisure purposes by this time.

The fellows' garden today consists of mature trees placed around a meandering circular walkway. Those trees include copper beeches, amelanchier, ginkgo, *Davidia involucrata* and fruit trees, in addition to the great oriental plane. Until the 1930s even the plane was upstaged by an ancient elm said to have been planted by Chaderton. An 1889 plan by Joseph Morden shows the fellows' garden in basically this layout but in earlier times it was much more formally arranged.

In David Loggan's engraving (1690) it appears to be divided into two principal compartments by a long tunnel arbour, with a remnant of the fellows' orchard to the north-west and the bowling green to the south, where the entrance to the garden is today. Divided from the fellows' garden by a wall on the western side is the master's garden, and west of this is the grand entrance on Emmanuel Street. Loggan also shows a tiny garden in the north-west corner of the college site; this was probably the cook's garden next to the kitchen, which is first mentioned in 1612. But to return to the fellows' garden, there are a few other details worth noting. In the north-east section is a small pedimented classical summer house or covered seat, erected in 1680, that has now disappeared, and also a roughly square body of water with rounded edges that most decidedly has not. This piece of water, which at the time was probably an additional ornamental pond, later became the fabled fellows' swimming pool and today is a jealously guarded amenity, strictly for college use. A plunge pool or cold bath is recorded at Emmanuel from the mid 18th century, but there has been some confusion as to whether this was the same feature as today's swimming pool (it would not have been).

It was the extension of Hobson's Conduit along Regent Street in 1631 that allowed the college to channel water into its three main water sources: an open channel (later pond) in Chapman's Garden,

the old fish pond in the Paddock and the new pond in the fellows' garden. Plunge pools became popular only in the 1730s and 40s so it is unlikely there was a pool at Emmanuel used for this purpose until then. (Then as now, a brief immersion in cold water was seen as bracingly health-giving and somehow morally improving.) The habit of bathing at Emmanuel almost certainly began after 1745, when money donated by a college member was 'applied to the making of a Bath and the building of a House over it'. It has been inferred that this refers to the conversion of the existing pool into a kind of swimming pool *avant la lettre*, but this is unlikely. Swimming in open water was considered dangerous and undesirable whereas plunging into a small pool with reachable sides was not. Outdoor plunge pools were small and circular, usually sheltered by a small building, sometimes with a larger body of ornamental water adjacent – to enhance the theme, as it were. That was the case with the plunge pool at Wrest Park in Bedfordshire, for example, and it seems to have been the situation at Emmanuel. The brand new plunge pool was mentioned in

ABOVE RIGHT Emmanuel is one of a handful of colleges to keep bees, an old tradition in Cambridge.
OVERLEAF The great oriental plane tree in the fellows' garden is one of the university's arboreal glories.

The Foreigner's Companion (1748), which states that in the fellows' garden 'there is a Bowling Green and a Cold Bath…over which is a neat Brick Building, sash'd in Front, and containing also a commodious little Room to dress in.' The author, Thomas Salmon, adds that bathing was quite a craze: 'Cold-baths are much resorted to by the Students of Cambridge at present.' The building is captured in a watercolour painted almost exactly a century later by a Miss Cooper, who was then engaged to an Emmanuel fellow. Her painting shows an elegant little building with three arches forming a loggia below and three windows above, clearly a reference to the Wren chapel. Such architectural-academical jokes are not unknown in Oxbridge colleges. The pool in Miss Cooper's watercolour does not appear suitable for bathing, having what look like waterlilies on its surface. The bathing house was also mentioned in an 1814 *History of the University* by George Dyer, who records the fellows' garden as being 'diversified by many plants, a bathing-house, bowling-green, and piece of water'. (Note that the bathing house and piece of water are enumerated as separate features.) Dyer, who was an alumnus of the college, mentions a fine old cedar in the garden and a former mount from which you could see into Christ's – 'but this pert peeping ornament has been very properly removed'.

The ornamental pond was renovated in 1855 and the old bath house 'repaired', though in actuality it was replaced by the current thatched hut, more rustic than elegant. Presumably at this time the old plunge pool or its remains were also filled in. It is not clear when bathing began in the main pool; most likely it would have been the 1920s or 30s. One college member recalled of this period: 'In the May term the dons would frequently take coffee in the fellows' garden, and…the butler, Page, carrying the silver coffee pots at shoulder height, and advancing with stately tread, was a sight to be remembered.'

Things had not changed all that much by the late 1960s, when one fellow remembered daily games of bowls in the fellows' garden after lunch:

Life, perhaps especially for a resident fellow, was extremely comfortable materially; the delicious breakfasts served in the elegantly redecorated fellows' breakfast room, the hours in the swimming pool jealously preserved for fellows' use alone on summer afternoons, the circle around the generously stoked Parlour fire on winter evenings, are some of the memories I retain of what was virtually life in a first-class country hotel.

The master's garden is still situated adjacent to the fellows' garden, a continuation of the classic arrangement which is rarely encountered nowadays, since masters' lodges have so often been rebuilt, generally in other parts of college. Emmanuel's current master's lodge stands on the same site as the original, the garden of which, according to George Dyer, contained a sort of poetical summer house

'surrounded with the prints of some of our principal old poets, a very agreeable nook'. The lodge was reconstructed in 1963 as an attractive modernist building in pale brick and glass with a small rear garden designed by the architect, Tom Hancock. This consists of a lawn rising to a prominent mound created by a Second World War air-raid shelter, and several trios of birch trees. There are small paved terraces to both kitchen and dining room, while the entrance front features a stylish paving design of concrete discs with gravel infill. All in all it is a notable example of a surviving modernist integrated house-and-garden design.

Hancock also designed South Court (1966), a modern accommodation block that meshes less happily with its garden setting. It overlooks – or overbears – Chapman's Garden, which is the most extreme historical example in the university of fellows commandeering areas of college as their own private space. In this case the eponymous fellow, who resided at Emmanuel from 1862 to 1913, was able to create a large garden for himself that until 1910 was only accessible through a door at the rear of his set of rooms in Front Court. Loggan depicts this area as densely treed, which seems to have been its character for some time. Essex's 1746 survey shows narrow rectangular planting beds and the rill-like conduit channel widened into a pond. The earliest photographs of the space, dated 1892, reveal it to have been quite open in aspect under Revd Chapman's care, with circular beds, rose standards and a prominent dovecote. Latterly it has taken on the character of a rather outgrown shrubbery and small arboretum, with tulip trees and a *Metasequoia glyptostroboides*. It would benefit from a revamp; the potential is for a landscape scene with willow-pattern appeal.

Some of John Codrington's suggestions for the college gardens in the early 1960s were thrown out, such as his idea for a vibrant alternating green and gold hedge for the master's garden. Cambridge colleges tend to be timid when it comes to such matters, which makes it all the more pleasing to discover that one such bulletin from Pimlico, Codrington's proposal for a Futurist-style herb garden in New Court, was actually realised and is carefully maintained today. It is a dynamic arrangement of sharply triangular box-hedged compartments filled with herbs and also roses and perennials, clearly designed to look its best when seen from above, though also effective at ground level. One more cherishable element in a garden that has so much more going for it than a fine old plane tree and a swimming pool.

TOP RIGHT The enticing rose-embowered entrance to the fellows' garden belies its entirely private character.

RIGHT *Jester* (1994) by Wendy Taylor is situated in a quiet spot near the pond.

FITZWILLIAM COLLEGE

ISITORS TO THIS MODERN COLLEGE are presented with a leaflet describing special areas of interest. Half the document is devoted to the college's architecture, which is distinctive and of high quality; the other half celebrates the gardens. That equal split is indicative of a journey the college has been on since it arrived on this site in 1963 to occupy buildings designed by Denys Lasdun, best known as the architect of London's National Theatre and the Royal College of Physicians overlooking Regent's Park. The weighting towards the gardens at Fitzwilliam would have pleased Lasdun, who was always sensitive to the possibilities of landscape, or as he rather vaguely put it, 'the even larger order of context and conspectus within which the building finds itself'. A recent in-house exhibition about Fitzwilliam's design history pointed out that the college environment 'enjoyed today by staff, students and visitors alike was not envisaged from the outset and has evolved only gradually — perhaps even fortuitously'. It appears that the impact of the gardens on the inner life of Fitzwilliam has taken the college somewhat by surprise. In effect its garden has indeed been made by its head gardeners, but its appearance is the result of skill and discernment, not mere happenstance.

Fitzwilliam had no premises, officially, for some time – because it did not want any. Founded in 1869 as a non-collegiate institution, it provided the opportunity of a Cambridge education to those who could not afford the college fees for bed and board and needed to stay in lodgings instead. But after a few years of this, it made sense to the college to find a building that it could use as a social centre and a base for teaching, and a house was duly acquired in the centre of town on Trumpington Street, opposite the Fitzwilliam Museum – hence the eventual name of the college. The house was serviceable, with a dignified frontage, but to judge from contemporary photographs the garden around the back was, frankly, grotty.

LEFT The auditorium (2004) is one of the first sights to greet visitors to college. Its glass walls reflect the mature trees and shrubs of the garden, and there is a sunken 'moat' of mainly blue-flowered plants (alliums, salvias) running next to it.

Fitzwilliam remained on Trumpington Street from 1887 until 1963, when after more than 20 years of discussion by the university authorities it secured a much larger permanent home where students could at last avail themselves of accommodation and meals on site, and a few years later became a fully fledged college of the university. The site found for the college was a 3.2-hectare/8-acre plot of land between the Huntingdon Road and Storey's Way that had previously belonged to The Grove, an address famous in Cambridge as the last home of Charles Darwin's widow, Emma, and one of several houses in the immediate vicinity associated with that great Cambridge family. The house itself was not part of the acquisition, as it was still in private ownership at that point, but as the name of the property suggests, there were a number of grand old trees on the estate, mainly wych elms and beeches. These were retained as part of Lasdun's plan, and were even depicted on his architectural drawings as individual rather than generic trees, indicating how well the architect understood that the 'genius of the place' should be respected.

Lasdun's idea was to develop a perimeter of buildings around the rectangular site – what he called 'an inhabited wall' – and to leave the central area relatively open, almost as one great court (the same idea had recently been essayed at Churchill College). Funding was tight, so the college's growth was going to be a gradual process, and the architect developed a 'snail' metaphor to describe the way the college would expand like the whorls of a shell. In the event the ground plan was notably geometric from start to finish, so perhaps this conceit was more of a selling tool than a real design idea.

The first building to go up, the hall, remains the college's signature, specifically its extremely tall roof, with clerestory windows framed by hooded parabolic pods that repeat and ripple like billowing sails or frothy waves, improbably high above the ground. There is an unreal quality to the sight which is immediately arresting and almost unsettling in its vaunting idealism. The whole college space seems to gravitate towards this roofline. By 1966 Lasdun's perimeter ranges on three sides formed Fellows' Court and Tree Court (named for its one existing mature tree, an oak), with the hall complex dividing them. At this time the courts were almost bare save for several trees dotted around, and some rose bushes on the mound outside the Old Senior Common Room, a striking trapezoid building attached to the hall complex in Fellows' Court. The south side of the two courts was open but for a short lateral accommodation range in the south-west corner. This was intended to serve additionally as the entrance, though no concession would be made to the traditional monumental Cambridge gateway. The proposed entry point from Storey's Way, some distance south, was reached by an exposed zigzag drive next to an open field. In fact the real entry to college, right up until the late 1990s, was on the north side via Huntingdon Road as it was more convenient. Unfortunately, Lasdun's northern range had not been designed to function as an entrance facade, so looked rather dark and forbidding from the roadside, with its massy expanses of the utilitarian brown

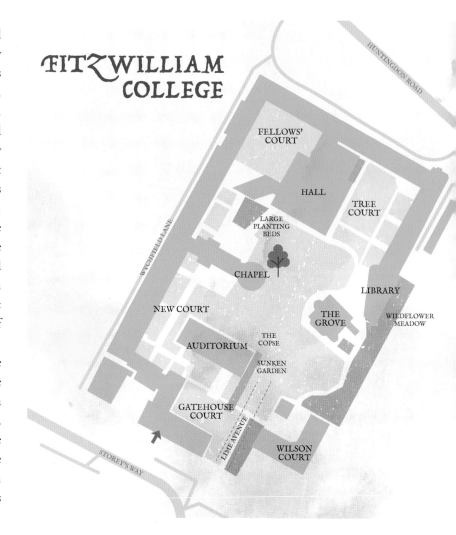

brick used to construct the college. One old member recalled coming up for interview in 1970: 'The taxi from the station dropped me off outside the college on the Huntingdon Road. I didn't see a sign and rapidly concluded that the building in front of me could not possibly be a Cambridge college. I actually thought it was a warehouse.'

For the time being it was not possible to 'complete the square' and enclose or semi-enclose the two courts, as The Grove and its garden occupied the south-eastern corner and was still in private occupation, separated from the college by a 1.8-metre/6-foot timber fence. The owner, Mrs Winifred Armstrong, the widow of a Newmarket brewer, was a great supporter of the college. The head gardener at the time, Andrew Peters, who often took tea at The Grove, recalls finding the mature garden set in the midst of college tantalisingly out of reach, 'over the fence'. Mrs Armstrong was a friend to students and reportedly allowed them to use her own garden for parties on occasion.

By the 1980s the lack of available accommodation within the college had become a problem and it was decided to expand south of Fellows' Court to create New Court, which was designed in 1985 by Richard MacCormac in a rhythmic style sympathetic to Lasdun's work. This established the principle that the college would now reach almost down to Storey's Way, diverging from Lasdun's original plan. He had intended to extend buildings down the east side and two-thirds

along the south, with a large rectangular piece of water linking the south range to a porter's lodge at the south of what is now New Court. Visitors to college from Storey's Way would have had a surprise view of the water as they rounded the corner of the south range and proceeded up to college. Perhaps too much time had elapsed for the college to honour Lasdun's initial proposal; either way, the entire Fitzwilliam project is glossed as 'unbuilt' in the major monograph on Lasdun's work (1994). This seems a little ungenerous as an assessment.

The college took possession of The Grove in 1988, when the challenge of integrating a late Victorian woodland garden with the modernist college growing around it gave sudden impetus to the issue of landscape design. Andrew Peters was invited back as a consultant and continued in this role into the late 1990s, advising on the planting around all the new buildings. During his time as head gardener he had overseen the creation (1983–84) of the large beds around the hall, which remain the college's horticultural showpiece, while among his recommendations as consultant was the easing of the slope between the college and The Grove. Some of the formal planting around The Grove was retained, and a little later a box-hedged formal garden was created on its east side, so as to shore up its domestic character. Tree Court was completely redesigned by Peters, with large 15 x 20-metre/50 x 66-foot beds on the eastern side, allowing for a path system which was

not adjacent to the building (privacy had been an issue), while across college a great many more trees and shrubs were planted, and more connecting paths made to increase the variety of landscape experience.

None of this work encountered any opposition from staff or students, who evidently appreciated the complementary character of the plants against the architecture. As more buildings were added to the college estate, extra garden areas were created, and today Fitzwilliam truly is a 'garden college' thanks to head gardener Steve Kidger and his team, who are working to a high level in the contemporary naturalistic mode, deploying a greater range of plants than is seen in most Cambridge colleges. The scale of the open spaces at Fitzwilliam is gratifyingly large, leaving considerable potential for horticulture, and the garden committee here is 17-strong, an indication of the commitment of the fellowship to the idea of the garden (even if the number of opinions involved makes decision-making somewhat laborious at times).

The college's long-standing problem with its entrance arrangements was addressed definitively in 2003 with the creation of Gatehouse

ABOVE The spring blossom and complex branch system of a *Prunus incisa* 'Praecox' contrast pleasingly with the clerestory windows which form the hall's distinctive roofline.

Court on Storey's Way, a two-storey accommodation block realised in dark brick with grey horizontal banding, in keeping with the overall tonal aesthetic. The path to the lodge is lined with yew hedges as backdrop to a range of plants which assure the horticulturally minded visitor that this is a college worth seeing. Apparently the security-minded bursar liked the idea of using *Colletia paradoxa*, 'living barbed-wire', in the beds here, and there is further excitement provided by spiky trachycarpus. These are offset by the stately ornamental grass *Calamagrostis* 'Karl Foerster' and mounds of *Pittosporum* 'Tom Thumb', while that connoisseurial plant *Lobelia tupa* is prominent alongside equally strident kniphofia. This is also the first sighting of vivid blue-flowered *Ceratostigma willmottianum*, which Mr Kidger describes as a signature plant across college, as it looks attractive all year round.

Passing through the entrance lodge, the visitor emerges into a straight run of modernist brick cloister against the western side of Gatehouse Court. The architects Allies & Morrison were responsible for this development as well as the partly glass-walled auditorium building to the north, which semi-encloses the space, its tan-coloured brick setting it apart from the other buildings in the modern college ensemble. Two huge copper beeches lend considerable character to the court, but this often shady area appears darker still when seen from within the cloister, making it a rather low-key experience. It has

to be questioned whether this is the very best prelude a college could have. The court is however lit up in spring by bulbs such as aconites and crocuses, and again in autumn with *Cyclamen hederifolium*, while dicentra and primulas grow among ferns at the edges of the space.

Originally, the auditorium was to have been complemented by a long, wide canal that dramatically cuts across its eastern side, extending into Gatehouse Court where it is crossed by a low bridge. This was a nod to Lasdun's plan for a large 'water garden' in this area. The structure was completed, but it was decided not to fill it with water. Instead, plants have been deployed to create the illusion of a pool: blue salvias, *Agapanthus* 'Midnight Star' and purple alliums are interplanted with pennisetum grass 'Hameln'. Large areas of purple pittosporum are intended to mimic the shadows cast by the beeches overhead, and a liquidambar in the small copse at the northern end of the canal provides a useful focus. As an imitation of water, though, the feature signally fails; the garden team seems slightly flummoxed, and understandably so. Perhaps one day the water will arrive.

ABOVE LEFT The Olisa Library (2009) is fronted by plantings of grasses and perennials in the contemporary naturalistic manner, with seed heads and stems left *in situ* until early spring.
ABOVE CENTRE Next to The Grove, the Regency building at the heart of the college, a great plane tree plays an important role in the garden scene.

At this point the visitor has a choice whether to go left or right around the auditorium. The Grove is to the right but the main route is left, into the modernist heart of the college, first passing through New Court, which is kept fairly simple, with panels of lawn and shrubs around the south side of the curvaceous chapel. MacCormac's design of this court is a fine complement to Lasdun's original buildings, the complexity of the rhythmic, stepped facades with their distinctive slot windows requiring very little by way of horticultural ornamentation (only some plantings of grasses near the doorways). Across the piece at Fitzwilliam there is an evenness in the height of the buildings and a respect for the unity of materials which characterises the work of all the architectural practices involved here. Bob Allies of Allies & Morrison remarked on the way new buildings have been developed 'out of the kind of language which Lasdun established at the beginning', with the different architectural teams working together, in effect, to conserve and contribute to Fitzwilliam's 'particular identity'. The garden team regards each space as a discrete episode within the college ensemble, a wise approach given the variety of architectural voices, albeit all singing in the same key.

The north side of the chapel harbours a packed winter border where bulky heather plantings are lifted by cornus, witch hazel, epimedium, *Lonicera fragrantissima*, *Viburnum carlesii*, *Rubus thibetanus* and callicarpa. The hall and its roofline hoves into view, with the well-stocked borders in front of it creating an irresistible gathering point for all college members in summertime. These deep and detailed planting beds contain naturalistically arranged drifts and large clumps of perennials. *Melianthus major*, *Eryngium alpinum*, yucca, *Stipa gigantea* and big shrubs such as buddleias and the white-flowered New Zealand daisy bush (*Olearia × haastii*) create structure, while all around are the firework colours of salvia, lychnis, tricyrtis, phlox, solidago, asters, knautia, achillea and ceratostigma. It is easy to feel pleasantly enveloped in flowers and foliage.

Fellows' Court, to the west of the hall, is kept relatively austere, with specimen trees ginkgo and *Acer griseum* in the grass. The evergreen shrub sarcococca, with *Allium cristophii* and the grass *Miscanthus sinensis* 'Flamingo', create visual interest and scent around the doorways.

Over to the east of the hall borders, one begins to get tantalising glimpses of the old garden of The Grove and its mature trees (a blue cedar first in view), as the college seems to lose itself, somehow, in the past – a pleasing sensation. Emma Darwin was delighted with The Grove when she moved in as an elderly woman, living there from 1883.

ABOVE RIGHT An impressive heather border erupts, just north of the chapel, one of several horticultural surprises engineered by the garden team.

The house is an attractive Regency villa of sandy-coloured Cambridge brick, with an elegant central staircase and pretty verandah. But it was the garden Emma enjoyed the most, as 'being the very place for an old person, such nooks and corners for shelter and seats'. Her daughter Henrietta remarked on the 'old walls and spreading wych-elms which gave it charm and individuality'. Emma was reportedly 'more interested in landscape gardening than furnishing, and the cutting down of the trees was entirely decided by her'. She took great delight, for example, in the felling of a huge old elm which did not fall in the direction predicted and crushed a sycamore in the process. Natural selection?

The Grove has been extremely skilfully absorbed into the Fitzwilliam scene, despite its apparently anachronistic presence. A decision was taken to respect the historic character of the house and its garden, while blurring the edges at its boundary so that it melds with the wider college, an ambitious approach that depends on the kind of subtle and skilful garden maintenance practised at Fitzwilliam today. Trees and shrubs are used as screens to control vistas, while large areas of planting link the distinct architectural episodes, interventions which are designed to be 'invisible' or 'natural' and which may therefore go unappreciated. It is not clear whether Lasdun's choice of brick as the material used for the college was consciously influenced by The Grove, but either way it is a subtly effective way of uniting the buildings.

The new Gatehouse Court was sited so that it does not impinge on a short mature lime avenue leading up to the house from Storey's Way, creating a vista through gates just east of the college entrance that most visitors miss but is quite beguiling. Wild flowers flourish in the long grass here in early summer, while in spring the avenue is ornamented by chionodoxa, snake's head fritillaries, wild daffodils and the relatively rare white helleborine orchid (of which there are also some examples next door at Murray Edwards College). There is a spring border on the way up to the house with daffodils followed by foxgloves and poppies.

The most striking addition provided by The Grove's old garden is a magnificent plane tree (*Platanus* × *hispanica*) situated between the house and the chapel, which it is thought was planted around the time the house was constructed in 1813. It has a strong presence and creates a sense that here lies the college's secret heart. In its way this plane is just as 'important' to the Cambridge scene as the more celebrated examples at Jesus and Emmanuel. MacCormac worked closely with Andrew Peters when designing the chapel, with the aim of integrating the tree and making it a focal point in views out. The relationship is highly successful.

On the south side of The Grove is a homely scheme of wallflowers, dahlias and chrysanthemums alongside a trio of snail-shaped clipped-box topiaries, perhaps a sly reference to Lasdun's original 'snail' plan for the college. There is a Paulownia tree in the lawn. The north side is like a quotation of a classic English garden – which is of course what The Grove formerly was – with formal box enclosures containing little sedums, ferns, Solomon's seal and aruncus for shade, early summer plants such as aquilegias and knautia, with the bright flowers of midsummer rounding it off – *Monarda* 'Cambridge Scarlet', daylilies,

red salvias, lychnis and showy *Centaurea macrocephala*, with bronzy furled flower heads which resemble a flapper's haircut before growing out to become big yellow thistles beloved by bees. Directly east of The Grove is the box parterre created in 1989 as a form of ornamental potager (at that time a fashionable interpolation). Vegetables are still used but bright flowers are the mainstay: tulips in spring followed by begonias or another bedding plant in the four triangular beds that radiate from a central sundial. This side of the house was under scaffolding in early 2019; in a controversial decision on the part of the college, which might have considered The Grove to be an inviolable element of Fitzwilliam's fabric, a wood and glass extension is being constructed in order to provide more space for the graduate students who use it. At least this generic modern addition is sited on the least exposed side of the building. The lawn in front of the house has a big curving border with plants suited to the woodland setting, such as macleaya, geraniums, cephalaria and lysimachia.

The Grove is sited on a slight mound and there is a sensation of descent across the grass, back into the different reality of the college precincts. Beeches have replaced elms as the tree typical of Cambridge's environs and there are several in the transition space leading down from The Grove, with wood rush (*Luzula sylvatica*) and *Brunnera macrophylla* 'Jack Frost' to complement them. Tree Court, in the north-east portion of college, was one of the first areas laid out by Lasdun and is the section of the modern college with the most established feel. Lasdun's courts are somewhat bigger than those in many other of the modernist colleges of Cambridge and Oxford, and this has paid off in terms of atmosphere. The court itself contains a big old English oak, specimens of American red oak (*Quercus rubra*) and a trio of peel-bark birches. Mr Kidger took out an existing mix of berberis, old cistus and lavatera and installed instead showpiece borders on three sides. The west border has a shrub backbone of beauty bush (*Kolkwitzia amabilis*), with buddleia and spiraea, along with 4.5-metre-/15-foot-tall clumps of the reed *Arundo donax*. Tall flowers include foxtail lilies (*Eremurus*), verbascums and heleniums, with sedums, *Geranium psilostemon*, euphorbias, *Salvia nemorosa*, white lychnis, sisyrinchium and heuchera lower down, mingling with the grass *Stipa arundinacea* (now known as *Anemanthele lessoniana*). This border is nicely complemented by one of David Harber's spherical slate sculptures entitled *Dark Planet*. The border on the east of the court is much broader, more open and 'embroidered' in style, the detail provided by penstemon, knautias, phlox, daylilies and geum around a central *Prunus incisa* 'Praecox' flanked by *Euonymus alatus*. The repeat rhythmic planting here is accentuated by the use of *Persicaria microcephala* 'Red Dragon' and euphorbias. The border to the south, in the woodland zone, also features euphorbia – the scintillating 'Excalibur' variety which crops up around college – with the addition of scarlet roses to presage the historic formality of The Grove just beyond.

The western edge of college incorporates several other major architectural additions which have been successfully absorbed into

Fitzwilliam's overall composition. There is a new palette of plants to enjoy in front of the Olisa Library designed by Ted Cullinan in 2009. A distinctive corner turret negotiates the point of transition with Lasdun's east wing, with a complementary planting of grasses and perennials – *Deschampsia cespitosa* 'Goldtau', perovskia, rudbeckia, ceratostigma, *Miscanthus sinensis* 'Flamingo' and pampas grass. The slatted oak panels of the library's main facade are offset by huge clumps of *Persicaria alpina* and several *Cornus controversa* 'Variegata' trees, with osmanthus and *Viburnum* × *burkwoodii* behind, echinaceas for late-summer colour, and dryopteris ferns and Corsican hellebores in front – a beautifully scaled composition. Around the back of the library is a small wildflower meadow.

A path past the east side of The Grove leads into a shrubbery walk with flowering cherries *Prunus* 'Kanzan' and 'Shirotae', and behind them the attractive twisted stems of an overgrown box plantation among the yews and *Robinia pseudoacacia*, with hellebores, geraniums and ferns interplanted. Unfortunately none of these plants obscure in any way a bronze figurative sculpture entitled *The First Undergraduate* commissioned for the college's 125th anniversary. He is a rather diminutive fellow, leading to the college joke that the statue is 'not to scale'. Behind here is the eastern perimeter fence, where the garden team likes to wave at their counterparts at Murray Edwards, at work

in their glasshouse. Finally, the south-western corner of the college is occupied by Wilson Court (1994), a respectfully recessive postmodern design with well-appointed concrete details (pillars and benches), a small lawn with the purple *Acer palmatum* 'Sumi-nagashi', and two large *Euphorbia mellifera* specimens with salvias in flanking beds by the path.

In terms of both garden and architecture, Fitzwilliam College is far more complex than it may first appear. But it wears this complexity lightly. The site has a compact feel, yet the spaces within are nicely balanced, while all the architecture has a quietly stylish air. There is a pleasingly delimited feel to the open-sided courts and other spaces, an aesthetic which is carefully controlled by the garden team. Ted Cullinan, who had worked with Lasdun on the original college before contributing work in his own right, commented that Fitzwilliam is 'very graceful and very calm' – a feeling that has been retained despite the beaverings of a troupe of eminent architectural practices.

ABOVE LEFT The curving walls of the college chapel provide the backdrop for rich shrub plantings and the purple autumn flowers of Michaelmas daisy, *Aster* 'Little Carlow'.

ABOVE RIGHT David Harber's slate sculpture *Dark Planet* has a dignified presence in Tree Court.

GIRTON COLLEGE

GIRTON IS OFF THE MAP. At least that's how many people in Cambridge see it. But its apartness is an important part of its character. Two miles (3.2 kilometres) down the road from the city centre, just south of Girton village, this is the farthest flung college in either Cambridge or Oxford. With particular seriousness of purpose, Girton's website informs us that it is situated on latitude 52.22877100 and longitude 0.08501608, as if we might get lost on the way. Yet the off-centre location seems to suit the individualistic, slightly bloody-minded flair of the place. It is apparent that Girtonians, like Hercules, shun the smooth and easy path – on the understanding that the rocky one is more virtuous and rewarding in the long run. At least this is what the undergraduates can tell themselves as they pedal to and from lectures twice a day along the busy Huntingdon Road.

The approach to college is from the south-west, along a straight entrance drive lined with mature horse chestnuts, where snowdrops, aconites and leucojums appear in spring. The saplings of these trees, along with so much else in the gardens here, were an early gift from a well-wisher. Most of these benefactors were alumnae of Girton's first incarnation at Benslow House, near Hitchin in Hertfordshire, a women's college founded in 1869. Looming large at the end of the entrance drive is Girton's tall and imposing gatehouse tower, realised in somewhat vivid red brick and flanked by multiple white-painted, half-timbered gables. This row of gables projects a domestic air which today seems incongruous and ungainly at such a massive scale and in such an unmistakably institutional context, an impression arising from our familiarity with the form of mock Tudor architecture later appropriated by suburban housebuilders in the interwar years. (The severe Gothicism of Girton's tower also brings to mind that other monument to Victorian female self-improvement: Holloway Prison, 1852.) Mixed borders, including a *Ceanothus* 'Cascade', stand either

LEFT The shrub plantings against Girton's distinctive rich red-brick buildings have been carefully selected so that a variety of greens sing out.

ORCHARD

HONEYSUCKLE WALK

FELLOWS' GARDEN

YEW WALK

WILDFLOWER MEADOW

POND

ASH COURT

EMILY DAVIES COURT

DINING HALL

CLOISTER COURT

ELIZA BAKER COURT

HUNTINGDON ROAD

GIRTON ROAD

WOODLANDS COURT

CHAPEL

CAR PARK

CHAPEL LAWN

CAMPBELL COURT

LIBRARY

MARE'S RUN

LIBRARY LAWN

GIRTON COLLEGE

RIGHT A cross from 'Cox's Orange Pippin' is one of the apple varieties grown in the college's famous orchard, established in 1893.

FAR RIGHT Memorial sundial to Caroline Penrose Bammel, who came up to Girton as an undergraduate in 1959 and remained there as a PhD student and fellow until her early death in 1995.

side of the gatehouse and there is an open view through the arch to the greenery of Cloister Court beyond. But the entrance gate is not the place to gain an authentic impression of the original Girton, since this range, completed in the 1880s, was only the second phase of building at the new college.

To experience Girton as it was envisaged a decade earlier by its architect, Alfred Waterhouse, one must head left, to Emily Davies Court, named after the college's founder and comprising its initial suite of accommodation. (Construction was speedy: the first 13 students moved into Old Wing in 1873, the year after the land had been acquired.) This large lawned court of almost 0.4 hectare/1 acre, dotted with specimen trees, including two pairings of Atlantic and deodar cedars, is formed by just two built ranges – well, two-and-a-quarter, if one counts the Stanley Library which protrudes on the south-eastern side, complementing Old Wing adjacent and Hospital Wing (1879) opposite. It can hardly be called a court at all, but its openness is actually the key to its success, resulting in a wonderful feeling of freedom. This is one of the only parts of the college (the other being the area to the east, around Mare's Run field) that conveys something of the atmosphere of a large country house of the later Victorian period, which was perhaps part of Waterhouse's intention.

Showing uncharacteristic restraint, in the context of his *oeuvre* to date (his buildings at Pembroke College, for example), Waterhouse managed to combine seriousness of purpose, expressed in the relentlessly regular fenestration and utilitarian brick, with just a frisson of romanticism lent by details such as the Bavarian round tower, topped by a 'fairytale' conical turret, which faces into Emily Davies Court (a touch of Neuschwanstein or Hohenzollern, perhaps). A frisson of fairytale, certainly, but there was to be nothing frivolous about Girton's outward appearance: the first women's colleges had to work hard to be taken seriously by the male establishment. Emily Davies herself, Girton's first mistress, wanted 'dignity in every way' and was notably circumspect about the idea of a garden, considering it to be a luxury. In 1866, however, she had written to a colleague expressing admiration for Waterhouses's work in Manchester, 'with gardens and grounds and everything that is good for body and soul and spirit'. The two long ranges of Emily Davies Court have due south as their apex, apparently to allow for suntrap herbaceous borders along their entire lengths, like the butterfly wings of an Arts and Crafts house, though such horticultural ambition prevailed only for a short time at the college, during the 1920s and 30s. Today, these borders are dominated by bulky shrubs, in particular wisteria and cistus.

The internal organisation of Girton's accommodation wings plays its own subtle part in the landscape. The architect adopted the concept of the corridor, new in collegiate design. It meant that far fewer doorways were necessary in courts compared to the traditional system of staircases, where each staircase has its own entrance. This in turn leads to a calmer and more tranquil ambience than in the

typical Oxbridge quad or court, with its endless comings and goings from multiple doorways. It is an arrangement that does not suit all tastes, it has to be admitted, since it can lead to a feeling of starkly institutionalised desolation, and a sense that one is being constantly surveilled. This is indeed the most school-like of the Cambridge colleges.

It is often suggested that Girton was sited so far away from the town centre because of 'prudery' – concerns about the virtue of the female students being compromised. There is no evidence for this. In fact Miss Davies initially tried to buy a plot of land considerably closer to town. However, since the college was not built as a citadel surrounded by high walls, like those in the city centre were, it might be fair to say that the corridor arrangement made it easier to detect unwanted (male) visitors by providing fewer ways for them to get in to the premises. Long vistas along the corridors also mean that intruders – or escapees – can be spotted more easily (reminiscent of the panopticon principle, which was the very latest in contemporary prison design when the college was built). The strategy seems to have worked: there is a tale of one mistress discovering a party of young men clambering into a college corridor through a window; she politely suggested that they must have 'lost their way' before briskly escorting them out of the front gate.

Waterhouse had to provide plenty of student accommodation, and on a tight budget; the danger as ever with such utilitarian developments was a 'barracks' feel to the buildings. He understood that this style of architecture might become over-institutional in the context of a conventional enclosed court, so he deployed the substantial grounds of the new college (covering 6.4 hectares/ 16 acres when he arrived; today 20 hectares/50 acres). He considered the landscape a foil to the architecture and used the sense of enclosure created by a band of trees around the perimeter of the site. These trees were planted for purely practical reasons in the first place, as shelter belts, since Girton's exposed site is prone to high winds (a revolving summer house was blown away in 1931, according to the minutes of a gardens committee meeting), but they soon matured into a key element of its landscape design. Still today there is a sense that the college is set in open pasture and semi-natural woodland, rather than hedged around with enclosed gardens.

The fact that Waterhouse was thinking about the landscape aspect at Girton is revealed by a note in the college archive stating that in August 1872 'Mr Waterhouse [was] asked to submit a design for laying out the grounds at Girton' and that his plan was accepted in November. No record of the plan survives, but it is likely that

Waterhouse's main recommendation was to plant the shelter belt. Surviving plans of the college by Waterhouse's office dating from the late 1880s show the perimeter woodland walk augmented with thick, sinuous shrub beds, and a continuing ambition to encircle the expanding college site with trees.

If all this sounds perfectly sensible and natural, it was not deemed so in the early years of the college, when there was a conflict of opinion over the desirability of a garden setting for the college. The land on which Girton was built had been agricultural: it appeared as if the first college buildings had simply been dropped down from a height on to the open countryside of Cambridgeshire. There were hayricks in the tenanted fields around the college, and it was the consternation caused by a fire on one such rick that led to the college fire brigade being formed. (An early photograph shows young women brandishing pails, pumps and hoses.) The open setting, coupled with the builders' materials strewn around the place, made for a depressing prospect for students arriving from the much more established and bucolic college setting in Hertfordshire. Some must have wondered why the move was deemed necessary. There was not even the kudos of belonging to the university: Girton (like Newnham) became a full college only in 1948. In 1879 the *Cambridge Chronicle* quoted an American visitor's report that the grounds were 'scanty and rough…

There is almost nothing that is attractive in the external appearance of the establishment.' The trees would grow up in time, but the first students would be long gone by then. Several in the group became depressed and surly, clashing with the autocratic Miss Davies and inciting younger students to insubordination. The poor quality and meagreness of the food did not help, and students often went down with minor illnesses (perhaps this is why Girton is the only Oxbridge college with its own hospital wing).

The college's early supporters became seriously worried that it was in danger of collapsing in on itself because of these ructions, which were only magnified by the low number of students and the intransigence of the mistress. Women's educational institutions at this date were up against it, subject to attacks and prejudice from traditionalist women as well as men. Students and staff alike in the women's colleges were often isolated and thrown back on each other's company, which could cause complications. These institutions were usually stricken with financial problems and hampered by social restrictions, such as the necessity for chaperoning in town. There were doubts as to whether the female sensibility could cope with

ABOVE White irises beneath the pergola, planted with crab apple 'John Downie', in the fellows' garden designed by Penelope Hobhouse.

'difficult' intellectual topics. On one celebrated occasion during the dissection of a human brain, all the young men in the lecture theatre turned around to see if any of the Girtonians on the back row would faint. (They did not.)

Even among the no-nonsense educationalists in charge of the college, an incipient maternalism could surface on occasion. When Girton was apparently threatened by a German Zeppelin seen looming overhead in 1915, the mistress agonised over whether to alert the parents of the students so they could withdraw their daughters from the war zone if they saw fit. Given such problems and confusions to contend with, it is little wonder that the atmosphere became somewhat intense at times. Girton has a complex relationship with the memory of its founder – a mixture of gratitude for her vision and tenacity, and an acknowledgment that pastoral care of students was perhaps not quite her forte.

Arguably as important as the college's founder was Barbara Bodichon, the artist and women's rights campaigner. She took on the nascent Girton College as one of her 'projects', donating a large amount of money and time. Interestingly, she had recently struck up a close friendship with Gertrude Jekyll, the great Arts and Crafts planting designer, whom she met while on holiday in the Swiss Alps in 1872, subsequently travelling with her to Algeria.

Jekyll was more interested in painting and interior design than gardening at this time, and provided ideas for decorating the college – ideas rejected out of hand by Miss Davies. Bodichon felt that a garden was perhaps even more of a necessity than interior decor. Later she recalled that what they had wanted in 1871 was 'an old-fashioned and useful garden with autumn and spring hardy flowers all about', adding that 'we ought to plant a belt of trees as soon as we can around our own domain.' (Perhaps the wooded perimeter was her idea, not Waterhouse's.)

Bodichon's own garden in Sussex was taking shape very much in the modern style promoted by William Robinson in his book *The Wild Garden*, published just a few years before Girton's foundation, in 1870, and the early plantings in the college's perimeter woodland walk appear to echo his prescriptions. In Robinson's vision, there was to be nothing too obviously 'exotic' on display, the look dependent instead on natural-looking shrubs and trees such as crab apples, medlars, thorns, box, yew, pears and wild service trees – as were planted at Girton. *Pinus nigra* (black pine) was the key tree in college, and groups of pines still play an important role in the gardens today.

ABOVE The recently planted wildflower meadow next to the sports pitches on the west side of college.

The species is not native to Britain, but it looks as if it could be – which is all that mattered in the Robinsonian aesthetic. His was a highly fashionable if not radical horticultural approach at a time when geometric patterns of annuals, ornamental urns, raised gravel terraces and great banks of colourful rhododendrons were still seen as the *ne plus ultra* of the High Victorian garden. It took a while for Robinson's ideas to enter the mainstream. This means that quietly, in its own way, and thanks to the efforts of Miss Bodichon, Girton was at the cutting edge of garden design in the 1870s and 80s.

There is some evidence that flower borders were also being thought about at Girton at this time. Apparently in a spirit of mollification, Miss Davies asked Miss Bodichon to bring a copy of *The Wild Garden* with her to a meeting in 1872 so they could discuss plants. A list exists – in Davies's hand – detailing candidates such as poppies, mulleins and phlomis. But it appears nothing came of this. In one of her letters, Davies responds tartly to Bodichon's horticultural suggestions by stating: 'We will get around to grounds as you and Miss Jekyll want' – meaning that their ideas for the garden would be considered only when more important matters had been dealt with. What can also be inferred is that Jekyll was involved with the garden aesthetic at this point. She did not begin gardening seriously herself until 1877, but had become fascinated by plants on her trip to Algeria with Bodichon. Clearly they were now engaged in creative discussions about the Girton garden. This could well have been the very first occasion when the great Gertrude Jekyll thought seriously about the practical aspects of garden design – though we do not know what she might have proposed.

The 'no garden' situation did not improve even after the resignation of Miss Davies in 1875, after just a few years in post. The second mistress, Marianne Bernard, was also quite slow to acknowledge the desirability of a garden, to the frustration of Bodichon and her principal ally in the campaign, Fanny Metcalfe, headmistress of a Hendon girls' school and a member of Girton's executive committee. In 1881 Metcalfe wrote to Bodichon: 'I am quite of your opinion that it is useless to give gifts to a garden so utterly uncared for…I am certainly not tall, but the weeds are taller than I am…I think the Committee are very short-sighted in leaving the garden as the last thing and doling out such scanty supplies, when I believe if it were fairly kept it might be a powerful attraction to students.' (This was a prescient statement indeed, given that a good college garden is now seen an important asset by both prospective students and conference organisers.) Ultimately, and despite her own reservations with regard to the college's commitment to horticulture, Metcalfe forced the issue. In 1881 she presented the college with £400 which she had raised expressly for the purpose of improving the college's grounds.

Matters moved apace after that: the lawns around the college were turfed, and grass tennis courts marked out on Emily Davies Court – the beginning of a long tradition. This work led to the discovery of an Anglo-Saxon burial ground, and the urns unearthed at this time are still on display in college. (Girton also acquired a mummy dating from the 2nd century AD, which is known in college as Hermione. Somewhat improbably, Hermione is the actual name of the embalmed person: it is inscribed on the mummy case.) The most telling innovation at this time was the appointment in 1883 of Elizabeth Welsh, the vice-mistress, as the college's first garden steward, a role unique to Girton among the Oxbridge colleges at the time, hovering as it did somewhere between head gardener and college fellow. (Homerton later adopted the appellation, as did several other colleges including Selwyn and Christ's). The garden steward tended to come from a similar social background as the academics, and to be just as opinionated.

The creation of this post reflects the development of horticultural education for women in the late Victorian and Edwardian period, when a number of gardening colleges were set up to provide training for middle-class women who might otherwise become teachers, nurses or governesses. Horticulture was seen as a respectable alternative means for them to earn their own living. (For men, meanwhile, gardening remained an almost entirely working-class profession.)

The year 1883 saw the planting of the Honeysuckle Walk against the garden's north-eastern boundary; it remains an iconic feature at Girton, now backed by hazel and with a carpet of periwinkle. The following year it was decided that an ornamental pond would be made out of a pit left over from the construction works, slightly to the north of the college buildings. As ever at Girton, practicality was the trump card: the pond was given the go-ahead because it was to double as a water-source for the college fire brigade. One other curiosity is that a golf links is recorded on the Girton site from 1891 to 1900, at the height of the game's fashionability.

Ostensibly the chief reason for appointing the garden steward was not to make the place more beautiful but to feed up to 80 students and staff. Not since the medieval period had an Oxbridge college aspired to this level of self-sufficiency. Miss Welsh laid out a 'home garden' on land north-east of the college, near the pond, so beginning concerted market-garden activity at Girton. Until the end of the Second World War there were 5–5.7 hectares/12–14 acres of land devoted to food production, both on the home garden and on an additional area next to Grange Drive, on the north-western side of the estate. There was grazing for livestock and a piggery – and how

many Oxbridge colleges have engaged in ferret-breeding as a way to combat rats?

Associated with this drive for self-sufficiency was the orchard laid out in 1893, also in the north-western part of the estate, on a portion of the 7 hectares/17 acres of additional land the college had acquired in 1886. The orchard would in time mature to become the jewel in the crown of the college gardens. Girton's head gardener in the 1960s and 70s, William 'Mac' Stringer, won numerous prizes for the college's apples at Royal Horticultural Society shows. Varieties growing today include 'Blenheim Orange' (one of the original plantings), 'Beauty of Kent', 'Laxton's Superb', 'Egremont Russet' and 'James Grieve', as well as pears, plums, medlars, quinces and cobnuts. In the late 1990s the old orchard was rejuvenated using the rootstock MM111. It's a shame the apples are not currently used for juice or any other purpose, though windfalls may be collected by students and visitors. The Yew Walk, consisting of tightly clipped hedges, was created in the 1890s and still runs along the edge of the orchard, dividing it from the pond and fellows' garden. A second orchard was planted in 1948 farther to the north, but it was recently grubbed up to make way for more sports pitches, to the disappointment of those in college who prefer horticulture to hockey.

In 1913 a book about Girton by the mistress, Emily Elizabeth Constance Jones, was published, by which time the 'large garden and half-wild grounds', encircled by a sheltering band of trees known as the Woodlands, could be described by the garden steward as well established: 'Surely among the happiest recollections of former students must be memories of the beautiful garden: of the many walks round the woodlands; of the games in the fields; of tea-parties in the orchard or on the lawns; of quiet hours of study in sheltered nooks.' The perimeter walk around the college is described as being about a mile (1.6 kilometres) in length, as it is today (though few seem to walk it). Herbaceous borders and a bed for rambling roses are also mentioned, but not the kitchen garden or its beehives – there was a clear distinction by this time between agricultural and horticultural activity at the college. The first head gardener was appointed in 1916, working under the garden steward, and the college garden committee was formed in the same year. After an uncertain beginning, Girton's garden had become one of the college's greatest assets.

By 1920 the college's horticultural ambitions had extended as far as commissioning the now-celebrated

Gertrude Jekyll to design new flower borders. Miss Bodichon had died 30 years previously, but Jekyll's connection with Girton evidently remained clear in the memory after all those years. One of her nieces had even attended the college. Jekyll's original planting plans for Girton College are housed in the Reef Point collection at Berkeley, in California, and they show two garden areas that were realised and two that were not. The first idea the college decided not to take up, perhaps unsurprisingly, was also the boldest: a horseshoe-shaped formal water garden for the centre of Cloister Court (which Jekyll calls Middle Court), with a circular pool and a cross-walk with seats at either end. Her second unexecuted suggestion was for shrubberies against the walls of the court – hardy, serviceable things such as skimmia, aucuba and berberis, and laurels in the corner, with jasmine and honeysuckle on the walls and veronica at the front of the beds.

Her other two – realised – ideas were for borders against the two 46-metre/150-foot ranges of Emily Davies Court, and a fairly narrow – but richly planted – Mediterranean-inspired bed in pastel shades along the far wall of Cloister Court, against the enclosed cloister corridor (which is incidentally a garden feature itself, in the way it communicates so tangibly with the exterior spaces). The garden historian Jane Brown, who has published a small book

on the gardens of Girton, describes the Cloister Court border in its time as 'typically Jekyllian, a scented rhythm of silver, greys, bluey-mauves and soft pinks with touches of purple, delicately understated'. It included long drifts of cotton lavender, catmint, pinks and campanulas.

The borders in Emily Davies Court were richly romantic in the cottage-garden spirit, with an emphasis on grey-leaved foliage and pink or purple shades, but more highly coloured than the Cloister Court plantings. They had stachys, lavender and bergenia drifting at the front, with nepeta, erigeron, lavatera and hyssop mingling above. Shrub structure was provided by ceanothus, pyracantha and escallonia. Vines, clematis and jasmine were planted against the walls. On the warmer, south-west facing Old Wing range there were additionally groups of poppies, snapdragons and the creamy yellow daisy flowers of *Chrysanthemum* 'Morning Star'.

There has been some doubt in college as to whether any of Jekyll's work was ever actually realised, but the minutes of the garden committee meetings from 1921 to 1923 show that some of

ABOVE Mature trees on Chapel Lawn provide a visual link with the college's perimeter woodland plantings, bolstering the illusion that this is a country house set in substantial grounds.

it certainly was. The initial reaction, in September 1921, was not wholly positive: 'the plans are rather too elaborate to be carried out in full'; they were also described as too costly. But in February 1922 the plans for Jekyll's flower beds were 'adopted with some modifications'. A gift of £100 from a college alumna to realise the work is recorded. The garden steward's report for October 1923 mentions that 'The improvements made last year, in accordance with the plans suggested by Miss Jekyll, have given very good results.' As is often the way with planting designs, it appears that these borders were relatively short-lived in this form – they lasted for perhaps 10 to 15 years and were described merely as 'mixed borders' by the garden steward in 1933. Jekyll's contribution was forgotten quite quickly, it seems, as it never gets mentioned later in college documents. Paradoxically, Girton makes less of its Jekyll credentials than does Newnham College – when at Girton her planting plans were actually realised, while at Newnham they were rejected.

The garden continued to be the subject of quite considerable expenditure: in 1923, £200 was spent on clearing the woodland and planting wild flowers – foxgloves, Solomon's seal, campanula – while the borders in Emily Davies Court were to be 'trenched, manured and replanted'. A substantial rose garden was made in 1926 by the well-known rosarian Revd J. S. Henslow, on the site of Woodlands

Court but now long gone, though its outline remains visible. It was later relocated to a position between the library and chapel (known as 'the hyphens' because of their protrusion), and was finally done away with during the construction of Campbell Court (2004).

As the college's general floriferousness increased, so did the desire among its members and staff to plunder the herbaceous borders for their own flower arrangements. This practice infuriated the garden steward and other high-ups in the college, and also some influential alumnae. It engendered a dispute that rumbled on for nearly 20 years and led to a series of diktats which do nothing to allay the impression that Cambridge University can be a bit of a 'bubble' at times. It all started in 1917, when the domestic bursar ruled that no roses were to be picked and that Cloister Court was entirely off-limits to flower-arrangers. In 1919 that stricture was extended to Emily Davies Court. But flower cutting seems to have been endemic at Girton. When Chrystabel Procter, the college's most celebrated garden steward, arrived in 1932 she recalled being told by her predecessor '*Don't waste your time trying to grow flowers.*' She was warned that the fellows 'had the right to pick flowers for themselves for their rooms

ABOVE *Rhus typhina* in front of the colonnade in Ash Court (2013), one of several recent developments.

whenever they wanted to and almost wherever they wanted to'. Even 'breaking branches off the flowering and other trees was permissible and commonly done by certain fellows!' To begin with Procter trod carefully, noting in an official memo that picking flowers was 'a privilege greatly appreciated by members of staff'. But by 1935 she had established her authority and the gloves came off. A typewritten memo on the subject was issued, prohibiting any flower-cutting in the principal courts and insisting that 'Scissors should always be used' and that 'no bulb should be deprived of more than one leaf.' Quite who would police these regulations is not made clear, but one imagines no one would dare pick anything when Miss Procter was around. The issue was still 'live' as late as 1937, when Lady Stephen (a great benefactor of the college) wrote a polite but firm letter to college suggesting that flower-picking in the gardens should be further discouraged. The letter was nine pages long.

Another bone of contention was the noise made by lawnmowers (considered a problem at Cambridge – though curiously, not at Oxford). Having consulted a body named the Anti-Noise League, in 1936 Miss Procter was engaged in a long correspondence with Wing Commander T. R. Cave-Browne-Cave, a professor of engineering, about his prototype 'silenced mowers' and whether the college could have several on loan. It is not recorded whether they ever appeared, or truly were silent (one suspects not). The wing commander was the brother of an eccentric and naturally dishevelled Girton tutor who cultivated her own 'wild garden' in the college grounds; she was once mistaken for a vagrant by someone visiting from the village and offered the gift of a florin (which she accepted).

In the mid 1930s the formidable but evidently likeable Chrystabel Procter pursued a policy of dramatic flower gardening with the express purpose of 'wowing' the students – and their parents – when they arrived at college in Michaelmas term. There are photographs of huge beds of tall lupins in Woodlands Court in 1937, for example, and the list of flowers grown especially for cutting in the fellows' garden includes lupins, delphiniums, aquilegias, penstemons, irises, pinks and daylilies. The Honeysuckle Walk was completely replanted and returfed in 1936. Procter had announced her intentions for the garden in the college newsletter soon after her arrival, describing them with typically quirky humour as a Soviet five-year plan.

But Miss Procter's gorgeous flower displays ended with the outbreak of war. In her report for Michaelmas term 1940, she proclaimed: 'College has become potato-conscious!... We *may* be bombed, we *must* be fed.' The college was already well-placed to Dig for Victory, having substantial areas devoted to food production, but efforts were redoubled with advice and encouragement from the Ministry of Agriculture, as well as the help of volunteers. Miss Procter appreciated the assistance: 'Huge sweeps of beautiful Brussels sprouts, cabbages, savoys, broccoli and kales owe their present health – perhaps their very being – to certain public-spirited dons and students who attacked the progeny of the Cabbage White Butterfly during the Long [vacation]'. Later that year it was decided to remove all the herbaceous material and instead plant carrots and beetroot in the borders on either side of the entrance arch, leaving only the shrubs in place. In 1941 there were 1.4 hectares/3½ acres of potatoes (producing 20 tons per year) and 0.6 hectare/1½ acres of cabbages and greens in the home garden, while the college was also growing leeks, onions, broccoli, beans, spinach and a range of herbs. There were three tomato houses and 43 frames for lettuce and watercress. Photographs in the college archive show salad crops growing in the borders below the windows of principal college buildings. Three land girls appeared and the fellows' tennis court was symbolically turned over to grazing. No other college in Oxford or Cambridge was able to contribute as much in this way during wartime. There were problems – complaints about visiting evacuees running wild when left unsupervised by students, and marauding soldiers stationed nearby, scrumping apples and trying to requisition some Girton sheds – but there were also pleasant memories of visitors, such as the Free French in Cambridge who held a morale-boosting garden party at Girton in 1942.

As at many country houses in England, the gardens at Girton never quite recovered after the Second World War. Despite an anonymous gift of £500 in 1945, everything had to be reined in (although tennis was still well catered-for, being the college's chief sport). Just before she retired, Miss Procter produced a plan for the rationalised garden which included borders denuded of all but peonies. Easier-to-maintain shrubs began to be favoured over herbaceous material and whole borders, such as those in Emily Davies Court, were forgotten about. Vegetable production was dramatically reduced. The minutes of the garden committee in 1950 reported that parts of the garden were 'in a very bad state' due to lack of labour, with the passive-aggressive addendum: 'It was suggested that

members of the high table might be asked to volunteer to help with the weeding of the Fellows' Garden.'

Girton's longstanding head gardener, Robert Bramley, has recently retired, and a successor has not been immediately appointed. The college has said that it is 'considering the best way to secure a future for the gardens and grounds that is as innovative and distinguished as the past'. The current garden staff have a large acreage to cover and several areas of intensive horticulture, and there are a number of high points. One is the fellows' garden, situated north of Emily Davies Court, beyond the pond. This was remade in 1992 by the garden designer and Girtonian Penelope Hobhouse, and has been kept up immaculately in recent years. It is in the form of a 'green theatre' of the type found at Villa Marlia and Villa La Pietra in Italy, with yew blocks forming the wings of the stage and a semicircular lawn as the auditorium. A pergola, planted with crab apple 'John Downie', bisects the space, with *Pyrus salicifolia* 'Pendula' at each end, and plantings below of white irises and pale pink sedums. It is an enchanting spot.

The college pond is linked to the fellows' garden by a bridge and is another highlight. From the 1920s a substantial rock garden was built up on the mound overlooking it, with a walk through lined with santolina. This was achieved largely under the direction of Kathleen

Butler, who went on to become Mistress of Girton in the 1940s. The feature is still known as Miss Butler's Mound. (Until the 1970s there was a tradition in college of individual fellows having their own portion of garden.) The ducks on the pond had a close shave in 1957, when they were blamed for the disappearance of the waterlilies; but a delegation from Cambridge Botanic Garden concluded that they were innocent and should be reprieved. Today the pond is fairly wild in aspect and gardened for ecological ends; it is shaded by willows, laburnum and a large thuja, with plantings of *Buddleja alternifolia*, choisya, phlomis, euphorbia, eryngium and vinca below. The soil at Girton is gravelly with bands of heavy clay on top of what the former head gardener described as a 'concrete-like' chalk marl.

The main courts at Girton are less distinguished and are frankly in need of a revamp. A substantial portion of Cloister Court is used as a car park, while a central planting bed, simplified in the 1980s, contains overgrown shrubs along with several limes and a walnut tree (survivors of the original 1901 planting), as well as birches and a cherry tree. It's a pleasant enough space but lacks definition. Woodlands Court, to the south-east, was originally a two-sided court open to Girton's lawns and woodland, much as Emily Davies Court is now. In 1931 it was 'completed' by being enclosed on all four sides to the designs of Michael Waterhouse, grandson of Alfred. This was

not a good idea as it created a rather stark and open central space which is difficult to landscape effectively. In fact it resulted in the very problems that Alfred Waterhouse's original designs for the college, as shown on his plans of 1886, expressly avoided. In the 1930s a central paved terrace was added to the enclosed space, apparently for the purposes of discreet sunbathing (then newly in vogue), with Mediterranean plantings of lupins and catmint. Today it is a nondescript area with park benches and simple groups of grasses, though students do like to use it. (Those students include men nowadays; they were admitted from 1976.) A slightly ragged copse of limes nearby adds to the sense of confusion here. The wall plantings are more inspiring: the climbing pink rose 'Madame Grégoire Staechelin' grows along the north-west range, with white centranthus, cistus and a bed of peonies, while the deeper pink rose 'François Juranville' can be found on the north-east wall, along with catmint and stachys. All the flower and foliage tones have been carefully chosen to complement the 'difficult' colour of the red brick behind, and overall success in this regard at Girton is one of the garden's subtle triumphs.

One other historic area worthy of mention is Eliza Baker Court, hidden away behind the eastern corner of Cloister Court. This small space was designed in 1932 by Michael Waterhouse as a sunken pool garden, with an elegant blue lias paved surround, York-stone terrace and low walls of Bath stone. The planting in the beds flanking the pool initially achieved by Miss Procter was Mediterranean in theme, using herbs such as lavender, rosemary and catmint, and creeping thymes in the paving. Today it is usually planted up much more simply with a single variety of a brightly coloured annual. More could be made of this as a garden feature. The court is overlooked by the prominent windows of the mistress's flat (David Roberts, 1962), a distinguished modernist design which has recently been restored and extended. There has never been a distinct mistress's garden at Girton; a principal's garden is always a good idea because at least then the head of college has some personal interest in the upkeep of the gardens.

The most recent addition to Girton is Ash Court (2013), a red-brick and concrete accommodation court (with indoor swimming pool) designed by Allies & Morrison, with a sleek modernist landscape design by Bradley-Hole Schoenaich Landscape Architects (BHSLA) featuring calamagrostis grasses, clipped box panels and young ash trees around an elegant colonnade. The college's other

ABOVE LEFT *Girton Column* (2012), a sculpture in Corten steel by Paul de Monchaux on Chapel Lawn.

recent intervention, Campbell Court, on the south-western side of Woodlands Court, incorporates block plantings of lavender, poppies, and a green roof on the library extension. As is so often the case with additions to colleges since the 1990s, these areas have a rather corporate air, perhaps partly because of the perceived need to look 'modern' and 'professional' in the context of the conference business, which is now such an important element of colleges' income.

Perhaps the principal pleasure at Girton's garden has always been the ability to roam the pasture and woodland encircling the college. The lack of terraces around the buildings enhances the bucolic atmosphere, as the grass comes right up to the brickwork. This has not been overly compromised by the addition of a large car park on the south-eastern side of college, adjacent to the field known as Mare's Run (until the 1940s the college owned a carthorse, Daisy, which made two trips per day into Cambridge on a sort of shuttle run). The perimeter walk is still maintained and cleared, with chestnuts, limes, field maples, fine old beeches, hollies, yews, box, sycamores, spruce, ash and oak. Black squirrels can be spotted among the trees. There are several lovely mature specimen trees on the lawns, including *Larix decidua* 'Pendula', with pretty pink flowers in spring and small barrel-shaped cones later, and a group of *Magnolia* × *soulangeana* at the woodland edge.

In Emily Davies Court the huge cedars help define the garden's Victorian atmosphere, even if several rooms in college are in their shadow, while good trees on the Chapel and Library Lawns include a monkey puzzle, a weeping copper beech, a ginkgo, a tulip tree and a *Sequoiadendron giganteum*. A large abstract sculpture in Corten steel, *Girton Column* (2012) by Paul de Monchaux, is a well-chosen addition in terms of colour and scale. Hidden away behind Hospital Wing, to the west, is a wildflower meadow covering part of the college's old vegetable gardens, formerly an integral part of Girton's identity. Something of that old identity may reassert itself yet: in this era of food-security concerns, the college's historic 'home garden' could suddenly seem a rather progressive idea, perhaps resulting in more apples, pigs, potatoes, flowers and – who knows? – ferrets.

ABOVE CENTRE Students and visitors are encouraged to collect windfalls.
ABOVE RIGHT The crab-apple pergola and associated border in the fellows' garden, which is hidden away beyond the pond.

GONVILLE & CAIUS COLLEGE

ATES AND CAIUS, CAIUS AND gates…It's all about those gates, at Gonville and Caius (pronounced 'keys' – and yes, the pun was intended). Like a condemned car in a crusher, the college is squeezed on all sides by the city, its courts shaped into rhomboidal contortions. But those gates stand firm: Humility on the east, Honour to the south, Virtue in the middle – bulwarks against the encroaching urban fray.

How much of gardens, then, in this constricted domain? Not a great deal, it has to be said, though the college does not quite deserve George Dyer's dismissive summary, given in his 1814 *History of the University*: 'No college has less of a *Rus* in *urbe* than this; everywhere surrounded with the town, and public buildings; with little of garden, no agreeable walks, overshadowing groves, or refreshing water, and not a single outlet into the adjacent country.'

That was perhaps truer in the early 19th century, when the space now known as Tree Court consisted of an avenue hemmed in by the high walls of disparate garden enclosures. Today this court is much more open and, as its name suggests, provides a pleasant arboreal overture to the austere and ancient courts beyond, as well as some lively horticulture, while the college's major architectural set pieces are also nicely framed by garden elements.

The college is generally known simply as Caius – poor Gonville often gets forgotten. Its curious double name derives from the fact that the old Gonville Hall, founded in 1348 by a Norfolk rector of that name, was refounded and expanded in 1557 by John Keys in his own image as Gonville and Caius College (he Latinised his surname and also appointed himself master). Tiny Gonville Hall consisted of just one court – today's Gonville Court – with provision for four fellows and a handful of students. From the mid 15th century there was a garden more than twice the size of the court, attached to the master's lodging behind its south-west corner, though we do

LEFT The Gate of Honour with Senate House beyond. The gate is elegantly framed by box clipped into swags, with lollipop-clipped privet above.

GONVILLE & CAIUS COLLEGE

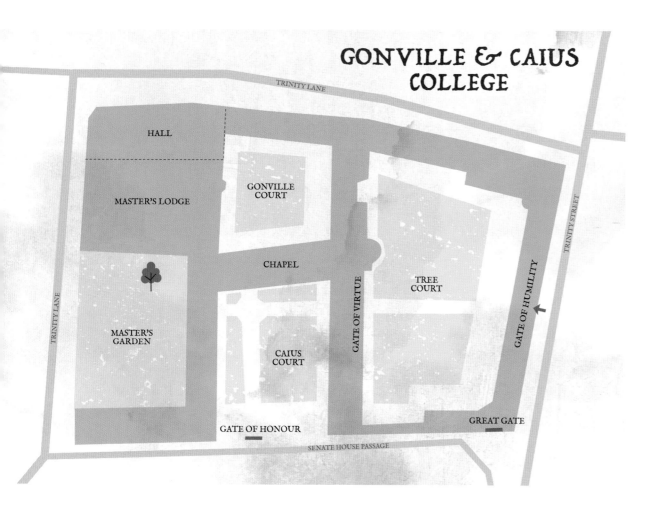

RIGHT An avenue of whitebeams in Tree Court is complemented by an unusual decorative device: rings of ivy at the bases of their trunks.

not know precisely what form it took. In all likelihood it followed the pattern of other college gardens of the period, beginning as essentially a productive space for growing vegetables and fruit, then gradually taking on modest ornamental elements such as seats, gravel paths, flowers, arbours and clipped evergreens, which all members of hall would have enjoyed.

In the early 1560s Keys commandeered the eastern section of this old garden and added it to land he had acquired south of Gonville Court to create Caius Court. In his own detailed account, the new master noted that the area reserved for Caius Court was 'previously occupied by four gardens divided by three walls and a wooden paling'. The remainder of the old Gonville Hall garden was retained as the master's garden, where it still stands (making Caius' master's garden potentially the oldest on a single site in either Oxford or Cambridge). At this time Keys also bought some old tenement gardens east of Gonville Court, a space that would eventually become Tree Court. The north-western part of this court was at that time taken up by a small cook's garden, while south of it a rectangular walled fellows' garden was made; Keys knew that a proper college needed a fellows' garden, however diminutive. In addition he created a small square walled plot in the south-west corner, designated the president's garden (Keys had decreed that his

college was to have both a master and president – the former running the college, the latter presiding over meetings of the fellows). None of these little gardens exists today, as all the walls were taken down in stages during the mid 19th century, when Tree Court was opened up. But its central axis, the avenue of trees leading up to the gateway into Caius Court, remains the dominant feature.

Keys' most notable addition to the college was the series of symbolic gates and associated spaces which mark a student's passage from humility to virtue, then wisdom and finally honour. Keys' Latinisation of his surname followed a fashion among Renaissance scholars, and an awareness of this pun involving keys and gates would certainly have played its part in the way he chose to ornament the college. The master's own character played as decisive a role in this arrangement, in that John Keys was – to descend to contemporary parlance – a control freak. His statutes for the college include absurdities such as a ban on Welshmen (though this may have been a scribal error), strictures against the lame or sick, as well as a rule that any college member of any rank who did not use his new gates in the manner he had prescribed should be expelled. The symbolism of the gates was embedded in the very structure of the college, so that Keys could be sure that his vision would continue long after his death.

With his gates, Keys was working in the classical tradition of the triumphal arch, while making architectural play with their complex design, which was intended to reflect the virtues they symbolise. The original Gate of Humility (since replaced) was a simple doorway flanked by Corinthian columns. The Gate of Virtue is much more substantial – built on the solid blocks of morality – but still plainly decorated, as befits the virtuous. The Gate of Honour, on the other hand, is a tour de force in the tradition of the 'frontispiece' for a Renaissance building, with a sophisticated piling-up of architectural features.

The architectural design of the gates was important; but one's physical progress through the spaces of the college is equally demonstrative. There is the point of entry at the Gate of Humility on Trinity Street (the college's main entrance today), then quite a long, constricted 'journey' through what is now Tree Court up to the Gate of Virtue, followed by one's emergence into the wide Arcadian simplicity of Caius Court, which was dedicated to 'Wisdom' in a foundation ceremony choreographed in 1565. Finally, the student turns 90 degrees to exit via the decorative Gate of Honour, on Senate House Passage. This is but a few short steps away from the Old Schools, where students receive their honours degrees, and to this day the gate only opens for graduation days and other special occasions.

The student has learned humility on a long and difficult path, displayed virtue through hard study, achieved wisdom and dwelt in the heart of the college, and finally leaves to enter the outside world, garlanded with honours. In Keys' scheme, the college itself is transformed into a physical metaphor: its fabric becomes meaningful and dynamic as the scholar progresses through its courts, whether that be over the course of a day, during years of study, or indeed across an entire lifetime. In this sense the vision of the college is realised as much by its spatial and landscape setting as by its architectural adornment. It is as relevant on the first day of the student's life in college as it is on their last, and an awareness of these virtues is intended to remain embedded in the Caius student for life. The symbolic scheme works in reverse, too, in that every student leaving the precincts through the Gate of Humility is reminded of the comportment expected of college members when 'out' in the world.

Caius Court (1565), with the old Gonville chapel on its north side, is often described as innovative in its 'three-sided' design, the south side consisting of a plain wall framing the Gate of Honour, as opposed to a conventional building range. This system has become known among architectural historians as a 'sanitary court', because it was apparently devised by Keys specifically for healthful reasons and to mitigate the threat of plague, being open to circulating air and to sunshine. As the college's refoundation statutes state, somewhat dramatically:

> We decree that no building be constructed which shall shut in the entire south side of the college of our foundation, lest for lack of free ventilation the air should become foul, the health of our college, and still more the health of Gonville's college, should become impaired, and disease and death be thereby rendered more frequent at both.

The theory has gained credence, but it is equally possible that the motivation for the 'open' south side of the court was to emphasise the architectural set piece which is the gate at its centre. This boundary abutted one of the busiest and dirtiest parts of the old town centre, so it is unlikely that it would have been seen as a genuinely hygienic alternative to the traditional enclosed court or quadrangle. It is also moot whether this court would have been seen as 'open' at all, given the architectural fantasia of towers, spires and noble edifices on view immediately to the south – something emphasised in all the old prints and engravings of the college, and which would also have been apparent in Keys' time (though this gate was only completed several years after his death). This was a 'borrowed view' of the heart of the university, a rather elegant – and economical – alternative to building a south range for the court. There was also the simple prerogative of space, in that Keys wanted an elegant, modern court to house the students for his new, expanded college, avoiding the appearance of a cramped little medieval court, like Gonville Court adjacent. The desire for an impression of size is evident elsewhere, notably in the long straight passageway Keys created through Tree Court, partly as a means of exaggerating the dimensions of the college estate.

It is, however, true that the three-sided court became something of an architectural typology in Cambridge, in a way that it did not in Oxford. There were early three-sided courts at Sidney Sussex, Trinity Hall, Peterhouse, Pembroke and Jesus, and in the 19th century the system was reprised in the form of the pierced screens along the front of King's and at St John's New Court, though enclosed courts were also constructed in Cambridge throughout this period. Arguably this had as much to do with the overall plan of the town as it did with the Caius Court exemplar, for the look and feel of Cambridge is characterised by large areas of open space – the commons and 'pieces' – situated just at the edge of the city centre,

areas which suddenly open up into view at unexpected moments. One has exactly the same sensation inside many of the Cambridge colleges, where the corners of courts provide tantalising glimpses of open space beyond. In fact Caius Court does not operate at all in this manner, given its cramped city-centre situation.

Tree Court remains the most horticulturally interesting part of college, traversed by the multi-stemmed whitebeams (*Sorbus aria* 'Majestica') that today constitute the avenue running from the entrance gate due west to the Gate of Virtue. Set in cobbled panels flanking the main path, these trees with glossy leaves, white flowers and red berries are elegantly and unconventionally ringed with ivy at the bases of their trunks. It is claimed that Keys himself oversaw the plantation of the original avenue of lime trees, but there is no evidence of its existence until 1658. Up to that point, the 'journey' from the Gate of Humility was a simple path squeezed between two high walls for half of its length, not unlike the 'chimney' walk leading up to the entrance at Jesus College. Most of the continuous wall to the left (south) abutted a property the college did not own until the late 18th century, while its western end hid the president's garden, which in Loggan's engraving of 1690 appears to have been an orchard with fruit trees trained on the walls. (This is almost certainly the orchard 'for the fellows' that Edmund Carter mentions in his 1753 history of the university.)

North of the avenue was a rectangular open court associated with the Perse and Legge accommodation blocks, which were added in 1618 and 1619 (to be replaced by Alfred Waterhouse's ranges in 1870). At the time of the Loggan engraving this was a simple lawn with a specimen tree. The north-west area was the walled fellows' garden, where a 'bouling green' was added in 1623, according to the bursar's accounts. It was a rather narrow affair flanked by a line of trees, to judge from Loggan's engraving and his city map. There are also references to a cold bath in the fellows' garden in the mid 18th century, when such amenities became fashionable.

Tree Court was transformed in the late 1860s with the addition of Waterhouse's overbearing new ranges and gatehouse, all achieved in a lofty French Renaissance style, including two substantial towers. In Waterhouse's defence, he somehow had to squeeze in 60 sets of rooms, so four storeys were deemed necessary. This was when the fellows' garden and the other walled spaces were done away with, and the court took on the open aspect we see today. There is a walnut tree on the

RIGHT Tulips and forget-me-nots are one of the spring plantings in front of the chapel in Caius Court.

BOTTOM RIGHT The most intensive horticulture in the college is found in Tree Court, around the chapel's east end, where a tree fern presides over the border.

north side of the court, while on the south is 'the president's apple tree', commemorating the president's garden which once stood on the site. The well-stocked borders in the northern part of the court feature tree ferns, alchemilla, salvia, alliums, stipa grasses and astrantia, with crocosmia, penstemons and daylilies following on. The shadier walls on the opposite side of Tree Court have *Hydrangea petiolaris*, holly, and variegated cornus. Wisteria and roses have been trained against the walls to form geometric panels, as is the style in the Cambridge colleges (the wisteria used to reach the roofline).

Entering Caius Court, the eye is immediately drawn to the Gate of Honour, which has recently been blessed with a framing device along the south wall on either side. This consists of lollipop-clipped privet standards and sentinel cupressus above a box hedge that has been shaped to create a swagged effect. The chapel dominates the north side of the Court, and a wide bed in front of it is planted up with tulips and forget-me-nots, and then a changing display of bright annuals. The panels of lawn in the court are of delightfully irregular form, adding to the amiably eccentric air the college as a whole imparts. Caius was long known as a college for 'reading men' as opposed to 'rowing men', and traditionally specialises in medicine; as such it managed to hold on to its dignity in the mid

19th century when some of the other smaller colleges descended into complacent decrepitude amid a dearth of students. Its roster of 14 Nobel laureates (second only to Trinity College, Cambridge, across Oxbridge) attests to its intellectual character.

Gonville Court is wonderfully atmospheric, and the only place where students are permitted to sit or walk on the grass. There is not much room for horticulture, though a number of window boxes (geraniums, petunias, verbena, diascia) contribute colour and there is a small bed for annuals such as begonias. At the time of Loggan's engraving and city map (1690/1688) there were trees at each corner of the court; these would have been severely cut back every year to keep them at a reasonable height. Contemporary squeamishness about such tree management would make them an impossible adornment today.

The master's garden was gradually reduced in size – by the time of Custance's map of 1798 it consisted only of a simple lawn with small flanking shrubberies – and was eventually halved by 19th-century building additions in the north-west corner of college. Today it has a strikingly domestic air, with a large tulip tree, a mature variegated acer and an old silver birch, pink and white roses and a terrace with pots. In 1868 the original Gate of Humility was replaced by Waterhouse's new gatehouse, and it eventually ended

up in the master's garden. It is kept hidden away in obscurity today, almost as a guilty secret.

The college was able to expand across Trinity Street in 1901, where it built several accommodation ranges wrapping around St Michael's Church, the most notable being the south range of 1934, which is usually described as the first modernist college building in Cambridge. The redundant church has housed a popular cafe since 2002, while outside it the Caius garden team look after shrub plantings and a small lawn with maples and *Prunus × yedoensis*.

After the fellows lost their garden in 1868 there were efforts to find an alternative private leisure space for senior members of college, and this came to fruition in the 1890s, when a site off Sidgwick Avenue was secured. The fellows' garden, paid for by subscription by the fellows themselves, was laid out in an L-shaped acre (0.4 hectare) of this block, where it remains today – yet sadly enjoys little usage. It consists of a lawn fringed by mahonias, with limes, walnuts, a huge plane and a tulip tree, and the remains of a large rose garden with concentric beds. There is a 'bowling green' – used for croquet today, as most former greens are – with a pavilion and an old *Prunus serrula* by the tennis court. A little brick hut next to a catalpa tree at the bottom of the garden is the exclusive domain of the fellow in music.

A modernist accommodation block, Harvey Court, was built on the adjacent land in 1960, and this is where most first-year Caius students are housed today. There is a substantial garden component to this site, with many mature trees and large planting beds around a sunken lawn (formerly the lily pool of Thorpe House, which existed here before the new development). There are also three other houses (for fellows), each with its own garden, kept up by the gardens team. The latest addition to college, in the north-west corner of the Harvey Court site, is the Stephen Hawking Building (2007), built in honour of one of the most celebrated Caians of our time. The S-shape of the building was conceived partly to accommodate three mature trees, which have been carefully integrated into the design. But S is for Stephen, too, an appropriate continuation of the college's long-standing tradition of telegraphing messages through architectural form.

ABOVE Harvey Court, developed from 1960 on a satellite site, includes the gardens of several existing houses and the Stephen Hawking Building (*centre*), designed in an 'S' shape so as to retain three mature trees.

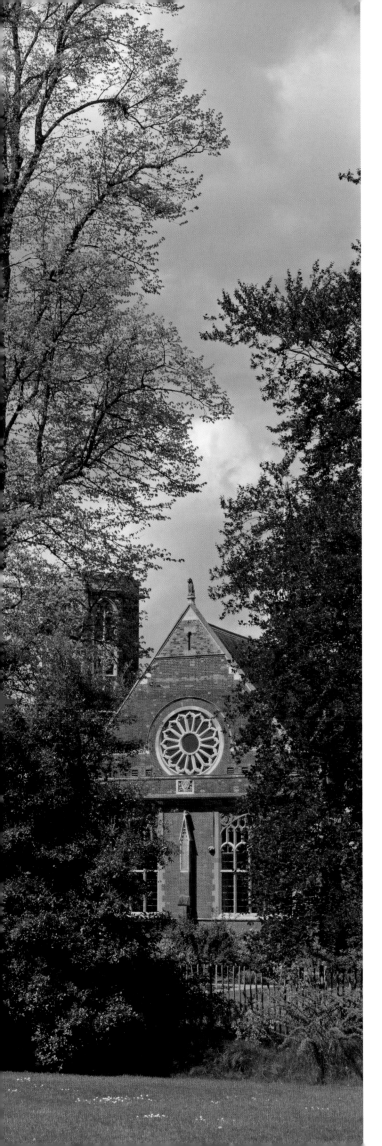

HOMERTON COLLEGE

Q UIETLY IMPRESSIVE, HOMERTON MAY NOT benefit from lovely old buildings or vistas along the Backs, but this pragmatic college has constantly striven to make the best of itself. It has never lapsed into complacency, having been engaged in a continual process of refashioning since well before it landed up in Cambridge, a process that continues apace to this day with an ambitious new commercial development next to the railway lines (three apartment blocks, eight houses, a sixth-form college and a cookery school). On the garden front, the acreage is huge – 9.7 hectares/24 acres including sports pitches – with a number of set-piece herbaceous borders and several hundred metres of deep shrub beds, but there are only three ('and a half') gardeners to keep it all looking presentable. This makes Homerton easily the most understaffed garden in Cambridge University, and its garden team therefore among the most effective. Understandably, the policy has been to concentrate on certain key areas while keeping the rest in check. Yet some of the horticulture here is of the highest quality.

Homerton is thought of as one of the newer colleges, as it gained collegiate status only in 2010. But its foundation can be traced back to 1695, when the Congregational Fund Board was set up to help Calvinist and other Nonconformist ministers excluded from mainstream education. The fund enabled young men to attend dissenting academies in and around London. Its reputation and assets grew and from 1768 it was operating from premises of its own, an impressive former school building in the High Street at Homerton, then a quiet village north-east of London. Homerton Academy (renamed 'College' in 1824) was highly successful, and was the alma mater of several notable writers, radical politicians and evangelising explorers. The college was absorbed into the new London University in the 1840s but in 1850 was refounded by the Congregational Board of Education and became solely concerned with training teachers

LEFT A fibreglass cast of Henry Moore's *Locking Piece* (1964) sits on the college meadow, in front of a line of limes and horse chestnuts.

HOMERTON COLLEGE

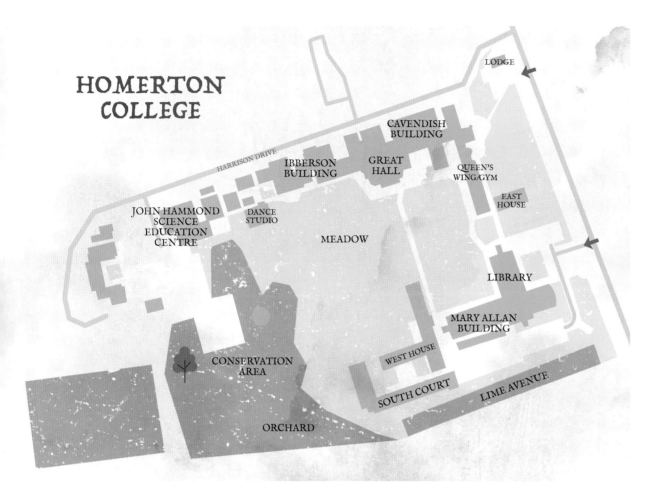

HARRISON DRIVE

LODGE

CAVENDISH BUILDING

IBBERSON BUILDING

GREAT HALL

QUEEN'S WING/GYM

JOHN HAMMOND SCIENCE EDUCATION CENTRE

DANCE STUDIO

EAST HOUSE

MEADOW

LIBRARY

MARY ALLAN BUILDING

CONSERVATION AREA

WEST HOUSE

SOUTH COURT

LIME AVENUE

ORCHARD

RIGHT The evergreen shrub *Sophora microphylla* growing against the brickwork of the old buildings of college.

FAR RIGHT Lilac blossom in the wider garden.

– this time both men and women – for Board schools. Homerton railway station opened in 1868, a century after the college had arrived in the area, and the atmosphere of the locality gradually altered as more speculatively built streets of terrace houses were packed in and light industry arrived. Homerton was being absorbed into the East End of London – so in 1894 the college relocated to the more salubrious and conducive environs of Cambridge.

Expeditiously it took up residence, initially as Homerton New College, in a series of Gothic Revival red-brick buildings (1876–89) on the Hills Road about a mile (1.6 kilometres) from the city centre, in the parish of Trumpington. This site had recently been vacated by Cavendish College, an experiment in socially enlightened education founded in 1873 as a hostel for university undergraduates who might be unable to afford college fees. Cavendish lasted until 1892, when it closed down in financial disarray, blighted by poor management and a lack of facilities. This defunct college, a valiant early attempt at 'widening access', is rarely mentioned and remains something of a skeleton in the university's cupboard.

Homerton has fared much better on the site. Almost immediately it switched to a women-only policy, since the university could not countenance mixed education at this time. It established itself as Cambridge's teacher-training centre, its academic reputation

growing until finally – and controversially – it gained 'approved society' status from the university in 1976. Now that it has full college status, Homerton offers the normal range of academic subjects to undergraduates, but it still has a speciality in education, accommodating some 280 PGCE (trainee teacher) candidates each year. Homerton has tried every permutation of intake: it started as an all-male college in 1768, accepted women from 1850, switched to female-only in 1895, and finally reverted to a mixed intake in the 1970s. It even accepted children, in a sense, from 1941, when the pioneering Homerton Nursery School was built on the premises.

When the college moved to Cambridge in 1894, various Cavendish College facilities, including hall and kitchen, were still brand new, but the 4 hectares/10 acres of grounds had not been developed. The college had been constructed on fields leased from Trinity College and the land around it had been left with an agricultural character, partly because of the aspiration that Cavendish students should learn land-management skills alongside the academic curriculum. There was a vegetable garden which grew over time and was an important part of Homerton's identity into the late 20th century. Early photographs show the college buildings in around 1900 in their smart livery of red Suffolk brick with Bath-stone dressings, surrounded by grass and simple gravelled paths, with little by way of horticulture besides some

shrubs and climbers. Yet the grounds were certainly used by students – there are several reminiscences about pleasant picnics on the grass. The regime at Homerton was, however, somewhat austere at this time. There was an injunction that students should dust their rooms every morning at a quarter to seven (how many did?). Male visitors were not encouraged and the college gate closed every day at teatime. As late as the 1930s a Homertonian recalled how 'The corridor prefect had to knock on each door at 10 o'clock and we had to answer: "In and alone. Goodnight." ' Homerton felt cut off from Cambridge; little wonder that the cycling club rapidly grew in numbers – it was a means of escape. The overall atmosphere was described as akin to a rural girls' boarding school – a genteel establishment, to judge by photographs of the homely, attractively furnished drawing room, with a gramophone.

Within a decade the Homerton estate had grown to nearly 12 hectares/30 acres, thanks to the acquisition from Trinity of more land south and west of the college, including parcels of woodland formerly used as a shoot. The copses and rough grass here further diversified the college grounds and are still very much part of the character of the place today. By 1903 student numbers had reached 200; the 'new' college was a success. It became known for its caring atmosphere, despite the evident privations, such as no heat or gas lighting in student bedrooms. ('Oh, the appalling coldness of that

top corridor,' remembered one student.) A support system developed whereby new students were assigned 'mothers' from the higher years. One dreads to think what psychologists today would have to say, but most Homertonians seem to have appreciated it.

Over time, young trees that had been planted on the estate grew up, lawn tennis courts were laid out in the fields around and the college gradually colonised the grounds for leisure purposes. In the 1930s and 40s Chrystabel Procter, garden steward of Girton College, came to Homerton to oversee students' horticultural examinations. The college's market-gardening activities accelerated from the mid 1930s until vegetable beds took up a substantial part of the west and south-western reaches of the estate. As at Girton, these activities contributed to the college's war effort, when several Homerton students metamorphosed into land girls in order to help. Even then, a 'homely' atmosphere prevailed. One student reminisced of the period 1944–46: 'Huge arrangements of flowers were always prominent in the entrances to the college, in Hall, and in the drawing rooms.' A key decision was to engage Joan Salter as the college's own garden steward in 1962; she stayed on until 1984 and made a significant impact. As it matured, the orchard she planted became a favourite place for picnics and quiet study. Generations of Homertonians have enjoyed the unburdening sensation of roaming the fields around the college to relax and collect

their thoughts – not quite the same as pacing around some ancient cloistered court, perhaps, but certainly possessed of its own charm. In the 'alternative prospectus' to the university, Homerton's beautiful grounds are cited as the chief reason for applying there.

There are two contrasting characteristics to the gardens of Homerton College today. The first is the sense that it is enveloped in expansive grassland and trees. Homerton's student body is the largest within the university, with 700 residents and around 1,000 people using it as their daily workplace. The garden team spend time each day directing students and visitors around the site, which is spread out and (happily) irrationally organised. The buildings inherited by the college were slightly oddly oriented not facing the road but east to west, so that even today visitors approaching from the Hills Road side do not encounter a grand frontage but the east end of the original building range, and an archway leading through into the college proper. This was the only way the architects could squeeze the necessary buildings into the long rectangle of the estate as it was then. As more land was acquired south, the college opened itself up to the great meadow that today occupies the heart of the Homerton site. Thankfully, given the college's recent desire for expansion, this has not been built upon.

An informal line of mainly copper beeches, horse chestnuts and limes straggles from east to west, extending about halfway across the meadow. To the south are the college's newer accommodation blocks, West House and South Court, constructed in the 1990s and 2000s. A recent addition for these lawns is *Locking Piece* (1964) by Henry Moore. The meadow is left as wild as possible, with recent birch and field maple plantations and older beech trees (many planted in 1947). An avenue of hornbeams, their multiple branches giving them an air of coppice, has beehives beneath. There are around 120 different grass and wildflower species in Homerton's meadows, including pyramidal and spotted orchids and an abundance of bee orchids, while the rare adder's-tongue fern is found in the woodland areas. Grass snakes are common and all three British native woodpeckers – the great spotted, lesser spotted and green – can be seen (and heard). Brightly coloured jays are regular visitors, too. The site is also a haven for moths such as the crimson-coloured elephant hawkmoth, the burnet moth and the hummingbird hawkmoth.

To the south-west, Joan Salter's orchard survives in fine condition, with a good show of blossom in spring and an abundant crop in

ABOVE Generations of Homertonians have appreciated the generous space provided by the college gardens and the meadow at its heart.

autumn which is pressed to make some 1,500 bottles of juice annually (there is an aspiration for college cider). There are around 30 different old varieties of apple here as well as newer plantings of plums, quinces and medlars, including the Cambridge gage (excellent). Nearby, to the south of South Court, just beyond a specimen tulip tree, is one of the true secret treasures among Cambridge's college gardens. Suddenly, out of nowhere, a fine mature avenue of lime trees materialises, running almost to the eastern border of the estate, where a wrought-iron gate formerly marked an entrance. Planted in 1909, the avenue follows the line of an 18th-century brick wall constructed by Trinity College to mark the southern boundary of the land. There are snowdrops and aconites here in springtime, followed by frothing cow parsley, while mistletoe hangs in the trees. Richard Thompson, the recently retired head gardener, said he discovered this avenue forgotten and smothered in ivy, which he removed to reveal a hidden arboreal delight.

The east side of the college, abutting Hills Road, is also possessed of a woodland character, creating the sensation that it is set within its own grounds, as a country house might be. There is no entrance drive to speak of, but a red-brick entrance lodge enhances the notion of an escape into a different world. Today there is a bike park next to the lodge, a necessary amenity which is considerably dignified by the presence of a little rectangular box-hedged planting with lavender

and alliums bubbling up around a small columnar yew. York-stone flags and cobbled paving contribute to the impression of smartness and organisation at Homerton. Further along Hills Road, a diagonal pathway lined with lavender and roses runs towards the archway into college, across smooth lawns with specimen trees and clumps including beech, catalpa and phillyrea. Extending south of the archway is the Queen's Wing (designed by Seeley & Paget in 1956), adjacent East House (1998) forming an L-shape with it. There is a big lime tree, a lovely ailanthus, a monkey puzzle and a *Pinus wallichiana* in the lawn here, and shrubs hugging the bays.

Another characteristic of the college gardens is the creative horticulture in the immediate vicinity of the buildings, which is first-rate in several places. Near Queen's Wing is a little space overlooked by a huge robinia with cardoons, variegated miscanthus grasses and nepeta below, while a mulberry in one corner was a gift from a fellow. A big border against East House includes geraniums, dicentras, daylilies, thalictrum, persicaria and filipendula. But the main horticultural interest is found along the south front of the old Cavendish Building.

ABOVE Small courts set against the old college buildings develop horticultural themes including dry Mediterranean plantings.
OVERLEAF An avenue of hornbeams near the orchard.

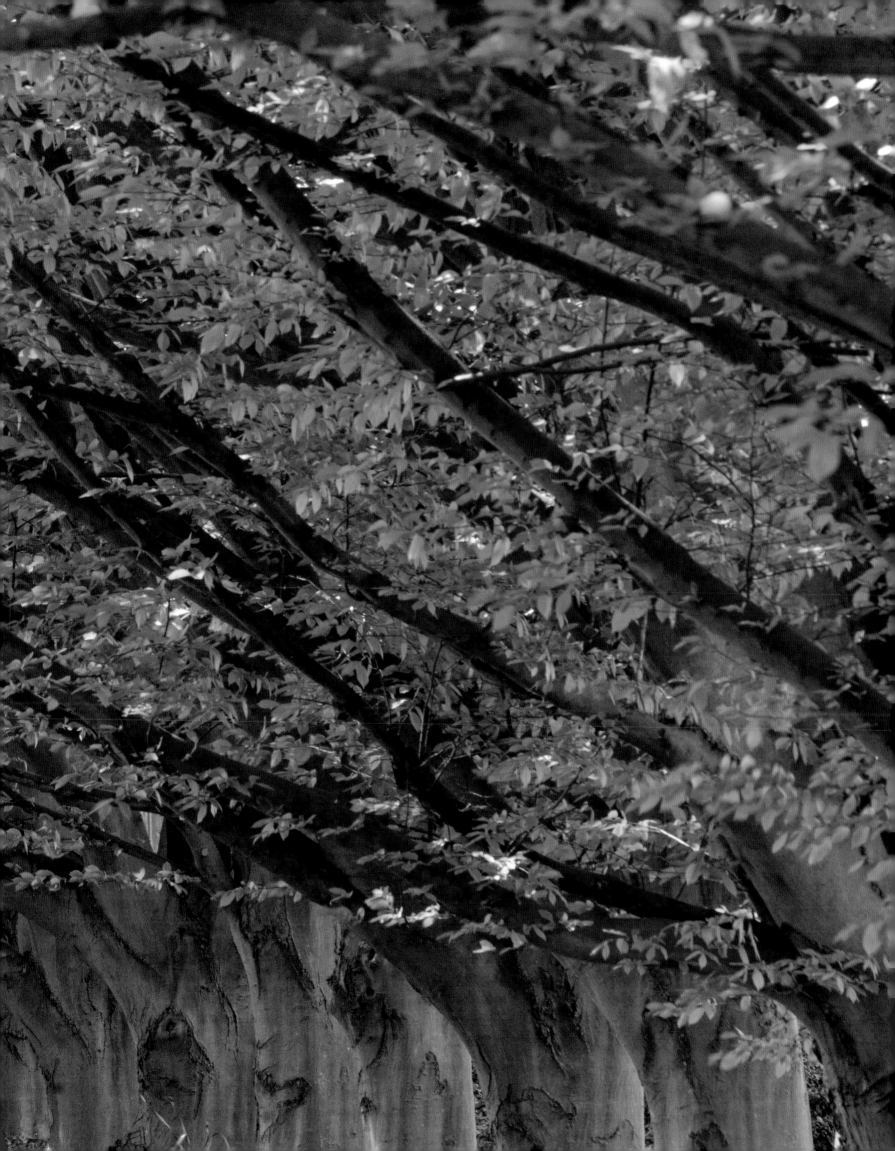

This range contains two substantial alcoves or courtyards in a mixture of pavers and grit, which have been planted up with a thrilling range of architectural subjects on a generally Mediterranean theme. These are suntrap spaces and the soil is a light, sandy loam. The alcove nearest the arch features a sculpture entitled *Stretching Figure* (1959) by Betty Rea, a friend and contemporary of Henry Moore who taught art at Homerton from 1949 to 1964. A *Magnolia kobus* grows up one wall and the entire space is occupied by an exuberant mixture of self-sown echiums mingling with carex grasses, verbascum, lavender, alchemilla, euonymus, heucherella, daylilies, fuchsia, daphne and astrantia, supported by hostas and variegated ivy. A golden catalpa sits in the middle, backed by *Cotinus coggygria* (smokebush). The silvery and glaucous-leaved plants look well against the rich red brick of the building.

The second alcove is even larger and more exuberant, with a quartet of clipped columnar Irish yews marking the centre, around which are other small trees including an olive, sophora and medlar. Climbing trachelospermum and magnolia grow against the building, and there are more echiums, cistus, rosemary, alliums, stipa grasses, spiky cordylines, *Phlomis fruticosa*, lavender and a diminutive form of *Pinus wallichiana*. Bulbous plantings here include crinums, *Cyclamen hederifolium* and *C. coum*. There is also a sundial in this space, and a

generic vertical sculptural piece in stainless steel. Clipped variegated ilex in pots stand sentry in the fellows' entrance to the hall.

Running along the south range in front of these alcove gardens is a long border of shrub roses, mostly Bourbons and old English varieties, including 'Louise Odier', 'Saint Swithun', 'Molineux' and 'Abraham Darby'. At the south end of the dining hall the planting morphs into a great surging border realised in classic English style, with more roses including *Rosa gallica* 'Versicolor' (rosa mundi), centaurea, salvia, phlomis, yellow-flowered peonies, *Lythrum salicaria* 'Feuerkerze', angelica, fuchsia and a large blue-flowered *Solanum crispum*, together with cannas and hedychiums for a subtropical note. Around the corner, towards the college bar, is a magnificent old oak and shadier borders containing foxgloves, cotinus, fatsia, *Stachyurus praecox* and clumps of dicentra. The whole south side of the Cavendish Building is something of an extravaganza.

West of the dining hall is the Ibberson Building, designed by Herbert Ibberson in 1914 as the college gymnasium (now the Senior

ABOVE LEFT A large area of mown pasture at the heart of the college is left wild at the fringes.
ABOVE CENTRE These plantings are designed as much for contrast in shape and form as for flower colour.

Combination Room) and the only building of real distinction on the site, with a steeply pitched Arts and Crafts roof and exaggerated bays. Symmetrical beds on the terrace in front of it comprise clipped box cones and 'Hidcote' lavender, while the intense fragrance of *Rosa* 'Blanche Double de Coubert' fills the air in summer. The college is about to embark on its plan to build a new dining hall slightly farther west, the V-shaped roof of which is intended to complement the Ibberson Building.

The large accommodation blocks on the south side of college – South Court and West House – were built to replace a cluster of late-1960s modernist buildings to the north, in the grounds of the old Trumpington House. These were colloquially known as the 'black-and-white' buildings because of their black steel frames and white-painted concrete panelling. Also in this area was the modernist nursery school by Maxwell Fry (1941). All these buildings were demolished in the late 1990s to make way for the new Faculty of Education that now occupies the site. South Court and West House are not distinguished works of architecture and the gardens team confess it is sometimes a struggle to keep up the plantings that encircle them. But their ambition is admirable and largely fulfilled. These borders were formerly stocked with generic shrub landscaping of berberis and viburnum, since replaced by shrub roses, *Hydrangea quercifolia*,

thalictrum, clipped box balls and euphorbia. The aim is to make the atmosphere more 'homely' by horticultural means. On the northern side of West House is a muscular, big-scale border replete with carex, epimediums, ferns, fatsias, ligularia and mahonia. The western wall of West House features ceanothus, cistus, macleaya, euonymus, bamboo, phlomis, *Hydrangea arborescens* 'Annabelle' and shrub roses, with *Verbena bonariensis* at the front. (Hummingbird hawkmoths love the ceratostigma here.) Detailed interest in these borders is provided by eryngium, helenium and penstemon, which one hopes that at least some of the college's members notice and appreciate. Inside South Court is a paved courtyard with verbascums, echiums, cordylines, sages, cistus and red achillea, while against the building is a little box-hedged border with hydrangeas, a golden catalpa and a trio of silver birches framing views to the Ibberson Building across the meadow, where fritillaries and field scabious flower in spring and early summer.

Homerton strives for effect in every regard, including the horticultural. The level of detail and quality achieved by the small gardens team at this college is truly astonishing.

ABOVE RIGHT Common spotted and other orchids are a familiar sight in the college gardens.

JESUS COLLEGE

J ESUS STANDS APART. PHYSICALLY, IN that it is set in its own spacious grounds, a little way from the epicentre of the city. Conceptually, in that of all the colleges in Cambridge and Oxford, this is the one which most closely resembles the monastic institutions whose ground plan had such an influence on their form. Certainly there were other, secular models to draw from – the country house, or the inner-city court – but the medieval monastery and priory must be considered the parents of the Oxbridge colleges.

Jesus is unique among all the colleges, then, because it retains at its heart a complete medieval monastic cloistered court, incorporating a chapel, refectory and other appurtenances (such as an almonry) whose usage has changed. This complex belonged originally to the Benedictine Priory of St Radegund, which had declined almost to extinction, with just two nuns in residence, and was dissolved by the order of Henry VII before the college's foundation in 1496. Several other Cambridge colleges developed out of monastic institutions: Emmanuel, St John's, Sidney Sussex, Magdalene and Christ's. But in these cases, little physical trace of the monastic legacy remains. Christ Church in Oxford preserves a portion of monastic cloister next to the cathedral (now a small garden), but only at Jesus College in Cambridge has an old monastic complex survived more or less intact. A German visitor commented in 1710 that the college 'lies quite out of town. It looks just like a monastery.' That's not quite true today, since large red-brick accommodation blocks built in the 19th century conspire to create a semblance of the typical Cambridge college court structure – but there is still something different about Jesus.

The key to that difference is the setting: the college's spacious, open-sided courts are surrounded by playing fields fringed by woodland. Several colleges founded more recently, such as Homerton and Churchill, may be similarly blessed with expansive meadows and groups of trees, but the palpable sense of antiquity at Jesus creates its distinctive atmosphere. Richard Harraden caught something of

LEFT The view back across the cricket pitch on Jesus Close, towards the 1880s east range of Chapel Court.

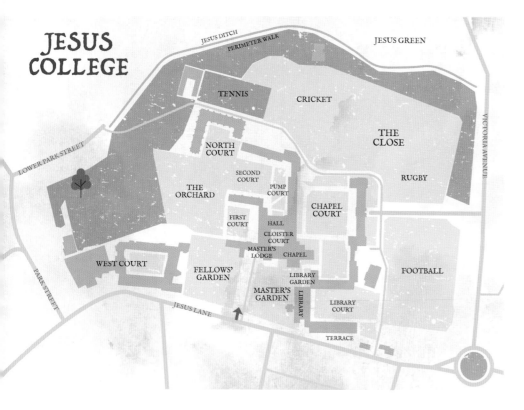

RIGHT A quartet of bulbous yew topiaries frame a central specimen tree, *Parrotia persica*, in Second Court. The topiaries are the overgrown remnants of a late-Victorian scheme.

BELOW David Loggan's engraving of 1690 shows the walnut in First Court (left, central) which was for many years a celebrated Cambridge tree. At that time the site of Chapel Court (top right) was used as the master's paddock.

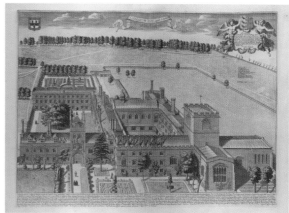

the place when he remarked in his *Descriptive Guide Through the University of Cambridge* (1800) on its 'air of calm retirement to many minds far more interesting, than the proud display of studied avenues and splendid structures'. It is said that James I liked to pray at King's, to dine at Trinity, and to sleep at Jesus. In times of plague and disease, it was considered to be slightly safer here than in the city-centre colleges, just a few hundred metres away.

Gardens were laid out at the new college almost as soon as the first scholars arrived. The college statutes of *c*.1516 stipulated that 'the Master will have a Garden', and both the master's and fellows' gardens are mentioned in the college records by the mid 16th century. These probably developed out of gardens originally created by the priory nuns, possibly on a site occupying the western side of what is now the fellows' garden. The old priory accounts for 1450 reported: 'Katherine Rolfe paid 4 pence for four days weeding in the garden'; a man was paid for mending 'the wall of the garden' the following year. In addition to the nuns' garden there were landholdings of some 31 hectares/77 acres belonging to the priory north, east and west of the college, and these were built up over the centuries following various bequests. Today's Jesus Close is the remainder of that estate, which was managed for centuries as Radegund Manor. The college tenanted out all of this land to farmers who used it mainly for grazing even into the early 20th century, while it also reserved an area north-east of the chapel as the master's paddock (this is Chapel Court today), and two plots to the south and south-west of Cloister Court as the master's and fellows' gardens. We know that these two college gardens existed early on because they are specifically mentioned as excluded from a lease of some Jesus land to a farmer in 1553. The spaces are divided from

each other by the high brick-and-masonry walls which also create the college's dramatic and distinctive entrance drive, a long straight alley known as 'the chimney' running up to the impressively castellated gate lodge. It is generally supposed that this name has arisen because of the chimney-like narrowness of the brick-lined entryway formed by the walls, and perhaps from the fact that the south range of First Court once boasted elaborate brickwork chimneys. These factors may have contributed to the nickname sticking, but its ultimate derivation is most likely to be the French word for path, *chemin*, which had been used since the time of the priory.

As at other colleges, the master's and fellows' gardens took the form of orchards in their earliest incarnations. That is how they appear on the city maps of Richard Lyne (1574) and John Hamond (1592), where they both look well established. Fruit was an important crop economically and also potentially something of a status symbol, which is one reason why a college would generally plant an orchard if it could. There are mid-17th-century references to the fruit from the fellows' orchard being stored in attics at Jesus. Grapevines, providing fruit for the dessert course, were seen as perhaps the ultimate high-table delicacy, and the college's accounts show that frames for vines were put up by the same man in both the master's and fellows' gardens in 1596. Fruit long remained a speciality at the college; George Dyer, writing in 1814, considered that Jesus had 'the best fruit gardens in the University'. The master's large orchard also came in useful during the English Civil War, when the college plate (silver) was buried there for the duration.

The master was able to substantially extend his garden eastwards after around 1570, across the site of the old priory chapel burial

ground and also over the area historically reserved for the Garlick Fair, an annual event that had taken place on 14 and 15 August since the mid 12th century at least. Garlic imported from the Middle East was just one of the commodities traded at this jamboree, which was moved over to the western edge of Jesus's land, where the college houses at Park Street stand today. The last fair was held in 1801.

By the time of David Loggan's city map of 1688, the gardens had diversified: the fellows' garden is shown as four roughly equally sized beds in a cruciform, with a bowling green (made in 1630) occupying the western portion of the space, while the master's garden, double the size of the fellows', had some nine beds, with at least half of the garden still reserved for orchard trees. By the mid 16th century a bowling green was seen as a necessary addition to any college garden, though the game was not to everyone's taste. Edmund Boldero, master at Jesus from 1663 to 1679, was a rather spartan person. A college fellow recalled of him: 'After dinners and in evenings, he kept company with the fellows and fellow commoners in the garden; but not long, for he could not be pleased with such insipid pastime as bowls, or less material discourse, such as town tales, or punning, and the like.' ('Dinner' at this period was the main meal of the day and would have been taken between 2 and 4 o'clock, after which the fellows would have had recourse to their garden.) The fellows' garden was walled

in 1608 and the master's garden in 1681, so creating the 'chimney' effect at the entrance. In 1703 a fine new gateway designed by Robert Grumbold (of Clare Bridge fame) was erected at the Jesus Lane end, when the old wooden door was replaced by a wrought-iron screen.

There is more detail of the master's garden on Loggan's college engraving of 1690; it was clearly a carefully maintained area. The illustration shows ornamental topiary forms clipped into tiers as the centrepieces of two garden squares, and a fir tree in a small grass plat by the entrance to the lodge. A huge tree growing in First Court was a walnut famous for its size, while farther north, beyond the new range forming the north side of First Court, lay another hedged-in formal garden space of narrow strips of grass focused on another centrepiece fir tree. This space had been a garden since at least the time of the late-16th-century city maps, though its earlier form is unclear. Close examination of the original Loggan map suggests that some of the beds here were used for vegetable-growing, perhaps making it an early form of ornamental potager. Just east of it a service court (now Pump Court) is shown, with several small buildings at its north end. One of these was the college's (indoor) tennis court, first mentioned in 1566 and rebuilt in 1603 at the expense of the scholars. The fenced-in master's paddock enclosed a substantial area north-east of Cloister Court, while a fringe of trees at the northern perimeter was

Jesus Grove, which would have been mature ash (planted in the 1570s) at this time.

By the time the 19th century dawned, the productive elements of these gardens had been much diminished, with only the western part of the master's garden reserved for fruit and vegetables. William Custance's 1798 map shows the master's garden as having two large planted areas and two smaller ones, with wide pathways around them; the section closest to the lodge appears to be a small 'wilderness', probably made of evergreen plants, with serpentine walks (it would have been a very old-fashioned feature at this date – something which does not tend to bother Oxbridge colleges overmuch). The fellows' garden by this time was thickly wooded with mature trees and appears to have taken on the character of an arboretum; George Dyer noted in 1814 that the trees and plants were all labelled in Latin 'to assist the botanical student'. Around this time somebody in college was knowledgeable about horticulture, judging by an 1829 bill of sale drawn up by the Norwich Nursery, which included numerous connoisseurial choices including a strawberry tree (*Arbutus unedo*), two tulip trees, *Daphne bholua* and *Hydrangea arborescens*. Most items in this big plant-order were single specimens, and therefore probably destined for the botanically organised fellows' garden. The old bowling green had simply become lawn by this point, as was usual, and a neoclassical summer house was put up in 1800 (it still stands, flanked by bright crocosmias, sedums and fuchsias).

The fellows' garden continued to take on the form of a little arboretum, which is its character today. The centrepiece has long been a large oriental plane planted in autumn 1802. The genesis of this plane tree is helpfully adumbrated by a label carved in slate:

—

PLATANUS ORIENTALIS CUJUS SEMINA THERMOPYLARUM FAUCIBUS DEPORTATA HUIC HORTO COMMENDATA SUNT AB **EDWARD DANIEL CLARKE LLD** ANNO **MDCCCII** FLOREAT INCOLUMIS SENSIQUE NEPOTIBUS UMBRAM PRAEBEAT ET GENIO CRESCAT AMATA LOCI

This says it all. But for those like me with little Latin and less Greek the gist of it is that a Jesus College fellow called Clarke collected seed of the plane in Greece – to be exact, from a tree standing next to the fountain in the Pass of Thermopylae. It is said that Clarke raised 11 such plane seedlings, including one specimen growing now in Jesus's master's garden and one on the north side of the hockey pitch. It is a moot point whether he also provided, as is sometimes claimed, the seed for the plane tree in Emmanuel fellows' garden, which is the greatest tree in Cambridge; but its habit is rather different to those at Jesus, with the branches reaching down to the ground. Emmanuel does not know exactly when its plane tree was planted but Jesus does, and took the opportunity to celebrate its 200th birthday on Midsummer's Day in 2002 with a lavish party including a jazz band, morris dancers, a toast from the head gardener, a talk from the fellow in botany and a choir singing the aria known as 'Handel's Largo' from the opera *Serse*: 'Never was dappled shade granted more lavishly, more lovingly.' Serse, or Xerxes, was the Persian king who defeated the Spartans at Thermopylae. Herodotus recounts how he came across a beautiful oriental plane tree at the town of Kallatebos (in modern-day Turkey) and ordered that it should be hung with golden ornaments and protected for ever by a guardian he appointed. To top off the celebrations, Dr Anthony Bowen, a classics fellow who then held the post of university orator, composed a Latin ode which he declaimed to the tree. It ends with the words (in translation):

We did not see you in the years of your youth, when your trunk began its upward climb, and your branches stretched down in pliant curves and your green leaves spread ever more widely, but how we admire you now in your full maturity; how we admire you now in your two hundredth year! O plane tree, you came here originally as a tiny guest, but now you play the part of host yourself.

There are several other notable trees growing in the fellows' garden, which would be a fine and private preserve were it not for the fact that anyone travelling on the upper deck of a bus along Jesus Lane can see straight in. Numbered among the trees are a holm oak planted in around 1780 that was destroyed down to the ground by frost in 1860 but survived to produce new stems; a mulberry planted in 1608 which at one time yielded enough fruit to provide each fellow with a pot of jam; a black walnut (1912); and a much more recent *Davidia involucrata*. Growing against the east (chimney) wall is birthwort (*Aristolochia clematitis*), generally held to have been grown in the time of the priory; as its common name suggests, it was traditionally used to terminate pregnancy. The greenhouse against the wall in this garden was erected in 1871 after an extremely lengthy correspondence now preserved in the college archive. A recent innovation is a potting shed in the shape of an inverted terracotta pot, which is an amusing novelty for the fellows but according to the gardeners is not fit for purpose. In spring the grass is covered with cowslips, primroses, crocuses, daffodils and aconites. One has the impression that the fellows of Jesus College actually use and enjoy their garden, which is not always the case in Cambridge.

The master's garden, on the other side of the wall, is rather dominated today by a straight gravel drive that runs parallel to the 'chimney', with a vehicle entrance on to Jesus Lane. This drive allows the master to park right in front of the lodge, a convenience whose necessity is debatable. The opportunity has been taken to create a border on both sides of this drive, backed by a large and attractive wooden tracery screen in Gothic style along the eastern side, with drifting late-summer plantings of hollyhocks, persicaria, thalictrum, miscanthus, phlomis, veronicastrum, polygonum, pinks and *Crambe cordifolia*, all 'inspired by Piet Oudolf', the Dutch plantsman. The other side is more of a shrub border, punctuated by tall Portugal laurels clipped as 'lollipops'. There are some good trees in the master's garden, including a *Cercis canadensis*, a monkey puzzle, a tulip tree, a eucalyptus and the characterful bristlecone pine (*Pinus aristata*). Near the lodge are two flower beds with tulips in spring followed by pretty summer flowers such as phlox and cosmos, offset by the foliage of purple millet (*Pennisetum glaucum*). A Mediterranean-themed terrace includes fruiting olive trees, pots with rosemary and a hot border dominated by salvias. A herb garden has been made against the chapel wall. The size of the master's garden was significantly reduced in the mid 1990s by the construction of the college's new library, which stands on the site of the master's vegetable garden and orchard, to the east. Yet this garden remains generously appointed.

Moving past the bicycles stacked along the walls of the 'chimney', and then through the porter's lodge, the visitor emerges into First Court, where Barry Flanagan's sculpture *San Marco Horse* (1983) makes for a superb counterpoint to the varied architecture and the backdrop of the wisteria-covered north range of 1638. The western side of the court is open, with a low wall fronted by a long border kept colourfully planted at all seasons, with red and yellow tulips in spring and in summer mainly annual plants such as pelargoniums, helichrysum, nicotiana and purple millet. Any sense of 'municipality'

RIGHT Barry Flanagan's *San Marco Horse* (1983) stands poised in First Court. In 1988 this was the first contemporary sculpture to be introduced to the college, the beginning of a notable collection.

associated with these massed plantings is eliminated by the quality of the gardening, which is first-class across the piece when it comes to these display beds. Huge clipped forms in yew and bay create an extremely pleasing sense of scale and balance. *Abutilon* 'Thompsonii' is among the shrubs along the walls.

A passageway in the east range leads into Cloister Court, the innermost sanctum of the college and one of the most special places in all Cambridge. One might not suppose that colourful hanging baskets would be an adornment to cloister arches and I confess I am still in two minds about them, but they certainly enliven the space. In practice this is a small cloister, not particularly conducive to extended meditation. The arches themselves were made in the 1760s as replacements for the original windows. In earlier times there were plantings in the middle of the court: sweet briars are mentioned in 1665 and laurels seven years later. It appears that at one stage there was an arbour, too, for in 1596 the college accounts state that 'Nadde the carpenter' had been engaged to make 'the frame of the Arbere in the quadrangle'. (Cloister Court was known by various names, including 'quadrangle' and 'inner court'.) Today it is simply laid to lawn, with *Vitis vinifera* and *V. coignetiae* growing on the walls alongside Boston ivy and Virginia creeper, creating an attractive 'living wall' inside this palpably ancient precinct.

Second Court lies north of First Court and is the site of the garden shown on the Loggan engraving and the late-16th-century city plans. For a time it was known as the Ha-ha Garden, because the ha-ha made to keep the grazing animals in Jesus Close out of the college ran across its north and west sides. In the 18th century the space was used as a kitchen garden; it was only with the construction of Alfred Waterhouse's fine north accommodation range of 1869 that the garden's design was again addressed. At that time it was evidently decided to return it to something akin to Loggan's engraving, which depicted a garden made in 1658 – an excellent idea. The only remnants of this formal garden, which was almost entirely removed in the 1970s, are the bulbous pairs of yew topiaries that are now marvellously marooned in the grass and keel over at deliciously precarious angles. They are a memorable adornment to the college and one hopes no one will ever attempt to reform or improve them. A *Parrotia persica* tree stands in the centre of the court.

Pump Court, at one time known as Third Court, lies just east of Second Court (formerly the site of the tennis court and, obviously

---

ABOVE LEFT Wisteria growing on the north range of First Court.
ABOVE CENTRE Evelyn Herring's *Mortal Man* (1960) sits amid snowdrops and crocuses in the Orchard.

enough, the college pump and well). The St Radegund Garden made on this site in 1996 commemorates the college's patron saint, a Thuringian princess who had been forced to marry a Frankish king in the 6th century. The garden contains medieval-period plants such as herbs and fruit trees, but is not particularly successful.

West of the Waterhouse range is North Court, a mid-1960s modernist accommodation block by David Roberts characterised by large angled balconies. In front of it are four beds with phormiums and *Stipa gigantea*, and 'hot' plantings in high summer. Interesting trees in this area include yellow birch (*Betula alleghaniensis*) and paperbark cherry (*Prunus serrula*).

South of North Court lies the Orchard, which is more of an arboretum now and has no connection with the old orchards in the master's and fellows' gardens. Growing in the grass here are a number of walnuts, an old copper beech, a weeping ash and a Lucombe oak, and more recent plantings of ginkgo, wingnut and *Quercus rubra*. More importantly perhaps, this is the principal site for the college's constantly evolving sculpture collection. The Flanagan sculpture in First Court is only the fanfare for the finest curated display of modern sculpture in any Oxbridge college, which is a beacon for others to follow. The Flanagan horse was the star of the college's first sculpture show in 1988, inaugurated by the then master Colin Renfrew, and it

has never departed. Since then the college has consistently attracted work by the most highly regarded contemporary sculptors for its temporary annual show, and has acquired around 30 notable works to remain *in situ*, both inside and outside. The artists represented include Antony Gormley, Barbara Hepworth, Richard Long, Henry Moore, David Nash, Eduardo Paolozzi, Cornelia Parker and William Turnbull. Only Pembroke College in Oxford and Churchill in Cambridge have modern art collections of comparable stature.

Chapel Court lies east of Cloister Court and is a difficult space to negotiate aesthetically. It is extremely large, open on its north side, with a wide variety of architectural styles on display, from the east end of the medieval chapel to a great brute of a late-Victorian brick accommodation range to the east, and Percy Morley Horder's almost apologetic range to the south, realised in an insipid fawn brick. Today there are big shrub borders against the chapel and ranges, and a couple of mature trees such as a lime and sycamore. The Victorians had opted for pleached limes across the wrought-iron screen on the north side, and a central fir tree surrounded by low shrubs, which had the virtue of providing a focus to the scene, but this garden was

ABOVE RIGHT Cow parsley dotted with orange 'Ballerina' tulips in the shade of a copper beech in the Orchard.

returned to lawn in the 1920s and the limes removed 60 years later. There is a story in college that the old Victorian path system, which looked like an X from above, was removed during the Second World War to deter German bombers from using the college as target practice or for wayfinding.

The landscape design of such areas within college are difficult to deal with, and Jesus has sought advice on several occasions, perhaps most notably when it commissioned a complete redesign of the college estate from Sir Geoffrey Jellicoe in 1946; he was then near the beginning of his highly successful career as a landscape architect. His plan was radical and not acted upon. The sage advice which Sir Harold Hillier (of the Hillier arboretum in Hampshire), communicated after his visit in 1931, would perhaps have been of even more benefit to the college. His long letter noted the low-lying, waterlogged land and also the danger of frost and drought pockets. 'I was struck by the very slow growth made by trees planted from ten to twenty years ago,' he wrote, adding that he was 'impressed by the lack of colour at Jesus College'. Hillier recommended iris, peonies, roses, phlox, delphinium and other 'old-time English Flowers', and suggested replacing the ivy on the court walls with wisteria. He clearly felt that the college needed 'cheering up' at this point, and it seems Jesus College has been cheery with colour ever since.

The college's new library has a few associated garden areas, designed by the landscape architect Janet Jack. A small garden at the entrance has a curved yew hedge with sturdy shrub plantings and a mulberry tree. A large and intriguing sculpture by Keir Smith, entitled *Coastal Path*, has been placed in the grass to the west. Another well-realised area associated with the library is a sunken garden with gravel and a variety of climbers, while 'around the back', behind a new accommodation block on the south side, is a broad terraced garden against Jesus Lane with shade-tolerant shrubs and more climbers. The space formed by these buildings is named Library Court, where the columns are festooned in clematis, honeysuckle and golden hop, with daphnes below.

Jesus Close envelops the college buildings on three sides and is now an area almost entirely dedicated to sports, with cricket, rugby and football pitches. A charming thatched cricket pavilion (1924) designed by Morley Horder sits at the top of the site, surveying all this Corinthian activity, for Jesus has been an excessively sporty college

---

ABOVE LEFT Narcissi in front of the red-brick Waterhouse Building of 1869.
ABOVE CENTRE Birthwort (*Aristolochia clematitis*) grows against the wall of the fellows' garden. It is believed to be a survivor from the time of the Priory of St Radegund.

since the mid 19th century. Jesus Grove originally occupied only the northern perimeter of college, against the watercourse known here as Jesus Ditch but which is in fact part of the King's Ditch that ran through Cambridge as an open sewer until the late 19th century. Later the Grove was extended west so that it formed a 'semicircular figure', or so it was described in the late-18th-century guidebooks to the university, when the Grove was high on the agenda for visitors. This woodland walk was being considered for its aesthetic properties by 1700 (we know seats were put up in 1717) and it was replanted in 1780 and again in 1905.

Hazel and other native hedgerow plants have recently been added to the woodland walk in the Grove, along with log piles to encourage newts and invertebrates. Red admiral and orange tip butterflies are regularly seen, jays and woodpeckers are common, and water voles live by the ditch. The Grove becomes closer and darker at its western end, lending it a different atmosphere. Reconceived as a perimeter walk, the Grove is now being 'marketed' by the garden team as the Coleridge Path, in an effort to entice more college members into its environs. The new name arises because Samuel Taylor Coleridge, one of the college's most famous sons, was fond of the college's grove. After he had run away from Cambridge and then returned, he was obliged to remain in college and translate certain texts – 'a thin quarto of about 90 Greek

pages', as he said. He made light of the punishment in a letter to a friend. 'The confinement is nothing. I have the fields and grove of the college to walk in, and what can I wish more?' Coleridge wrote a poem inspired by the place in 1792. The first two stanzas envisage a placid and content life akin to this quiet realm of wood and stream, where one feels refreshingly detached from quotidian concerns:

A Wish:
Written in Jesus Wood, Feb. 10, 1792
Lo! through the dusky silence of the groves,
Thro' vales irriguous, and thro' green retreats,
With languid murmur creeps the placid stream
And works its secret way.
Awhile meand'ring round its native fields
It rolls the playful wave and winds its flight:
Then downward flowing with awaken'd speed
Embosoms in the Deep!
…

ABOVE RIGHT The 'chimney' or entrance path up to the college, with the master's garden over the wall on the right, and the fellows' garden to the left.

KING'S COLLEGE

KING'S IS NOT ALL IT may seem. The magnificence of the chapel, the imposing physical size of the college and its prime position in the beating heart of the city would seem to place it at the very core of the university. It was founded by Henry VI in 1441, with early links to Eton College, and gives its name to King's Parade, the showpiece street of Cambridge. But King's does not see itself in quite that Establishment sort of way. It is, appealingly, not so easy in its grandiloquence. Over the past century it has presented itself as a 'progressive' institution, with a good proportion of its members espousing liberal or leftist views (most notably the economist John Maynard Keynes, who might now be regarded as the archetypal Kingsman). Evensong may be sung every night in chapel, just as it has been for more than 500 years, but this is a college that strives to be modern.

The college's rather wonky ground plan today is the result of its back-to-front development. The land on which the King's College of Our Lady and Saint Nicholas was built was, in the mid 15th century, a busy industrial zone, with wharves, warehouses, shops, a school, an inn, a parish church with walled graveyard and several notable houses. Nearly all of this was swept away after the 19-year-old king acquired the site for his new college, leaving a blank canvas for an institution whose courts were presumably going to extend westward, perhaps all the way down to the river. That was the plan, at least – but for various legal and civic reasons it was never realised. For the first 300 years of its existence, the college's buildings remained clustered to the north of the great chapel in a rather cramped quarter known as Old Court (now the site of the University Old Schools). Prints of the 18th and early 19th century – including Thomas Rowlandson's 1811 caricature of the fellows in raucous disarray, singing along to a harpist – depict Old Court as the social centre of the college.

LEFT The west end of King's College Chapel viewed across Scholar's Piece, with the Gibbs Building to its right and Clare College to the left.

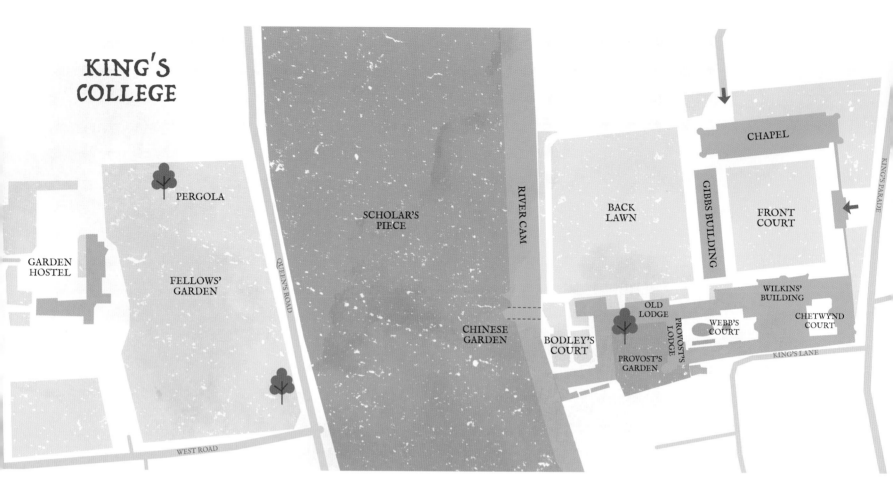

KING'S COLLEGE

As it proved impossible to construct college buildings next to the river, the land to the west was left largely open, with the exception of a wooden belfry outside the chapel's west door (which survived into the 18th century); there was also a walled enclosure containing two gardens (the first fellows' garden) and a stable with its own enclosed yard next to a central bridge on the college side of the river by the time of Hamond's 1592 map of Cambridge. The bridge across the Cam, first recorded in 1472, led to the area of rough pasture now called Scholar's Piece but which at that time was a tree plantation or orchard (the college archives record apple-pressing in the late 15th-century). There was a square pool in the middle – probably a stew pond for stocking fish – with a building, possibly the dovecote, adorning an island; this substantial building lasted for some time, and was clearly shown on maps of 1574 and 1592, though it appears to have gone by the time of Loggan's city map of 1688. There is a record of a garden being laid out at King's as early as 1451–52, and of seeds and saffron bulbs being bought for it in 1467–68; this was probably a kitchen garden, but it is not clear where it was exactly. There was also a large vineyard somewhere on King's land: we know that verjuice was being made from the grapes in 1483.

Most of these features remain recognisable on Loggan's 1690 bird's-eye plan of the college, though the mature plantation was by

that time named King's Grove and there was a tree-lined walkway, which we know was planted in 1580, leading up from the bridge through the centre of the meadow or 'grene' in front of the chapel, towards what is now Front Court. Another tree-lined walk ran parallel to it, heading towards the chapel's west door. The main, central walk provided a pleasant perambulation down towards the river and the bridge, passing by the enclosed fellows' garden on the near side of the river. The presence of avenues indicates that the grounds at King's were from the late 16th century at least designated partly as a space for leisure and relaxation.

Both the Hamond and Loggan maps show the old fellows' garden (called the 'little garden' in early references) divided into two sections. It is also shown on Richard Lyne's bird's-eye view of Cambridge in 1574, with the stable enclosure adjacent. By the time of Loggan's plan the southern part of the old fellows' garden was labelled as a bowling green; this had been made some 30 years before, in 1658, and was known as the junior fellows' garden. Barnabas Oley of neighbouring Clare College bequeathed £50 for a (new) wall to divide these gardens in 1689, though whether this was to benefit the juniors or seniors is not clear. All these plans also show a building overhanging the river; this is the wooden gallery mentioned in the college accounts from 1468 onwards, along with a water gate and stone seats shaded by a

vine. The old fellows' garden at King's sounds like a pleasant private resort, with bowling green, gallery over the river and agreeable walks.

The main college entrance remained north of the chapel until the 1820s. The chapel itself was still hemmed around by old houses, its east end poking into the town. What we think of as King's College today, south and south-west of the chapel, was at this time essentially a large area of green space, which the college developed only very gradually. Finding itself unable to contemplate a series of semi-enclosed, connecting courts as its neighbours had done, the college instead constructed discrete buildings on the available land over a long period across the 18th and 19th centuries. The result is that King's is constituted as a group of showpiece buildings of different periods standing in more or less open space. Most people would not describe these spaces as 'gardens', exactly, yet they play a vital role in the aesthetic of the college. The Gibbs Building was finished only in 1732, creating Front Court in the process, but even this space does not function in the usual way of a Cambridge court – the buildings here are simply too large and imposing to allow for any real sense of enclosure. Front Court in any case remained open to the street, barring a line of trees along its east side (as along its south), until as late as 1828 and the addition of William Wilkins's effective Gothic Revival frontage, including the celebrated screen that now separates the college from King's Parade, as if protecting the modesty of the chapel.

The most innovative aspect of the Gibbs Building lies not in its architectural quality, which even the most ardent Palladian could not deny is somewhat bombastic, but in its scenographic placement in the context of the river and the view from the Backs. Before this time, the western ends of the riverside colleges had not really been considered for their aesthetic possibilities, beyond their function as the site of walks, groves, orchards and small walled gardens. The river itself was seen as an industrial zone rather than an adornment, the colleges still described their nether regions as 'the backsides', as opposed to the more decorous 'Backs', and there was no effort to emplace college buildings or garden features within an overall designed landscape vista. The Gibbs Building changed all that by introducing the principle of picturesque composed views back to college from across the river. Up until that point, this way into the riverside colleges had been seen as the tradesman's entrance.

King's, then, occupies a large site in the middle of the city, but operates spatially in a quite different manner to other colleges. As

ABOVE The buildings along the college's southern edge are adorned with clipped shrubs such as *Osmanthus × burkwoodii* and *Viburnum carlesii*.

we have seen, this is largely the result of the halting way the college developed architecturally over the centuries. Perhaps it is fitting that the gardens at King's are also to be found at one remove from what is apparent. One previous guide to the gardens of the colleges omitted King's altogether on the grounds that 'it has no garden'. But this is palpably not the case, if one allows the term 'garden' to extend beyond the realms of ornamental horticulture. There is the fellows' garden, which opens one or two days a year for the National Garden Scheme charity, and several gardened spaces in the enclosed 19th-century courts. And then there is also of course that iconic view across the Backs, taking in the chapel (1515), the Gibbs Building (1732) and, at a right angle, the south range of neighbouring Clare College's Old Court (1642). These three buildings form a felicitous ensemble when seen across the green sward of Back Lawn, with cattle grazing prettily in the foreground on Scholar's Piece. It is the view that in 1779 inspired Capability Brown to suggest amalgamating the gardens of all the colleges on the Cam into something approximating a country-house landscape design, linked by a serpentine river and with the Gibbs Building as its centrepiece. It is generally agreed to be a good thing Brown's plan was never adopted, for it would have swept away the idiosyncrasy of the college gardens along with their boundary divisions, and their bridges, too – and would probably also have ushered in centuries of inter-collegiate strife with regard to horticultural decisions.

More heretical perhaps is the opinion that the iconic vista would have been even better if the Gibbs Building had never been interpolated, for then the whole south side of the Gothic chapel – the best building in Cambridge – would have been visible, rather than 'long-back'd', as Wordsworth put it in *The Prelude*. The contrary view holds that the oddity of the proportional arrangement of the trio of buildings lends it distinction: the grandiose breadth of the light-coloured neoclassical Gibbs Building next to the tall and elegant, ship-like presence of the west end of the chapel, which is realised in a completely different style and material, and then the recessive, complementary character of the Clare range, somehow balancing it all out. One of the characteristics of Oxbridge college chapels is that they are rarely free-standing, as King's Chapel is. In addition, the rectangular or square character of courts and quadrangles generally requires the principal – as in most visible – facade of the chapel to be one of the long sides, while the narrower east and west ends are frequently obscured or curtailed, or perhaps left facing a public street (as at Pembroke). In this vista from the Backs, the west end of King's College Chapel plays the starring role, magnificent in its vertical isolation, flanked and framed by the long horizontals of the neighbouring buildings.

That the college should have a garden was stipulated by Henry VI at the outset and a garden is mentioned in the college mundum (account) books from the 1450s on. The area described as the 'new garden' was situated west of the Cam, on the site now occupied by Scholar's Piece, and was early on bisected by a raised causeway planted with trees (removed in 1819, its remains piled up to form the two curious mounds which are still visible today, topped by hornbeams). It was needed because the area was criss-crossed by streams and ditches and was most likely waterlogged much of the time. This problem has beset all the colleges with land near the river over the centuries. In fact there are as many references to ditching in college accounts as there are to gardening itself, almost up to the present day (for example, King's availed itself of the services of four Austrian POWs for this purpose for a month in 1944). It is probable that Capability Brown was consulted as much for his skills as a water engineer as a landscape aesthetician.

This early garden was characterised as a 'grove' to the south and a 'meadow' to the north, though the names varied at different times: the northern section was used as a paddock for horses, while the southern part, for a long period known as Laundress Yard, would have been used as a drying ground but was also reserved for the fellows' leisure. Hops were grown here, too, from the 1570s. (Early gardens in the Oxbridge colleges were generally put into multiple use in this way, as productive or service areas as well as places of pleasurable retirement.) This southern section also contained a dovecote and tree-lined walkways known as 'le crouches'. One of the chief pleasures offered by a garden was long considered to be the sensation of walking in the shade of files of trees, as Sir Francis Bacon's essay on gardens attests (and he was a Trinity man). The early history of all the college gardens in Cambridge should be considered in that light. There is some evidence to suggest that over time the tree-lined walkways on the far side of the Cam were the resort of ruminative senior fellows, while junior (usually younger) fellows and students were given the run of the old enclosed fellows' garden, with its bowling green. (The site west of the river was being described as 'the fellows' pleasure ground' in internal college documents by the 1750s.)

As for bowling, in Oxbridge colleges until the late 18th century, when they finally fell from favour, bowling greens were places where young men could cut loose a little and let off steam; they became associated with drinking, gambling and in some places (though not the colleges) prostitution. Swans were another accoutrement in the garden at King's – or rather on the river at King's. They are first mentioned in the accounts in 1554 and in 1570 there are references to a James Beckwith being paid for 'uppyng ye Swannes and wynteryng them' and also to one Cole of Horningsay being prosecuted 'for kylyng a colledge Swanne'. A swan-house was built soon thereafter and in 1641 there is a reference to the college owning nine of them.

The principal architectural adornment to the garden at King's was long considered to be the elegant two-arched stone bridge across the Cam constructed in 1627 to the designs of George Thompson, a sturdier replacement for various earlier wooden structures. The simple (but lockable) Friar's Gate on the bridge led into what was by then the mature 90-year-old avenue extending east across the middle of the Back Lawn, and west into the college's walks, as far as the ditch at the western extremity of the estate, where there was another (wooden) bridge at Field Gate. It is recorded that the eminent landscape designer Charles Bridgeman was consulted in the 1720s to reorganise and ornament the college's walks and waterways west of the Cam, but there is no evidence that any of his suggestions were acted upon. Eight years after the completion of the Gibbs Building in 1732, and two years after the death of Bridgeman, the Cambridge architect and antiquarian James Essex published ambitious plans for a formal landscape garden to complement Gibbs's architecture. This included canalising the river and expanding it to form a great central basin. Essex, who had been a pupil at the grammar school attached to King's and whose father had worked for James Gibbs, would have been 18 or 19 years old at this time, and the suspicion has to be that the designs he published were substantially based on those earlier submitted by Bridgeman, since they were in his style

and would certainly have been well out of fashion by the 1740s. (Though if he did indeed reprise Bridgeman's work, it is likely he did so with the full knowledge of the college, where they would not have been forgotten.) Only a few subsidiary elements of Essex's plans were implemented: in 1749 a new lime-shaded walk was planted next to the river on its western side, as well as another new walk on the college's southern boundary, along what would later become the principal 'back route' into college. The young lime walk is shown in an engraving in *Cantabrigia Depicta* (1763) by Peter Spendlowe Lamborn, as viewed through a short avenue of elms on Queens' College land. A small gate is visible next to the bridge, on the walk on its western side; this would have led into the northern, 'paddock' section. Loggan's engraving (1690) of neighbouring Clare College depicts this area as relatively open, with an avenue of trees running straight across it, south to north.

Most things seem to have happened rather gradually at King's College, and this is certainly true of the metamorphosis of the old Chapel Yard area into the Back Lawn we see today. At some point

ABOVE LEFT Autumn colour from *Tilia tomentosa* in the fellows' garden.
ABOVE CENTRE The provost's garden is characterised by soft shapes contrasting with spikier forms.

in the mid 18th century (possibly as early as the 1730s) the central avenue of trees was felled, though the path itself remained *in situ* for several more decades. The walled enclosures near the river, including the now outmoded bowling green, were cleared away in the 1770s, along with the wall running along the riverbank and the portico of Friar's Gate on the bridge, which was replaced with iron railings. The ground was then levelled, and by a college vote of 14 April 1772 it was agreed to

> proceed in the further improvement of the Chapell yard on the West side of the New Building, by laying down the same with Grass seeds and afterwards feeding it from time to time with sheep as occasion may require in order to get it into good and ornamental condition; to compleat the Gravelling of the Walks round the same as now laid out, and not for the future to put any horses there.

At around this time Front Court was also grassed over. It appears that King's was being pastoralised in the approved 18th-century manner.

The next major decision came in 1818, when the somewhat decrepit stone bridge was removed. A new single-arched ashlar bridge was designed by Wilkins to be positioned at the college's southern boundary, where it remains today. A winding, tree-lined walk up to it from a grand new iron gate on the Queen's Road to the west created the dramatic scenography visitors now enjoy, with the diagonal surprise view across to the chapel suddenly opening up. Today, the path is celebrated, too, for its spring bulb display – aconites, crocuses, chionodoxa and narcissi – shaded by a great beech tree beside the bridge. This path was extended so that it hugged the southern edge of the Back Lawn, under the trees planted earlier according to Essex's plans. Wilkins further enhanced the scene by replacing the riverbank's reinforced edge, a remnant of the waterway's previous workaday character, with a gentle grassed lip.

In the 1830s the enclosure of ancient fields surrounding Cambridge meant that the college was able to acquire land west of the Queen's Road. In 1836 a resolution was passed for a new fellows' garden to be made there which would be 'planted and a walk made through the plantation; the interior to be secured by an iron fence and enjoyed by the Provost rent free: the Walk to be accessible to the Provost and his family, and also to Fellows by keys not transferable'. Initially 1.25 hectares/3 acres were reserved as a paddock for the provost's coach horses, with a separate shrubbery walk for fellows winding through an adjacent plantation – this was around the time that the new provost's lodge was constructed on the south side of college, sweeping away the old provost's stables. But in 1851 the provost agreed that the entire area should be treated as a fellows' garden. It was duly laid out by the bursar, Mr Bumpsted, in a gardenesque manner of lozenge beds on smooth lawns which has survived until today.

As one emerges into the sunlit interior of the space, passing a group of Lucombe oaks and a very old *Catalpa bignonioides*, a true 'secret-garden' moment can be enjoyed. A fine oriental plane at the far end of the garden provides a focus. The magnificent wellingtonias (*Sequoiadendron giganteum*) here are believed to date from this early period, making them among the first tranche of introductions of this tree. The garden has a perimeter walk through evergreens and two large island plantings of specimen trees, including what is generally reckoned to be the best example of *Koelreuteria paniculata* (golden rain tree) in Cambridge. Other notable trees include *Quercus × hispanica*, *Thuja orientalis* f. *flagelliformis*, Judas tree, *Corylus colurna* (Turkish hazel) and a *Gleditsia sinensis* with a very beautiful trunk. The college's growing seriousness about horticulture at this time is reflected in the governing body's decision in 1861 to separate the offices of porter and gardener. However, a letter dated 1882 in the college archive recalls the fellows' garden thus: 'We revelled in a feeling of complete isolation. The gardener was no better than a farm labourer and took no trouble.' The northern part of the garden was early on taken up by a lawn used for croquet, bowls and 'occasionally lawn tennis'. The original college set of bowls dated from the time of the creation of the garden in 1851, when they were marked up with fellows' initials (not uncommon in Cambridge; Pembroke has some bowls dating from the 1760s). A few decades later, a handlist of 1904 made by Arthur Hill (then a fellow, later director of Kew) reveals that there were several unusual plants here at that date, including *Halimodendron argenteum* (Siberian salt tree), *Eccremocarpus scaber* (Chilean glory flower), two species of calycanthus and *Xanthoceras sorbifolium* (yellowhorn, from China), as well as numerous spiraeas and a large collection of veronica species.

The Victorian idea of a garden of specimen trees, shrubs and some herbaceous material has clearly been kept up at King's almost without interruption since the 1850s. A photograph of the fellows' garden taken in the 1920s or 30s shows an immaculately tended space with a wide, smooth lawn and trees fringed by herbaceous planting. A college fellow has annotated the print, suggesting that a figure seated in a deckchair on the lawn is J. M. Keynes himself. A recent innovation in the fellows' garden is a large, cross-shaped pergola at the northern end, donated in 2012 by Hugh Johnson, garden and wine writer and honorary fellow. The feature looks a little isolated set in the middle of the lawns but is well planted with lavender, *Verbena bonariensis*, rudbeckia, sedum, verbascum, asters, echinaceas and masses of climbing roses, including 'Madame Alfred Carrière', 'Crown Princess Margareta' and many others.

In recent years head gardener Steven Coghill has added more botanical interest to the fellows' garden, including *Edgeworthia* and *Pinus pinaster*, while a new greenhouse range being constructed nearby will function as a display area for tender plants. To the west of the fellows' garden is the brick Garden Hostel (1950) and a partially wood-clad extension known as New Garden Hostel (2001). Here in 2015 a permaculture orchard was established with apples, pears, plums, nectarines, peaches, figs, nuts, greengages and a mulberry at the centre with turf seat. A brightly exotic planting scheme associated with the newer hostel includes *Musa basjoo*, dahlias, *Solanum crispum*, euphorbia, orange coleus, echiums, eremurus, salvia, bamboos and abutilon. To the south is a large student allotment which the garden team have embellished with square raised beds, cordon apples, beehives and an extremely smart greenhouse. Mr Coghill is the intellectual among the head gardeners of Oxford and Cambridge, with wide knowledge and interests beyond horticulture and a strong pedagogical streak (in the fellows' garden he teaches Royal Horticultural Society students techniques such as pruning and plant identification).

But to go back to the beginning for a moment, the visitor to King's is faced with Wilkins's imposing gatehouse and screen, which most will imagine is far older than the early 19th century. Between this and King's Parade are a wide, paved entranceway and two triangles of lawn; the larger of these, to the north, boasts a magnificent horse chestnut. Front Court is simply laid to lawn (strictly out of bounds to all except senior fellows) with a central fountain incorporating bronze figures by H. H. Armstead, added in 1879. The fountain is of little aesthetic merit but is listed in its own right and cannot

RIGHT Echiums make a dramatic show along the substantial (but sometimes overlooked) border which runs along the southern boundary of Clare College.

easily be removed. Here as at other colleges, the gardeners use special 'silenced' lawnmowers so as not to disturb students in the run-up to exams; when the new organ was being installed and tuned in the chapel, King's gardeners were forbidden to mow the lawns at all. The screen wall is planted up on both sides with old-fashioned roses but otherwise Front Court is left to speak for itself.

There are three courts with garden elements along the southern edge of the college, where most of its common buildings now lie. The first is Chetwynd Court, adjacent to the dining hall and bar. This space functions as an outdoor dining area in summer, with a pond and jolly exotic plantings including daturas and the strappy leaved banana *Musa basjoo*. A little farther along, about level with the Gibbs Building, is Webb's Court, with a large oval of grass at its centre and the portico to the provost's lodge on its west side. Next is Bodley's Court, named after the Gothic Revival architect who designed it in 1899. The centrepiece is an old quince tree which has been struck by lightning several times. There are box topiaries by the building, and lines of pots with figs brightly underplanted with begonias. Growing against the south wall, adjacent to Queens', is a *Campsis grandiflora*, while another border features stipa grasses and a catalpa at one end. This court is easily overlooked but offers some dramatic vistas.

Views across King's Backs from its bridge have long been dignified by the sight of grazing livestock. The tradition is kept up at the college in a small way in that cattle are still grazed on Scholar's Piece by a tenant farmer (at a rent of £1 per year). Currently the 'herd' consists of two Suffolk cattle, a picturesque adornment to the scene.

The Gibbs Building is left pristine and unadorned, though there have been occasional discussions at the college as to the desirability of having plants against it. In the post-war period the garden committee at King's was extremely active, even dictating to the head gardener lists of individual plants to be used in beds (a habit among fellows at other colleges, too) and today is one of the largest, at 15-strong. In 1950 there was a suggestion that the bays on the west side of the Gibbs Building be planted up with roses and wisteria, to replace a rather random assortment which had grown up there. The question split the committee, as a memo attests: 'Will members of the Committee please inform me whether they would agree to reference to the Council. I cannot see that further discussion on the Committee, which is clearly divided, can be very helpful, and it is not really a question of any technical knowledge of flowers.' In the event it was

ABOVE LEFT A London plane complements the west end of the chapel.
ABOVE CENTRE The autumn foliage of an oriental plane tree in the fellows' garden.

decided to remove all the existing plants and leave the walls bare.

At the entrance to the chapel, near the college's side entrance into Trinity Lane, there is a bed of 'Hidcote' lavender and a tulip display in spring. A long 'hot' border runs down the length of the Clare building, with rush-like restios, salvia, melianthus, echiums and a grass area at the far end with logs for insects.

There is one more historic garden area at King's and it is perhaps the most beguiling in college. This is the provost's garden, expressly kept private as most principals' gardens are, though it can be partially seen through an iron gate down a passageway south of the back lawn. This garden has recently been revamped to jaunty effect, with rose standards ('Wedding Day') on handmade ironwork supports leading up to the low terraces in front of the Georgian-style lodge. A medlar and a quince flank a subtropical border against the house, with purple ricinus, dahlias and at one end a low planting of purple *Verbena rigida*, *Musa basjoo*, calochortus, kalanchoe and orange-red *Kniphofia* 'Timothy' (an excellent choice). The supports marking the edge of the lower terrace are very nearly monumental, with the pillar rose 'Strawberry Hill' growing up them (a reference to Horace Walpole, who was a Kingsman). At the end of this putative avenue, swags of 'Winchester Cathedral' roses have been set up on synthetic ropes on 5-metre-/16-foot-high green-oak posts, slung laterally across the

garden. Beyond here, at the western end of the garden, is a curious but charming little enclosed area bounded by a woven willow fence with a seat. A small potager of box-edged compartments is tucked in, redesigned by Yasmina Keynes and named the Keynes Garden. There is a line of limes against the wall with Queens' and a large *Magnolia grandiflora* on the northern side.

Just across the bridge to the Backs the visitor can discover a new Chinese garden designed by Mr Coghill and installed in 2018. The impetus was the popularity of a memorial stone placed on this spot ten years earlier in honour of Xú Zhìmó, the Chinese poet whose most celebrated poem is a wistful and mysterious paean to Cambridge. Conventionally translated as 'Second Farewell to Cambridge', it is compulsory reading in Chinese schools and is one reason why so many Chinese tourists are attracted to the city and to the prospect of being punted along the Backs. (The poem may also owe something to William Mason's 'On Expecting to Return to Cambridge, 1747' – see page 202.) Xú Zhìmó spent a year studying at King's in 1921–22, where he developed a lifelong love for English poetry and for Cambridge itself. He wrote the poem after revisiting the city in 1928,

ABOVE RIGHT Foxgloves and roses abound at the Garden Hostel, on the western edge of the fellows' garden.

and the memorial stone quotes its first and last lines. Here is my own free translation:

On Leaving Cambridge for the Second Time

slipping quietly away
from that riverbank again
the pink and vivid sky
is murmuring its goodbye

but see that willow there
she is a bride arrayed in gold
the silvered threads of the water
are winding me back towards her

the rushes beckon from the bank
my willow dips her tresses
the weed is swirling down below
I long for the water's caresses

to lie down there on the smooth still green
where duckweed makes a bed
and pools of secret shadows make
dark circles 'neath the yews

why don't you punt a boat as far
as the fields where the green wheat grows
flat on your back and forgetful
gazing up at the murmuring stars

don't ask me to come along with you
I am leaving and cannot go
the insects have all gone quiet now
in the silence of the grove

and up above the trembling limes
the night clouds make no sound
I am leaving, now, for the second time
and I am rooted to the ground

LEFT Narcissi and tulips by the winding path and lime avenue which leads up to King's Bridge and back to college.

LUCY CAVENDISH COLLEGE

FOUR HOUSES, FOUR GARDENS. ACQUIRED, altered, amalgamated, augmented – and now a college. It took 46 years for the germ of an idea to become fully recognised by the university, but Lucy Cavendish College is now an institution with its own buildings set within 1.6 hectares/4 acres of special character. What is more, 'Lucy' began and for a long time has remained a resolutely all-female institution. (It was announced in 2019 that men would be admitted from 2021.)

The embryonic Lucy Cavendish College coalesced in 1951 as the Dining Group, with three female academics, all graduates of Newnham, at its core. The group gained in strength and clarity of purpose until in 1964 the Lucy Cavendish Collegiate Society was formally recognised by the university, at a time when women could not become fellows of male colleges or affiliate to them. The society sought to provide a way forward. It initially operated from a two-room office at 20 Silver Street, moving the following year into a pair of 18th-century cottages in Northampton Street (and thereby gaining the nickname 'the college in a cottage').

The new society was named in honour of a supporter of women's education who was at one point invited to be Mistress of Girton. Lucy Cavendish was also a great-aunt of the philosopher Margaret Braithwaite, one of the Dining Group's founders. As *The Times* reported in 1965: 'without tower or turrets, without chaplain or porters, without a building of its own or even a foundation grant, Britain's first graduate college for women has come quietly into being.' (Undergraduates aged 21 years and over have been accepted since 1972.)

In 1969 St John's College offered the society a house it owned off Madingley Road in north-west Cambridge. Built in 1883 as a home for the university professor of anatomy, in 1920 it was leased to the Oratory of the Good Shepherd (a chapel built

LEFT The college took up residence on its present site in 1970 and has gradually expanded to incorporate the garden plots of a number of existing houses. The tone is informal and shrub-dominated.

LUCY CAVENDISH COLLEGE

inside is now the tutorial office). The warden of the Oratory, Wilfred Knox, was a keen gardener and was sometimes joined by other residents (numbering about 10), including the social critic Malcolm Muggeridge. Subsequently the house was assigned to the Society of St Francis, but was vacated in 1967 and was near-derelict when the college arrived in February 1970.

Lucy Cavendish immediately dubbed its new home College House: a sturdily unremarkable Victorian villa with an attractive porch. The garden, of about 0.4 hectare/1 acre, was overgrown with ground elder and even patches of giant hogweed, though the remnants could be seen of an old rock garden, a rose garden and a vegetable patch. There was a pair of planes on the lawn near the house (one was subsequently taken down), and specimen trees such as catalpa, blue cedar and ginkgo. Mature limes, beeches and chestnuts formed a belt against Madingley Road. There were various climber-covered sheds and outbuildings, as well as all sorts of detritus strewn around, such as old sinks, birdbaths and abandoned bicycles.

The nascent college lost no time in appointing a garden steward and subcommittee to oversee the clearance needed. There was no money for a full-time gardener and so in the early years college fellows volunteered their services to supplement the work of a casual gardener employed for a day and a half each week. This regime continued even after Lucy Cavendish took possession in 1973 of a neighbouring house and its substantial but overgrown garden. The property had once (1908–40) been owned by J. D. Duff of Trinity College, another keen gardener,

who had also leased that part of Trinity's fellows' garden still known today as Duff's Garden.

Lucy Cavendish's second president, Kate Bertram, imported a small herd of guinea pigs in the spring of 1970 as a novel way of keeping the grass under control. They grazed and multiplied but unfortunately all escaped in July. Some were evidently still at large, however, for the garden steward's report for October 1970 states: 'Ginkgo and balsam poplar turning colour – decide to burn leaves where possible. Last apple picked up Oct. 14. No frost yet. Ginger guinea pig seen on 17th.' There was a further guinea-pig purchase in April 1972, but their escape marked the end of the experiment.

Roses, asters, dahlias and petunias were planted on the heavy clay soil, and there was an attempt to revivify the vegetable garden (with a strong emphasis on rhubarb). But it was difficult to achieve much, horticulturally, given the resources available. Contemporary photographs show the garden to be 'relaxed' in style.

A third Victorian villa became available in 1975 and the following year 'Lucy' acquired the freehold of what amounted to, with the boundary fences taken down, one continuous plot of 1.4 hectares/3½ acres. It now owned outright the three houses with their gardens, but was lacking basic collegiate facilities. Formal hall could not be held in the dining room, so once a week 'Lucy' accepted the hospitality of neighbouring Churchill College.

The 1980s and 90s saw numerous new buildings going up, and Lucy Cavendish became a full college in 1997. It was a confusing time for the garden team (permanent staff were taken on around this time), with trees being moved around to make way for these amenities and a general atmosphere of flux. It took a while for the gardens truly to be taken in hand. A report by the bursar of Corpus Christi in 1984 described the grounds as 'mature, heavily wooded, with thick and unkempt undergrowth both front and back... Round the main buildings are a few formal flowerbeds. The lawns are pitted and rutted, and in some areas poorly drained.'

During this period the shrub mix was extended and the prevailing naturalistic atmosphere of the garden was maintained, a look which became gradually more fashionable over the years. Today, meadow-like areas have replaced the formal lawns and an emphasis is placed on wildlife gardening. In 1981 John St Bodfan Gruffydd, the landscape architect responsible for Robinson College, visited and gave (unrecorded) advice. Corpus Christi's head gardener was a formal advisor from 1983, and in the early 1990s the landscape architect David Brown was consulted in the light of new buildings such as Oldham Hall (1989). The 'rather random' appeal of the gardens was preserved, and the impression persists of buildings set within the remnants of established gardens.

One more Victorian villa was acquired in 1991, though Marshall House has a rather different air to the college's other properties, and is certainly the most distinguished architecturally. Designed in 1886 by John J. Stevenson, it exhibits that architect's exuberant style, with a wooden balcony and unorthodox fenestration (similar to his work at what is now Darwin College). Since its refurbishment in 2001, the house has served as the president's lodge. The college's new library of 1999 was another catalyst for garden improvements, with a *Parrotia persica* and an *Acer capillipes* planted nearby.

Today the gardens have a decidedly woodland feel. Apart from a few cottagey borders (peonies, foxgloves, lupins) against the buildings, the accent is on wild flowers and cranesbill geraniums beneath the trees. A small pond, attractively ringed with primroses and irises, is focused on a lead statue of Ceres. Five thousand bulbs were planted in 2016, much enlivening the spring scene. The college's new accommodation site (2014) a few minutes away on Histon Road also has a garden element; the noted garden designer Arabella Lennox-Boyd advised on the planting, which features *Dianthus carthusianorum* and tall *Allium sphaerocephalon* together with lavender, nepeta, thalictrum and achillea.

The most talked-about aspect of Lucy Cavendish's setting is the Anglo-Saxon Herb Garden. Made in 1987 at the instigation of fellow Jane Renfrew and a Newnham colleague, Debby Banham, it reflects their respective areas of specialism in palaeoethnobotany and early medieval medicine and diet. Archaeological evidence and Anglo-Saxon literature provided inspiration for the planting, and a small cruciform garden was laid out with edges of feverfew and violets, daisies and strawberries. One of the texts used was a collection of medicinal and magical recipes known as the *Lacnunga*, which includes an extract from the Nine Herbs Charm. Perhaps a garden of charms and remedies is a fitting horticultural diversion at this college of wise women.

ABOVE Wildflower meadow plantings are now encouraged across the college site, where sculptures and other features are incorporated into the scene.

MAGDALENE
COLLEGE

OVER THE BRIDGE AND OUT on a limb, Magdalene – pronounced 'mawdlin' – is the last of the colleges along the Backs, after St John's. It is not really on the Backs at all, but slightly askew in its position beyond Magdalene Bridge as the Cam bends from north to north-east, beginning its slow exit from the city. The river frontage here is the longest of any Cambridge college, but this has not been exploited as an aesthetic asset at Magdalene, historically, since the character of the Cam changes as soon as it leaves St John's land. The river by Magdalene Bridge was always a busy industrial hub and a major point of loading and unloading, teeming with river workers who slaked their considerable thirsts in local pubs such as The Pickerel on Magdalene Street; the Victorian coal-bargemen liked to refer to Magdalene as 'our college'. Almost the only commercial traffic today is punts for hire by the hour, but the area on the southern side of the river, opposite the college and in its ownership, is still known as the Quayside.

On the Magdalene side, for centuries most of that river frontage was screened out by walls, houses and even a public lane, with the fellows' garden somewhat set back. The river was not just visually unsightly to collegiate eyes, there was also the smell to contend with: until a modern sewerage system was introduced to Cambridge in 1895, the river was the recipient of effluent and rubbish of all kinds, and the stench on and around it could be remarkable, especially downstream – and Magdalene was about as downstream as you could be, with both its courts almost immediately adjacent to the water. The college in fact made its own contribution in this regard, since for many years the college 'heads' or toilets gave straight on to the river, causing James II to tease, during a dispute with the college master in 1687, that 'he would go stool there'. In fairness, most of the waterside colleges had to put up with noxious odours from the river, but such was Magdalene's reputation.

LEFT Looking back across First Court, with *Isotoma axillaris* 'Blue Star' and *Salvia* 'Mystic Spires Blue' in the bed to the left.

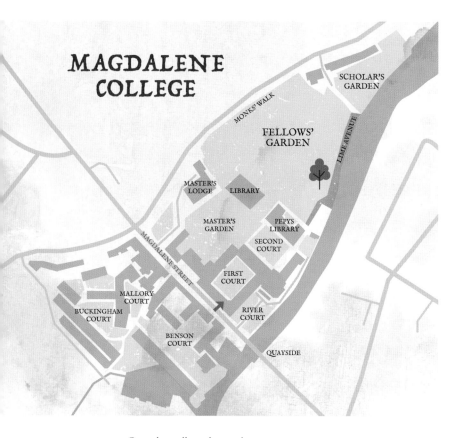

MAGDALENE COLLEGE

SCHOLAR'S GARDEN

MONKS' WALK

FELLOWS' GARDEN

LIME AVENUE

MASTER'S LODGE   LIBRARY

MASTER'S GARDEN

PEPYS LIBRARY

SECOND COURT

MAGDALENE STREET

FIRST COURT

MALLORY COURT

BUCKINGHAM COURT

RIVER COURT

BENSON COURT

QUAYSIDE

RIGHT Over the wall on the south side of Second Court is a planting of smokebush (*Cotinus coggygria* 'Royal Purple') and purple-leaved corkscrew hazel

OVERLEAF Wisteria on the walls of River Court, with dahlias and blue salvias in the foreground.

Yet as the river's old industrial identity was lost during the past century, Magdalene has gradually turned itself around and opened itself up to the river. The waterside avenue of old lime trees in the fellows' garden is today one of the quiet gems among college gardens, offering exhilarating long views down the widening Cam, where its character is quite different to that along the Backs. Still, one feels that the picturesque potential of the spot has slightly taken the college by surprise and that even more could be done.

Magdalene College was founded in 1542, but it began as a hostel for Benedictine monks in 1428. As at Worcester College, Oxford, the four local abbeys who sent their young monks to the college also built their own staircases in which to house them. Three are in the south range – south-east in actuality: compass points have been simplified here – and they each have differing doorways and staircase designs, though they can no longer be individually associated with specific abbeys. Some of the rooms, notably in Staircase E, have been reconstituted in 15th-century form and are among the oldest such examples in Cambridge or Oxford. From the 1470s the hostel was sponsored by the 2nd Duke of Buckingham and duly became known as Buckingham College, when lay students were also admitted. It was during this period that the chapel in First Court was constructed, and in 1519 the 3rd Duke commissioned the hall. But Buckingham College's fortunes were waning by the 1530s and hit a low point during the dissolution of the monasteries. It was then reprieved expediently by Thomas Audley, the lord chancellor, who it is believed was educated at the old Buckingham College. He refounded the institution as a college dedicated to St Mary Magdalene, that curious biblical character who barely appears in the scriptures but who has played so decisively into the Christian imagination. It was she who first saw the resurrected Jesus Christ and initially mistook him for a gardener.

Second Court took shape from the 1580s with the construction of the library building, enlarged and embellished in the mid 17th century and renamed the Pepys Library after Samuel Pepys's donation of books to his old college. This is not a conventional court, in that the north and south sides are simply high walls rather than building ranges, but this only increases the impact of the library facade, which was decorated to good effect at moments in the late 17th and early 18th centuries. It is a curious building but a handsome one, effectively free-standing in this open court. Five arches at ground level create an elegant loggia effect as the base of a centrepiece, while the windows above each of them, though extremely large and heavily decorated with Ketton-stone pediments above and cartouches below, succeed in combining lightness and sophistication. It is the breadth of the building that allows for such levity, along with the sturdiness of the relatively plain three-storey wings, which act as sensible bookends to the central confection. Hanging baskets with changing displays of single plants, such as orange begonias, are suspended in the arches, and are one of the few instances in Cambridge where these suburban staples are a good idea in a college context. The real horticultural opportunity here lies in the two borders

against those high walls, which have a pleasingly rough texture, being made of ashlar and rubble with brick runs above. To the left of the library is the south-facing, 'hot'-themed principal border, with rudbeckia, heleniums, cosmos, sedums, achilleas, tithonias, crocosmia, geums and macleaya at the back, all making a valiant effort to compete with the presence of the characterful wall behind. The border to the right is themed cool or blue, with delphiniums, hostas, cardoons, alliums, asters, verbena and foxgloves. All that is lacking is a sense of scale and structure at the library end of these borders, where a small tree (perhaps a malus or cornus?) would be welcome.

Behind the library, and extending northwards, is the 0.8-hectare/2-acre fellows' garden, which is Magdalene's great secret treasure. The earliest reference to this land is in the 1420s, at the time the monastic hostel was founded; it is referred to as the 'pondyerds', for which an annual rent was paid to the college between 1432 and 1521. The 'Old Book' of Magdalene refers to the charter given by Henry VIII to Thomas Audley, when this part of the estate is described as 'those two gardens or parcels of grounds together with the ponds therein, called two pondyards, lately belonging to Buckingham College'. These multiple small ponds – there were seven in 1554 – would have been for freshwater fish for the table (important in monastic institutions), and the name recurs until the late 16th century, when the ponds were finally filled in or had silted up. Being on the floodplain, it appears this was the obvious and possibly only use for the land, which would have been boggy much of the time, though at one point early in the college's history a hard path was made across the space. The problem of flooding was also the most likely reason for the raised bank which still marks the northern boundary of the fellows' garden, along what is now Chesterton Lane. It was probably dug during the Roman occupation (in around the 4th century AD), though there are other theories – that it was either part of an Anglo-Saxon defensive embankment, or a remnant of the rubbish dump associated with the castle, situated just uphill to the north. (In the college archive there is a tin biscuit-box containing 54 items retrieved from the fellows' garden by a fellow in 2002, including buttons, six musket balls and several Roman coins from the 3rd century.) At this early date there was also a navigable channel made from the area of the St John's punt dock to the west, cutting across what is now Bridge Street and the college courts, to rejoin the river at the far end of the fellows' garden (it had silted up by 1300 but still exists, flowing underground, at one point following the line of the lime avenue).

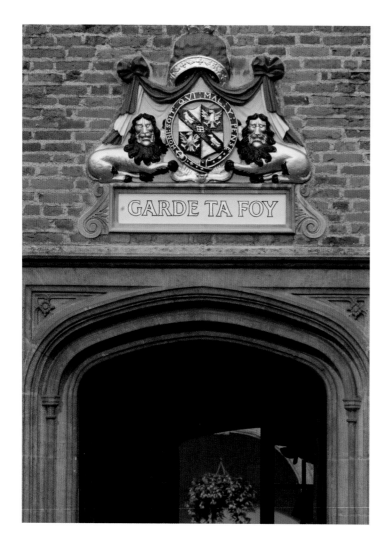

The college statutes of 1554 mention three gardens: a 'garden into which the master's chamber looks', a small garden near the college gate and the 'largest garden, otherwise called the Orchard, situated behind the College'. So it appears that fruit trees were being grown here at this early date. At other times the Magdalene fellows' garden was referred to as the close, the grove, the field or the backsides (a term common to all the riverside colleges, later shortened to 'the Backs'). It was also referred to as 'the great garden' in the 1550s, which suggests that it was beginning to be thought of as a potential space for leisure purposes as opposed to a mere pond yard. As late as 1578 a local fishmonger was renting the ponds from the college (he paid in a mixture of cash and fish – pickerels – for the hall) but the ponds disappeared and the college was generally smartening itself up by the late 1580s, with a new street frontage and library. It is therefore possible that at this time an avenue of trees (probably limes), doubled on the north and south sides, was first planted around the perimeter of the garden. Trees in this arrangement can be seen on Loggan's engraving published in 1690, though they appear quite young – not more than 25 years old – so the tree-lined walks may date from only around 1660. In the Loggan engraving, the bank to the north is clearly integrated into the design as a raised walkway (given the fanciful name Monks' Walk in the 19th century). The centre of the space is left entirely open, an indication that

it was used as pasture and as a valuable source of hay. The cows of one late-16th-century master were said to have come into the hall at meal times, and the masters of the college continued to exert their grazing rights into the 1910s.

The master's garden occupies the space north of both courts and in the Loggan engraving is quite densely treed with different specimens, including a pine at the western end. To the north-west of the master's garden is an enclosed bowling green, while – unusually for him – Loggan depicts the industrial life of the city in the form of numerous boats plying the river or moored downstream. First Court is shown with two rectangular grass plats of different sizes, surrounded by a post fence. It is interesting to find that Edmund Carter, author of a history of the university in 1753, emphasises the rural qualities of the college garden in his brief description of it: 'The Lodge, Gardens, and Terras-Walks, which commands a View of the River Cam, and adjacent Country, are very agreeable and wholly Rural.' William Custance's city map of 1798 shows how this was achieved: the riverside avenue of trees effectively

---

ABOVE LEFT The college motto is derived from the Old French meaning 'Keep Your Faith'.

ABOVE RIGHT Hanging baskets in the library's arches are planted up with *Begonia* 'Dragon Wing Pink'.

screened off the river and its traffic until the far eastern end of the garden, at which point a surprise view downriver opened up. By this means, the college had successfully created an impression of bucolic ease – an impression which persists today.

The basic form of the fellows' garden has remained unchanged since the 17th century, the main addition being various specimen trees. Several of the larger trees which survive here today were planted in the late 19th century, including a magnificent plane tree; there are also walnut trees and a ginkgo. An 1830 engraving by Richard Harraden was made from the perspective of Monks' Walk, where the original limes had by then grown venerable. The centre of the fellows' garden was still open at this date, while a line of young elms and a hedge divided it from the master's garden. By this time the fellows' garden was sometimes being described as Magdalene Walks, given its character as tree-lined avenues around a central grassy space; at least that is how it is referred to in the sale particulars of a house on Chesterton Road in 1832.

The rear elevation of the Pepys Library is remarkably different from its front: a far simpler, red-brick affair. In the space created by its protruding wings is an attractive garden of foliage effects, with hellebores, epimediums, philadelphus, hydrangeas and variegated hollies at the back. An orchard near the boundary with the master's

garden on this western side of the fellows' garden has recently been removed, along with several oval flower beds made in around 1906, to make way for the new £15-million library, which straddles the fellows' and master's gardens. The work of 2017–19 caused temporary chaos but the character of the fellows' garden will no doubt reassert itself in due course. At least one of the fruit trees removed was a mirabelle plum, source of fruit (not commercially available) for a traditional pudding in college hall. One hopes new specimens might be planted elsewhere in recompense, since such traditions surely ought to be kept up.

In the north-west corner of the fellows' garden, under the yews, is a pet cemetery instituted by a 19th-century master's wife, and above here are steps up to Monks' Walk. Bounded by a high wall (1667) against Chesterton Lane on the northern side and a dense fringe of yews below a row of limes on the opposite side, this *allée* is a shady and atmospheric excursion. At the western end is a green man fountain designed by college member Bevis Sale and installed in 1996. There are laburnums along the way and in spring hosts of primroses on the bank below, along with scillas, *Iris reticulata*, narcissi and tulips. At the far end of

ABOVE The west front of the Pepys Library, constructed in the mid-17th century and later embellished.

Monks' Walk is a rather curious terrace made in 1990 on the site of the old college bonfire (banned nowadays) where a huge elm stood until the 1980s; a fine young cut-leaf beech replaces it. The statue of Mary Magdalene which terminates the eastern end of the walk dates from 1876 and formerly stood on top of the college chapel. Apparently it fell off in the 1950s and struck an undergraduate – but survived. (The statue, that is. The status of the student is not recorded.) The whole southern side of the fellows' garden is covered in narcissi each spring, while the eastern end is left to grow slightly wild. This area is now delineated as 'the wilderness', which is a modern term in this context, unlike the 18th-century Wilderness at neighbouring St John's.

The best aspect of the fellows' garden today is not the dark and atmospheric Monks' Walk, which according to one Magdalene don 'only the fellows know about', but the bright avenue along the riverside, consisting of fine old lime trees pleasingly interrupted by alders, Japanese cherries and willows. At the end of this straight yet informal walk is a bend in the river and a sudden vista downriver which is quite thrilling. At the moment the avenue rather peters out at each end, with an uninspiring, black-varnished wooden utility building to the west and no focus or end point to the east, which is nevertheless a pleasantly shady retreat with ferns, epimediums, primulas, foxgloves and peonies. It is unfortunate that the college has chosen to install ultra-modern metallic lighting posts along this walk, which compromise its atmosphere, while intrusive, over-large signage is also an issue across Magdalene's domain. Although it is certainly charming now, there is much potential on this southern side of the fellows' garden, and the head gardener has great ambitions for it.

Beyond the lime avenue to the east one reaches an area that has been recently – and perhaps slightly pretentiously – named the Scholars' Garden. It consists of the back gardens of several cottages along Chesterton Lane which are owned by the college and have now been amalgamated. One cottage garden has raised beds for vegetables and a pergola with a rambling rose, while elsewhere a black-and-white border is planned. The head gardener describes the Scholars' Garden as 'a work in progress'. The front gardens of these houses are filled with floribunda roses in various colours, another instance of the level of horticultural detail at this college, where the garden team is of modest size for the scale of its operations. Over the road is Cripps Court, a college extension with well-maintained gardens.

The fellows' garden connects with the rest of college via a gate in its south-west corner, by the library, where the charming brick gardeners'

ABOVE The lime avenue in the fellows' garden, with narcissi beneath.

bothy stands, jauntily bedecked with hanging baskets and tubs, with glasshouses behind. The entrance to the fellows' garden was adorned in 2006 with Latin inscriptions relating to Mary Magdalene on both sides of the gateway. Going in, the inscription reads *VIDI DOMINUM* or 'I have seen the Lord' – which is, according to St John's Gospel, what Mary Magdalene said to the apostles. Leaving the garden, the inscription reads *IN SAPIENTIA AMBULATE*, meaning 'Walk in wisdom'. There is no more apposite or elegant inscribed addition to a college garden in Oxford or Cambridge.

River Court is the name given to the sliver of land between the river and the southern range of First Court. Formerly this was a warren of little courts and cottages around a dirty lane which was only cleared away by the college in the 1870s. Recently it has become celebrated in Cambridge because of its plantings, in this highly visible spot next to Magdalene Bridge. The grassy bank sloping down to the river here is known as 'the beach' by students, because of its summer sunbathing potential, but in spring is covered by around 4,000 crocuses. Against the back wall of First Court are a huge wisteria and 'hot' plantings of dahlias, heleniums and tithonias, which come into their own in late summer. In front of it is a panel of lawn with a border of alternating salvias and rudbeckias. Fine wrought-iron gates, with a run of railings and gate piers surmounted by urns, face on to Magdalene Street.

Back in the college proper, First Court may be relatively small but it is one of the most attractive in Cambridge, with its warm red-brick tones and palpable atmosphere of antiquity. In the east range facing the entrance lodge, the great window in hall presides over the space, while gilded crests above the doorways add to the impression of ancient dignity. The path layout is almost exactly as it was when the Loggan engraving was made in the 1680s. The tradition here is for wallflowers in the wide southern bed, followed by geraniums and fuchsias, though today the fuchsias are joined by dark salvias, while the other beds in the court might feature nicotianas, phormiums and cosmos, with euphorbia and box on the shadier eastern side. First Court was stuccoed over in the 18th century in an attempt at modernisation – and restored back to brick in the 1950s. These toings and froings are emblematic of the fact that this college has long struggled to assert its intellectual identity. Magdalene still indulges in bouts of self-laceration over a mistake it made in the 1570s when it let go of 2.8 hectares/7 acres of valuable land in the City of London, bequeathed by founder Thomas Audley. With this pot of gold lost, the college settled back into an acceptance that it was the poorest college at either university, 'enjoying' a reputation

ABOVE The characterful old clunch walls of Second Court threaten to upstage even the golden flowers of *Rudbeckia fulgida* 'Goldsturm'.

as a place where anyone of the right background could get in as long as they paid the fees. It is true that its assets were stretched: in 1880, when the university began to levy a contribution from the colleges proportionate to their wealth, it was decided that Trinity College would pay more than 32 times as much as Magdalene, which was at the bottom of the rich list.

The college had nurtured a reputation for toughness and sportsmanship since the early 19th century. The concept of 'sport' apparently encompassed fighting in the street, where Magdalene students frequently clashed with the rivermen who also felt they should rule this area by Cambridge's docks. The boorish Marquess of Queensberry, of boxing rules fame, who led the charge against Oscar Wilde, was a Magdalene man. The situation was not helped by Audley's requirement that the master should be a member of his family in perpetuity, which led to a succession of masters with little ambition. (The college finally – and controversially – rescinded this rule in 2012.) For a period in the late 19th century the college was dominated by Etonians and Harrovians who had found the intellectual environment at Trinity rather too taxing, with too little opportunity for extra-curricular activities. 'Switching to Magdalene' became an established habit, with the college referred to as a 'transpontine refuge for fallen undergraduates'. Many Magdalene men were obsessed by

hunting and horse racing, to the exclusion of other sports (this was not a rowing college, despite proximity to the river). Some kept their horses tethered at the gate on hunting days and even the dean was censured for keeping foxhounds in the college courts. One buck, Harry de Windt, recalled in his memoir:

> When I went up to Cambridge [in 1875] Magdalene was essentially a riding college, and certainly not a reading one. I suppose there were reading men…but I never saw them… Magdalene was a little oasis of idleness and insubordination to the University rules and regulations. It was indeed more like a club than a college…There was a dinner-party somewhere nearly every night…Then there were the Newmarket meetings only a few miles away, very fair hunting with the Cambridgeshire, and three days a week with the Drag…

These undergraduates were in many cases rich, and were only too happy to pay any fines relating to non-appearances at tutorials or chapel, while the impecunious college in its turn found this a vital source of income.

When A. C. Benson arrived at Magdalene in 1904 he found there was no organ in chapel, only four fellows on the staff, elderly gentlemen from the town lodging in some rooms and no one at all in the college

LEFT The eastern end of Monks' Walk is terminated by a statue of Mary Magdalene, which formerly stood on the chapel.

BELOW A statue of the Chinese examination god in the Ivor Richards Memorial Garden.

library. First Court itself was partly boarded up, covered in ivy, with the stucco falling off. As master from 1915 to 1925, Benson resolved to revolutionise the college and in this he had some success. Walter Gardiner, fellow in botany at Clare College, had been invited to assess the condition of the college gardens in 1905. His recommendations amounted to a scorched-earth policy with regard to the fellows' garden, which he could not bring himself to name as such, describing it as little more than a boggy 'paddock' filled with old and diseased trees. But he also lit upon the riverside walk as a prime asset and suggested it be replanted and redefined. In his diary in May 1917 Benson noted (with a characteristic overlay of self-aggrandisement): 'I never really saw a more entirely lovely place than the Garden is. It is all that the greatest monarch could desire.'

Benson Court, hidden behind the shop frontages on the other side of Magdalene Street (the oldest run of houses in Cambridge), directly opposite the college, is the chief physical memorial of this reforming college master. There are actually three large courts in this complex of accommodation blocks over the road, which occupies as much space as the college proper. Students call it 'the village' on account of the homely feel imparted by the cottages (and former vinegar brewery) of Mallory Court, which was redeveloped in 1925. Wisteria grows on the walls and the head gardener says he is aiming for a 'Himalayan feel', as the court is

named after George Mallory, the celebrated mountaineer and college member who died on an attempt at Everest in 1924. To the south, Benson Court itself is dominated by a massive, barrack-like brick accommodation block (1932) by Edwin Lutyens, probably the worst building he ever designed. The interior is better than the exterior and there are fine river views from the west windows, but arguably it is a mercy that the college did not find the funds to realise the other two ranges in this putative semi-enclosed court (the south end was to be open to the river). There is a *Malus × floribunda* here, some weeping willows, a mulberry, a cherry, a cornus and a sycamore with attractive bark. The southern end of Benson Court is a much-appreciated riverside lawn with a punt dock and tranquil views upstream through St John's. To the north is Buckingham Court (1970) consisting of low-slung brick blocks. An ash and a catalpa provide arboreal relief in this uninspiring zone.

As ever in the colleges, the master's garden is rather off-limits to outsiders, and at the time of writing it is difficult to know in what form it will emerge after the completion of the new college library, which is being built over part of it. The lodge was constructed in 1968 in pale yellow brick in a vaguely neoclassical style, and struggles to compete with the surrounding architecture. The best aspect is the view to the chapel on the south boundary, where there is a fine group of philadelphus, across a lawn dotted with trees including mulberry, hazel, paulownia, robinia and a huge multi-stemmed holm oak (though again, it is unclear which of these will survive the construction works). On the western side of the garden is the old master's lodge (1835), built on the site of the bowling green. It contains Benson Hall, a large function room that was formerly the master's drawing room, realised on a positively ducal scale. Among the adornments of this garden are a sundial, some fine Chinese metal lanterns doubling as lights and a statue of the Chinese deity K'uei Hsing, known as the examination god. It was installed in 1986 in a little space grandly titled the Ivor Richards Memorial Garden, commemorating this celebrated college fellow who pioneered the study of English literature at the university. The exam god is traditionally represented as a rather unprepossessing character and is sometimes depicted as holding what looks like a whip, apparently to keep students in line. In fact he is holding a brush, which we are told he uses to sort out the best candidates. This diminutive deity is perhaps emblematic of 'the new Magdalene', where hunting and horse racing have been swept away and a rather stricter academic regime ushered in.

MURRAY EDWARDS COLLEGE

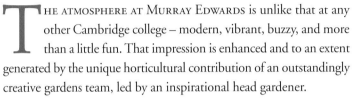

THE ATMOSPHERE AT MURRAY EDWARDS is unlike that at any other Cambridge college – modern, vibrant, buzzy, and more than a little fun. That impression is enhanced and to an extent generated by the unique horticultural contribution of an outstandingly creative gardens team, led by an inspirational head gardener.

Murray Edwards was founded in 1954 as New Hall, a women-only institution, as it remains today. It was originally housed in the Hermitage, a mid-19th-century building on Silver Street which now belongs to Darwin College. The mature garden at the Hermitage – including a large pear tree that still stands – was reportedly enjoyed by students, several of whom volunteered to work in it, though a gardener was seen as surplus to requirements. Then as now, that garden's greatest asset was the romantic presence of two river islands. (See pages 66–70 for the full history of the Hermitage.)

In 1965 the college relocated to a 2.5-hectare/6-acre site on the Huntingdon Road, land belonging to a house named The Orchard which was donated to the university by Nora Barlow and her sister Ruth, great-granddaughters of Charles Darwin (the aquilegia 'Nora Barlow' was named in honour of the younger sister). The new college buildings were designed in modernist style by the noted firm of Chamberlin Powell & Bon (architects of the Barbican complex in London), with a futuristic domed dining hall at the centre and a spinal walkway running down the middle of the buildings and grounds. Behind the Dome is Fountain Court, an entirely architectural conception.

As at many of the other newer colleges, such as Churchill, there was little gardening ambition early on, the entire focus being on making the place habitable for students. Photographs of the official opening by the Queen Mother show the Main Walkway in an almost bare setting. There had been a substantial garden at The Orchard but nearly all of this was churned up during the building programme (a few mature trees survive, notably the beeches which grow well here). The college's

LEFT The college facade is almost futuristic, with the dome and curved entrance lodge furnished with pots. The circular planting bed (left), with *Musa basjoo* and ricinus, is nicknamed 'the magic roundabout'.

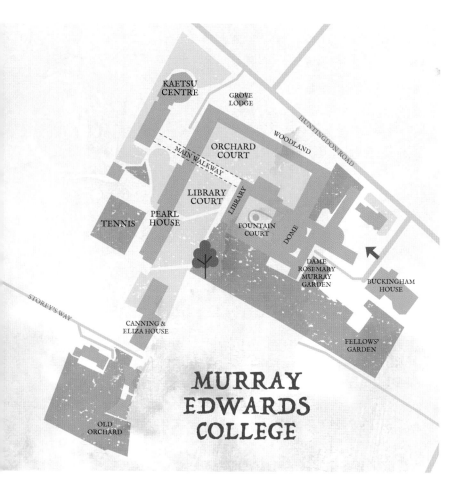

MURRAY
EDWARDS
COLLEGE

RIGHT The college consists of a range of buildings constructed during the past few decades, with the richly planted gardens creating a sense of unity.

FAR RIGHT Some of the 6,000 plants grown annually by the garden team are raised in the greenhouse, which is fronted by a cloud-pruned box hedge.

first president, Rosemary Murray, planned and planted the area around Library Court and gardened a border there – but she does not mention this in her own published history of the early college; a garden has now been named in her memory.

In 1988 the college site was substantially enlarged to around 5.5 hectares/14 acres by acquiring neighbouring land, part of The Grove estate, another famous Cambridge address in the 19th century. The Grove was the home of Emma Darwin, widow of Charles; the main house stands today within Fitzwilliam College. Two of Emma's sons built houses on the estate: Wychfield, now owned by Trinity Hall, and The Orchard, demolished to make way for New Hall. Since this increase in acreage, various accommodation blocks have popped up across the site, the latest in 2006, all suitably in scale with the setting as a whole. In 1972 New Hall attained full college status and in 2008 was renamed Murray Edwards in honour of its founding president and Dr Ros Edwards (née Smith), who with her husband donated £30 million to the college.

Most of the garden areas on the site are south-facing and the soil is good, if a little shallow in places. The avowed policy of head gardener Jo Cobb is for 'diaphanous, colourful and unstructured' planting, with Great Dixter and East Ruston Manor cited as inspirations. White flowers are avoided, as they might get 'lost' against the near-white concrete of the buildings, and everything is geared seasonally to work with the academic year: peaks of interest in spring and the third week in June, and then again at the end of September.

As visitors approach the entrance down a spur off the Huntingdon Road, the observatory-like dome of the dining hall hoves into view. A prim line of six hornbeams creates a formal note to suit the architectural style; they are soon to be replaced by Mongolian limes or liquidambars. The horticultural vivacity at this college is announced right at the outset, in the form of a large circular bed nicknamed 'the magic roundabout': in high summer, its dramatic changing displays feature huge-leaved banana plants (*Musa basjoo*), ricinus, amaranthus, dahlias and salvias. The last are a considerable speciality of the college and Ms Cobb's favourite genus, with scores of different varieties to enjoy. Their high colour sets the general chromatic tone. Large clusters of pots around the wide, glass-walled entrance porch contain anything from wisteria and azalea to flowering almond trees and lilies in profusion, together with seasonal displays of tulips and narcissus. A favourite tulip is the huge, almost peony-like 'Yellow Mountain'. In the Dixter manner, bright colour is seen as a positive virtue.

There is a small cutting garden for flowers behind the lodge, and an ikebana arrangement on display inside, which changes weekly. All these details raise the general impression and make the college feel special. On the other hand, the garden team is not precious about what they do: students and staff are encouraged to pick flowers for their rooms, and to eat any of the fruit (including cherries, figs and mulberries, as well as apples and pears). In this sense, Murray Edwards is the most generous of all Cambridge college gardens towards its community.

Immediately behind the Dome is Fountain Court, which Ms Cobb and the garden committee have decided to keep decidedly minimal, horticulturally speaking. (For a period from the 1980s to the early 2000s this court was allowed to get rather 'bushy' with trees and shrubs.) The furniture here is blue and the only planting is in cobalt blue pots chosen to match: bulbs in spring and dahlias in summer. With its low bubbling fountains and chunky central circular pool, this space makes a fine exterior pendant to the dramatic and inspiring dining hall interior, featuring an ingenious servery which rises up out of the floor. Architecturally, this is Cambridge's most successful modernist college.

The Main Walkway extends north-west from interior to exterior, continuing as a covered passage between Orchard Court and Library Court. These two lawned areas immediately create a sense that one is in a collegiate setting, where architecture always oscillates with greenery. Across the large lawn of Orchard Court are ranged various sculptures, including Barbara Hepworth's *Ascending Form (Gloria)* (1958); there are plans to relieve the openness here with more shrub plantings, while a programme of massed bulb displays in the grass has been embarked upon. There was 'a slight row' with the housekeeping staff about the shrubs growing against the buildings here and elsewhere in college. Apparently mice were climbing up them and then jumping into student rooms through the windows. As a result many of the shrubs around the accommodation blocks have been cut down slightly to make them less mouse-friendly.

Library Court has more of a woodland feel, with beeches, yews, hazels, limes and oaks across the whole college site. The main bed has been replanted with peonies, *Aruncus dioicus*, various hellebores, *Aconitum carmichaelii* 'Arendsii', bergenias and eurybias (an 'unknown species' donated by Christ's College garden), as well as a succession of spring bulbs and biennials. For late summer the standout plant is the single red *Chrysanthemum* 'Venus'. The area named for Rosemary Murray is occupied by elements of the garden created for the Chelsea Flower Show in 2007, entitled 'Transit of Venus'. Designed by alumna Sue Goss, it features a swirl of box hedge, a central glass sculpture and a cordon of pleached whitebeams. The college also participated in the Chelsea Fringe Festival in 2015, with a poetical-horticultural collaboration perhaps better suited to its 'funky' style.

The Walkway itself is planted up with clematis (including 'Polish Spirit' and 'The President') but mainly with climbing roses such as 'Kew Rambler', 'Cécile Brünner', 'Maid of Kent', 'Dublin Bay', 'Francis E. Lester', 'François Juranville', and 'The Albrighton Rambler'. They help relieve what can otherwise be a rather dark passage on a dull day.

Adjacent to Library Court is the fellows' garden, an even woodier area which has a private air. It also incorporates a large, sunny terrace,

with low Versailles-like tubs (dubbed 'Sceaux tubs') filled with masses of salvias in season. There are swathes of *Geranium macrorrhizum* under the trees, as well as flag irises, purple loosestrife and bistort. A small wooden pavilion is secreted in a shady spot. One rarity here is the Chinese shrub *Dipelta floribunda*, similar to *Kolkwitzia*. A rose garden was created by the late Liz Acton, a fellow in engineering, with classic varieties such as 'Duc de Guiche', 'Mousseux du Japon', 'Cardinal de Richelieu' and 'Ferdinand Pichard'. To avoid a 'sherry-trifle effect', yellow or coral roses were not mixed with the pinks. There is also a pond. As the head gardener explains: 'The fellows wanted a pond and they dug it themselves.' There are good views across the water towards the rich autumn colour of a mature *Parrotia persica* which was planted before the college descended on the site. A damson grows next to it.

These are the gardens and courts associated with the heart of college. It is in the slightly farther-flung areas that the garden team can really cut loose, and the character of the place comes to the fore. Although architecture tends to dominate the impression garnered by the one-time visitor to a college, or online browser, for those who get to know the place better, or who reside there, its gardens can be just as affective and memorable. This is certainly the case at Murray Edwards.

The Huntingdon Road frontage is a lengthy, wooded expanse in the shade of mature horse chestnuts which are reaching the end of their lives, with seedling beech, lime and hornbeam growing up beneath to replace them. This rectangular section has been made into a woodland garden with the expected cow parsley and wild garlic growing in the shade of the trees, but also aquilegias, a few peonies, polyanthus, hellebores, euphorbias and cranesbill geraniums. The grass is left long here and the leaves are not collected in order to increase the site's biodiversity, especially beneficial to wild bees and other insects. Native plants include cowslips, restharrow and violets. This process is now being talked of as a 'rewilding project'. Elsewhere there are large groups of bee orchids and a few of the stately white helleborine (*Cephalanthera damasonium*).

Local people nip into college and walk through the woodland strip to avoid using the pavement next to busy Huntingdon Road, entering by a gate next to The Grove's old entrance lodge. The cottagey garden

ABOVE LEFT The pond in the Murray Edwards fellows' garden was dug out by the fellows themselves.
ABOVE RIGHT A small wooden pavilion is a private retreat for the fellows.
RIGHT The Kaetsu Centre, with its glass-walled stairway, now dominates the northern part of the site. The placement of a bench in front of the border indicates that this college wants its students to enjoy the gardens.

here has *Phlox* 'Clouds of Perfume', tulips, irises, carex grass and many annual flowers. Nearby, in the far north corner of the college site, is the Kaetsu Centre, where paths are mown through a small meadow area fringed by trees including a young Cambridge oak (*Quercus × warburgii*). Around the back of the building is a small Japanese garden of artfully placed rocks, river pebbles and grey gravel, which is easily missed. The Chōshū Five Garden was designed and built by the Japanese Garden Society to commemorate five young men who escaped Japan in 1863 and studied in England before returning home to help form the modern state. It is an intriguing 'inside-and-out' garden in that the clipped yew balls morph into ceramic spheres indoors, visible through a glass wall. Like everything at this college, it is immaculately maintained.

South-west of the Kaetsu Centre is some concentrated herbaceous gardening, including a fine June border with huge red poppies ('Beauty of Livermere'), cardoons, valerian, salvias (of course), sages, forget-me-nots and euphorbia, lent structure by box pyramids. A May border adjacent includes alstroemeria, geraniums, achilleas, aquilegias and more euphorbia. These borders give on to a 'teardrop lawn' (triangular) shaded by a beech tree. A little farther down this perimeter edge of the college estate is the tennis court, which is screened on this side by a border with a subtropical theme, and on the far side by grapevines. The

college's greenhouse, inherited from Emma Darwin's garden, can also be found here, next to the old coach house. It shelters numerous tender salvias – which all get lifted, pruned and potted in autumn – as well as daturas, cannas and dahlias in pots. The garden team grows on some 6,000 plants a year, mostly in the polytunnels in the more serviceable garden yard, where a cactus collection is also kept up. Along the west side of the tennis courts is a secret space, a narrow hedged walkway with a tree named 'the kissing willow' along it. A group of incense cedars can be found on the other side of the tennis court.

Beyond the tennis court is the college car park, which is not an area generally included in descriptions of college gardens. Murray Edwards is different, as ever, in that the trees used are interesting and varied, including *Picea omorika*, *Pinus wallichiana* (Bhutan pine), a Monterey pine, variegated hollies such as 'Golden King', *Cornus mas*, *Malus* 'Evereste' and fastigiate oak. In addition there are plantings of variegated choisya, alliums, euphorbias, asters and several grasses. A grove of *Betula utilis* 'Doorenbos', with an evergreen backdrop to accentuate the white stems, has recently been added, an idea borrowed from Anglesey Abbey. In 2018 the maize variety 'Fiesta' was grown

ABOVE The rose garden and pergola in the president's garden, which is situated just outside the college proper.

in the car park as part of a collaborative art project focusing on the concept of the 'jumping gene' (which 'Fiesta' exhibits).

Occupying the southern part of the college site is 69 Storey's Way. Ranged on the stepped terrace in front of the house are cacti, euphorbias, succulents and geraniums in pots, as well as poppies and creeping rosemary. There is a scheme here aimed at encouraging students to grow, for which small cactus plants are handed out. Behind the house is a remnant back garden with a lawn and clay oven, as well as the fellows' allotment. (There are also communally gardened student allotments in college.) At the far end, behind a Glastonbury thorn, is what remains of an old orchard of apples and pears.

A discreet gate in the southern corner is the way to the president's house, a late 1930s building. There is a little sunken garden with box pyramids and a rose pergola festooned with 'Treasure Trove', 'Paul's Himalayan Musk', 'Seagull', 'Penny Lane' and 'Climbing Peace', along with viticella clematis and golden hop. At the far end is a meadow area. This land was originally part of a 'guinea garden' complex comprising third-acre (0.1-hectare) plots, and some of the old paths remain.

Emerging back into college proper, some lively planting can be enjoyed around the Canning and Eliza accommodation block, including asters and chrysanthemums along the front of the building, a multicoloured iris border bolstered by nepeta and cardoon, and a subtropical border which reverts to spinach in winter. (A sign says 'Spinach – Please Pick'). A square of lawn behind the block contains more sculpture and several specimen trees, including a ginkgo. There is a lot of gardening betwixt and between at Murray Edwards, and a herb garden in this area, planted in containers, features only edible (no 'medicinal') plants. The garden team makes home-made herbal tea to welcome the 'offer-holders' who visit the college while waiting for their exam results in summer. Perhaps the herbal element does ease their trepidation somewhat. Another annual garden event is Happy Apple Day, held in October, with apple-pressing, fires and a band, at a moment when a third of the college are 'freshers'. Most Cambridge garden teams are divided as to speciality, but it is unusual to find someone deputed specifically to run the garden's social media presence. Yet another unusual feature at Murray Edwards is a noticeboard listing recommended tracks to listen to on headphones in the garden; the list is updated at least twice a week.

This is an exceptional college garden in every way. It is also fast-moving, so the preceding description can only be considered a snapshot.

ABOVE Orchard Court, with the Main Walkway running along one side, is the principal venue for the college's collection of art by women. Perhaps the best-known piece is *Ascending Form (Gloria)* (1958) by Barbara Hepworth.

NEWNHAM COLLEGE

'FEMININE' AND 'DOMESTIC' ARE AMONG the epithets commonly used to describe Newnham's visual appeal, which is defined above all by a series of buildings (1875–1910) designed by Basil Champneys in the 'Queen Anne' mode – soft orange-red brick, tall windows and dormers, white-painted wooden details, high chimneys, steep-pitched roofs. This look became fashionable in the final decades of the 19th century as a lighter, airier alternative to the sometimes dour and muscular presence of the Victorian Gothic Revival and the rather intense idealism of early Arts and Crafts. Perhaps the less gender-specific 'handsome' might be a better word to describe these buildings, as it captures more of their inner dynamism and verve. The early college was somewhat caught up in the craze for Aestheticism, and Newnham's buildings might be considered in that light – as an expression of a contemporary attitude to both art and life where the two were seen as indivisible.

The grounds spread out across 7 hectares/17 acres, the vivid green of the spacious lawns proving to be a marvellous tonal foil to the rich colour of the brickwork, while the now mature trees create a relaxed ambience which seems to grant every student the permission to consider these grounds their own personal domain. All college members regardless of rank – there is no separate fellows' garden – are free to lie on the benches or grass, sit beneath the trees, or simply wander around the herbaceous borders.

Newnham was founded in 1871 as a direct result of the university's decision the previous year to allow women to attend certain lectures. Henry Sidgwick, a forward-thinking philosopher and professor of Trinity College, had been one of those leading the charge for women's higher education – organising the so-called 'Lectures for Ladies' – and it was he who pushed for a hostel for women who lived at a distance from Cambridge and therefore required overnight accommodation. A detached villa in Regent Street

LEFT The box parterre at the foot of the Memorial Mound, with Clough Hall and the great oriel windows of the dining hall beyond.

189

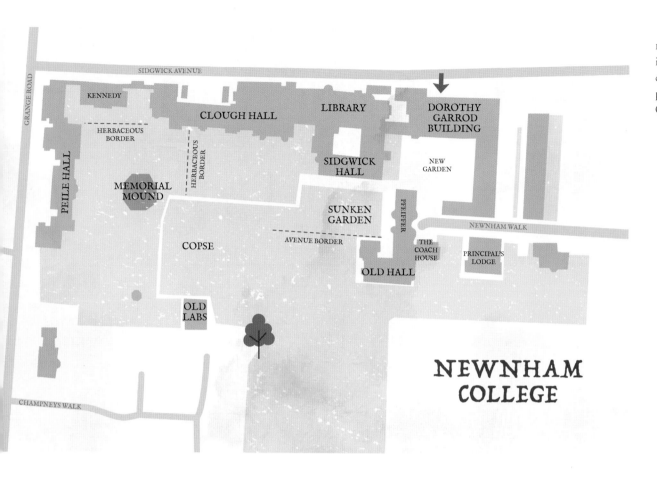

was the college's first home, personally rented by Sidgwick, for just five students, and then as numbers increased it moved twice more before ensconcing itself in brand new premises in the fields of west Cambridge in 1875. The college was named after the village in which it was sited, though Newnham village would soon be subsumed as a suburb. Sidgwick himself had appointed Champneys as the architect and also persuaded Anne Jemima Clough, who had set up a school in the Lake District in 1852, to preside as first college principal.

As so often with colleges founded and built in the 19th and 20th centuries, at first Newnham appeared somewhat isolated. An early photograph of Newnham Hall (later renamed Old Hall) shows it alone and starkly silhouetted against a grey sky. The building is stranded in open fields, its boundary marked simply by an agricultural wooden fence. But the college principal had an interest in gardens and was soon overseeing the planting of trees and shrubberies. The blank canvas was given a late-Victorian structure comprising substantially scaled, semi-enclosed garden features linked loosely together by serpentine paths. (Newnham is sometimes described as an Edwardian Arts and Crafts garden. While it is true that the planting detail is realised in that spirit, the garden layout has retained its Victorian structure, lacking the strongly directive quality associated with the cellular 'garden of rooms'.) Newnham feels emplaced in its

garden in a way that few other colleges do, because the gardens have grown up around the buildings in this relaxed and informal manner, even if there are relatively formal episodes contained within. At the older Cambridge colleges, traditionally the garden areas were rigidly divided from each other, and even while 'hard' divisions such as walls may have disappeared over time, the ghost of that structure lingers and one has a strong sense of moving from one distinct garden space to the next. Newnham is more 'joined-up'.

The early college had a rural air which students enjoyed, to judge from one letter home written in May 1876: 'It is just like country here. We are completely private in our garden, and quite surrounded with country sights and sounds – cows and sheep in the fields round us, and birds of all sorts just outside the hedge.' Lawn tennis and croquet were played – but not cricket, to the consternation of some students who had invested in a bat. A tutor had said 'it would spoil the grass', and after a little hesitation, that 'there were other reasons'. One wonders what these 'other reasons' could possibly have been, but Newnham was not alone among the early women's colleges in considering the game improper for young ladies.

There was a decidedly Aesthetic atmosphere to the college in the late 1870s, with a particular emphasis on fashion and interior decoration. Students were encouraged to choose their own wallpaper,

and when it came to dress the tutors set the style, as one Newnhamite reminisced: 'A good many students wore aesthetic green gowns & the harmony of colours against the green and blue walls was quite delightful.' The Aesthetic creed placed natural beauty to the fore, and there are accounts of students embroidering their tennis frocks with flowers, fronds, tendrils and Virginia creeper. The college's second building, North Hall (now Sidgwick Hall), was built in 1880 just to the north of Old Hall, on the other side of Newnham Walk. This public road running east to west was a quiet thoroughfare, but it split the college in two. (The problem was not solved until 1894, when the college persuaded the town to build Sidgwick Avenue just north of its own line of buildings, and to close Newnham Walk to traffic.) As the gardens and lawns began to establish themselves, and as more of Champneys' buildings went up, the college felt the need, by 1888, to employ a head gardener. An illustration in *The Builder* magazine the following year shows the college grounds as natural parkland, with young trees and clumps of flowers. One of the saplings pictured was planted by former prime minister W. E. Gladstone in 1887. In a scandalous action, this was dug up soon afterwards by students in the night as a prank, but the 'Grand Old Man' good-humouredly despatched an oak from his Hawarden estate. The replacement stands today in front of Sidgwick Hall.

A sea-change came over the gardens at Newnham with the appointment in 1892 of Blanche Athena Clough, a niece of the principal, as chair of the college's garden committee. She steered the garden's development for several decades. Almost her first action was to employ the venerable Yorkshire firm of James Backhouse & Son, one of the pre-eminent nursery companies of the day. Like most larger nurseries at this date, in addition to plants the firm offered a garden design-and-build service. An unknown designer at Backhouse's produced a plan for the garden which overlaid a geometric design on the existing structure. These straight paths, realised at a cost of £900, have been retained to this day: one principal axis extends due south from Clough Hall (1888) and another bisects it at a right angle, following the line of the old Newnham Walk.

The most prominent feature of the garden in early photographs is a white-domed observatory containing a telescope (a gift from the wife of the master at St John's College), sited on a mound south-west of Clough Hall. (The Mound remains; the observatory has been moved to the playing fields area.) One student recalled the 'small observatory, where Miss Stephen, Vice-Principal of Sidgwick Hall, made mysterious observations every morning after breakfast'.

There was a different mowing regime in the rectangle of grass in front of the great twin oriel windows of the dining room and staircase

of Clough Hall, suggesting it was considered a putative 'court' for the college. This area still feels like the heart of the garden, while those oriel windows were always the best element of Champneys' architecture, so the instincts of the Newnham sorority, and the Backhouse designer, were well founded.

Various elements of the Backhouse plan were not implemented, including an avenue of cedars of Lebanon along the main axis south from Clough Hall, but photographs from around 1910 indicate that there were some serious herbaceous borders at the college by this date. The overall structure of the garden may have been Victorian but the planting style was very much in the romantic Arts and Crafts vein, with herbaceous perennials jumbled up together as opposed to height-graded in smart rows. This had been partly inspired by the college's commissioning of the architect Alfred Hoare Powell to come up with a new design for the garden, in around 1906. Presumably it was realised by some that the Backhouse plan was already 'old-fashioned'; garden style was moving fast at this time. Powell suggested a complete revamp along Arts and Crafts lines, and although only a few of his ideas were implemented, they were decisive. The sunken rose garden in front of Sidgwick Hall was Powell's design, as was the form and placement of the double herbaceous border and the yew exedra which terminates it. Finally, a simple flower parterre in front

of the Kennedy building eventually evolved into the long herbaceous border we see there today.

The garden had loosened its stays, as it were, but there was potentially more to come. In 1910 the great garden designer Gertrude Jekyll was approached about designing the area in front of Peile Hall, Champneys' last building at Newnham, which semi-encloses the college garden on its western side and overlooks the Mound. The decision had been taken to relocate the observatory and create in its stead a memorial garden feature in honour of the college principal, Eleanor Sidgwick, who was about to retire. A large sum of money (£1,000) had been raised for the purpose. Jekyll's innovative proposal comprised a pair of hexagonal pavilions, one of them on top of the Mound, linked by a walk flanked by wavy yew hedges, with an area of hedged enclosures behind the southern pavilion. There was no trademark herbaceous border; this was to be a dignified and restrained memorial. The plan was initially voted through college council – but was then abruptly shelved. It appears

ABOVE LEFT The sunken rose garden designed by Alfred Hoare Powell in 1906.
ABOVE CENTRE Trees planted early in the life of the college contribute a verdant dignity to the garden.

possible that this was related to the fact that Edwin Lutyens, Jekyll's usual architectural collaborator, was going to be involved as the architect of the pavilions. Lutyens had recently caused an upset at a dinner at Clare College when, apparently 'in his cups', he had poked fun at the colleges and dons, and reportedly used bad language at high table. Such transgressions are not forgotten in Cambridge. Lutyens was firmly 'off the list' – and so was Jekyll's proposal.

Newnham's alternative choice for the revamp of the Mound proved disastrous. A little-known Scottish architect named W. C. Watson came up with the memorial we see today: a tall, narrow obelisk with stone seats at its base, the Mound itself treated as a kind of terrace with flights of steps leading up to it. As a garden feature this overblown monument is wholly irreconcilable with the landscape surrounding it. It looks like a war memorial to thousands of fallen soldiers, when in fact it commemorates one person. The sentiment attached to it makes any alteration problematic, but really the Mound should simply have been flattened and the memorial relocated. In 2009 an attempt was made to beautify the feature by means of a new knot garden paid for by alumni, but unfortunately this does not resolve its problematic relationship to the rest of the garden. The best one can say is that it is an idiosyncratic moment which speaks of the college's strident individualism. A photograph

taken in 1919 shows the Mound closed in by trees that had grown up on it, and this suggests the ideal approach to the issue: turn it into a glade feature, like a miniature version of the Mound in the garden at New College, Oxford. Those trees near the mound had a double purpose, as a former student recalled of her time at Newnham in 1918:

One of the most attractive features of college life in my time, which I believe is not allowed nowadays, was the 'sleeping-out' in the open air. Every dry night in the summer term processions of students could be seen carrying a load of rugs and eiderdowns, heading either upwards to the lead flats on the roof, or downwards through the windows to occupy the hammocks slung between the trees in the garden near the raised Sidgwick Memorial. This was of course against the regulations, but was winked at, provided that the hammock occupiers got themselves in again at dewy dawn before the College was well astir.

ABOVE RIGHT A double herbaceous border extends on an axis from Clough Hall. The vibrant colour scheme across college replaces an earlier emphasis on white and pastels.

The old entrance into college was via the Pfeiffer Arch on the east side, along the line of Newnham Walk, and its fine black iron gates remain a notable adornment. Just beyond is a ribbon of 'Iceberg' roses underplanted with the almost-black tulip 'Queen of Night', with white foxgloves following on. One wonders how many visitors see the gates nowadays, as the college's main entrance has been moved to Sidgwick Avenue. The lodge is now definitively established there thanks to the smart new Dorothy Garrod Building, opened in 2018, containing the porter's lodge, a cafe and student accommodation. Visitors progress through this sleek, modern environment, redolent of a corporate HQ, and come out into a new court with a garden designed by BHSLA, a partnership recently formed between Christopher Bradley-Hole and Brita von Schoenaich. This garden consists of clipped yew hedges and beds of perennials arranged in a geometric pattern on the new turf, focused on an existing birch tree.

The college gardens are ranged across the area of lawn south of the Champneys' suite of buildings, which hug the northern boundary of the site. A row of mature limes cuts across the centre of the garden and there are various other trees to discover, including a fine cut-leaf beech, a mulberry, an ailanthus, *Sorbus latifolia* and yews. The first of the formal episodes encountered is the sunken rose garden next to the Pfeiffer building and directly in front of Sidgwick Hall.

It functions as a memorial to the college's paterfamilias, the circular central water basin encircled by an inscription carved by Eric Gill which reads: 'The daughters of this house to those that shall come after them command the filial remembrance of Henry Sidgwick.' This is a slightly queasy moment now, given the revelations around Gill's treatment of his immediate family, and our general misgivings about the replication of family relationships in institutional surroundings. The borders around this well-proportioned formal feature are planted with modern shrub roses, *Verbena bonariensis* and marigolds, edged with lavender 'Vera', and the cerise tulip 'Maytime' for early in the season. Arts and Crafts sunken gardens, sometimes labelled as 'Italian', were generally highly architectural features, but here there is no balustrade and a minimum of stonework, so the feature pleasingly recedes into the surrounding lawn.

The horticultural highlight of the garden must be the romantic double border aligned on the entrance to Clough Hall, conceived in Arts and Crafts spirit. Cardoons, alliums, aquilegias, cirsium, *Paeonia mlokosewitschii* and oriental poppies play off the foliage of

---

ABOVE Frosted *Crataegus* 'Paul's Scarlet' around the Memorial Mound. An effort has been made to create link features such as this between the garden's successive episodes.

dusky macleaya and frothy thalictrum. A *Magnolia × soulangeana* 'Alba Superba' is framed by the yew hedge at the far end, while at the college end *Campsis radicans* grows around the door to Clough Hall. The long border in front of the Kennedy building is equally impressive, with a pronounced subtropical note, the rich oranges and yellows of cannas, heleniums of various types and tithonia mingling with tall foliage plants such as ricinus. It used to be that Newnham's planting was mainly white and pastel-toned, to complement the orange-red brick, but these borders show how strong colours can also be used to good effect with this backdrop. South of here, hawthorns have been planted in front of wisteria-festooned Peile Hall, while a little further on is a long Nut Walk of coppiced hazels, the dappled shade beneath underplanted with ferns and bluebells. Wild orchids grow along here and several species of daphne for winter scent have been planted by head gardener Charlotte (Lottie) Collis, who achieves a great deal with a small team of three, and also plays an understated leadership role in Cambridge horticulture, having instigated regular meet-ups between the head gardeners of the colleges.

The western parts of Newnham's garden are much wilder, with mature trees including cherries and orchard trees dispersed around the long grass. The Old Labs, all on its own in this area, was one of the first buildings to go up on the site, a necessity because at that time women were not allowed to use the university laboratories. Perhaps it was placed in this isolated position because of the danger of explosions? There is a fine bulb display here in spring – camassias, cowslips, fritillaries, *Anemone blanda* – with masses of cow parsley following. En route to Old Hall are huge old clipped hedges and another 'surprise' herbaceous border on the boundary with the college playing fields, which expand southwards. The college's memorial orchard is in this area, as is the blue Atlantic cedar planted to mark its centenary, and the popular student allotments, complete with raised beds and polytunnel. There is also a specialist iris garden including several varieties co-raised at Newnham: 'Henry Sidgwick' (red-brown), 'Old Hall' (orange) and 'Peile Hall' (white and lavender), which are all available commercially.

Newnham has not been laid out with any particular logic, and it can be tackled in any order. This is one garden where the pleasure lies in just drifting from place to place, in making new discoveries, or simply stopping for a while to enjoy the scents of the flowers, the long vistas across the lawns and the sweet sound of birdsong.

ABOVE A new garden designed by BHSLA in the court behind the Dorothy Garrod Building, which also acts as the college's main entrance.

PEMBROKE
COLLEGE

PEMBROKE HAS A GREEN HEART. Most of its buildings are situated at the edges of its rectangular, 2-hectare/5-acre estate, leaving a collection of ten distinct garden areas in the centre. All the courts in Pembroke are open or semi-open, meaning that it is the garden space which defines the site physically, much more than the bricks and mortar (chiefly Victorian). The garden areas, though nominally distinct, flow into each other with little sense of a formal transition, at least when compared with the physical fabric of most other colleges. This set-up makes Pembroke a most relaxing environment in which to live, lending its verdant interior, replete with mature trees and shrubs, a pleasantly bucolic, unbounded atmosphere.

Pembroke was not always like this. Founded in 1347, it is the third oldest college in the university, after Peterhouse and Clare. It began life as a squashed-up medieval college with a tiny front court consisting of a right-angle of two brick ranges, which was expanded in the 15th century to form two courts (really a small court and a yard) where today there is only one – Old Court. Formerly there was a range running east-west across the middle of what is now Old Court, with the old hall occupying the east range, its three large arched windows and four tall buttresses dominating the scene. (For simplicity, the line of Trumpington Street in front of the college is treated as running due north; all other compass directions given here follow suit.) The master's lodge was tucked away at the southern end of the hall, adjacent to the second court, where a little later St Thomas's Hostel (part of college, leased from St John's) stood on the site of today's chapel. The whole area beyond, to the south – perhaps an acre (0.4 hectare), where the Library Lawn is today – was taken up by the master's garden. This was extremely large in a Cambridge context (in relative terms, only Corpus Christi, Christ's, Queens' and Sidney Sussex colleges have been as generous towards their principal). It is likely that the Pembroke master's garden followed

LEFT The view from Library Lawn to Old Court, with Wren's chapel at left. A line of *Rosa* 'La Sévillana' forms a divide.

a similar trajectory to other early Oxbridge college gardens, starting as a chiefly productive space and gradually acquiring elements associated with leisure, such as flower beds, walkways and shady arbours. The garden is shown in some detail on Loggan's engraving of 1690; by this period it has a fantastical sundial laid out in one of the little parterres and also what look like rows of vegetables. We know that in 1454 the master planted saffron 'to the public advantage of the college' – but this was probably east of the hall (now Ivy Court).

There was also a large orchard on a separate acre of land, across a public lane to the east, which the foundress had explicitly desired. This land was acquired in two stages, in 1363 and 1401, as long, rectangular 'messuages' or plots, and is labelled as Pembroke's orchard on Hamond's city map of 1592. It formed the basis of what later became the fellows' garden, and then (with the dividing lane erased) the nucleus of the whole expanded eastern part of college, where so many students live today, some of them in the Orchard Building. In Loggan's 1690 engraving, this garden is divided into three, with the orchard itself now occupying only the far section, a bowling green in the middle and a fellows' garden consisting of trees, rows of vegetables and a summer house at the west end. There was a wall and a gravel path running around the entire perimeter. Ivy Court (1614–70) had been constructed by this time, while the old lane which formerly ran through the college site can still be traced as the path that crosses the court's eastern end; it also marked the boundary of the original master's garden. William Custance's 1798 map of Cambridge shows that the fellows' garden had by then been simplified into a long rectangle with the bowling green, or the smooth lawn it had become, occupying the central section and parcels of orchard trees at each end, with a line of elms along the southern boundary. Ivy Court, open to the east at this point, had a double line of trees flanking a central grass panel.

The basic medieval structure of the college lasted for some 450 years before it was abruptly disturbed. The east-west range across Old Court was taken down in the 1870s, and the master's lodge demolished in the process. This happened during a phase of rebuilding overseen by the aptly named John Power, a dynamic master who tripled undergraduate numbers after a century or so of collegiate somnolence. (This had reached its nadir in 1858 when the single undergraduate admitted to Pembroke decamped to Caius after five days.) Obviously the college had to change, but it is likely that even today thoughtful members privately regret the extent of the master's ambitions and his cavalier approach to Pembroke's medieval fabric. The most controversial decision taken at the time was to demolish the old college hall, constructed in around 1350. It was admittedly too small, at 12.5 metres/41 feet by 8 metres/27 feet, to serve that function any longer but could have been put to other uses. If it had survived it would have been a gem to rival Peterhouse's hall, which dates back to 1290. But following the alterations to Old Court, the building was described as 'forlorn' and 'isolated'. It had no chance.

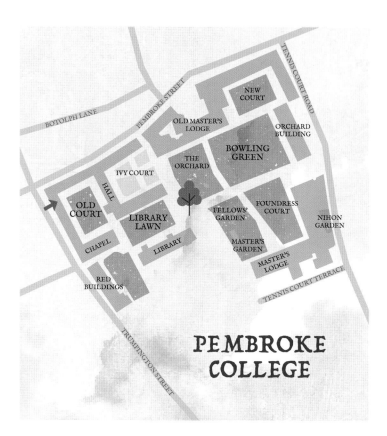

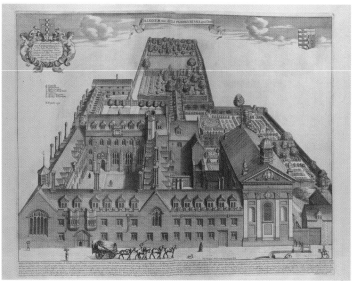

ABOVE David Loggan's 1690 engraving of the college shows the old form of the fellows' garden (at the top), with the bowling green in the middle section of the tripartite space.

TOP RIGHT Yew topiaries in Ivy Court. The gateway is the 17th-century doorcase of the college's old hall.

One of the positive outcomes of opening up Old Court was the opportunity to show off to better effect the college chapel (1665), Christopher Wren's first built work, which lies on the western edge of the college, against Trumpington Street. Pembroke's chapel generously offers its elegant Corinthian pilasters and a richly carved pediment to the world as it rushes by outside. Superficially a dutiful exercise in Renaissance neoclassicism extrapolated from the 16th-century architect Sebastiano Serlio, the building nevertheless displays felicitous balance, proportion and restraint in its decoration, with four refined elevations and a flash of individuality in its prominent cupola. Although not large, it projects a convincing impression of loftiness in the context of the other college buildings and can be considered the second finest chapel in Cambridge, after that of King's.

Power's confederate in the 1870s rebuild was the architect Alfred Waterhouse, whose best known work was the Natural History Museum in London. He was given almost free rein by a majority of Pembroke's fellowship (though there were dissenting voices) to 'modernise' the college and create superior accommodation for all those extra students. Waterhouse was an outstanding architect, one of the most successful of his generation, but like many in his profession he did not suffer from a lack of self-confidence in his own abilities. The free-standing buildings he constructed in Pembroke in the

1870s, which were realised in a variety of exuberant, continentally influenced neo-Gothic forms, a milieu Waterhouse revelled in thanks to his travels across Europe, now appear bombastic and self-indulgent. Waterhouse's work often has a glued-together look, and can seem unremitting in its decorative stridency. There is a sense, especially with his smaller buildings, that he was trying to cram in too many good ideas. At Pembroke the overall impression created by features such as prominent clock towers with a municipal air (the library), a pseudo-palatial facade with French pavilion roof (Red Buildings), and round chateau-towers on top of what might otherwise be an English rectory (Old Master's Lodge), is that the college is a motley assemblage of 19th-century Belgian town halls. One blessing is that Waterhouse did not get his way with regard to Wren's chapel. He opined that 'though it would be a matter of regret', its demolition was necessary for his own vision to be fully realised. The fellowship finally baulked at that.

One conclusion from all this is that a Pembroke fellowship, cowed by an ambitious master, had allowed a Victorian 'starchitect' to use their college as a playground for his own ideas at the peak of his creative gravity. Another factor possibly of relevance is that at exactly the period Waterhouse was 'rebuilding' Pembroke, his close contemporary William Butterfield was creating Keble College, in Oxford, in polychrome red brick (work commenced on Keble's

gigantic chapel in 1873). Perhaps there was an element of varsity rivalry here, as well as conventional professional competitiveness. There would have been a religious edge, too. Waterhouse was a Quaker while Butterfield was High Anglican, and they viewed each other with mutual suspicion, Butterfield's attitude being religiose, lofty and evangelical and Waterhouse's ecumenical, liberal and somewhat more down-to-earth. (In fact their work comes together – or collides – in the Front Quad of Balliol College in Oxford.) While it is no longer acceptable to exercise the condescension of history, and in doing so to vilify 'the wicked Victorians' for their arrogance, it is difficult to find much merit in Waterhouse's destructive impulses at Pembroke at this period.

In 1879 the fellowship decided to appoint another architect, Sir George Gilbert Scott, who had a different view, immediately stating: 'I have no doubt at all that what remains of the ancient buildings of the College should be religiously preserved.' He delayed submitting plans for the remodelling of the Old Library (formerly the medieval chapel) in Old Court in the hope that the fellows would reverse their decision, which they did. With a fine plasterwork ceiling of 1690, this remains one of the university's great interiors. And rather than destroy Wren's chapel as Waterhouse would have, he remodelled it internally with subtlety and panache. It was indeed 'religiously preserved'.

Gilbert Scott also created New Court, in the far north-east corner of the college's estate. This range represents a kind of jumbled-up neoclassicism with a frisson of Arts and Crafts. It has a long balustrade to the roof, Dutch gables and heavily pedimented windows, all overlaid on to the proportions of a building of the English Renaissance. It's an intriguing facade, and looks over the old bowling green beyond, which is still used for its original purpose. In order to get there one must walk through Pembroke's other courts and gardens, just as the fellows would have in the 14th century.

The constricted proportions of medieval Pembroke had been blown apart by the overhaul of the 1870s and a gaping hole created in the south-east corner of the newly expanded Old Court. This opened up new views not just to the chapel but also tantalisingly beyond into the green space that had been the master's garden, setting the tone for a college where no court would ever be entirely enclosed again.

Old Court today is the first in a series of perfect lawns. Head gardener Nick Firman has been at Pembroke since 1965 and is by some

ABOVE LEFT A statue of William Pitt the Younger, an alumnus of the college, can be found in a shrub border by the library.

ABOVE CENTRE A croquet pitch is marked out each summer on Red Buildings Lawn.

distance the longest serving head gardener employed in a Cambridge college. The care of turf is one of the traditional Cambridge gardening skills still highly prized in this college, and the sward everywhere in Pembroke is kept up to an exacting standard. In the narrow beds on the east side of Old Court and against the chapel, tulips and forget-me-nots in spring give way to standard fuchsias with pelargoniums below, again highly traditional and most welcome in context. Mr Firman knows the varietal names of every fuchsia in the beds – indeed of every plant in the garden – and here we find 'Mrs Popple', 'Mrs Marshall', 'Phyllis', 'Lena' and 'Rufus'. Square corner tubs contain bright mixes such as pansies and ivies, or geraniums and flax, while around the chapel entrance is a shrubby blend of ceanothus, abutilon, trachelospermum and plumbago. A large *Magnolia grandiflora* grows at the south-east corner of Old Court, where the first master's lodge once stood, marking the beginning of another phase of the garden. A long raised bed between the chapel and Library Lawn consists of red *Rosa* 'La Sévillana' underplanted with catmint (*Nepeta* 'Six Hills Giant'), all fed by mushroom compost. *Prunus* 'Shogetsu' blossoms well near here in spring.

Library Lawn itself was the site of the original master's garden until the changes of the 1870s. Perhaps the most remarkable master the college has seen was Roger Long, who served from 1733 until 1770. An astronomer with an interest in engineering, Long created a kind of paddle-boat diversion in this garden, as described in Edmund Carter's *History of the University of Cambridge* (1753):

> But the chief beauty of this Lodge is (in my opinion) the Gardens, and therein the Water-Works, contrived by the present Master, (and here let me tell you, he is a very great Mechanic) which supplies a beautiful and large Bason in the middle of the Garden, and wherein he often diverts himself in a Machine of his own contrivance, to go with the Foot as he rides therein.

This was not the only invention of Long's to be found in the garden. In the 1750s he built a large metal sphere, about 7.5 metres/25 feet in diameter. Up to 30 people could clamber into it and observe the movements of the planets and constellations on the interior walls, which were activated by means of a winch. This planetarium, or 'globe' as it was known in college, was initially housed in a specially designed room next to the master's lodge (this would have been an

---

ABOVE RIGHT The east-facing herbaceous border between Ivy Court and the Orchard, with delphiniums and crocosmias.

extremely large room) but was later moved out to the west end of Ridley's Walk, where the sundial is today. It survived until 1871, by which time it had disintegrated beyond repair. It is said that its dismembered remains are still buried somewhere in the garden. Long's assistant in these projects was the college butler, Richard Dunthorne, who became a noted astronomer himself, specialising in the moon.

The fellows' garden with its bowling green was divided from the master's garden by a wall built in 1693, which was a serious barrier designed to keep undergraduates out of both areas. One Pembroke scholar who particularly enjoyed the garden 'over the wall' was the poet Thomas Gray, who would become something of a connoisseur of garden design. He settled at Pembroke in 1756 and stayed there all his life, in rooms overlooking Ivy Court, remarking: 'I'm like a cabbage, where I'm stuck, I love to grow.' He apparently always planted his own window box with sweet-smelling plants. His particular friend and fellow Pembrokian, William Mason, was the author of *The English Garden* (1772–82), an influential poem in four books that took gardening and the aesthetics of nature as its prime theme. We can understand something of the appeal of the garden to such a sensibility from Mason's poem 'On Expecting to Return to Cambridge, 1747':

Lo, where peaceful Camus glides
Through his ozier-fringed vale,
Sacred Leisure there resides
Musing in his cloyster pale.
Wrapt in a deep solemnity of shade,
Again I view fair Learning's spiry seats,
Again her ancient elms o'erhang my head,
Again her votary Contemplation meets…

Mason is making explicit the connection between the natural environment of the garden and its suitability as a place in which to study, very much in the tradition of Aristotle's Lyceum or the Garden of Epicurus. This is an ideal that has always been kept up at Pembroke, with college fellows encouraged into the garden to play at bowls, and with a convention of fellows choosing and planting their own trees, or even cultivating their own areas of the garden.

Library Lawn is blessed with a long, south-facing border on its northern side, where Gray had lived. Richly planted with a variety of shrubs and perennials, highlights include *Nandina domestica* 'Richmond', red-flowered (with small fruits later) *Punica granatum*

ABOVE Spenser's Mulberry on its mound in the Orchard, with narcissi.

'Albescens Flore Pleno', vibrant purple *Indigofera heterantha* as well as a huge *Phlomis fruticosa*, photinias, pittosporum, philadelphus, melianthus, hebes, daylilies and more fuchsias. A rarity is the pineapple guava (*Acca sellowiana*), which does bear fruit here. To the east of the lawn, behind a small seating area with benches, is a handkerchief tree (*Davidia involucrata*). The shadier side of the court, against the library itself, features a sturdy mix of mahonia, sambucus, rhamnus, sarcococca, berberis, various viburnums and several actinidia species, including *A. polygama*. Around the corner, south of the chapel, is Red Buildings Lawn, which has a well-stocked border on its east side featuring flowering cherries, an acer, verbascums, geraniums, *Hydrangea quercifolia* and a *Berberis darwinii* that self-seeds itself around.

The old division between the master's and fellows' garden, originally defined by the ancient lane that cut through college, is still strongly emphasised by the tall iron railings and gate running across the east end of Library Lawn. Wisteria climbs the pillars here, and there is a heliconia growing against the west-facing wall. It is possible to pass from here into Ivy Court, where the buildings were indeed smothered in ivy until the 1970s, when it was all removed in line with the general fashion for 'clean-shaven' courts in Cambridge. The centre of the quad is taken up by four perfect lawn plats, fetchingly raised up on plinths, while the east end is closed not by buildings but by a line of columnar yews, which are clipped once a year and are complemented by the old wall passing behind. Annual bedding – wallflowers followed by petunias – is used on the west side. Apparently Pembroke's garden committee likes to select the colour scheme. Somewhere in the vicinity of Ivy Court was the college's cold bath, which in the mid 18th century was in the private garden area of one of the fellows and flowed out into Pembroke Street along the King's Ditch.

East of Ivy Court, the visitor passes through a fine old gateway – in fact a 17th-century doorcase to the medieval hall, moved here in the mid 19th century – and enters Ridley's Walk, which passes along the front of Waterhouse's master's lodge, now the Junior Parlour (common room). The walk is named after Nicholas Ridley, Master of Pembroke and one of the Protestant martyrs. While in captivity in 1555, Ridley wrote final letters to various friends and family members, and also to Pembroke College:

In thy orchard (the walls, butts, and trees, if they could speak,

ABOVE The college 'globe', or planetarium, was constructed in the 1750s and could hold up to 30 people. This photograph possibly dates to 1871 when it was dismantled.

would bear me witness) I learned without book [i.e. off by heart] almost all Paul's epistles, yea, and I ween all the canonical epistles, save only the Apocalypse: of which study, although in time a great part did depart from me, yet the sweet smell thereof, I trust, I shall carry with me into heaven.

Possibly Ridley was making reference here to the likely manner of his own impending execution, which included being burned (suffocated) at the stake; we can only hope that the sweet smells of Pembroke's orchard did indeed accompany him in some way at the time of his death. The butts Ridley mentions were archery targets; another Pembrokian, Dr William Turner, recalled that Ridley's demeanour in his younger days at the college 'was very obliging, and was pious without hypocrisy, or monkish austerity: for very often he would shoot in the Bow, or play at Tennis with me'. Archery butts were set up in the orchard at Christ's College, too, and we know that arrows also flew at King's, Queens' and Peterhouse (despite the university statutes theoretically prohibiting the sport, probably because a sharp arrow can be a murderous weapon in the hand). The Pembroke tennis court where Ridley played was at the east end of the garden, and is possibly the large building depicted in Richard Lyne's bird's-eye view of Cambridge of 1574. It appears orchard trees took up most of the space at that time, and there was no master's garden, to speak of.

Ridley's Walk is smartly edged with cobbled panels and contains the principal set-piece border at Pembroke, with a large *Musa basjoo* in the centre. This specimen actually fruited in 2015, attracting press coverage; Mr Firman now describes it as 'our famous banana'. The exotic theme continues with fan palms (an offshoot from Selwyn College), echiums, strobilanthes, cannas and fremontodendron. The planting continues in an east–facing border against the wall of Ivy Court, where it is bolstered by the likes of *Buddleja crispa*, *Crambe cordifolia*, persicaria, pennisetum, perovskia, acanthus and *Eupatorium purpureum*, while additional colour comes from *Delphinium* 'Lord Butler', malva and lythrum. But as ever in this traditional garden, the prime effect is from interesting and unusual shrubs; there is a fine red-orange flowered *Abutilon* 'Patrick Synge' by the entrance to Staircase N.

Along the southern side of Ridley's Walk, in the part of the garden known as the Orchard (though there are only two old pear trees remaining), is the site of a rock garden created in the late 1930s by Revd Meredith

Dewey, who was Dean of Pembroke until the 1970s. 'I had found a lot of old stones behind Red Buildings which were evidently the remains of the 14th century hall,' he later recalled. One day he saw from his window Ellis Minns, another fellow, 'burrowing like a badger in the rockery to extract an enormous stone, less globular but almost as heavy as himself, and then scuttling across the lawn to the Master's Lodge. I couldn't see what he did with it but shortly after he came back for another, like a squirrel burying nuts against a rainy day.' Minns told him afterwards that 'they were important and precious and illustrated in Willis and Clark' (this being shorthand for the standard architectural history of the university).

The rockery was extended in 1946, after which, according to Dewey, he and the head gardener looked after different portions of it on an entirely amicable basis. Mr Firman says that the rockery often had coal in it in the dean's time, because he used to throw lumps from his window at the birds on it to scare them off. Today the rockery is largely covered in a range of evergreens, including several dwarf conifers. An olive tree has recently been planted in this area, while other trees and plants in the Orchard include a purple plum, a robinia, gunnera and a *Sequoia sempervirens*. This lightly wooded sector is covered with narcissi in spring and colchicums in autumn, to enchanting effect. A small pond dug during the Second World War is fed by a pipe that connects to Hobson's Conduit, Cambridge's famous water supply; this in turn feeds a smaller pond in the rockery area. Spenser's Mulberry can also be discovered here on a mound, this tree a cutting taken from the original in 1978. It commemorates the Pembrokian poet Edmund Spenser but is unlikely to have been planted by him.

Ridley's Walk continues east, with thick but low yew hedges abutting the bowling green, which now appears ahead. Damage to these hedges (the student bar is adjacent) is the bane of the garden team's lives here, as at other colleges. (According to one head gardener: 'students and hedges don't mix.') A recently planted specimen of + *Laburnocytisus* 'Adamii' marks the transition into New Court, to the north, with yet another pristine lawn and a large bed of mixed magnolias at its western end. *Verbena bonariensis* and *Teucrium fruticans* grow on the northern side of the court, and there are plantings in the crevices of the low drystone walls on three sides of the sunken lawn – santolina, muscari, horned poppy, muehlenbeckia, echeveria, ivies. An *Akebia quinata* (chocolate vine)

RIGHT The avenue of London plane trees that divides the bowling green from modernist Foundress Court (1997).

flourishes in the north-east corner. This court, with its principal building by Scott (described earlier), was for many years cut off from the college proper and accessed via a separate entrance on Pembroke Street, as undergraduates were not permitted to pass through the fellows' garden. The 3.5-metre/12-foot wall which ran east-west dividing New Court from the bowling green was reduced to just 90 centimetres/3 feet in the mid 1950s, when the fellows' garden as a whole was finally opened up, and it is now a favourite spot to perch while watching a game of bowls. The bowling green itself has raised banks and also a ridge (or 'rub') down the centre, which are both used strategically by bowlers – Pembroke is the only college in either Cambridge or Oxford where the game is even half-seriously pursued. It still has in its possession some fellows' bowls (marked with initials) dating back to the 1760s.

A mature *Liriodendron* (tulip tree) marks the transition from New Court over to the bowling green, with the neo-Gibbsian Orchard Building (1957) on its eastern side. The material used, buff-coloured Dutch brick, jars rather in the Pembroke context and the building was not universally admired; Revd Dewey commented that a paperbark birch was planted here to partly screen the building and calm the sensibilities of certain fellows. *Aristolochia clematitis* (birthwort) thrives in front of the building, with wisteria, *Coronilla valentina* subsp. *glauca* and *Garrya elliptica*.

The south-eastern stretch of the fellows' garden was bought from Peterhouse in two tranches in 1854 and 1861, after which the whole eastern section of the college was reconceived as a pleasure garden. The far side of the bowling green is defined by a path known as the Avenue, a characterful line of London planes, some of them leaning decorously. Originally that row of trees was matched by the line of elms on the other side, as Revd Dewey recalled:

In 1925 I reckon there were still three elms standing to the north of the Avenue out of an original five or six. In the thirties we used to take wine under the most westerly one, always in style with the whole outfit of linen, cut glass and plate, insisted on by Albert Bell, the high table waiter. That elm is now replaced by a ginkgo. The last of the line was cut down in 1974.

Today a slightly random assortment of trees (an arboretum?) has replaced the elms, several of them being the gifts of fellows, since the college got into the habit of marking the tenth election of fellows in this way.

Beyond the planes, which act as a screen, is Foundress Court (1997), the college's latest addition, an exercise in recessive modernism by Eric Parry, faced in a light Bath stone instead of the expected concrete. Rather quaintly, Pembroke deferentially refers to Marie de St Pol, widow of the Earl of Pembroke, as 'the foundress', in a way that other colleges with female benefactors (such as Clare, Christ's, Jesus and St John's) do not. A few years ago an all-female Foundress's Society was formed within college, its members recorded in faux-Victorian group-portrait photography.

Today, the master's and fellows' gardens are conjoined into a long north-south rectangle and can be found at the west end of the Avenue, near a spreading copper beech. Both gardens are firmly closed to visitors, though this is no great disappointment, as they are not spectacular. A rectangular lily pond is half in each garden, the master's end a rectangle of lawn ornamented by circular lead planters with roses, crocosmias and delphiniums. There are dahlias, alchemilla, daylilies and other plants in a west-facing border, while a long pergola of rambler roses leads up to the door of the master's lodge itself, which is attached to Foundress Court. The fellows' garden has a black-painted summer house, two robinias (one gold and one green), an incense cedar and *Acer pseudoplatanus* 'Brilliantissimum', whose foliage is as complex as its name. A bed of delphiniums looks fine against yew hedges at one

end of the garden. A stone torchère finial 'rescued' from the roof of Wren's chapel sits in the lawn as the principal ornament.

There is one more garden area tucked away at Pembroke. Immaculately maintained, the Japanese garden on the east side of the Foundress Building comes as a considerable surprise and is one of the real secrets among Cambridge college gardens. It is a legacy of the fact that the building was partly paid for by Nihon University, in Tokyo, in exchange for a promise that its students could continue coming to Pembroke for a summer-school for 60 years. The garden consists of grey-white gravel, black bamboos, acers, clipped box balls, small pines, skimmias and, as a centrepiece, the compact flowering cherry 'Asano'. One wonders how many college members use and enjoy this garden. The fact it is so well-maintained is testament to the high standards of the garden team here.

It may not have a vista over the Backs, but Pembroke is one of Cambridge's great garden colleges.

LEFT The lily pool is half in the fellows' garden, visible here, and half in the master's garden.

ABOVE Hedges around the bowling green create a semi-formal divide typical of the garden's structure.

PETERHOUSE

THE OLDEST COLLEGE IN CAMBRIDGE necessarily has the oldest college garden, though Peterhouse's Grove, with its wonderfully fresh annual displays of narcissi and other bulbs and blossom, perhaps does not quite fit the venerable and antique stereotype. A 'house of scholars' was founded in 1280 by Hugh de Balsham, 10th Bishop of Ely, as an institution modelled specifically on the example of Merton College, Oxford. Hugh's predecessor as Bishop of Ely had shown an interest in the culture of scholarship in 13th-century Cambridge by making a bequest of 200 marks to the Priory of Barnwell. This represented a subsidy of 10 marks annually to two priests studying divinity in the city – effectively the first Cambridge scholarships. Links between the diocese and the scholars of Cambridge continued during Hugh's incumbency and, on Christmas Eve, 1280, he gained royal assent for a group of scholars to live together in Cambridge as an organised body.

The chief function of the college was to provide priests for the Church, as remained the case at all colleges in Cambridge until the late 19th century. But there was a slight yet decisive change in emphasis at Peterhouse, towards a subtly more secularised attitude to the education of scholars, a widening out of the concept of education so that those in religious orders were not being trained up to be ordained priests only, but to fulfil a variety of roles within the organisation of the Church, including – vitally – legal positions. If the bishop did but know it, this was the start of the gradual displacement of the religious houses as seats of learning in Cambridge, an usurpation finally and brutally achieved during the dissolution of the monasteries in the 1530s.

To emphasise their status, Bishop Hugh's scholars were initially lodged in an institution with strong diocesan links, where the monastic rule of St Augustine was considerably more relaxed than

LEFT The chapel (1632) stands at the centre of Old Court, a simple grass lawn with lamp posts at each corner.

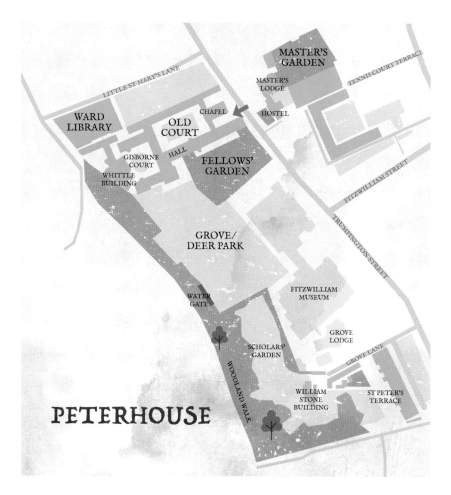

PETERHOUSE

TOP RIGHT Flowering cherries on Trumpington Street outside the master's lodge. The college entrance is visible over the road.

BOTTOM RIGHT The vivid autumn colour of *Malus trilobata* in the Grove (Deer Park), with a strawberry tree just behind. The Fitzwilliam Museum looms beyond.

at other houses: St John's Hospital, the precursor of St John's College, north of the city's centre. Nobody knows exactly why, but this experiment of placing the bishop's scholars at St John's Hospital was not deemed a success, and three years later, in 1284, they left to take up residence in two hostels leased by the diocese on the south side of the city centre, just outside the Trumpington Gate.

Bishop Hugh solidified his benefaction at his death two years later in 1286, by leaving 300 marks for the erection of the hall which stands to this day in Peterhouse's Old Court (it was remodelled later and can be seen to best medieval effect from the fellows' garden on the south side).

The two hostels of the early Peterhouse, containing 17 chambers in all, survived in the northern part of the college site until the early 17th century, even as the rest of the college took shape around the hall. Various bequests and acquisitions of land meant that the college's garden was extended to the south, with the Grove (also known as the Deer Park today) reaching its current size of about 1 hectare/2½ acres by the early 14th century (Peterhouse's garden acreage is now about 1.8 hectares/4½ acres in all).

In about 1270 one Walter de Brasur of Shelford and his wife, Audreada, had bequeathed to the monastic brethren of the Order of the Brothers of the Sack, who had their friary on the other side of Trumpington Street, some land to the south of Peterhouse's hall. The nascent college gradually acquired all the property of this ailing order adjacent to their own site, including, in 1570, the land which became the 'new garden' and ultimately the Scholars' Garden, as it is known today. The college in turn leased this land out to tenants on the understanding that Peterhouse scholars could walk in it. Later, the eastern portion was used for building Grove Lodge (1798) – now the residence of the director of the Fitzwilliam Museum – and in around 1851 St Peter's Terrace, which remains in college ownership. Some houses against Trumpington Street had been cleared away in the 1820s to make way for the construction of the Fitzwilliam itself from the 1840s, an edifice which is today the college's rather overbearing neighbour.

The entrance to Peterhouse is via an 18th-century gate on Trumpington Street, where a screen with railings (1848) imparts a semi-open appearance. This portal is a relatively recent innovation, however: until the 1820s there was a line of houses along this part of

the street and the only way in to college (Old Court) was from the north, via a passage off the lane running past the Church of St Mary the Less (also known as Little St Mary's). This little 'introit' or entry was quite as obscure and insalubrious as the entrance to Corpus Christi at this time, when both colleges were looked upon as decrepit relics of the medieval period. (Both were completely revamped in the 1820s.)

Richard Lyne's map of Cambridge of 1574 shows a small square garden, to the south of the hall and old master's lodge, laid out in quarters, which John Hamond depicts in 1592 as a grid of trees, probably indicating an orchard. This would have been the master's garden, at this date. There are references in the college account rolls for 1374–75 to vegetables and culinary plants such as parsley, cress, garlic, leeks and saffron, which would most likely have been grown in a cook's garden either close to the hall or to the west of the court, where Gisborne Court is today. A reference at this time to fairly large plantations of clover and vetch suggests that the bulk of the land known as the Grove today was then used as pasture for haymaking and possibly grazing. On Hamond's map the area is fringed at the edges with trees and labelled 'Peter Howse backeside & walkes'. This indicates that by the end of the 16th century it was certainly being used for leisure purposes – for 'walkes' under the trees and probably also as an area for archery practice, since butts are mentioned in the college records in 1588 and 1613.

Old Court itself was originally a simple, unadorned open space which would have been compacted earth or possibly hoggin (sand mixed with gravel). It is shown as open on early maps but there is a record of privet bushes being planted there in 1600–01 and hawthorns in 1611–12, presumably as a hedge. However, by the time of David Loggan's city map (1688) and engraving of the college (1690), Old Court has been ornamentally planted up with trees in a strikingly formal manner. In his book *Cantabrigia Illustrata* (1690) Loggan generally depicts the colleges by means of a bird's-eye view, but in the case of Peterhouse he chose to show only Old Court, and from an almost ground-level perspective. Loggan's illustration shows Old Court divided into four grass plats surrounded and crossed by gravel walks. An avenue of columnar trees (ten in all) leads to the chapel door and another ten of the same kind stand on the north and south perimeters of the lawn plats.

Between these lines of trees, cutting across the middle of the grass plats, are two lines of specimen conifers, three on each side. It was not uncommon for colleges to have single trees (often walnuts) in their principal courts, and occasionally more than one (as with the corner trees in Gonville Court). But nowhere else has a layout which is anything like this elaborate.

Over time these trees were removed and in 1775 the cross-paths were done away with, and Old Court took on its current form of a simple grass lawn with lamp posts at each corner (these were replaced in 1830 and again in the 1980s; there is an incongruously municipal air about them). Today the most striking horticultural intervention is the spring and summer window box display – there are 59 in all, with the ivy-leaved pink pelargonium 'Vinco' the dominant theme, complemented by petunias. The colour scheme is non-negotiable, according to the head gardener: 'It has to be pink, not red.' Against the dining hall on the shady south side of the court is a well-chosen selection of shrubs (red-leaved hazel: *Corylus avellana* 'Fuscorubra', prunus, a small magnolia) together with hostas, hellebores, foxgloves, ajugas, saxifrages, monkshood and *Hydrangea petiolaris*. This part of college also boasts a fine display of flowers – tulips, marigolds, begonias – in pots arranged around the door of the porter's lodge, which is festooned with runner beans. This display, unique to Cambridge and Oxford, has been nicknamed 'Gerald's Bower' because it is the handiwork of the head porter, Gerald Meade.

To the west is the college's second court, Gisborne Court, which was formed in 1826 by building ranges to north and south and more recently (2015) has been

ABOVE David Loggan's engraving (1690) depicts Old Court with an elaborate tree parterre.

RIGHT The view into Old Court from the cloisters adjoining the chapel.

completed by the Tudor-Gothic Whittle Building on its west side. This building was designed by John Simpson, the neoclassicist who has been to this college what Quinlan Terry has been to Downing. The arched windows of its facade echo the form of the screen that once defined the court's western side. The old Cambridge tradition of planting trees in courts, now almost lost, is continued here with a central crab apple, underplanted with tulips in spring, on the octagonal lawn plat. The beds around the edges of the court are crammed with plants, mainly shrubs and small trees including magnolias, mahonia, fatsia, *Hydrangea quercifolia*, spruces, maples and paulownia, with a strong contingent of Mediterranean-style subjects – broom, sages, box, olive, phormium – and even a dominant trachycarpus palm. Hostas, bergenias and geraniums provide cover at the lower levels.

The garden areas in the southern part of the college are accessed by an ancient passage next to the dining hall in Old Court. A small hedged and enclosed herb garden with a sundial is the way in to the Grove proper, via a laurel-edged walk. But there are some distractions along the way, including roses and a large magnolia against the south-facing wall.

The Grove itself has been much augmented by tree and shrub plantings over the past 20 years, with specimens such as prunus,

magnolia, *Parrotia persica* and sweet chestnut among old oaks and limes as well as existing and recently planted apple and pear trees (the older trees being the remnant of a Second World War Dig for Victory orchard). A line of columnar yews, replacing a lime avenue, has been planted against the boundary with the Fitzwilliam Museum. The glory of the Grove is its spring bulb display – mainly narcissus, with aconites and crocuses, which students living in the southern accommodation blocks enjoy as they walk the path through the Grove to college.

The Grove has always been a relatively informal area. A dovecote and the tennis court against the western wall are first mentioned in the 1570s (the tennis court is described as 'now fallen down' in 1727). A building mentioned in 1544–45 and described as the *spectaculum* may have been a viewing pavilion built on the west wall to provide views across Coe Fen, the boggy 'wilderness' on the college's western perimeter (this building was demolished in 1859). It is likely the *spectaculum* – possibly a castellated building shown on Hamond's map of 1592 – was built on top of a now-bricked-up water gate, the outline of which can still be seen on the western wall of the Grove. The arms of two bishops of Ely are clearly visible on top of the arch on either side of the wall. In earlier times a tributary of the Granta flowed here, and it is believed a shallow runnel across the Grove was used to convey provisions to the door of the college kitchen. A wall at the southern edge of the Grove (first erected in 1501) creates a decisive boundary between it and the Scholars' Garden.

Before we proceed further, it is necessary to comment upon the alternative name for the Grove, which is possibly in more common usage today: the Deer Park. It is often supposed that this is an ancient appellation but in fact the first deer to be put in the Grove arrived in 1857. It seems numbers were always low and the deer afflicted. In 1892 the college master wrote:

> The late Duke of Devonshire, Chancellor of the University, about 1870 sent us a buck and does from one of his deer-parks, and the late Earl of Rosslyn, a year before his death [1890], sent us from Easton Lodge, Dunmow, half-a-dozen young deer; but they disliked so much the confinement within our small grounds, that they nearly all died. At present we have only two, but in the proper season we shall endeavour to replenish our stock.

By 1910 there were perhaps nine deer in the Grove, but numbers steadily declined until the 1930s, when the last of them perished. It was discovered they were infected with Johne's Disease, which could have been a reason for the longstanding failure of the herd.

The fellows' garden, which occupies the north-eastern section of the Grove where it abuts the college, was until 1725 the master's garden. It is shown as two square plots, with some orchard trees, on Loggan's map of 1690 and as three sections, the central one an orchard, on William Custance's city map of 1798. Today it is a spacious lawn, not fenced around but hemmed in by a thicket of old yew trees, with plane trees above, and box-edged paths leading into the Grove. Black gravel is used here as a reminder of the old habit of using coal dust to make 'black walks' (also recorded in Christ's and Queens' Colleges). There is a mulberry in one corner and a bed on the east side with diascias, sedums, sweet peas and geraniums. Primroses and wild flowers grow under the trees in the long grass in this characterful little retreat, with its tangibly antique air.

As has been mentioned, the land for the Scholars' Garden was first acquired by the college in the 1570s,

when the early tenants were enjoined to keep the walks 'fair and passable and well graviled'. The college later managed the garden itself. Loggan's 1688 map shows the layout in great detail; it is clear these were kitchen gardens, with vegetables, orchard trees and even what look like arable crops or plantations of grass for haymaking. A pair of buildings faces each other at the centre of the cruciform layout; they were most likely greenhouses. The layout does not appear to have changed much by the time of Thomas Salmon's *Foreigner's Companion* of 1748: 'There is a Grove South of College, and a large Garden beyond, abounding with all manner of Wall-fruits, and a Cold-bath, much frequented by the Students.'

This cold bath, fed by a brick culvert from Hobson's Conduit on Trumpington Street, is drawn and labelled on Custance's map of 1798; it is situated about halfway along the western wall. It was overhauled in 1799 and is last mentioned as existing in 1819. By this time half of the Scholars' Garden had been obliterated anyway by the construction of Grove Lodge and its garden on the eastern side. In the 19th century this area was known as the Fen Garden, and it continued to be used for fruit and vegetables until the 1840s, when it was re-landscaped in the informal manner we see today. There is an unsubstantiated suggestion that the designer and watercolourist William Sawrey Gilpin was commissioned at this time to draw a layout for both this and the fellows' garden.

Today the most noteworthy feature of the Scholars' Garden is a modernist accommodation block, built entirely in brick, named the William Stone Building (1964), which has a pair of huge beech trees behind it. The Scholars' Garden has a slightly more formal feel than the Grove, with specimen trees dotted around including a sweet chestnut, parrotia, weeping lime, mature oaks and a lovely copper beech. The old yews on the western side are perhaps its defining feature, with wild wisteria growing up and through them. Behind these yews and hollies is a dark woodland walk on the western boundary, next to the ditch which was once a tributary of the river; there are plans to plant it up with wild flowers. A croquet lawn has been made in one corner, where a herbaceous border is brightly planted with penstemons, kniphofias, wallflowers, sedums and variegated ivy, while clumps of peonies appear around the yews.

The master of Peterhouse was granted new lodgings thanks to the generosity of Charles

Beaumont, a former fellow and son of a master, who in 1725 gave to the college a handsome red-brick townhouse he had built in 1702, just across Trumpington Street. The lodge has a large garden which is shown as divided into quarters on Custance's map and was described in a contemporary publication as 'handsome' and 'walled around'. The college hostel next door to the master's lodging is prefaced by a small knot garden with foxgloves growing in the compartments, while around the back the master's lodge is a pleasantly tranquil space with a big, double herbaceous border – peonies, roses, osteospermums, perovskia, kale, penstemons, aquilegias – leading on to shrub roses and lime trees beyond. A conservatory containing a vine and a vigorous fig leans against the wall with Pembroke's garden, and there is a robinia in the corner. Overall it feels like a garden which has evolved rather than been designed, which is something that might be said of Peterhouse's gardens as a whole. The relaxed attitude helps to imbue this ancient college with a pleasingly timeless ambience.

QUEENS' COLLEGE

T HERE ARE SEVERAL GREAT GARDEN colleges in Cambridge, but Queens' cannot be numbered among them. No, Queens' is something rarer: a great garden*ing* college. It has been a hive of horticultural activity almost since its foundation in 1448, with any available land used intensively for fruit and vegetable production, for timber, for leisure activities such as bowling and archery, and as a place where agreeable walks might be laid out. While not the most prettily sited of the Cambridge colleges, Queens' has made the most of its riverside position by means of walks along the banks of the Cam which link it to the Backs, unfolding to the north. Early on, it even expanded across the road (Queens' Lane) by making a kind of annexe to the fellows' garden there. As a result, there were no fewer than three separate fellows' gardens simultaneously in existence at Queens' from the early 16th until the mid 19th century, which is definitely an Oxbridge record. Latterly, the increase in student numbers experienced by all the colleges has meant that Queens' has had to turn its gardens into courts with accommodation blocks. Yet it has still managed to preserve a sense of its original layout, as a series of walled gardens extending north and west from Old Court and Cloister Court, the ventricles of its beating heart.

Queens' – as its apostrophised name suggests – was founded by queens, plural. It was Margaret of Anjou who formally petitioned her husband, Henry VI in 1447–48 for permission to refound the existing College (formerly Hostel) of St Bernard, adding St Margaret as a patroness and emphasising her own patronage as a woman through the name of the new college. Seventeen years later, in 1465, the college was refounded by Elizabeth Woodville, Edward IV's queen, who codified its statutes and affirmed a long-standing association between the college and the queens of England.

LEFT The turreted gatehouse in Old Court, completed by 1448. This is generally held to be the best example of a medieval court in Cambridge.

Following its foundation, the college rapidly expanded out of the old St Bernard's site towards the riverside by the acquisition of four tenements and their gardens, providing space for Cloister Court and Pump Court to be built. In 1475 the college's first master and prime mover, Andrew Dokett (sometime rector of St Botolph's Church), was able to purchase from the Corporation of Cambridge a plot of land across the river; this would become the site of the tree plantation known as the Grove, the glory of Queens' gardens today. As with most of the Backs on the west side of the river, this was a waterlogged zone, prone to flooding, and a ditch dug along the plot's south side effectively made it into an island, given the presence of the river and existing watercourses on the other boundaries. It was at this point that the college's first bridge across the Cam was built to link the two parts of Queens', establishing it as the only Cambridge college which truly has the river at its heart. A mud wall was soon built (1499) around a central portion of the island site, and this is first described as a kitchen garden in 1505.

In the 1530s, the college obtained a substantial area to the north of the main site from the Carmelites, whose monastery was about to be suppressed during the dissolution period. This surrendered land would become the location of the president's and fellows' gardens, which are shown in detail on David Loggan's engraving of 1690. Both are set against the river (the fellows' garden divided into two sections – one half was the bowling green), and east of these are two large walled areas, densely planted with trees, one of which was an extension to the president's domain. The modest wooden bridge linking the fellows' garden with the Grove was *in situ* between 1555 and 1793. The disposition of the four gardens in this part of college, and the need for privacy, led to the construction of a tiny 'court' at their intersection which on the Loggan engraving looks like a roofed and windowless shed. This was essentially an empty room with four locked doors.

Loggan was able to depict only about half of the garden space at the college on his engraved view – he did not have room to show the island site across the Cam, which from the 1530s incorporated the stables, the brewhouse and the Grove, as well as the walled fellows' vegetable garden and orchard. Walks were laid out in this kitchen garden in 1539, and the term 'Grove', indicating an ornamental plantation with walks, was first used in 1555.

Another space not shown on Loggan's engraving was the garden squeezed between and behind the townhouses across Queens' Lane, opposite the college gate. This land, mentioned as an orchard in 1511, became a sports area for fellows. The (covered) tennis court was in use before 1531 and archery butts were also set up there (before being moved to the island site in 1580). In 1629 the college got into trouble with the civic

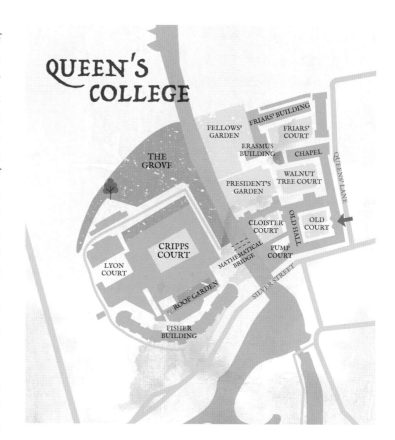

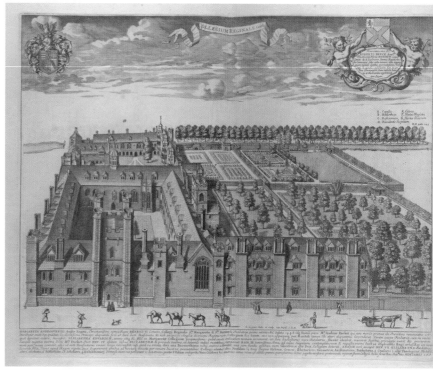

ABOVE David Loggan's engraving (1690) shows the bowling green (top right) and the small windowless building with four locked doors at the intersection of four gardens.

RIGHT The half-timbered President's Gallery (*c*.1540) in Cloister Court. Queens' was the first college in Cambridge to introduce cloister walks.

authorities for digging up turf sods 'in the Green by Newnham for the repairing of their butts, without any leave or license'. The last mention of arrows flying at Queens' is in 1682–83. (The 'tennis court yarde' over the road was eventually bought by the expanding St Catharine's College in 1836.)

The importance of trees at Queens' in the early days is indicated by the controversy that erupted around Humphrey Tindall, president from 1579, who proposed felling a number of the college's trees for timber in order to fund a new brewhouse. This prompted a protest from his immediate predecessor, William Chaderton, who opined that the trees were the 'ornament, bewty, and defence of the Colledge' and hoped that 'the long row of goodly ashes' might be saved. It is not clear where these ash trees were, precisely, but that does not matter – this was a question of principle, affecting the character of the college. It is interesting that Chaderton refers to the trees as a 'defence'; obviously in some sense they were seen as a bulwark against the town and its noisomeness. The college's arboricultural impulses were demonstrated again in 1685, when it collaborated with neighbouring King's College in planting Erasmus's Walk as a memorial to the celebrated scholar. This avenue of elms straddling

a boundary ditch would become a noted sight at the university until the mid 19th century.

The obvious portal to college, the monumental four-turreted gatehouse which faces out towards the town on Queens' Lane, no longer serves as the main entrance – in 1975 the porter's lodge was moved to the other side of the Silver Street Bridge, where most students live. Old Court is extremely quiet, for a 'front court', as a result, and an atmosphere of suspended antiquity prevails. The entire ensemble was complete by 1450, making this the most unified example of a medieval court in Cambridge. There is a south-facing flower border against the north range with suitably cottagey subjects such as delphiniums, campanulas, alchemillas and achilleas, while ceanothus and akebias adorn the wall in the north-east corner. Astrantias and toad lilies (*Tricyrtis*) thrive in the shadier south-western portion of the court, and there are climbing hydrangeas and a spring-flowering cherry around the door in the west range.

The lovely sloping lawn of Cloister Court is a perfectly imperfect foil to the splendid half-timbered President's Gallery of *c*.1540, where orange-red crocosmias, potentillas and burgundy-leaved physocarpus offset the ochre walls, while hostas, mahonias

and a massive pittosporum 'tree' add bulk. Tiny Pump Court, to the south, is planted up with pink hydrangeas, ferns and rhododendrons in saucer-shaped pots. Growing against the walls are corkscrew hazel, lilies, tiarellas, lonicera and more hydrangeas.

The northern part of college retains the basic form established in the 16th century, of four roughly square garden compartments, but a number of buildings have been added, converting these spaces into semi-open courts in the process. At the centre of these northern courts and gardens is a circular plot treated as a Mediterranean gravel garden, where cannas, *Verbena bonariensis*, pulsatillas, erigerons, and alliums can bask in the sunshine of the Cambridge Riviera.

Today the bays of G. F. Bodley's chapel (1891), which forms the northern range of Walnut Court, are planted up with spreading shrubs – ceanothus, fremontodendron, buddleia, sophora, *Rosa banksiae* and other climbing roses – all carefully clipped into shape in the Cambridge manner. The court's south side is shady and damp; in the south-east corner is an exotic border with tree ferns, maples, astilbes and heucheras, while the old chapel adjacent is adorned by *Cornus kousa* 'China Girl', *Hydrangea quercifolia*, fuchsia and euonymus. Roses on the Jacobean building to the east – 'Madame Alfred Carrière' and 'Dublin Bay', all smartly labelled

with metal tags – are mirrored by a complementary rose bed on the western side, against the president's garden, which was replanted in 2015 with 'Meg' and other varieties.

The college's most striking modern architectural addition is the Erasmus Building (1960) designed by Basil Spence, which now overlooks the bowling green in the fellows' garden. This caused a terrific controversy in the late 1950s but the fellowship should be congratulated for holding its nerve, as the building is one of Cambridge's most successful modernist moments. It was raised up on a colonnade to keep the fellows' garden intact, creating a cloister and allowing undergraduates to have views over the Cam. Of yellow-brown Stamford brick on its upper levels, the building seems to float above the green apron of the bowling green in a most satisfactory manner.

The style of the fellows' garden complements the building, with compositions featuring foxgloves, daylilies, ligularias, cotinus,

---

ABOVE LEFT The roof of Cripps Court is one of the greatest garden surprises in Cambridge, with colourful perennials such as rudbeckia, kniphofia and echinacea.

ABOVE CENTRE The mulberry at the heart of Cripps Court is a scion of the one in the fellows' garden.

geraniums, hellebores, hostas, sisyrinchiums and fuchsias, and a main border of salvias, phlox, delphiniums and other classic herbaceous flowers, set within columnar golden yew. Clematis, lonicera and jasmine are displayed on the wall behind. In the north-east corner, against the wall with King's, is a subtropical grouping with cannas, brugmansias, a ginkgo, ricinus and abutilon. A *Prunus serrula*, a large robinia and a pair of sophoras can also be found here. An old mulberry was possibly planted in 1609 as part of James I's efforts to start an English silk industry.

The college accounts refer to a 'black walk' in the fellows' garden. This was quite fashionable in the 17th century; Christ's College also had a black walk in its fellows' garden, as a contrast to yellow-brown gravel. In the Queens' accounts for April 1637, a labourer was paid 'for bringing seacoale dust into ye Fellows walks' and it seems the feature endured for some years, as there is a bill in 1678 for 'bringing back ye old door to ye black walke'. A reference to 'Cleansing the courts of ye cinderdust' in 1667 may indicate that the walk was rather messy to maintain. It is possible that this material was used partly because it was far cheaper than gravel and perhaps also needed less replenishment.

The private garden of the president, south of the fellows' garden, is lawned and has a large pergola with climbing roses along one side. There are herbaceous borders of mainly pastel shades, with white roses, box balls and a lovely acer against the river complemented by hydrangeas in pots. A sense of maturity is imparted by a pair of huge copper beech trees, a weeping birch (a favourite in Cambridge principals' gardens), a *Prunus serrula*, a catalpa and a robinia.

Now we must cross the river. And the only way to go is via Cloister Court and the so-called Mathematical Bridge. We alight on the island site, which today bears very little resemblance to its appearance between 1475 and 1972, at which point the massive Cripps Court was built over its heart. For most of its existence the largest feature here was the walled kitchen garden which would have made the college self-sufficient (and more) in vegetables and fruit well into the 20th century. Its character was rather different to the more modest kitchen gardens found at other colleges, as was remarked upon by George Dyer in 1814: 'its present appearance, it being open, and consisting principally of a kitchen garden, looks, perhaps, more like a country, than a college garden.' This quality was noted by various visitors over the years.

ABOVE RIGHT Narcissus beside the old walk by the river's edge, with the Mathematical Bridge beyond.

The vegetable garden was intensively maintained for the five centuries of its existence. In 1523 saffron was planted, and in 1575 we have the following record: 'paid for 3500 privie and 1000 of honeysuckles for the island and other places of the college, 19s 10d'. Among numerous references to fruit and flowers, there are bills for apricots and peaches in 1634, and in 1688 asparagus. The college's horticultural interests at this time are reflected by the fact that John Evelyn's *Sylva* (1664) and *Kalendarium Hortense* (1666) were both purchased on publication for the library, where they remain on the shelves today. Vines were also an interest from an early date, being first mentioned in 1510–11. A few decades on, in 1538, a frame was made at some expense (25s 10d) and by the 1570s there are references to what sounds like a substantial trellis, as squared stones for vertical supports are itemised. A series of payments towards the trellis at this time include a final bill to 'the frenche man' for setting up and planting the vine itself.

Photographs taken in 1932 show the fellows' vegetable garden with a cruciform path system and a dipping pool at the centre, when it was clearly still being kept up to a good standard. Next to the greenhouses and potting shed, the college's old stables were converted into Fitzpatrick Hall in 1936 (now demolished), and in the same year the great curved arc of the Fisher Building was completed along the southern side of the site. The walled garden was reprieved until 1972, when it was finally done away with.

The modernist Cripps Court was designed by Powell & Moya, the practice responsible for the sensitively placed Cripps Building at St John's College – but alas they seem to have missed the mark at Queens', especially with regard to the landscape setting. There is, however, an extraordinary and substantial roof garden on an upper level of this building. It was the brainchild of garden fellow Prof Allan Hayhurst and is now assiduously gardened by Steve Tyrrell and his team. A curving decked path wends through a swirling mass of burgeoning plant life, which comes as a mighty surprise in this place. There are rudbeckias, geraniums, dark penstemons, salvias, kniphofias, cannas, roses on supports, anemones, eryngiums, alliums, salvias, euphorbias and honeysuckles. The backdrop is a shrubby mix including photinia, wisteria, purple plum, even a eucalyptus tree and an olive. (The larger plants are in pots, as there is just 40 centimetres/16 inches of soil here.) The end of the path dissolves into a slightly oriental theme, with bamboos swaying in the near-constant wind.

RIGHT The Mathematical Bridge was first so-named in 1803.
It was designed in 1748 and reconstructed in 1905.

BOTTOM RIGHT
The rose collection against the outer wall of the president's
garden in Walnut Tree Court is one of the best such displays
in the university.

The Grove has remained mercifully untouched by the college's modernising impulses and retains a wonderful atmosphere. There are numerous references to planting trees in the Grove over the years, including 'fourscore oakes and ashtrees & five hundred quicsetts' in 1665. (Quicksets were used for hedging.) Today an avenue of beech cuts through the centre of the Grove and there are oaks, chestnuts, silver birches, willows and three liquidambars against the riverbank. In spring the ground lights up with tulips in multicolours, along with aconites and other bulbous plants (the tradition of tulips here was begun in the 1920s). But by far the most celebrated denizens of Queens' Grove are the two massive elm trees, at more than 44 metres/145 feet the tallest recorded in Britain, which somehow survived Dutch Elm Disease in the 1970s. These two great trees have been identified as Chichester elms, an earlier variant of the Huntingdon elm (*Ulmus × vegeta*) associated with Chichester Hall, Essex, a property owned by Lancelot Andrewes, who was Bishop of Chichester and also master of Pembroke College from 1589. Andrewes was ordained as a priest in 1580 by William Chaderton of Queens', so it is possible these particular elms came to the college through that connection.

At around the time that the Mathematical Bridge was built in 1749 the Grove was 'altered from its then nearly natural state to its present one', according to Robert Plumptre, a late-18th-century college president. Plumptre reports that this and other improvements were achieved by John Fortin, who was head gardener for some 40 years and 'a man of excellent skill in the

ordinary parts of his business, and of some taste and knowledge in these superior parts' – which is how several Cambridge college head gardeners might be described today. It is likely that the Grove was thinned out and the paths rejuvenated at this time. Richard Harraden's guide to Cambridge paints a vivid picture of the Grove and riverside in 1800:

> the beautiful scenery of this Spot, is agreeably diversified by the number of Barges passing and repassing from Lynn, and other Places, which unload at a Wharf a small distance from the College. The Meadows also, on the opposite side of the Cam, being often overflowed after heavy rains, present a pleasing variety from the sparkling of the water, as seen through the venerable grove of Elms, which peculiarly distinguish the Walks of this College.

The silvered complexion of a water meadow was a highly prized feature in the 18th century, and it appears that Queens' Grove could also offer up this sensation. Perambulations along the 'private walk' on the western riverbank next to the Grove were one of the chief advertised delights of the college, since they not only provided views across the water into the fellows' and president's gardens, but downriver towards King's College Chapel and Clare Bridge. George Dyer's advice in 1814 – 'Let no one leave these grounds without going to the end of that walk by the side of the river' – remains just as pertinent today.

ROBINSON COLLEGE

ROBINSON HAS COME IN FOR quite a lot of criticism, aesthetically speaking, since it was completed in 1980. Not many people seem to be persuaded by the architectural style, an austere essay in late-period modernism, shading into postmodernism by dint of its detailing. It is frequently condemned as 'fortress-like' and 'bleak'. The porter's lodge on Grange Road is approached along a sloping diagonal walkway that leads up to a modern take on a stubby medieval castle tower, complete with portcullis-like screen, as if visitors might expect boiling oil to be rained down on their heads by its defenders. Once inside, there is a monolithic quality to the architecture, with steeply tiered accommodation blocks stacked one on top of the other, and the same material – handmade Dorset bricks of a rich orange-red colour – used consistently throughout. That consistency is a virtue in many ways, and brick is certainly a 'friendlier' material than concrete. But the basic inner structure of two long parallel ranges forming a single narrow 'alley' creates a relentless, bunker-like feel.

In the architects' defence, it might be noted that there is a grand tradition of fortress-style building in Cambridge and Oxford; in fact, it can be considered as the unifying visual theme of the universities, with monumental gatehouses a particular speciality of Cambridge. And there are other compensations. A series of sturdy black trelliswork frames in a distinctively modern geometric pattern installed along the Grange Road frontage supports evergreen climbers which effectively counteract the monotony of the facade. Numerous trees and shrubs have now grown up along here and around the porter's lodge, mainly *Betula utilis* var. *jacquemontii* but also *Fagus sylvatica* 'Dawyck' and the unusual *Photinia davidiana*, along with hornbeam and Italian alder. The four inner courts are almost devoid of green, but they are relieved by well-maintained wooden planters opposite the college chapel containing clipped yew columns with bright plantings such

LEFT The garden front of the college features a thick shrub border which softens the edges of the architecture and provides a link with the characterful gardens beyond.

227

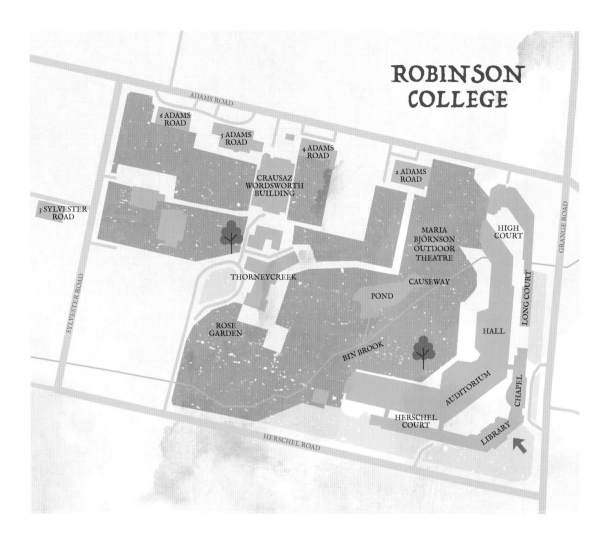

ROBINSON COLLEGE

ADAMS ROAD

6 ADAMS ROAD

5 ADAMS ROAD

4 ADAMS ROAD

2 ADAMS ROAD

CRAUSAZ WORDSWORTH BUILDING

3 SYLVESTER ROAD

MARIA BJÖRNSON OUTDOOR THEATRE

HIGH COURT

GRANGE ROAD

THORNEYCREEK

CAUSEWAY

POND

LONG COURT

ROSE GARDEN

HALL

SYLVESTER ROAD

BIN BROOK

AUDITORIUM

CHAPEL

HERSCHEL COURT

LIBRARY

HERSCHEL ROAD

RIGHT *Sailing into the Future* (2008) by Philip de Koning forms a counterpoint to Thorneycreek, the Arts and Crafts house visible beyond.

as iris and pelargonium, as well as hanging baskets (perhaps less well-advised). Then there is the chapel itself, with a great stepped triangular stained-glass window by John Piper. This building is a triumph when considered as a stand-alone work, as impressive without as within, its decorative brickwork revealing the potential of the material and providing an almost jaunty twist to the modernist idiom.

Robinson's aesthetic in any case should not be judged by its architecture alone. The college gardens, which are extensive, varied and unusual, are a memorable surprise hidden behind that apparently impregnable facade. The architects who won the competition to design Robinson, Gillespie Kidd & Coia of Glasgow, did not attempt to extend the architectural style across the whole site, which forms a 5-hectare/12-acre rectangle bounded by residential roads. Instead they suggested transforming five detached houses along Adams Road (north) and Sylvester Road (west) into lecture rooms (ground floor) and student accommodation (upper floors) while retaining the garden boundaries. They also set about preserving the country-house atmosphere around Thorneycreek, an Arts and Crafts house of 1895 that sits at the heart of the site. Its lawns lead down to Bin Brook, which lends the garden much of its considerable character. The importance of the brook was recognised by landscape architect John St Bodfan Gruffydd, who was engaged by the college in 1979.

He made the existing watercourse the central focus and guiding tonal principle of his design. This light-touch approach has paid dividends, since the college grounds have an attractively unproscribed feel; left to explore, visitors are not buffeted around by direction signs and compulsory routes, as is usual in a college environment.

The land on which Robinson now stands was once part of Carmefield, one of the four old West Fields of Cambridge. Owned largely by the colleges, this land was used for farming and riding following enclosure in about 1800. Carmefield formerly belonged to St John's College; Grange Road is so named because it once led to the college's Grange Farm. The Bin Brook flowing across Robinson's site eventually reaches St John's (where it has also been used as a defining feature in the garden), a neat physical link with the history of the landscape.

The architects' original idea was for a highly naturalistic garden scheme. It has been suggested that they were influenced by the Dutch *heempark* movement which developed from the ideas of J. P. Thijsse, who advocated a subtle enrichment or intensification of the indigenous flora. Gruffydd realised that this approach was probably inappropriate to a collegiate setting, which demanded a little more formality and a more straightforward maintenance regime, but he persevered with the concept of a naturalistic overall feel to the

demesne. At the outset he envisaged 'a wild woodland water garden across the middle of the site with a flood pond to buffer rising water levels… a park and informal woodland area with overtones of more sophisticated gardening beyond'. It has to be said that his wishes were almost precisely achieved – but more with the feel of a garden than the desired park-like setting. Gruffydd later crystallised some of his design principles in the book *Tree Form, Size and Colour* (1987). Sometime president of the Landscape Institute, by this point in his career he had also worked on both the Harlow and Crawley new town projects. (While one can certainly find parallels between Gruffydd's approach at Robinson and the design philosophy of the new towns, it's a bit of a stretch.)

The visitor to Robinson accesses the garden by descending Staircase G, near the chapel, and emerging on a lawn at the base of the dining hall. The deep-sunk garden here takes on the character almost of a moat beneath the looming 'castle' above. It's an oddly pleasing sensation, to be overshadowed in this way. A well-stocked border set against the hall contains interesting shrubs such as *Decaisnea fargesii* (dead man's fingers), *Osmanthus heterophyllus*, *Colutea orientalis* and purple-berried *Callicarpa bodinieri* var. *giraldii* 'Profusion'. As one looks across in the other direction, towards the lake and Thorneycreek, notable trees include an old mulberry, *Sorbus thibetica* 'John Mitchell'

(Tibetan whitebeam) and a pagoda tree (*Sophora japonica*) planted in honour of a former college member. At this scale, the tone of the garden is inevitably dictated by the trees and shrubs. Indeed, there are so many specimen trees now that within 20 years' time Robinson's garden as a whole will probably be regarded as an arboretum.

Gruffydd's chief 'hard-landscape' interventions were the small lake (or large pond) that acts as an overflow for Bin Brook and is an attractive asset in its own right, and a raised path or causeway in Indian York stone which takes the visitor across both water features via bridges and on to the terrace in front of Thorneycreek. This path is the only obvious way in to the gardens and visually links the new college building with the old Arts and Crafts house, so that the two feel almost naturally conjoined, despite their architectural divergences. The pathway literally cuts through the complexity of this site, which was previously covered by no fewer than ten large domestic gardens. It is a simple device but a clever one, since there will have been a temptation to introduce a more complex path system, given the nature of the space and the acreage. But in this case the landscape architect identified the chief qualities of the site, understood its limitations and the challenge of ongoing maintenance, and then came up with something that raises the garden space to a level appropriate to a Cambridge college – without it seeming effortful. Some of the

older colleges believe they can afford to be more complacent, given the splendour and antiquity of their architectural settings. They have tended to sit back and allow changes to happen almost by chance, or simply to evolve as head gardeners and garden committees come and go. But in reality most of them would benefit as much from a professional landscape designer's eye as Robinson has done.

As one reaches the bridge over the lake, on the left is a dragon's claw willow (*Salix babylonica* var. *pekinensis* 'Tortuosa'), one of the best trees in the garden, balanced on the other side by a *Magnolia × soulangeana* and Norway maple. The lake itself has two stepped terraces that serve as practical measures against flooding and also double as lakeside seats for students and visitors. There are enticing views up to Thorneycreek from here, which is offset to the left by an extraordinary weeping wellingtonia (*Sequoiadendron giganteum* 'Pendulum'), its form echoed by the silver arc of Philip de Koning's sculpture *Sailing into the Future* (2008), placed on the lawn. A small yew-hedged rose garden by the house provides a note of formality, with 'Rhapsody in Blue' and *Rosa gallica* 'Versicolor' (rosa mundi) in the corner beds, and yellow 'Freedom' and white 'Margaret Merril' along the edges. The lawns around Thorneycreek are thickly treed, mainly with unremarkable sycamore, yew, prunus and elder, but with the odd specimen at the fringes, including a tulip tree

(*Liriodendron tulipifera*), blue spruce and golden yew. The college's benefactor, Cambridge-born businessman David Robinson, was attracted to this plot because of the existing mature trees, having rejected another site due to the lack of them. The lake itself has proved a haven for wildlife, including water voles and the occasional night-time otter, and birds such as kingfishers and jays. It is an atmospheric place at sunset.

Robinson is certainly not unique among modern Oxbridge colleges in having commandeered a number of domestic gardens into its site, but it has dealt with the issue better than most, by identifying and then enhancing the existing character of each, rather than simply flattening it out for maintenance reasons. The number of specimen trees planted in these gardens in recent years means that over time they will effectively merge with Robinson's arboretum garden.

The easternmost house is 2 Adams Road, formerly the home of Lord and Lady Kaldor. The garden here still has a characterful, established feel, with substantial yew and lime hedges and an orchard set in a wildflower meadow. There is a large old lilac and mulberry,

---

ABOVE A bridge marks the beginning of the raised causeway which bisects the garden: a decisive move of landscape design.

while the steps up to the terrace are underplanted with erigeron. Various commemorative trees have been introduced in recent years, including a *Cornus kousa* and *Cercis siliquastrum*. Part of the garden is now taken up by an outdoor theatre made in memory of set and costume designer Maria Björnson. Next door is No. 4, another attractive Edwardian house, formerly the home of Dr Shillington-Scales, who pioneered X-ray techniques from the garage – which still stands. With the construction of an adjacent seminar building in 2015, this garden was redesigned and replanted by Robinson's previous head gardener, David Brown, and is very successful, with a simple pair of lawns, modern benches and a planting of azaleas and ferns. No. 5 was occupied by a Mr Rottenberg, a passionate collector of bulbs (notably *Narcissus bulbocodium*), many of which remain, and has been augmented by specimen trees including a Persian ironwood (*Parrotia persica*), pedunculate oak and black walnut. No. 6 belonged to Lady Thomson, widow of the Master of Trinity College. When she sold the house to the college she stipulated that her collection of *Cyclamen hederifolium* should be retained at all costs – and it has. There is one more garden around the corner at 3 Sylvester Road, at a house named Sellenger which was occupied until 1970 by Lady Barlow, the last surviving grandchild of Charles Darwin and the botanist for whom the exuberant double aquilegia

'Nora Barlow' is named. It can be seen flowering in the verge at the front of the house, and also at 2 Adams Road.

The garden at Robinson is a collection of romantic secret spaces which belie the college's outwardly austere architectural character. It is not entirely naturalistic in feel: institutional notes are created by the raised pathway, the terraces around the lake and lamp posts which would look more at home on King's Parade. But this is a college that appreciates its gardens, thanks to head gardener Guy Fuller and his team and Dr Stephen Trudgill, an exceptionally engaged garden fellow. One recent intervention is typically energetic: the Grange Road frontage now boasts a mass planting of some 6,000 bulbs. Dr Trudgill says he had the idea while walking through King's College, seeing the bulbs in flower there, and thinking 'Why can't we have this?'

Why not, indeed?

ABOVE As the trees and shrubs in the garden mature, the general character of the garden is developing into that of an arboretum.

SELWYN COLLEGE

I T MAY NOT BE TOP of the agenda for every visitor to Cambridge, but quietly, and in its own way, High Victorian Selwyn is one of the most satisfactorily formed of all the colleges. Its large garden has long been cherished and is currently replete with lively horticulture. What is more, it is extremely well-proportioned in relation to the site, framing good views back towards the college chapel – views modestly reminiscent of the great vista across The Backs to King's College and its chapel. All this from a college that began as the archetypal 'poor relation' – in that it was founded specifically to cater for undergraduates from financially constrained backgrounds – but which has strongly asserted its idealistic personality right from the beginning.

The college was founded and named in honour of George Augustus Selwyn, a churchman for whom the term 'muscular Christianity' might have been invented. Having been appointed Bishop of New Zealand in 1841 at the age of 32, on the recommendation of Gladstone (his greatest admirer), he spent the next 27 years travelling around the remote parts of his bishopric as a missionary. Strength and fitness were prerequisites for such a role, so it was appropriate that Selwyn himself was physically muscular, too: a St John's man, he had rowed at seven in the first Boat Race between Cambridge and Oxford, in 1829. One anecdote from his early life might serve to show the kind of indomitable person he was. While courting Sarah Richardson, his (equally impressive) wife-to-be, Selwyn on one occasion needed to cross the Thames near his home at Eton and found that the ferryman had finished work for the day. The river stood between him and Sarah's home at Bray, but he did not want to punt across and leave the boat on the wrong side of the river for the ferryman to find in the morning. That would have been selfish and immoral. So he punted across, took all his clothes off, punted back again naked, and then dived in the river and swam across it,

LEFT Old Court, with the impressive west end of the chapel as the centrepiece. The ironwork screen and gate leading to the college garden are on the left.

233

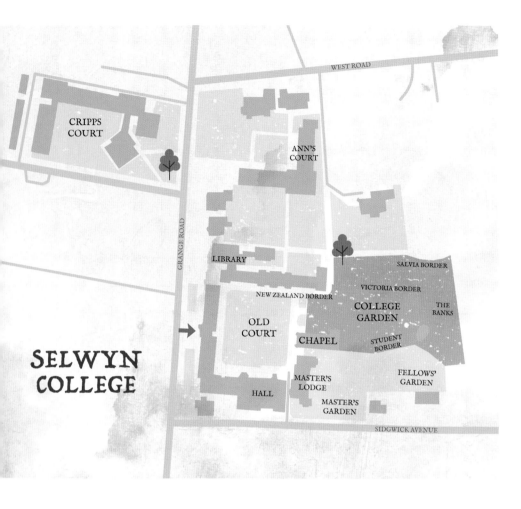

SELWYN COLLEGE

CRIPPS COURT

WEST ROAD

GRANGE ROAD

ANN'S COURT

LIBRARY

SALVIA BORDER

VICTORIA BORDER

NEW ZEALAND BORDER

COLLEGE GARDEN

THE BANKS

OLD COURT

CHAPEL

STUDENT BORDER

FELLOWS' GARDEN

MASTER'S LODGE

HALL

MASTER'S GARDEN

SIDGWICK AVENUE

RIGHT Looking back towards Old Court from the Victorian Border. A pair of huge incense cedars flank the gateway.

dressing again in his still-dry clothes on the other side. The Church of England felt that such resourcefulness and determination were precisely what was required in a faraway place like New Zealand.

In his lifetime Selwyn was an enormously inspirational figure, and the idea of naming a new Anglican college in his honour after his death in 1878 was not controversial. There was a slightly spiky political dimension, however: following the lead shown by Keble College, in Oxford, Selwyn was to be a denominational institution founded expressly to produce Church of England ministers and missionaries. A belief in the power of an education conducted according to Anglican precepts was integral to the project, but it did imply an understated militancy.

Funds were raised and a 2.5-hectare/6-acre site acquired on Grange Road. The architect Sir Arthur Blomfield was engaged in 1881 and within the year the west (entrance) range had been realised in a 17th-century red-brick Tudor-Gothic style. The college's architecture is nothing like as exuberant and distinctive as the polychrome brickwork at Keble – Selwyn's 'sister college' – but Blomfield's design is

serviceable and attractively proportioned, which is by no means always true of 19th-century work in the colleges.

The first 28 students took up residence in 1882, all of them bred up to the ideals of muscular Anglican Christianity (the junior common room at this time passed motions including a ban on horse racing, the refusal of the vote to unmarried women and a suggestion that smoking was 'morally and intellectually beneficial'). Needless to say, there was no garden at the cash-strapped college in its early days – just a 'straggly hedge' along the front, according to one description. But a kind of court was formed when iron railings were placed around a plot of land beyond the entrance lodge. A temporary structure made of white brick was created to house both the dining hall and library, and it became something of a totemic feature. The immediate environs of the college at this time were bare, open and almost treeless, with two substantial villas opposite, on Grange Road, the nascent Newnham College visible in the distance, and fields all around. The land west of Cambridge's centre was traditionally used almost exclusively for grazing animals, while most students would have known it only as the site of the polo field.

The other ranges around what is now Old Court went up during the 1880s, along with the master's lodge in its south-east corner, while work began on the chapel in 1893. As the college started to look less like a building site, attention turned to the land east of Old Court, which Selwyn's second bursar, Alfred Paget Humphry, had earmarked for the college garden. A Trinity man, Humphry did not live in college and when he visited, some of the fellows complained that he had a tendency to 'lord it' over them. Nevertheless he was an effective bursar for 17 years, overseeing the initial layout of the garden with trees and shrubs informally arranged around a central lawn. This remains its basic form today. At an early point a circular walk was added and there was also a fives court made in the 1880s, at the height of the game's popularity. This stands behind the master's garden and is now disused (the only playable fives court in Cambridge is at Magdalene; Emmanuel's is now a squash court).

The whole college including its garden revolves around the chapel, as well it might. Its tall, narrow western end stands to attention directly across from the entrance lodge and creates an irresistible focus for Old Court. Its soaring turrets impart a flavour of the Church Militant which is quite appropriate. The sheer size of Old Court, and its openness, catch something of the vaunting idealism of the place. The lawn here is a perfect square, 53 metres/174 feet by 53 metres/174 feet, and the repeated gables on Blomfield's ranges cast long and moody shadows across the grass. (As elsewhere in Cambridge, the garden team is engaged in a long-term battle with chafer grubs.) This lawn was originally 'sunken', like the main quadrangle at Keble – until the ground was finally levelled in 1961, using a cut-price consignment of soil displaced by Gonville and Caius's new development on West Road. This was controversial even though a level lawn had been Blomfield's original intention. In fact 'sunken' is not quite the right word, because Blomfield's first range was constructed on top of an embankment in order to obtain a perfectly level surface. The ground slopes away to the east, so that when the chapel was constructed it too had to be built on an even more substantial earthen platform. The result was a depression in the middle.

The walls around the court are swathed in *Parthenocissus tricuspidata* (referred to as Virginia creeper in college), which of course makes a great vermillion show in autumn, though it must be carefully controlled; the garden team uses a cherry picker to keep the top storeys and guttering clear of the plant. It is good to see these climber-festooned walls in Cambridge; most colleges got rid of the climbers on their buildings during the great 'ivy purge' of the 1960s and 70s, when eradication was equated with modernisation and building conservation. Selwyn wears its Virginia creeper with pride, like the bushy sideburns of one of its Victorian sons. Old Court is something of a suntrap, favouring subtropical plants such as the orange trumpet-flowered *Eccremocarpus scaber* (Chilean glory flower), *Echium pininana* from the Canary Islands (on the west range) and a silk tree (*Albizia julibrissin*) in the north-west corner, as well as more familiar plants such as *Melianthus major*, hostas, viburnums and agave. In the court's north-east corner, between E and F staircases, a New Zealand border commemorates Selwyn himself.

A fine pair of wrought-iron railings with elegant 18th-century-style gate piers topped by urns spans the distance between the chapel and the north range, marking the point of transition between Old Court and the college garden. The beds in front of the railings are planted up seasonally in colourful fashion, with tulips and then *Salvia splendens*, wallflowers, alyssum and

polyanthus, creating an explosive moment of horticultural temptation. The garden-minded visitor is drawn inexorably towards these heavenly gates and then descends the steps into the 'secret garden' beyond. A pair of huge incense cedars stand sentinel like archangels at the foot of the steps; one is larger than the other because of an unfair advantage: it was planted over a water-pipe that leaked. There is a *Davidia involucrata* on the lawn here and a rose garden of old-fashioned shrub varieties, with a small gloriette. In the 1970s Selwyn became known for its collection of shrub roses, which then numbered around 230, with many other interesting shrubs planted by Alexis Vlasto, a fellow in Slavonic studies who was also the college's garden steward and a considerable botanist and plant-hunter in his own right.

At just under 0.8 hectare/2 acres, Selwyn's is a proper garden with a beginning, a middle and an end, and not just a space between buildings, which is what has happened at some colleges, now that libraries and accommodation blocks have been thrown in. It is mainly laid to lawn and is shaded by mature trees, with a number of discrete garden areas waiting to be explored, all arranged informally so that it feels as if the visitor has just discovered them – a delight. The east end of the chapel towers over the scene, adding a note of drama. The garden's basic

structure, with the master's and fellows' gardens separated off to the south, is the same as it has always been, and the space as a whole has a pleasingly High Victorian atmosphere.

A verdant island outcrop in the middle of the lawn is named the Victorian Border for its subtropical interest but is in fact much more in thrall to the kind of 'jungle-connoisseur' horticulture essayed by the late Christopher Lloyd at Great Dixter, in Sussex, in the 1990s and early 2000s. Formerly a dahlia garden, in 1996 the border was revamped in this fashionable mode. There are several large *Trachycarpus fortunei* palms and yuccas at the heart of the scheme, which becomes denser and richer as late

FAR LEFT The winding path through the centre of the Victorian Border, which has been reimagined as an exuberant subtropical realm, with the strappy leaves of *Musa basjoo* (banana) plants, the orange flowers of cannas and the spikes of palms and cordylines.

ABOVE LEFT The 18th-century-style gate piers and flight of steps down to the college garden lend a dignified note and create a sense of arrival.

ABOVE RIGHT Virginia creeper, flame-red in autumn, clothes Old Court. (Strictly the common name for this species, *Parthenocissus tricuspidata*, is Boston ivy, but the college refers to it as Virginia creeper.)

summer progresses. A *Paulownia tomentosa*, valued for its large and shapely leaves, is treated as a shrub and cut down every year so that it can mingle at the desired height (eye level). Dahlias remain a key note, together with bananas (*Musa basjoo*), cannas, variegated cordylines, *Verbena bonariensis*, miscanthus grasses, three types of amaranthus, rudbeckias ('Prairie Sun' and 'Autumn Colors') and various abutilons, notably *A. pictum* 'Thompsonii'. The dahlias are lifted each autumn and overwintered in a store beneath the chapel. There is bright and rich colour from cosmos, crocosmia, penstemons, kniphofia, cleome, asclepia, as well as dramatic white-flowered *Sparrmannia africana* (African hemp), lemon-scented *Aloysia citrodora* and many different salvias, which were a speciality of former head gardener Paul Gallant. Varieties include *Salvia farinacea* 'Victoria', vivid blue *S. patens* and pinkish *S. coccinea* 'Coral Nymph'. All of this is played off intriguingly against the dark tones of *Sambucus nigra* 'Black Lace', castor oil plant (*Ricinus communis* 'Carmencita') and jet-black ophiopogon grass. It is possible to get enjoyably enveloped in this little paradise if one follows the north-south gravel path running through its centre. A nice touch is that the old tiles used to edge the borders were handmade from clay dug up on the college site; they were found buried during building work in the 1990s.

The north edge of the garden is fringed by a long shrub border which turns into a dahlia border at its eastern end, followed by a run of red and purple salvias next to the 'back' Sidgwick Gate to college. Just south of here is an area known as the Banks, site of a spring display of daffodils, the grass left to grow long in summer for a natural appearance and to encourage insects. There are many other early bulbs to enjoy at Selwyn, including scillas, aconites, snowdrops, fritillaries and chionodoxa, along with spring-flowering shrubs such as *Chimonanthus praecox*, skimmia, *Cornus mas* and *Cytisus* × *praecox*. An old holm oak and horse chestnut in the 'woodland walk' along the east edge of the garden are among the original plantings. A pond nearby provides a valuable wildlife habitat; apparently the garden is 'full of frogs', which is a pleasant idea if you like frogs, as most of us do. Just west of the pond is an early-summer border on a bank, with alstroemerias, lavatera, roses, viburnums, nasturtiums and astrantias.

The south-eastern corner of the garden is home to the small fellows' garden, where a sturdy wooden gate and several 'Private'

ABOVE *Prunus* 'Tai-haku' in flower in the garden along West Bye Lane.

signs help ward off intruders. A tunnel arbour leads to an irregular lawn fringed by chestnuts, with a little summer house and a recently revamped herbaceous border with unpretentious cottage plants such as foxgloves and geraniums, presumably selected to suit the simple and artless tastes of the fellows. The master's garden occupies a much larger area in the south-western corner, its entrance marked by a fine Weymouth pine (*Pinus strobus*) with large, cylindrical cones like green bananas. The 'Beware of the Dog' notice refers to a basset hound. The garden is bordered by yews, hollies, a beech hedge on two sides and a mature horse chestnut, while the terrace to the lodge is attractively planted up with salvias (of course), dahlias and other showy things suitable to this entertaining space. Around the front of the lodge is a shady walkway running south from the chapel to an entrance on Sidgwick Avenue, with ferns, black-stemmed bamboo, *Hydrangea anomala* subsp. *petiolaris* and variegated cornus.

In the 1960s there was a move to construct a second court on top of the college garden, but this was fended off by right-minded fellows. That second court, Cripps Court (1968), was in fact built on the opposite side of Grange Road. This is a forgettable modern development but there are some good trees, including *Phillyrea latifolia* and *Acer platanoides* 'Crimson Sentry'. Ann's Court, a

recent and ongoing development in the northern part of college, is similarly best placed in the 'has potential' category. It has fine specimens of cedar of Lebanon and *Catalpa bignonioides* 'Aurea', and (in the car park) a mature Scotch or wych elm (*Ulmus glabra*), which is less susceptible to disease than others in this genus. The front of college is prefaced by a rather magnificent line of the Japanese cherry *Prunus* 'Umineko', with pure white blossom in spring and orange-red leaves in autumn, while around the corner on West Bye Lane is a display of *Prunus* 'Tai-haku' which is arguably even better. It reminds us how far Selwyn College has come since the days of the 'straggly hedge'.

ABOVE Spring bulbs – snowdrops and aconites – appear at the front of college on Grange Road.

SIDNEY SUSSEX COLLEGE

'NOTHING BUT SINGING, AND FRAGRANCE, and seclusion'. That was George Dyer's verdict in 1814 on the garden at Sidney Sussex College, in his history of the university. Those sentiments still ring true, in that this sometimes overlooked college, hiding in plain sight in the middle of town, has a garden which is perhaps redolent more than any other of the intensely solemn loveliness that we associate with the older colleges of Cambridge. It is remarkable how closely the garden's atmosphere today accords with the romantically sequestered tone captured in 19th-century engravings and aquatints. With gently meandering walks hemmed around with shrubberies and mature trees, it is as if Sidney Sussex has been preserved, somehow, in the quietude of a Victorian dusk.

It is all the more remarkable to be able to plunge into this dreamy milieu straight from the maelstrom that is Sidney Street, now semi-pedestrianised but still one of the city's busiest shopping areas. Standing in one of the three courts, which are all immediately adjacent to the street and in places divided from it only by railings, the visitor is likely to be assailed by the noisy hubbub of lorries reversing, gaggles of summer-school students chattering and the incessant noise of buskers. Yet duck around the back of college into the fellows' garden, and that urban cacophony fades out. For here there are tall trees, birdsong, old-fashioned flowers and lengthening shadows across the lawn. If you are lucky – and you do not have to be all that lucky – you will have the garden completely to yourself.

There is another bonus: it is easy to visit 'Sidney', for there are no charges or restrictions or frowns, as at some other colleges. Visitors are asked to report to the porter's lodge and then they are free to wander wherever they wish, perhaps to enjoy a picnic lunch in the garden. If only all colleges were so hospitable.

Sidney Sussex College was founded in 1596 under the terms of the will of Lady Frances Sidney, Dowager Countess of Sussex, on

LEFT Cloister Court is an atmospheric space dominated by choice shrubs, a horticultural preference that extends across the college.

land formerly belonging to the Franciscan Order, the 'grey friars'. Their friary was established on this city centre site in 1240 and by the 1270s it had expanded to cover almost 2.5 hectares/6 acres, which remains the extent of the college to this day. The friary became an extremely important element of the university – its large chapel was used for the Commencement Ceremony, a significant moment in the university calendar, historically (though now lapsed). It also attracted some of the considerable scholars of the age, possibly including John Duns, known as Duns Scotus, the great 13th-century philosopher-theologian, who was associated with the Franciscans.

The old friary chapel occupied an area now covered by Cloister Court, but all of the Franciscans' buildings were dismantled during the mid 16th century, following the dissolution of the monasteries in 1538. Henry VIII then placed the vacant site in the care of his recent foundation, Trinity College (1546), which duly looked upon the old friary as a sort of builders' yard that could be freely plundered for stone – Trinity's chapel was constructed largely of material taken from the friary. (Therefore one can say that at least the fabric of the monastery was still being employed in the service of God, whatever the doctrinal differences. Duns Scotus himself developed the idea of haecceity, the argument that the particular individual essence of each thing exists and will endure, and in fact used a stone as an exemplar. In this sense it is appropriate to imagine that the house of the grey friars lives on in the stones of Trinity College Chapel.)

By the time the college was founded it was a more or less derelict site – unlike the recently founded Emmanuel College, also occupying the site of a friary, but with intact buildings above ground. The Sidney college site is shown on early city maps by Lyne (1574) and Hamond (1592) as a blank canvas, barring a straight watercourse which dramatically bisects the site north-east to south-west. On the Lyne map it looks like an onrushing river to rival the Wye. But this was not some babbling stream; it was the King's Ditch, a water supply and defensive feature of the town which, over time, became a noxious open sewer – hence the young college's care to gather its gardens on the western side, nearer its two courts and Sidney Street. The approximate line of the ditch can still be traced in the garden today as the path dividing the fellows' lawn from the fellows' garden, about level with the squash court against Jesus Lane.

The college statutes of 1598 specified a garden each for the master and fellows, with all produce in the garden going to the master (a perquisite that was usual in the colleges), barring the fruit from the fellows' orchard, which went to the fellows (also usual practice). It seems the fellows had a head start, as the Hamond map contains one other useful detail: an orchard on the western side of the site, an inheritance from the friary that appears to have formed the basis for the fellows' orchard. In that year, 1598, a gardener named John Simon was employed to lay out these spaces on the college side of the ditch and in 1607 a double line of sycamores was planted along either side of it (the last of these trees died in 1935). The avenue was

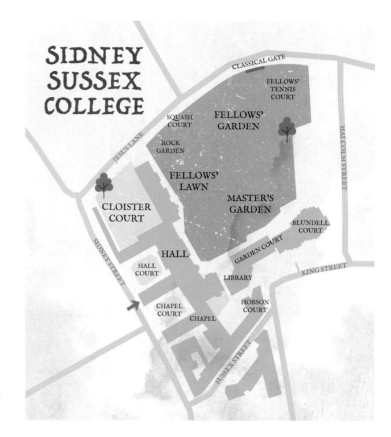

ABOVE The 1690 engraving by David Loggan shows the fellows' bowling green and garden (left) and the avenue of trees planted to adorn the King's Ditch which formerly ran across the college's land.

TOP RIGHT The long border in the fellows' garden is herbaceously classical in feel, with the addition of bold structural notes such as the acanthus looming in the background.

intended to transform the ditch from eyesore to amenity, becoming a 'walk' of sorts on college ground. This was only made possible after John Montagu, the first master, had cleared and widened the stagnant runnel. Thomas Fuller relates in his 1655 history of the university how Montagu 'expended a hundred marks to bring running water into it to the great conveniency of the University'. Fuller was an alumnus of the college so knew it well. He also reports how the friars continued to make their presence known in college, in the vicinity of their dismantled chapel: 'The area of this church is easily visible in Sidney College garden, where the depression and subsidency of their bowling-green east and west, present the dimensions thereof, and I have oft found dead men's bones thereabouts.' Skeletons – or at least bones – continue to be unearthed occasionally in the college grounds; several found in the 1950s are on display in an unregarded glass case in the college library. Bones are indisputably possessed of haecceity: the friars live on…

The 1598 college statutes are distinguished by a series of elaborate horticultural metaphors, as glossed in the official college history: 'The College was to be a *seminarium* for none but the best seed, which was to be watered with the streams of learning, the mature plants being transplanted to the Church, which would be nourished by their fruit.' The statutes also compared the college to a spacious meadow where young men, like bees, might gather honey from all kinds of flowers. 'And anyone who would not conform to the Statutes was to be harried with bites and stings, and driven forth from the hive as a drone.' A bee analogy was likewise deployed in the statutes of Corpus Christi College, Oxford, though not in quite such threatening terms.

We hear little more of the gardens until David Loggan's engraved plan of the college made in the 1680s, which reveals that the fellows were blessed with a far larger garden than the master (not always the case in colleges) and that it included an impressive bowling green adjacent to two compartments, one containing the orchard and the other an ornamental garden edged with lollipop-clipped box trees and centred on a low mound. The covered seat associated with the bowling green – there was always such a seat or alcove – was against the north end of the hall, as shown by a rare and rather wonderful depiction of four college members playing at bowls, which appeared in the university 'Almanack' or calendar for 1809. In the Loggan engraving there is also a two-storied hexagonal summer house glazed all around, which would have been a very smart resort for the fellows. The hall looked east across a simple pair of grass plats enclosed by a wall, while the master's garden next to the lodge to the south was a conventional parterre centred on a roundel, with a single specimen

fir tree. The master also had a small triangular kitchen garden to the south, complete with washing line (a detail Loggan included on other engravings). The line of sycamores flanking the ditch is prominent, and beyond that is the space Loggan labels as 'Sidney Coll Close' on his city map ('close' being a term used for open spaces at former religious houses). Within college this area was more commonly referred to as 'the back piece'; it was here that Oliver Cromwell as a very young man played football – that is, the extremely rough early version of the game – when he was an undergraduate at Sidney Sussex in the 1610s. In later life Cromwell is reported to have commented that 'he could remember the time when he had been more afraid of meeting Wainwright [an older student] at football than of meeting any army since in the field.' Football is not a game one hears of much in Cambridge at this date, but students were allowed to play it within a college's precincts. (Incidentally, Cromwell's head – still gruesomely impaled on its wooden spike – is buried at a secret location within college known only to a handful of senior members; rumour has it that it is in the antechapel.)

At the front of college, the two courts depicted by Loggan occupy the same space as they do today, with Hall Court acting as the front court, in that the old college entrance gate formerly led directly into it. The engraving also shows trees, probably limes, in Chapel Court which is fenced on the west and southern side, with carved finials on posts in the Tudor manner, while behind the fence on the south side by the path is a line of what look like severely pollarded trees. These are mature trees which have been cut down to size, having got too big and casting too much shade; Loggan shows trees in this state in several of his engravings of the colleges, leaving one in the row at full size to illustrate what work had been done. The bustle of Sidney Street at this period is indicated by a coach-and-four, dogs, horses and mules. Sidney Sussex has always been in the middle of things. One other garden detail on the Loggan print is a large walled kitchen garden in the south-east corner of college, beyond the 'back piece'.

The college buildings were remodelled by architect Jeffry Wyatville in the 1830s in an ebullient Elizabethan Gothic manner, characterised by raucous embattlements and crow-stepped gables along the parapets, later attracting a level of disapprobation from observers that does not seem entirely proportionate. For many years Sidney has been called 'the ugliest college in Cambridge'. But it has its moments. The college entrance on Sidney Street was moved at this time to a position between the two existing courts, creating a unique twin entrance which is one of the college's many quiet successes. On arrival the visitor is presented with an equal choice between two complementary courts, an agreeable dilemma to face.

And then of course there is the college garden. The aspect for which it is best known today in the city of Cambridge is the abundant purple wisteria which languidly drapes itself over the front railings of the college almost along its breadth on Sidney Street, a characteristically generous benefaction to town-centre workers, shoppers and tourists. The two old front courts are small, having retained their late-medieval proportions, and there is not much room for horticulture. Chapel Court to the south (right) is mainly climbers – Virginia creeper (pruned four times a year), *Campsis radicans*, *Vitis vinifera* – with a few characterful plants such as nicotiana and ricinus in the narrow beds below. Hall Court to the north (left) features rose 'Madame Grégoire Staechelin' on the south wall and the lemon-scented *Magnolia grandiflora* 'Exmouth' and *Ceanothus* 'Autumnal Blue' on the north wall. The ground-level beds here are also extremely narrow and head gardener Trevor Rees says he plants them 'almost like window boxes' with a varying palette of bright bedding plants such as cosmos, nicotiana, millet, ageratum and amaranthus. Near the entrance lodge is a festive mixture of purple-leaved Japanese basil (*Perilla frutescens*), 'non-stop' pink begonias and glaucous, spreading dichondra.

A passage in the north-east corner of Hall Court leads out to the site of the old bowling green and fellows' garden, now occupied by Cloister Court. The area is enclosed by the college's boundary walls to north and west, and to the east by a red-brick range added in the early 1890s, designed by architect John Loughborough Pearson. This is a large building which rather overpowers the court, seemingly

casting it in shade even when the sun is shining. Its design has been universally decried by commentators, and it is true that the run of cloister along the south and east sides of the court does not cultivate a convincing relationship with the space. But the repeated oriel windows across two storeys, topped with balustrades and faced with stone, alternating with Dutch gables, creates quite an elegant impression overall, as this Gothic Revival architect played with 'Queen Anne' effects at the very end of his long career. The style is perhaps rather intense and elaborate for contemporary tastes.

More importantly, the sensible horticultural decision to make the court's planting predominantly shrubby has resulted in some delightful contrasting effects between the tones of the orange-red brick and the grey stone, and the varying shades of green and olive exhibited by the multifarious species planted here, which must be managed energetically to be kept in check. Many of these shrubs are familiar – mahonias, variegated holly, viburnums, osmanthus, itea, privets – but the often exciting juxtapositions between them are a source of great interest to the horticultural eye; for example, a combination of the purple berries of *Callicarpa bodinieri* 'Profusion' with golden-green *Lonicera* 'Baggesen's Gold'. There are also unusual plants such as the Yeddo hawthorn (*Raphiolepsis umbellata*), with shapely, glossy leaves and delicate white flowers, and near the passage to Hall Court, *Citrus trifoliata* (Japanese bitter orange), with astonishing orange fruits. Of more familiar but serviceable trees there are common and copper beeches, a lime tree, a mulberry, a robinia and a trio of Himalayan birches against the north wall, which form a good foil for the darker leaf colours. The lawn has been used for croquet in the past; in the late 1980s the college team became serious about this endurance (arguably) sport and Sidney players won several championships.

From here it is possible to go 'around the back' of college to discover the fellows' and master's gardens, via a passageway and gate at the north-east corner of Cloister Court. The first feature the visitor encounters is the remains of an ambitious rock garden strung out against the college's north wall. This was constructed in the 1920s by B. T. D. Smith, a horticulturally minded fellow, and was later gardened with the assistance of William T. Stearn of Cambridge Botanic Garden, who grew up locally and did not attend the university but went on to achieve great and deserved eminence as a botanist at the Natural History Museum, founding trustee of the Garden History Society, fellow of the Linnean Society and honorary fellow of the college. A portion of the rock garden was sacrificed in the 1970s for the sake of a new gardeners' bothy and the planting was subsequently simplified to mainly dwarf conifers. It looks a little stranded as a feature today and one has to question why it is retained.

The fellows' garden is nominally divided into two sections, with the fellows' lawn on a raised area nearer to college and the fellows' garden proper extending to the east. It is conjectured that the platform on which the fellows' lawn sits was created by using the

rubble from one of the friary buildings, a hostel for the youngest monks, who would have been in their early teens. In practice the fellows' lawn and garden melds into one, with towering mature beeches, chestnuts and planes adding great character to the scene along with various specimen trees such as *Cercis canadensis*, *Cornus mas* and (on the fellows' lawn) *Prunus × yedoensis*. Arguably the garden is at its best in spiring, with a succession of bulbs carpeting the grass: aconites, snowdrops, crocus, chionodoxa and daffodils. The changing levels of the ground and the effect of the trees imbue it with almost the air of a natural open glade.

There are treats in store in the summer months, too; chiefly a great double border on the south side of the fellows' garden which is backed by a yew hedge. This is well stocked with flowers – delphiniums, heleniums, daylilies, verbascums, centaurea, alchemilla, aquilegia, solidago, penstemon, centaurea, nicotiana – while larger and more architectural plants such as acanthus, cimicifuga and persicaria provide structure. The delphiniums and other tall plants are staked using the cat's cradle method. At one end of the border is the brightly variegated maple *Acer platanoides* 'Drummondii', next to a scarlet oak (*Quercus rubra*). The whole effect is 'classic' or 'traditional' in the best sense. Trevor Rees has been head gardener at Sidney Sussex for ever ('for ever' in this

context meaning: since 1987) and there is a lot to be said for such continuity, as everything in this garden conspires to create its timeless atmosphere. Here as elsewhere, the subtler skills of the garden staff are not always understood or appreciated by college members preoccupied with their own academic business.

The visitor can drift freely around these spaces, which were 'naturalised' from the late 1760s with meandering paths and, in the early 19th century, island beds of shrubs and flowers. Certain old features such as the bowling green were still in existence at this time, when the fellows' garden began to take on its modern character, a process accelerated by the culverting (1812) and then covering over of the King's Ditch, which finally made the garden a seamless whole. Writing in 1814, George Dyer captured something of this transition in the description partially quoted at the start of this chapter:

Here is a good garden, an admirable bowling-green, a beautiful summer-house, at the back of which is a walk, agreeably winding, with variety of trees and shrubs

ABOVE A mulberry tree in Cloister Court, with spring bulbs coming up beneath.

intertwining, and forming, the whole length, a fine canopy over head; with nothing but singing, and fragrance, and seclusion; a delightful summer retreat; the sweetest lover's or poet's walk, perhaps, in the University.

And he was not even an alumnus of the college.

The far north-east corner of the garden is occupied by a 'secret' area hidden behind a thicket of yew and box, which is designated the fellows' tennis lawn, as it is laid out for the game during the summer months. A rather incongruous sight awaits in the corner of this semi-enclosed garden: a large classical stone gate standing on a small platform, apparently wondering what it is doing there (as do we). This gate served as the college's front portal into Hall Court from 1762 until the rearrangements of the 1830s; it has been placed into retirement here at the far end of college, like a racehorse put out to grass. It seems a little ignominious to go from being the very first thing visitors to college see, to the very last. A specimen of *Ginkgo biloba* has been planted next to it; this untidy tree is usually and erroneously thought of as rare. It is the shrub interest that marks out the Sidney garden – these woody plants which have been out of fashion for several decades but are now coming back 'in' again. If 'books do furnish a room', then shrubs furnish a garden,

maintaining their presence through winter as perennial plants do not. Around the tennis lawn one can find numerous euonymus varieties, sarcococca, huge fatsias, berberis, deutzia, osmanthus and pittosporum. The most interesting tree is an *Acer grosseri* var. *hersii*, a 'snakebark' variety with rich red autumn colour.

South of the tennis lawn is a woodland area which effectively screens Blundell Court (1969), one of the less inspiring 20th-century additions constructed all the way along the college's southern edge. Even where notable architects have been employed – in this case Howell Killick Partridge & Amis – Sidney has managed to commission mediocre buildings. There is yet another long and varied shrub border along the east edge of college against Malcolm Street. Part of the wall here is the only element of the 13th-century friary to survive above ground.

The master's garden is cunningly hidden behind a long shrub border and hedge which runs almost the length of the garden, dividing it from the fellows' garden to the north. Its substantial size may well come as a surprise. It is mainly laid to open lawn

ABOVE The Classical Gate was moved to the far end of the fellows' garden, in an enclosed area where a tennis court is made each summer. At one time it was the college's entrance portal.

ABOVE Spring plantings in the distinctively narrow beds of Hall Court.

TOP RIGHT The fellows' garden at Sidney Sussex is all about foliage contrast
in shrubs and trees – here there is ginkgo in the foreground and
a blue conifer beyond.

BOTTOM RIGHT An armillary sphere in Cloister Court, with the buildings
of busy Sidney Street visible beyond.

because it is in regular use for college functions, but the sward is interrupted by its greatest adornment, a fine weeping ash. Near it is a yellow buckeye (*Aesculus flava*) with good autumn colour, said to be the only example in Cambridge. The master's garden was in disarray in early 2019 because of the excavations underway to create a new subterranean kitchen. (Having shown itself incapable of commissioning noteworthy architecture for at least a century, it seems the college has hit upon an ingenious solution for its new buildings: placing them underground.) The plan is that the garden will be returned to its original form in due course.

Generally speaking in this narrative of the college gardens, the habit of listing notable alumni has been avoided; therefore the topic of fictional alumni might reasonably be supposed even less relevant. But perhaps an exception might be made for Sherlock Holmes. In 1934, the detective-story writer Dorothy L. Sayers published a lengthy paper in which she suggested that Holmes most likely attended Sidney Sussex College in the 1870s – she was obliged to speculate because in Conan Doyle's books the sleuth's alma mater is never specified, though there are tantalising hints. In one story Holmes mentions he was at a college which was clearly in either Oxford or Cambridge. Cambridge would have been preferred over Oxford, because of its analytical reputation and relentless seriousness of purpose. Sidney Sussex would certainly have suited Holmes's disposition, for he liked being at the centre of things while remaining invisible (hence the Baker Street apartment when he moved to London). The college's small courts and concomitant lack of exposure to public gaze would have afforded him privacy, while also permitting him to sally forth into any part of the town at a moment's notice. (In another story, Holmes explains that his earliest cases were conducted at university and concerned his college friends and acquaintances.) The college's quiet garden is suited to silent, solitary thought, one steady circuit allowing for the consumption of one pipe's-worth of tobacco. Indeed, the detective's palpable addiction to this stimulant, and his reliance on it for his deductive method, strengthen the case for Sidney Sussex as his choice of college: the famed tobacconists and pipe-makers Bacon Brothers (founded 1805) was situated a stone's throw away, on St Mary's Street. (Oxford did not have a tobacconist to compete.) Trinity was equidistant to the shop, but that college, with its open courts and extrovert nature, would not have suited a man of retiring disposition; neither would its high fees, for Holmes was not wealthy, and only found Watson because he was compelled to recruit a flatmate. 'Sidney' was ever a modest and moderate place which delighted in being a backwater, and small enough to be free of public-school coteries. Most likely it would have attracted Holmes as a place where one's contemporaries were less likely to exercise their critical judgment on a man's habits and inclinations, whether that be playing the violin in the early hours, examining the mud on the senior tutor's shoes, or hanging off Clare Bridge to ponder the mystery of its partial ball.

ST JOHN'S
COLLEGE

S T JOHN'S EXPANDS INTO THE Backs like no other college. It begins with a triple whammy of three old red-brick courts, all aligned on the same straight axis. There is little by way horticultural interest, and some feeling of constraint. Then it tantalises with snapshot views across pasture to the Backs through the stone windows of a covered bridge across the Cam – the Bridge of Sighs, no less. The visitor is then plunged for a moment into the cloistral gloom of the arcade which forms the southern side of New Court, where larger arched windows offer up yet more of the perfect green plain beyond, as well as glimpses of the flowers and foliage that are growing up beneath the windows on the other side. Finally, halfway down this arcade, a grand doorway releases the visitor into the green Elysian field which is St John's Meadow, and the most panoramic view of the Backs in Cambridge. There is also the considerable bonus of magnificent mixed herbaceous borders that span the entire south facade of New Court, hidden from view until this moment. We have travelled at speed from a world of trammelled brickwork into open skies and green fields. In the blink of an eye, *urbe* has become *rus*.

The processional scenography of St John's is a masterpiece of landscape engineering which is of course almost entirely accidental, since colleges have never given much thought to such matters. Nevertheless members of St John's are fortunate enough to be able to experience it every single day. Many of them, indeed, have even more to enjoy on their quotidian round, for if they are lodged in the Cripps Building, a zigzagging series of modernist blocks which carries the college across the Bin Brook in the north-west portion of the college's land, they will also experience the pleasure of sudden framed views across water and pasture towards the surrounding mature trees which lend such character to the place. And all that is without even crossing another bridge at the far side of the Meadow

LEFT The Bridge of Sighs, constructed in 1831 to link college with New Court, is framed here by a yew and a common oak.

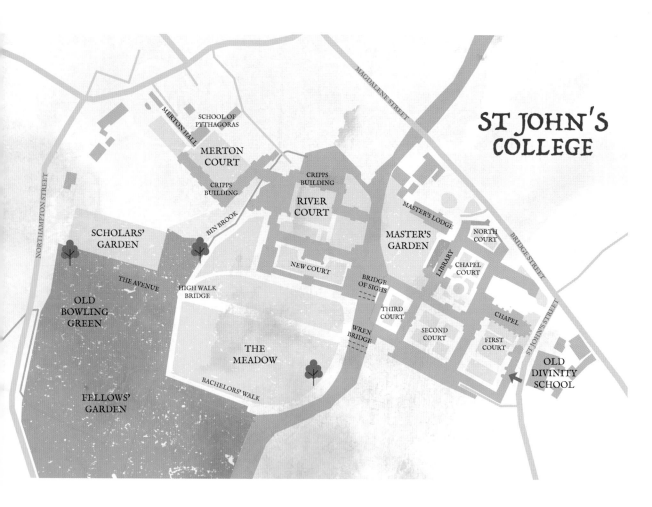

RIGHT Choristers making their way across the Meadow, with New Court beyond. A lone holm oak stands in the middle of the space.

OVERLEAF The long border in front of New Court is arranged symmetrically so that plants such as kniphofia, achillea, perovskia, echinops and sedum are repeated.

to discover the old fellows' garden, traditionally known as the Wilderness, and the 'secret' mid-20th-century Scholars' Garden.

Nature is never far removed from St John's and two animal symbols, one mythic and one real, dominate the college's iconography. The mythical symbol is the yale, a spotted, deer-like animal with rotating horns. A pair of these strange beasts is incorporated into the decoration of the college's spectacular gatehouse, where they rear up against a complex floral background consisting mainly of daisies (in a motif which later inspired William Morris). The yale is the symbol of Margaret Beaufort, founder of this college (and of Christ's College, and with a hand in Jesus College, too), that great lady who was mother of Henry VII and is credited with reconciling the houses of York and Lancaster, and thereby the formation of the Tudor dynasty. The daisy was also associated with Margaret, one common name for the flower being herb Margaret; it is also known as a marguerite. The other – and more important – symbol is the eagle, linked with St John the Evangelist, in whose honour the original monastic foundation on this site was founded. It is not clear precisely why St John and the eagle are symbolically connected; the proposition is that the eagle's soaring flight is akin to the lofty nature of St John's gospel, which contains some of the most visionary passages in the New Testament.

The Hospital of St John the Evangelist was founded in around 1200, by a local gentleman named Henry Frost, on the site of the present college's First Court (little trace of the original buildings remains). The word 'hospital' here applies in the modern sense, for this was an institution where the monastic brethren were engaged in healing the sick and aiding the infirm. The monks of the Hospital pursued their vocation over the ensuing centuries until by the late 15th century the buildings were in a state of some decay and the number of brethren much reduced. The state of the hospital had not improved by the first decade of the 16th century, and the ecclesiastical and university authorities concluded that something had to be done. It was John Fisher, Bishop of Rochester (and President of Queens' College from 1505–08), who took the initiative. The story goes that he raised the idea of a new college on this site during a boat trip down the Thames to Greenwich with 'my lady the king's mother' – that is, Margaret Beaufort. She pledged her support after due consideration and in 1509 the decision was made to dissolve St John's House and expediently to found the College of St John the Evangelist. There was a family interest, too: Margaret's stepson James Stanley was at that time Bishop of Ely, with responsibility for the Hospital; the dilapidated old hospital would have been his problem, as well.

At this point there were, besides the master, only three brethren in residence and they were all knights of the realm; one suspects that there was not much healing of the sick going on. The brethren were essentially paid off – promised eight marks a year for life – if they agreed to the disbandment and went quietly. Which they duly did. Margaret died a few months after making her pledge to St John's in 1509 but by then the wheels were in motion. The new college was founded two years later.

Building work began immediately and by 1520 First Court was completed, with the old hospital chapel forming its northern side (strictly the north-eastern side, but compass-point directions have been simplified here). This was demolished three centuries later to make way for Sir George Gilbert Scott's replacement, slightly farther to the north – the foundations of the original chapel are still picked out as flagstones in the grass of the court. The old infirmary building, referred to in college at the time as the Labyrinth, was initially retained but was later used as a store and stable before it too was demolished (there is not much architectural sentimentality about the Oxbridge colleges). The master's lodgings were situated in the north-west corner of the court, above the college's combination rooms, and were reached via a staircase in the Master's Tower, entered on the external (west) side of the court. The whole area west

from here down to the Cam was designated as the master's garden, overlooked by windows in the master's lodge at the top of that romantic tower. From John Hamond's city map of 1592 it appears the northern part of this garden was reserved as a tree plantation, possibly an orchard. It is probable that the garden was open to all members of college; there is a record of a tennis court being added in 1574. It seems this was removed during the construction of Second Court, completed in 1602, because a new open tennis court was built on the west side of the river the following year at a cost of £79; it is shown on the 1690 Loggan engraving of the college. (The college's copy of Loggan's *Cantabrigia Illustrata* was bought direct from the author – a payment of £10 15s was made to 'Mr Logan for his Booke of ye Cutts of ye Colleges in Cambridge'.)

Following the construction of Second Court on the site of the old master's garden, and continuing encroachment west towards the Backs, more use began to be made of this portion of the college's lands as a pleasure garden. A gallery building with windows overhanging the east side of the river had been constructed by this time; its 'decayed glasse' was being repaired in 1604, which indicates it had been in existence for several years already. (Or could it have been a rather superior privy, emptying into the river?) Another building, known as Rath (or Rats) Hall was built against

the river in the late 16th century to provide six more chambers. These appurtenances were swept away in 1669 when Third Court was added, with the old college library as its north side, but before then this area remained largely open in aspect.

In addition the early college owned a portion of land on the other side of the river, the northern part of which was – and still is – boggy and low-lying and the site of a number of fish ponds, a remnant of the monastic occupation of the site (this land west of the Cam had been given to the Hospital by Henry VI in 1448). Now the site of the Cripps Building, it was traditionally known as 'the pond yards' or, in the 17th century, as 'the fishponde close'. Such ponds were valuable stores of freshwater fish such as carp, perch and pickerel (young pike), necessary for the table on Fridays and other days designated as meatless in the Christian calendar. No fewer than seventeen ponds are shown in St John's on Loggan's city map of 1688, and that is not even counting a further six fish ponds and a dovecote the college owned on another piece of land across town, next to Jesus College.

Numerous watercourses and ditches flowed across the St John's site, in addition to the Cam, the most notable being the Bin Brook, which runs north-east through woodland and pasture until it joins the Cam at the college's northern boundary with Magdalene land,

and St John's Ditch, which at that time ran east from Bin Brook into the river through the middle of the Meadow, where New Court now stands.

The original letters patent of 1448 state the existence of a garden associated with the Hospital in the area east of the ponds, against the river. On Hamond's map of 1592 this garden is shown as a roughly square, open space bounded by Bin Brook to the north and a line of trees on its other three sides. The large area to the south of here – now the site of St John's Meadow in front of New Court – is marked on the map as 'St John's Walkes', indicating that at this early date this part of the college's land was reserved principally for leisure purposes, though the pasture would also have been used as grazing for horses (the stable was adjacent) and a valuable source of hay. A triple line of trees formed an avenue running west-east down its centre, while another parallel avenue divided this area of walks from the pond yards and square garden to the north. Lines of trees along the riverbank and along the banks of St John's Ditch to the south and Bin Brook to the west completed the tree-lined perimeter, a long loop which came to be known as Bachelors'

<small>ABOVE The view through New Court's central gateway towards Trinity College.</small>

Walk (today that name refers only to the line of horse chestnuts along the southern side).

The circumambulation of this roughly rectangular space would have made it the purest expression in either Oxford or Cambridge of college walks realised as an arboreal version of the quadrangle, court or cloister. It is notable that at this time the main central avenue was not yet aligned on the axis of the wooden bridge across the Cam (where the Wren or Kitchen Bridge is today) which then connected the Meadow with college. Members of St John's would cross this bridge and then turn left or right and continue their walk under the shade of the avenues that crossed and surrounded the space. Long axial views were not the point: the pleasure came from the sensation of walking under files of trees in leaf and flower. St John's Walks were finally cleared away during the construction of New Court from 1826, the area evolving thereafter into the open grassy Meadow we know today.

The early to mid 17th century was a time of considerable arboricultural ambition at St John's. In 1610 the college acquired yet more land west of the Walks, beyond Bin Brook, where an enclosed bowling green was made (in the northernmost section of what is the fellows' garden or Wilderness today). The bowling green is first mentioned in 1625, when it was planted around with

elm and sycamore. Ten years later a willow hedge was added to its western side, presumably to increase privacy, since bowling greens were places where the young men of the colleges could relax in private. The chunk of land south of the bowling green – which over time was developed into the Wilderness – was at this time leased from Corpus Christi College, though St John's did finally buy it outright in 1658. We can get a snapshot of Cambridge life in the early 17th century from a reference in the university archives to one Andrew Goodwin, who in 1619 was involved in a dispute with a pewterer over the non-payment of £5; the vice chancellor of the university stepped in to inform the justices that Goodwin had been a gardener at St John's for 20 years, illustrative of the solidity of the position in college life by this date.

A word on the term 'Wilderness'. To modern ears this sounds like a naturalistic if not wild-looking area, but it had a different meaning in the 17th and 18th centuries. That meaning changed over time and place but in this instance it referred to an area of straight, tree-lined gravel walkways, bordered by clipped hedges and interspersed with parcels of trees underplanted with fragrant shrubs such as roses, lilac and honeysuckle. It would have been a

ABOVE The rear (north) elevation of New Court is covered with Boston ivy.

much more formal layout than the term Wilderness would imply to us today – though it is worth remembering that on the ground such places would have felt more natural than they appear on plan. In larger Wildernesses (such as the one at Ham House in London), the interstitial areas of woodland might be penetrated by serpentine walks and decorated with statuary, urns or pools. But the St John's Wilderness was it seems too modest to stretch to such accoutrements – though as we shall find, fellows and visiting ladies and gentlemen were soon provided with covered seats for rest, rumination and possibly romance.

The college accounts for this period contain several references to tree planting in the 'new walks' or the 'upper walkes' and various alterations to the bowling green, including the construction of a series of arbours around it. In 1647 a man called Bright was paid £1 5s 3d for '8 Dayes worke for weeding the walkes and cutting the hedges about the bowling green', a further fee of 13s 11d for 'gravelling the walkes in the bowling close', and again later in the year for cutting the hedges in 'the new-walks'. The following year he is paid for 'hedging in the New Walks', while a molecatcher is engaged to work in the bowling green area. To begin with he is paid per mole (eight in 1648) but later, in the 1660s, this has become a more cost-effective rate of 8 shillings per year. A large bill of £6 1s

6d is paid in 1649 to a carpenter 'for three new seates set up in the New Walks' – these would probably have been large covered seats in the wooded area (or 'close', or indeed Wilderness) around the bowling green. In the same year there is a bill paid to one Clovis (sometimes Clove, or Cloves), for 'cutting the trees and making up the fences in the bowling close'.

It is clear that the bowling green demanded considerable care and expenditure at this time, and that the walks beneath the maturing avenue trees in the Wilderness were further defined by the addition of straight clipped hedges. In 1663 Clove 'and his men' were paid for about a month's work in all for their 'work in the walkes', which included cutting the hedges. Two years later Clove is paid specifically for, 'weeding the walkes and watring the young trees'. There is also a gang of ditchers at this time led by one Grubb. The year 1685 saw a major development, as noted in the college accounts: 'To Solomon Bones for 600 Poles to make ye Long Arbour in ye Inward Walks…£4. 1. 0'. The college clerk describes this as an arbour but with 600 poles it must have been a long covered walkway of some kind. Six years later there are further references to it being

ABOVE The master's garden viewed from River Court. The steps down to the private water gate can be seen.

raised up with bricks, presumably to create an assuredly dry walk for the fellows and their guests.

So, we have a picture of St John's in the mid-to-late 17th century with a cosseted and cherished bowling green, and the excitement of new tree-lined avenues, set in a more private, sequestered area of Wilderness. By the 1690s the visiting Celia Fiennes could opine: 'St Johns College Garden is very pleasant for the fine walks both Close Shady walks and open Rows of trees and quickset hedges. There is a pretty bowling green with Cut arbours in the hedges.' It is interesting to note how this visitor appreciated the differing aesthetic qualities of the walks in the Wilderness ('open rows of trees and quickset hedges') and in St John's Walks proper ('close shady walks'). The basic character of St John's Walks had not altered by the time Edmund Carter was writing his history of the university in the 1750s, when he noted the 'Courts, Bridge, long and spacious Shady-Walks, Groves, Canals, Bowling-Green, &c'.

It was at around the time of Celia Fiennes' visit to St John's that the college consulted Christopher Wren about rebuilding its bridge over the Cam. His advice, and that of his then assistant, Nicholas Hawksmoor, was to construct a new bridge in the centre of the west range of the recently built Third Court (where the Bridge of Sighs is today) to create an axis from the front gate through three courts to

the river, thus establishing a vista 'thro' ye body of ye whole fabrick', as Hawksmoor put it. This idea is clearly expressed on Hawksmoor's sketch plan for reorganising the centre of Cambridge. He criticised the existing arrangement as being

> without any regard of ye front or sides of ye Colledge so very ungracefull and inconvenient that seems rather by chance to belong to yr Coll: than by any intention: tis true it leads to a walk of trees which is an Avenue leading to nothing and would be no worse if ye Bridge was elsewhere, than in the present scituation which sufficiently condemns itselfe without any further evidence as being irregular unseemly and barbarous unfitt to be contiguous to so noble a house in a place where so many strangers come.

To this modernising architectural tyro, the place seemed intolerably old-fashioned – but he was ignored.

The new bridge (1709) was eventually built approximately (but not exactly) to Wren's designs but in precisely its original, off-centre

ABOVE Massive clipped yews create a sense of scale on the terrace in the master's garden.

position. Hawksmoor wrote a rather elegant if slightly exasperated letter to the college: 'Sir I can say no more but that my thoughts are still ye same as at first, but however I must confess your owne affairs are best known to yourselves, and must therefore submit ye execution of them to your owne wisdome.' One hundred and twenty years later college 'wisdome' finally caught up with Wren and Hawksmoor, and the Bridge of Sighs (1831) was constructed to join New Court with Third Court and the rest of the college.

There is a persistent story about Lancelot 'Capability' Brown designing (in fact redesigning) the Wilderness, and although there is no firm evidence, it does seem likely he had a hand in its 'naturalisation'. He was consulted by a modernising St John's master in 1772 and was later paid, in a manner befitting a gentleman, with a piece of plate worth £50 for his 'services to improving the walks'. One account suggests that Brown's initial estimate for the work, in February 1773, was £800 and that the master immediately put up £500 himself. The remaining £300 was perhaps too much for the fellows to bear; they were already in open rebellion over the master's plan to 'Georgianise' First Court to the plans of James Essex (only the south range was completed, in a rather bland neoclassical style). Either way, the suggestion that Brown softened the residual formality of the Wilderness seems credible. It had grown up to such an extent by this date that it was likened to a cathedral, complete with a 'nave' of tall trees. The bowling green was an outmoded feature by this time and it is easy to imagine Brown suggesting it be reconfigured as a smooth lawn in a glade, much as it is today. There is also a reference in 1772 to an order that 'the bank be repaired under the direction of Mr Brown', which suggests that here, as elsewhere, he was consulted as much for his expertise as a water engineer as for his aesthetic eye. This mention is also evidence that he did actually work on the site. The fact the college was concerned about the state of its gardens at around this time is further evinced by a reference to Charles Miller – son of Philip Miller, head gardener at the Physic Garden, Chelsea – being paid in 1765 'two guineas for his advice and plans for the improvements for the gardens'.

It was only several years after this experience at St John's that Brown was approached by the Duke of Grafton, the chancellor of the university, about coming up with a new plan for the Backs – the 'Alterations' of 1779 which, famously, never materialised either. Brown was paid for this work with yet another piece of silver.

By around 1800 the original trees in the Meadow and Wilderness had grown venerable indeed. The forest-like nature of the college's groves at this period is perhaps reflected by the fact that in 1777 a hunt allegedly pursued a stag right into the precincts of the college, eventually killing it on the steps of Staircase G. No less a poetic personage than William Wordsworth immortalised the prevailing bucolic scene in a stanza in *The Prelude* summarising his time at St John's, focusing on a favourite ash tree overhanging Bin Brook.

All winter long, whenever free to choose,
Did I by night frequent the College grove
And tributary walks; the last, and oft
The only one, who had been lingering there
Through hours of silence, till the porter's bell,
A punctual follower on the stroke of nine,
Rang with its blunt unceremonious voice;
Inexorable summons! Lofty elms,
Inviting shades of opportune recess,
Bestowed composure on a neighbourhood
Unpeaceful in itself. A single tree
With sinuous trunk, boughs exquisitely wreathed,
Grew there; an ash which Winter for himself
Decked out with pride, and with outlandish grace:
Up from the ground, and almost to the top,
The trunk and every master branch were green
With clustering ivy, and the lightsome twigs
And outer spray profusely tipped with seeds
That hung in yellow tassels, while the air
Stirred them, not voiceless. Often have I stood
Foot-bound uplooking at this lovely tree
Beneath a frosty moon. The hemisphere
Of magic fiction, verse of mine perchance
May never tread; but scarcely Spenser's self
Could have more tranquil visions in his youth,
Or could more bright appearances create
Of human forms with superhuman powers,
Than I beheld, loitering on calm clear nights
Alone, beneath this fairy work of earth.

In 1810 Wordsworth's sister Dorothy visited St John's, writing home: 'I was charmed with the walks, found out William's ashtree.' This favoured tree did not have much longer on this earth, however, since it was part of an old avenue felled in 1825 to make way for New Court. This decisive extension to the college – the largest building in the university at the time – was built over part of the old pond yards to a controversial neo-Gothic design and faced not in red brick, as had originally been planned, but in vibrant grey-white Ketton stone on three of its four melodramatic elevations (giving it a slightly Disneyesque appearance, to some tastes). The main, 'cloister' elevation faces south, towards Trinity, not west – a radical change of orientation not just for St John's but for the whole of the Backs. But it makes sense given the court's relationship with the Meadow, which was at this time largely cleared of trees so it became a prefacing greensward for the new building.

The fourteen bays and central arch of the cloister facade form the backdrop to what is perhaps the most impressive long border in Cambridge, recently redesigned and replanted by head gardener Adam Magee. The two 30-metre/100-foot sections on either side of the central gateway are planted as mirror images of each other, and are defined by spectacular splashes of orange kniphofia, yellow achillea, purple salvia, fresh green euphorbia, white phlox, purple cranesbill geraniums, yellow coreopsis and rudbeckia, asters, daylilies, echinops, potentillas and geums. Sculptural sedums bolster the border from below while the tall *Thalictrum aquilegiifolium* 'Thundercloud' forms a bushy backdrop. There are pomegranates as bookends and, at the far western end of the range, a fine old fruiting grapevine. The rationale? Mr Magee says he wants the border to be highly visible from Trinity College. It certainly succeeds in this regard.

The Meadow today no longer has the character of the old St John's Walks, with long lines of uniform trees, but now includes numerous specimens arrayed informally which add interest at different times of year. There is the elegant Mongolian lime (*Tilia mongolica*) next to the Wren Bridge (topped by recently restored yales), and then, in order southwards along the riverbank, the notable trees are a London plane, an oak, a willow weeping into the Cam, the so-called Wordsworth Oak and another weeping willow. West of New Court towards Bin Brook is a wellingtonia and then the massive weeping Babington Yew (*Taxus baccata* 'Dovastoniana'), named after the professor of botany who planted it in 1843.

The Meadow is bisected by an east-west thoroughfare which consists of an upper path and a narrower footway, lower down. There is a story that the lower path was designated for servants but this is unlikely; a mounting block at one end indicates that one is for riders and one for walkers. The spacious Meadow has been a venue for various sports including croquet, tennis and archery, with frisbee a recent popular addition.

The visitor is invited to progress over the iron High Walk Bridge across Bin Brook into a delightfully sequestered avenue of limes, known as the Avenue or formerly as the High Walk, flanked by panels of grass and with a yew hedge below. It leads up to the college's back entrance on Queen's Road. Several years ago the college made the decision to remove every other lime along the Avenue, which has enabled the trees to grow into shapely forms with good leaf. I was reminded in college that Trinity had decided against doing this in their avenue, and that the results are clear to see.

The fellows' garden, to the south, is entered directly from the Avenue, though many visitors will not even realise it is there. It is still a heavily treed area with a naturalistic feel – mainly horse chestnuts, oaks and yews, with a few specimens such as the walnut in one corner. Ditches criss-cross the woodland and cow parsley is allowed to run rampant in summer, while a young avenue of oaks with a yew hedge planted between is a nod to the formality of the old Wilderness. This can be a boggy area and there is a gravelled path encircling the whole, raised up in places. The focus, however, remains an open area of lawn at the northern end, formerly the old bowling green, now used for croquet. The first summer house was recorded here in 1695 and it has been replaced several times; the current incarnation is a charming lead-roofed, open pavilion festooned with the climbing rose 'Eden Rose '88' and a pair of hanging baskets. A long border along the northern side is 'due a revamp' (the garden team has been reduced from eleven to seven in a decade).

The Wilderness is most famous for its spring display of bulbs – snowdrops, aconites, swathes of Lenten daffodils, bluebells, scillas,

chionodoxas, and above all the martagon lily. The collection of martagons at St John's is traditionally considered the largest in Europe, though now the head gardener is honourable enough to call it the 'joint largest', because he has been told that a garden in Sweden vies with it. Another plant to look out for in the Wilderness, growing against the back wall, is the rare great tower mustard (*Arabis turrita*) an impressive and attractive plant. The Wilderness also boasts specimens of a rare epimedium, *E. × cantabrigiense*, a cross between *E. alpinum* and *E. pubigerum* which arose after the two species were planted next to each other here during the Second World War. It has elegant, nodding green and purple-red flowers.

Such matters as rare plants are noticed by the college's extremely active gardens committee, which conducts its meetings on foot as it perambulates the grounds (a good idea). For a period in the 1970s its minutes were recorded in verse form, which may not have been such a good idea. At times the committee's diligence has perhaps spilled over into over-prescription; the minutes of one meeting in 1937 include the following resolution: 'iii) to change the grouping

---

BELOW The arcade within New Court, where the play of shadows on grass precludes the need for plants.

of the delphiniums in the above border'. Such overbearing 'advice' seems all the more misplaced when one considers that at that time the college's head gardener was Ralph Thoday, perhaps the most celebrated person ever to have held such a post in Oxford or Cambridge. Thoday worked here from 1928 until 1973 and won numerous gold medals at the Chelsea Flower Show, notably for apples grown in the college orchards. He was also the recipient of the Victoria Medal of Honour, the highest accolade bestowed by the Royal Horticultural Society, an award held in considerably higher regard in the gardening world than OBEs, knighthoods, peerages, Nobel prizes – even professorships.

On the northern side of the lime avenue is the Scholars' Garden, formerly the college orchard where Mr Thoday's apples were grown, but which was grubbed up in line with some consultancy work undertaken by town planner Thomas Sharp in 1951–52. The resulting Scholars' Garden is a rectangular space bounded and bisected by chunky yew hedges with a perimeter path and mixed borders. The eastern side is more open, and laid to lawn (it was originally conceived as a bowling green), while the western end is planted with specimen trees and shrubs. There is a small summer house flanked by rose bushes at the eastern end, designed by David Wyn Roberts. The garden designer Sylvia Crowe is credited with this garden but it feels rather pedestrian for her style, and one suspects Thomas Sharp had a greater influence over it, while the original planting was the work of Cheal's Nursery of Crawley. Today the space appears a little tired and overcrowded, with gnarly fruit trees dotted around the lawn and overgrown shrub borders. One of the apple trees in here, 'Scrumptious', was donated by the Worshipful Company of Fruiterers.

From here the visitor can thread back northwards through pasture and woodland towards the dream of modernity that is the Cripps Building, designed by Powell & Moya in the mid 1960s and faced with Portland stone. This firm designed a number of distinguished modern buildings in both Oxford and Cambridge in the 1960s, of which the Cripps Building is perhaps the most successful in terms of its landscape component. The architecture is unusually generous towards its landscape setting in that it seems to respond sensitively towards the site, by means of its raised-up feel and the way that views out to pasture, stream and woodland are pleasingly framed all the way along the tranquil, slightly other-worldly promenade the linked buildings describe.

As in medieval times, a waterlogged feel persists in this part of the college, where the pristine terraces of the Cripps development appear somehow to carry us across a boggy realm where water never seems far away. A spinney of ash and sycamore has been left to

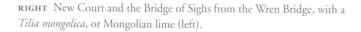
RIGHT New Court and the Bridge of Sighs from the Wren Bridge, with a *Tilia mongolica*, or Mongolian lime (left).

go pleasingly wild and would be a good place to keep rootling pigs. Indeed in the post-war period the college set up a hoggery in its kitchen garden, to offset the depredations of rationing, and a college Pig Club was formed. The hoggery was kept until 1954.

The college's interest in matters porcine may be in part a way of 'owning' and therefore taming an ancient nickname: Johnians have been known as 'pigs' by their collegiate neighbours since the 17th century at least, a slander repeated by Trinity fellow Joseph Romilly in his diary in 1843. The club itself was not disbanded with the end of rationing and election to its membership continues to be highly prized. The Pig Club has its own anthem, obviously, and holds feasts at which maupygernons (gaily coloured medieval meatballs) are consumed.

It is a grand and pleasing irony that the sight that greets the visitor who has traversed the modernist Cripps Building in its entirety, is 'the oldest house in Cambridgeshire', the evocatively named School of Pythagoras. This barn-like structure dating from around 1200 was only purchased by the college (from Merton College, Oxford) in 1959 and no one knows the derivation of its curious name, which came into use in the late 17th century. The best guess (by the college archivist) is that it was coined in an effort to exaggerate the antiquity of the college by implying that it was once a medieval mathematical school, or 'a society of gentlemen…living in a Pythagorean manner', as one writer speculated in 1730. It was a theatre from 1963 to 2011, at which point it was converted into the college archive. Adjacent is Merton Hall, a 16th-century building now used as accommodation.

There are some interesting garden areas associated with these buildings, including the remnants of the pre-1959 domestic garden of Merton Hall, with a pond and glasshouse, gardened in a naturalistic manner since 2006, and a bold new bed of salvias planted in 2016. Behind Merton Hall is a modern space with a rectangle of lawn, a copper beech and a birch, and plantings of clerodendron, osmanthus, photinias, cotinus and pomegranate. In the grass around and about the Cripps Building are two new wooden benches designed by Ian Heseltine, who was commissioned by the head gardener.

Bin Brook flows beneath Cripps at this point, re-emerging to the north as a punt station. South of here is River Court, with the massive, turreted but unremarkable brick 'back side' of New Court, covered in Boston ivy. Four dawn redwoods (*Metasequoia glyptostroboides*) flank its entrance, along with planted tubs. The best element of this large but difficult space, which feels like a backstage area, is a grassy slope at the eastern end with a view down to the Cam and across to the master's garden on the other side, with its magnificent plane tree, horse chestnut beyond and a young specimen of *Prunus* 'Shirofugen' on the lawn. Tulips and daffodils grow on the River Court bank in spring, though it is not a peaceful spot much of the time thanks to the constant traffic of commercial punts, the clank of metal poles and the running commentaries of the guides echoing around the brick river walls, making it into a veritable River of Babel. Near the point where the master's garden meets Third Court, the master's water gate and steps can be seen; the head gardener's daughter is on the garden staff, and it was from here that she and her husband 'went away' by boat on the occasion of their wedding in college.

Returning back over either the Bridge of Sighs (for college members) or the Wren Bridge (for visitors), the three 'brick courts' at St John's are not notable for their horticultural elements, which are hardly necessary anyway. One nice moment occurs in Third Court, where there is a surprise explosion of planting (pink and white Japanese anemones in high and late summer, foxgloves earlier on) against the eastern range, which one only notices on turning around, or when approaching from the Bridge of Sighs. Second Court has ferns to offset the salubrious severity of the architecture and its four pristine panels of grass. First Court is dominated by the huge bays and marvellous stained-glass windows of Scott's chapel, completed in 1869. It is possible that Scott's design was inspired by the choir of York Minster, whose fenestration it strikingly resembles. If so, this would be in homage to college founder Margaret of Beaufort, who is credited with uniting the Houses of York and Lancaster. In 2011 the path around First Court was extended so that it now encircles the space.

The tall buildings in St John's College, with their multiple turrets, gatehouses and embattlements, have proved irresistible to generations of amateur mountaineers in Cambridge. There was even a *Roof-Climber's Guide to St John's* published in 1921 which includes hard-won advice about conquering various 'peaks' in the college, including the tower of the main gate, where we are told: 'The foot-hold is precarious, but it enables a long stretch of the arm to be made up to the point where the pipe bends round a sloping ledge.' That sort of thing.

RIGHT Snowdrops in the grass near the modernist Cripps Building.

BOTTOM RIGHT Looking east back to college down the lime avenue, where every other tree was removed to allow for free growth.

To the north of Second Court lies Chapel Court, begun in 1885 and completed in 1942 along with the triangular North Court, just beyond, with railings on to Bridge Street. The architecture here is eminently forgettable, with the exception of the new college library on the west side of Chapel Court. Designed in a red-brick postmodernist manner by Edward Cullinan and completed in 1994, it picks up on many historic visual details within college. Chapel Court itself is a rather odd space, containing a sort of sunken paved amphitheatre with a lone bay tree in a pot in the centre, and a line of four sorbus trees in the grass plats beyond. There is a small, deep flower bed in front of the library which is planted up in a Victorian subtropical manner with orange dahlias, salvia, tagetes and cannas at the back, giving an impression of bands of colour. North Court is a space that only true exhibitionists would consider dawdling in, for it squarely faces the tourist maelstrom of Cambridge. There are some unmemorable shrub borders and two weeping cherries within the court itself, as well as a pair of good fastigiate 'Dawyck' beeches looking on to Bridge Street.

There is one more garden at St John's College worthy of note: the master's garden, arguably the finest in Cambridge. Closed to touristic visitors, this tranquil and immaculate garden occupies an area between Chapel Court and the river, a rectangle south of the master's lodge that was constructed to Sir George Gilbert Scott's designs in 1863–65. This is a remarkable building in its own right, and was the first example of a free-standing master's lodge in Oxford or Cambridge. Composed of red and blue-grey brick in a diaper pattern, with stone dressings including carved Barnack stone salvaged from the old St John's Hospital and chapel, it presents a complex facade on its southern side, where it looks on to a terrace and the master's garden. Below the oriel window is a coroneted achievement-at-arms with yale supporters against a thicket of germander speedwell.

The garden was subject to a redesign by Nevill Willmer of Clare College in the 1950s (Willmer is the professor credited with Clare's 'colour-theory' fellows' garden), but the garden as a whole has changed a great deal since then. The terrace of the lodge is a delight, with nicotiana in pots and yellow *Corydalis lutea* sprouting up from cracks in the shallow steps leading down to the garden. A pair of massive columnar yews stands sentinel at the top of the steps, with pots containing dwarf fuchsias flanking the treads. The great border against the building, which faces south, is a cornucopia of bright

ABOVE The college's gateway features motifs associated with foundress Margaret Beaufort, including the yales (mythical beasts) and daisies.

flowers including pink hollyhocks, cistus, cosmos, big fuchsias, crocosmias, bright blue delphiniums, tithonias, ceratostigma and roses, notably the white floribunda 'Margaret Merril'. Ferns, hebes and 'Hidcote' lavender help provide structure. On the spreading lawn below are the huge plane and chestnut visible from across the river (both were planted in 1868), together with a mulberry and birch. Another herbaceous border contains daylilies, verbascums, acanthus, rheums, rudbeckias and much else, while against the library on the east side is a semi-shaded bed with ferns, astilbes and astrantias backed by hydrangeas. At the western end of the terrace is a pleasingly old-fashioned, yew-hedge-enclosed rose garden with a pergola and hybrid teas in paired beds and beyond this, to the side of the lodge, is a cut-flower garden created in 2016 with sweet peas, dahlias, *Ammi majus*, cornflowers and sweet William.

The front facade of the lodge is far less interesting, with a turning circle and white hydrangeas in beds against the building. The head gardener's office is in the stable block adjacent to the master's lodge, close to the seat of all power in college.

Directly opposite the college, across St John's Street, is the Old Divinity School (Basil Champneys, 1879), another polychrome red-brick building intended to complement St John's older architecture. Since 1997 this building has been in the possession of the college

and in 2012 it was refurbished along with other buildings on the 'Triangle' site. Before work commenced, the remains of almost 1,000 people, including around 400 complete skeletons, were unearthed here by archaeologists. It was concluded that this must have been the medieval burial ground of the old Hospital of St John the Evangelist, taking our story full circle. The remains of gravel paths, a well and the seeds of flowering plants were also discovered, indicating that this graveyard may once have had a garden-like appearance.

At the heart of the new complex is Corfield Court, a sunken courtyard with grasses, ferns and hellebores around the perimeter, while another planted area around the Old School House comprises effective plantings of miscanthus grasses with tree ferns. This is just one more area of dynamic horticulture on an extremely large college site which comprises at least 25 distinctively gardened spaces. Fortunately the garden team here exudes the quiet confidence which is an integral part of the St John's College character. With this job in hand, they need it.

ABOVE The Cam as seen from the master's garden, framed by a weeping cherry and purple tulips in an urn.

TRINITY COLLEGE

PACIOUSNESS. EASE. CONFIDENCE. MAGNIFICENCE. This is Trinity.

The impression is created, above all, by Great Court. It is aptly named. Not only is it large, at about 100 metres/328 feet by 80 metres/262 feet (covering nearly 0.8 hectare/2 acres), it is architecturally varied to the point of palimpsest. Yet somehow it can contain all its variousness with aplomb. Great Court has the air of an elegant receptacle, since the space holds the ghosts of three earlier halls which occupied the site. The most important of these was the King's Hall, established in 1317, refounded by Edward III 20 years later and directly supported by eleven subsequent monarchs until 1546, when Henry VIII amalgamated it with seven other halls and hostels and refounded them all as Trinity. The college's special relationship with the monarchy has persisted. HRH the Prince of Wales was educated here, while in the 19th century the master of college enquired of the visiting Queen Victoria whether she might like to have a rest in 'my house' – as in the master's lodge – soliciting the imperious correction: '*My* house'.

The visitor enters Great Court via the Great Gate on the north-eastern side (originally the gatehouse of King's Hall), but perhaps the best vantage point is the Queen's Gate in the middle of the south range. From here one can survey the chapel straight ahead, the hall and master's lodge to the left, and the octagonal fountain with its fine decorative canopy in the centre of the court, the pinwheel around which everything else revolves, the very navel of the world for Trinity and its people. The fountain we see today, which has the air of an ornate wellhead, is a rebuilt version installed in 1716, but it was first constructed a century before, when painted beasts in green, gold and blue surrounded its canopy, as well as the rampant lion motif which still tops it. In the 17th century it even had a plasterwork ceiling. The water comes from a conduit engineered so that the flow rushes in with some force.

LEFT The west front of the Wren Library, prefaced by Scholars' Lawn. This space was previously occupied by a tennis court made in 1611.

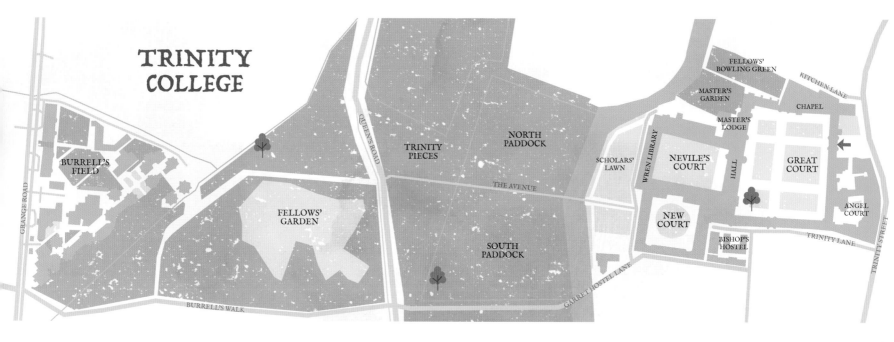

TRINITY COLLEGE

It is not clear when planting beds around the fountain were established (they are not shown on David Loggan's engraving of the college of 1690) but it is likely to have been the mid to late 19th century (the garden committee agreed to plant up the chapel bays in Great Court in 1862). There is a tradition of wallflowers followed by pelargoniums, though tulips, salvias and lavender may also be seen; the decision about this is one of the responsibilities of the college's current garden committee, which usually numbers eight to ten fellows. The bright red pelargonium 'Paul Crampel' has long been favoured by dint of its royal connections, as it is the variety most commonly seen planted outside Buckingham Palace. A few metres north of the fountain stands a simple stone baluster sundial (1704), marking the site of King Edward's Tower before it was moved adjacent to the chapel during the reorganisation of the court.

Six great rectangular and square plats of close-mown grass define Great Court, perhaps even more than the buildings do. These are the most closely policed of all Cambridge's lawns. Anyone can approach the high altar in Trinity Chapel, but not everyone can tread on its turf. Trinity's porters in their bowler hats are the most assiduous custodians of the college's boundary rules: Prince Charles as heir to the throne was told to 'get off the grass' just like anyone else on at least one occasion. Only fellows are allowed to carve a diagonal path straight across the court, and one occasionally sees them cleaving in this exclusive manner. There is a story about a 19th-century undergraduate who would often walk across the lawn of Great Court on the way to hall, in full view of the master's lodge. One day the master determined to reprove the delinquent, and, opening the window at which he was sitting, he called to the student: 'Sir, I never look out of my window but I see you walking across the grass plot.' 'My lord,' replied the offender, 'I never walk across the grass plot but I see you looking out of your window.' This says as much about the legendary self-confidence of Trinity men (and now women) as it does about the sanctity of Trinity's turf.

ABOVE Sir Isaac Newton's garden of plant specimens, which he had inherited from the botanist John Ray, shown in a detail of David Loggan's 1690 engraving.

Animals have been a feature at Trinity. A number of dogs are shown in Great Court in Loggan's engraving, while a payment lodged in the college accounts for 1654 is to a porter 'for keeping dogs out of ye Chappl', suggesting that they were tolerated out of doors. Sir Isaac Newton, the college's greatest alumnus, kept a dog when he lived in Great Court, though by the early 19th century the practice was frowned upon and even the college master was obliged to carry his dog across the courts. Lord Byron knew the rules and duly left his dog at home when he came up to Trinity in 1805, but at the start of his third term he arrived with a tame bear, which he attempted to keep in his rooms. That was his final term at Trinity. Another animal at large in Great Court was an eagle, shown on the Loggan engraving (a new perch for it had been purchased in 1683). An eagle was again kept in the court in the 1730s.

Trinity also owned swans on the river; the first reference to a swanherd is in 1592, and the last reference to the college swans is in 1782.

Great Court was the brainchild of Thomas Nevile, a great master of the college who in the 1590s set about demolishing various parts of the old halls and hostels to create a more unified space. John Hamond's city map of 1592 shows Trinity as it was 'before Trinity', with the southern range of King's Hall abutting straight into what was to be the centre of the court, while two ranges of another old hall, Michaelhouse (founded 1324), had also intruded on the west side. All of this had been removed by 1600, while the buildings in the perimeter ranges were either demolished or substantially modernised. Hamond also shows a tree growing in the middle of the court; the college accounts for the year before his map was drawn note an 'item for making railes about the trees in the Court, and mending the seate about the Walnutte tree'. The walnut was the traditional tree for the courts of Cambridge colleges (Jesus College had the most celebrated example).

Another horticultural particularity of Cambridge is well displayed in this and other courts at Trinity: the habit of training shrubs and climbers up the walls in geometric fashion, as living buttresses. Pale pink and white climbing roses, *Magnolia grandiflora* and ceanothus are among the plants deployed in this fashion on a suitably large scale in Great Court, while the chapel bays contain highly effective large-scale plantings of cannas, ricinus, *Dahlia* 'Bishop of Llandaff' and variegated euonymus. The narrow beds in front of the master's lodge on the court's west side are also a showpiece, with bedding plants backed by the purple leaves of ricinus and the vivid spikes of *Persicaria amplexicaulis*.

Trinity's other two courts could both fit into Great Court. Directly behind the college hall (1605) is Nevile's Court, an austere lawned space with cloisters to left and right, which is all that is needed to preface Christopher Wren's extraordinary library, designed free of charge in 1676. The library is a strident set piece, its power derived from the row of tall windows along its entire upper storey, supported by an open arcade which serves as a base, and a roof in perfect proportion with the whole. As a building it is wholly uncompromising and utterly dominant. It is at moments like this that one understands why Trinity considers itself the elite of the elite. The tribune or raised platform against the hall on the court's east side was expressly created as a means of admiring the Wren Library, while the building's undercroft is an atmospheric inside-outside space which offers surreptitious views out through the barred windows towards the Backs and Trinity Bridge.

ABOVE The east front of the Wren Library seen from Nevile's Court. The arcade below the library is an indoor-outdoor space.

South of Nevile's Court and connected with it via the cloister is New Court (1825), a rather stiff neo-Gothic confection in mustard-yellow by the versatile (perhaps too versatile) Cambridge architect William Wilkins. In the centre of this court, which is unfortunately used as a car park, is a large red-flowered horse chestnut (*Aesculus × carnea*) planted in 1885 when the garden committee decided to elaborate upon Wilkins's plain roundel of grass (he had wanted a fountain and basin). The borders here contain some excellent shrub plantings, especially on the north (south-facing) side, where a stupendous specimen of *Melianthus major* reigns supreme among cordylines, salvias, caryopteris and *Verbena bonariensis*, as well as more 'buttress shrubs' trained on the walls. This court is associated with Arthur Hallam, the subject of Alfred Tennyson's great elegiac poem *In Memoriam*. In it he describes returning to Cambridge in 1838, five years after Hallam's death, and how he re-explored the Backs and old avenue of limes which extends west from Trinity Bridge.

> And caught once more the distant shout,
> The measured pulse of racing oars
> Among the willows; paced the shores
> And many a bridge, and all about
>
> The same gray flats again, and felt
> The same, but not the same; and last
> Up that long walk of limes I past
> To see the rooms in which he dwelt.

Trinity's lime avenue was planted in 1671, when it was focused on the 14th-century tower of St Peter's, Coton. (In the early 19th century one university wit compared this walk with a college fellowship, in that it was 'a long dreary road, with a church in the distance'.) It was replanted in 1780 and again in 1949. It is the most beautiful avenue in Cambridge, a cathedral of luminescent green in spring and summer, while in autumn it is sprinkled with yellow-gold leaves. In winter a quiet dignity reigns. Beneath the trees, crocuses, small red tulips, narcissi and ox-eye daisies are planted in the grass, and there is more spring blossom from the lines of cherry trees (*Prunus avium* 'Plena'), which were inserted as flanking avenues in 1929, replanted in 1987 (when some fellows objected that these showy trees 'cheapened' the scene).

The pleasures of the Avenue are not only visual; college fellow Joseph Romilly, writing in July 1839, related how he went there specifically 'to see the walks & smell the Limes'. The open ground each side of the raised avenue is called the Paddocks, now used for May Balls and fireworks displays but otherwise kept refreshingly clear of activity.

The Avenue beyond Trinity Bridge started life as an access causeway, termed the 'causey into the feildes', which is first mentioned as being

LEFT *Tulipa* 'Apeldoorn' beside the lime avenue next to Scholars' Lawn, on the college side of the river.

repaired in 1589, indicating it must have been in existence for some time already. Ten years later it was shored up with 204 loads of rubbish topped by 60 of gravel. The accounts of this period reveal considerable expenditure on the 'close' or 'closes' – the fields on either side of the causeway – with bills for 'settes' (sapling trees or whips, used for hedge barriers) and 80 days of ditching work. Equipment was needed for all this activity, and in 1604 there is a bill for 'a wheelbarrow, a beetle [a mallet], and a Scoope'. Willows were purchased in the same year, and these would have been planted along the edge of the river. A decade later, in 1614, there is a reference to planting 81 elms, possibly the first trees to form the Avenue, and one of Nevile's last contributions to the college before his death the following year.

Gradually, as the trees matured and the walks became more alluring, a more ornamental picture begins to emerge. In 1650 there is a bill 'To Goodman Page for cutting the hedge, fencing the willows and Elmes'. Page was a sort of handyman who did various jobs at college; there was no dedicated gardener at this time and there are references to the porters mending hedges and suchlike. In the late 1650s a new man takes over from Page as the foreman of the work in the closes. The year 1657 sees payment 'to John Styles for setts, hedging & workemens wages about the College Closes' as well as more ditching. Two years later comes the first reference to the Avenue and the riverside area as the 'college Walkes', indicating that by this time they are beginning to be considered as spaces for leisure and relaxation, shaded from the sun, shielded from the rain.

If the first trees in the Avenue were indeed the 81 elms planted at the end of Nevile's time in 1614, it seems a little spendthrift to be replacing them with limes in the 1670s, as would have been the case. But perhaps the elms were failing, or fashion was coming into play, for the lime was the 'coming tree' of the late 17th century, valued above all others at estates for its beauty when planted as an avenue. The 'close' flanking the Avenue was now known as Trinity College Meadow, reckoned to be a pleasurable retreat in its own right, the northern section in particular offering views downriver towards St John's from an elevated viewpoint on its eastern side. In the 19th century Trinity's meadow was used for grazing the master's and fellows' horses, as well as for lawn tennis and hockey, which is when it came to be known, rather more prosaically, as the Paddock.

A word needs to be said about the area around Trinity Bridge, an elegant triple-spanned affair designed by James Essex in 1764, replacing at least two earlier structures. It connects with New Court via a short run of lime avenue, originally planted in the late 1670s to match the main Avenue. Before the Wren Library was built, Nevile's Court was

open to the river on its west end, where a walled open tennis court stood on the riverbank. The area was then known as Tennis Court Green, though before that it was probably used for in-college football (the rough, early version of the game), since a piece of riverside land at Trinity was mentioned in a vice-chancellor's diktat of 1580 as a space where the game was allowed. After the tennis court was finally taken away it became Scholars' Lawn, something of a cult destination for visitors to Cambridge from the late 18th century, when the grass was turfed as a perfect oval and the supplicant willows by the bridge lowered their branches into the river as it describes a languorous curve. This was also a favoured spot for ice-skating when the river froze over (as was Emmanuel's pond). In the mid 18th century the lawn had been levelled, and turf and gravel walks laid out, and in 1761 payment was made 'to Harrison the Gardner for Planting North-American Poplars, weeping-willows, and other Aquatics, under the wall next the river'. This is an early mention of weeping willows (*Salix babylonica*) in Cambridge. The willows remain a feature on this spot, with cyclamens and crocuses popping up below the bridge in spring. The openness of the walks along the Backs could lead to spectacular aeolian experiences, as related by the Gothic novelist Maria Edgeworth in 1813: 'Went next to Trinity College Library: beautiful! I liked the glass doors opening to the gardens at the end, and trees in full leaf…Shockingly windy walk: thought my brains would have been blown out.'

So, is that it, at Trinity? Three courts and an avenue?

That is not it. Hidden away around corners and down passageways are several other garden areas of note. The college is, famously, 'a mile long' (almost a mile) and there are several courts on the town side to the east, extending as far as Sidney Street, and a large new development on the far western, Backs side, against Grange Road.

But even within the historic college there are other gardens to discover (or perhaps just to read about, as most are out of bounds to strangers). The most fabled of these is the Fellows' Bowling Green, which was made in 1647 out of the old garden of King's Hall. It is reached via a passageway on the north side of Great Court and guarded by a locked wrought-iron door. It's not even worth risking the attentions of the porters to sneak a peek through, because the garden's main event is against the southern wall, out of sight. This is the giant clipped beech hedge, about 7.5 metres/25 feet high, which runs along one side of the bowling green, supposedly screening the master's garden (adjacent, to the south) from prying eyes in St John's next door. This feature began as a lime avenue in the 18th century and for a long time it was a mixed beech and lime hedge (the last lime died in 1947). The fellows fret that the hedge is too high, and historically it has been a source of tension with the master. The hedge is not actually against the wall of the master's garden, leaving a long, gloomy secret passageway between it and the wall that children love to explore (if they are permitted entry, that is). The green itself is not particularly smooth but that is perhaps part of the game: 'Trinity Rules Bowls' is played here using the old fellows' bowls, which come in sets of three.

This bowling green is one of the oldest parts of Trinity and was formerly known as the fellows' garden. There are references to it, and to the gardener's wages, at King's Hall as early as 1338–39, and in 1362–63 a new garden was made and beds laid out in the area between the hall and the river. A vineyard is mentioned as being somewhere on the King's Hall site by the early 15th century, and it appears to have been inherited by Trinity, for in 1550–51 there are charges for pruning the vines over the course of three full days. These grapes would have been pressed to make verjuice, an acidic form of grape juice generally used in cooking at this period, when the dichotomy of sweet with sour was still the apogee of gastronomy.

The Hamond city map of 1592 shows two ornamental or knot gardens surrounded by trees in the old fellows' garden, while by the time of the Loggan engraving a century later it is most definitely a smooth bowling green (a roller is depicted next to it). The fellows had a summer house at the western end, overlooking the river, and a few covered seats. The 18th-century antiquarian and garden-maker William Stukeley relates how whenever Newton

'took a turn in the Fellows' Gardens, if some new gravel happen'd to be laid on the walks, it was sure to be drawn over and over with a bit of stick, in Sir Isaac's diagrams; which the Fellows

would cautiously spare by walking beside them, and there they would sometime remain for a good while.'

Perhaps Newton was just working out the best angle for the next bowl.

Today the chief horticultural interest in the Fellows' Bowling Green is provided by a long, multicoloured herbaceous border against the north wall, with a wide range of plants including dahlias, acanthus, tithonias, rudbeckias, salvias and asters, arranged on no specific theme except the glorification of flowers. The deep pink and white blooms of *Lilium* 'Robert Griesbach' create a contrast with the saucers of achillea, the prickly purple balls of echinops and the grey-mauve froth of perovskia. The old wall at this eastern end of the garden is planted with purple *Erysimum* 'Bowles's Mauve' alternating with white centranthus, and white rose standards are formally aligned in the lawn in front. The Fellows' Bowling Green also contains a few surprises, such as *Poncirus trifoliata* (Japanese bitter orange). Perhaps the nicest spot, though, is

ABOVE LEFT The long, south-facing border in the master's garden is a multicoloured delight with salvias, achilleas, hollyhocks and many other flowers.

ABOVE CENTRE Acers, trachycarpus palms and clipped topiary in Duff's Garden.

the small terrace at the end of the garden by the river, with pretty views in all directions.

The master's garden is an extremely private inner sanctum which is nevertheless kept in tip-top condition by head gardener Tom Hooijenga, a Dutchman, and his team of twelve (including five women). This is another very early garden on the college site, first recorded as a plot of land named 'le Millestones' which was leased in 1434 by Michaelhouse. Sixteenth-century maps indicate that it was a highly decorative garden at this time, while the Loggan engraving of 1690 illustrates a formal parterre and a central fountain with statue (1677), and a summer house against the river which was built in 1684. There are intriguing references in the college accounts to various trees and shrubs being purchased in the late 1670s – phillyrea, holly, honeysuckle, juniper, tamarisk, holm oak – and their most likely destination was indeed the master's garden.

The amount of money a college spends on the master's lodge and garden can sometimes be a tricky matter. The days of overly extravagant college principals seem to have passed (cue a raised eyebrow in a senior common room somewhere), but historically there have been some terrific rows over garden expenditure, most notably at Merton College in Oxford in the 1660s (where the fellows blamed the master's wife) and, alas, at Trinity. As master, Richard Bentley got into a dispute with

some of the fellows about his expenditure in the decade from 1710. Possibly it did not help that he had transferred from St John's, their rival next door. It all started when Bentley complained that the fellows made too much noise in their bowling green, while they accused him of wanting to take over their leisure space as an extension of his own garden and also of planning to turn an adjacent laboratory into a greenhouse for his plants. They said he had 'exorbitantly and unnecessarily' spent around £2,000 of college money on his own lodgings (the mammoth cost, at least, was not in doubt). The disgruntled fellows appealed to the Bishop of Ely about the master's behaviour, directly accusing him of embezzlement, while the master in turn wrote to the bishop in the most sublimely complacent and self-confident terms, so sure was he of his position. The master was denounced by the fellows for 'ordering and causing your garden to be laid out and formed after a new model, and a terrace to be erected therein by the water-side; by building a summer-house, or room of entertainment, in the garden belonging to you as Master, and in that a bath, which you have caused to be supplied with water and other conveniences for bathing.' It did not stop there. In 1720 one fellow wrote about the master's new banqueting house 'and

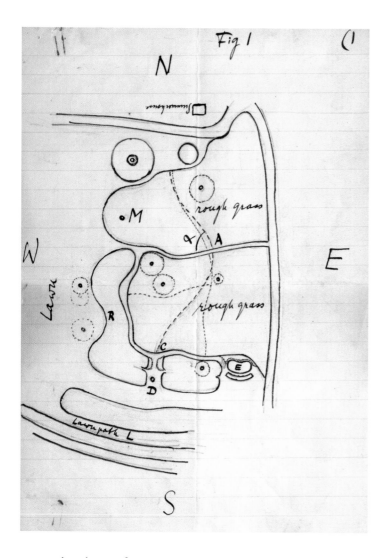

LEFT Planting plan for the fellows' garden drawn by philosopher Ludwig Wittgenstein in October 1934.

RIGHT Trinity Bridge – designed by James Essex in 1746 – and the lime avenue, looking west.

transition space between Great Court and New Court. This building was a rebuild of Garret Hostel, one of the institutions amalgamated into Trinity, renamed because its renovation was funded by a Trinity fellow who was Bishop of Lichfield. It is an attractively dainty exercise in neoclassicism, realised in red brick with buff stone facings. It also has a pleasant garden to preface it, with narrow panels of lawn and evergreen shapes in varied hues.

Even more interesting is the dog-leg passageway leading to student rooms behind the hostel, where a garden nicknamed 'the jungle' has been developed over the past decade or so. Tree ferns, tetrapanax, bamboos, albizias, cordylines, hydrangeas and fuchsias crowd into this narrow and atmospheric space, where sometimes the plant life becomes so rampant that students ask the garden team to clear the doorways so that they can get in (and out).

Outside Great Gate, the college extends itself across Trinity Street by means of a block of connecting courts of different dates. The first, Whewell's Courts (1868), is an attractively restrained neo-Gothic design by Anthony Salvin, nicely ornamented by plantings of young olive trees in low lead troughs and tubs. The postmodern Blue Boar development is more recent (1985–90), with a warren of small courts and alleys, several of which are well planted with hedges and striking plants such as aeonium, rudbeckia and *Verbena bonariensis*.

This part of college is not normally open to visitors and is in any case of passing interest only. But the area directly in front of Trinity's Great Gate does give pause for thought. Visitors will notice a single apple tree on the lawn to the right of the entrance gate, by the chapel. This is Newton's Apple Tree, supposedly grown from a cutting taken from the tree where the physicist dozed one day and had his eureka moment regarding gravity. This story has to be taken not with a pinch but with a dose of salts, yet the tree does mark a spot which has an extraordinary garden history.

Newton arrived at Trinity in 1661, a 'sober, silent, thinking lad', according to Stukeley. He had long been an assiduous cultivator of 'physic' (medicinal) plants, and when he was made a fellow he took a set of rooms in Staircase E on the east range, immediately north of the Great Gate, which offered the unusual amenity of an enclosed garden, one of a series on the outside of the college wall, ranged against the street but bounded by high walls. Loggan's engraving of 1690 shows these 'front gardens' in considerable detail – the greatest detail on any of his garden depictions of the colleges of Cambridge and Oxford. There are four gardens of varying sizes and the northernmost, which had been Newton's, where the apple tree is today, consists of a chequerboard pattern of small square beds,

some other things of great Expence and no Use to the College'. The fellows' complaints came to nothing and Bentley was not censured, though the offending bathhouse was pulled down in 1771.

All is calm in the master's garden today. It is mainly laid to lawn dotted with old fruit trees, getting wilder towards the river end, where it concludes with a gravel terrace and a charming old greenhouse. The beds in front of the lodge windows are planted up in 'hot' style, with cannas, crocosmias and rudbeckias backed by the foliage of ricinus, and there are pots of aeoniums and other choice specimens on the terrace. A herbaceous border along the entire north wall of the garden runs the gamut of colour from zingy yellow achillea, deep blue salvias, scarlet climbing roses and white hollyhocks and foxgloves earlier in the season, to the rich purples and pinks of alliums, dahlias, sedums, persicaria, verbena and lupins in late summer.

There is actually a fourth court in the old part of Trinity: Angel Court, an extension constructed in 1959 behind the south-east corner of Great Court, in the angle between Trinity Lane and Trinity Street. The buildings here are so bland that it is difficult for the gardeners to achieve great heights, but there is wisteria tumbling over a balcony, an immaculate lawn and shrub borders. Much more interesting is the garden associated with Bishop's Hostel (1671), tucked away in the

containing one specimen plant. There are also climbing plants, probably fruit, against the chapel walls. We are told that Newton was 'curious' in his garden, that it was 'never out of order', and that he 'would at some seldome time take a short walk or two, not enduring to see a weed in it'.

It seems likely that Newton had inherited this garden from another notable scientist, the botanist John Ray, who was at Trinity from 1649 until 1662, and so just overlapped with the teenage Newton. Ray was an assiduous plant collector, growing specimens in his own garden at Trinity, and in 1660 he published a flora of Cambridgeshire. We know Ray's garden at Trinity contained, by one reckoning, more than 700 different plants, and that the Master of Jesus College commended it as being 'as full of choice things as it can hold; that it were twenty times as big I could wish for his sake'.

One other botanist made his garden on this patch, though he was not perhaps quite as eminent as the other two. Trinity's vice-master from 1734 was the Revd Richard 'Frog' Walker – his amphibian nickname deriving from the fact he had spent so much of his life in the Fens. He was a noted horticulturist, as is mentioned in Thomas Salmon's guidebook *The Foreigner's Companion through the Universities of Cambridge and Oxford* (1748):

And tho' there be no public garden belonging to the University, Cambridge is not destitute of exotic Plants, the Trinity Gardener, Mr Harrison, having, by the direction of Dr Walker the Vice-Master, introduced several Species of foreign Fruits and Flowers, Natives of the warmest Climates; particularly the Anana or Pine-apple, the Banana, Coffee-shrub, Logwood-tree, the Torch-thistle, the Red Jessamine of the West Indies, &c. which are brought to great Perfection by the help of a Green-house and Stoves, which Mr Harrison has erected in the Doctor's Garden.

The four unfamiliar plants named by Salmon as being in Frog's garden are Coffee-shrub (*Gymnocladus diocia*, Kentucky coffee tree), Logwood-tree (*Haematoxylum campechianum*, grown for its dye), the Torch-thistle (*Cereus hexagonus*, a cactus) and the Red Jessamine (red jasmine: *Jasminum beesianum*). All these, except perhaps the jasmine, remain rarities in British gardens today. The greenhouse mentioned was probably erected against the south-facing wall of the chapel. These gardens at the front of college were finally done way with in 1856

ABOVE LEFT Dahlias by the lawn in the master's garden.
ABOVE CENTRE Groups of tightly clipped topiary are a feature of the fellows' garden and avenues.

when the walls were taken down. Only the apple tree stands there now, a memorial, perhaps, to three curious gardeners as opposed to one great thought.

Now let us leapfrog Great Court again and head westwards beyond the lime avenue, where the college stretches itself out across the land known as Trinity Pieces towards the current fellows' garden, on the other side of Queen's Road. This idiosyncratic hidden space was made in 1873 on land which had already been utilised as a private garden by the master 70 years earlier, with a circular path winding its way through trees and informally arranged shrub beds, and an area of paddock for his daughter's horse. The path was nicknamed 'the roundabout' and that name was to be retained for the area as a whole.

The garden designer William Broderick Thomas, who had worked on the lake at Sandringham, was brought in by the college to remake the space as the fellows' garden; his main recommendation was to retain the basic structure while augmenting it with flower beds and a wider variety of trees and shrubs. A thatched arbour in the south-east part of the garden was made on a mound which has been known since the 1880s as Monte Cobbeo, in memory of a college fellow named Gerard Cobb who successfully proposed to his wife inside it (such proposals were then a novelty, as fellows were permitted to marry only from the 1880s). A sundial was made during the First World

War to commemorate three fellows, all on the garden committee, who had been killed. Another fellow serving on the committee had had a vivid dream about a sundial in a rose garden, and it was decided to honour it. The sundial rose garden (themed around *Rosa rugosa*) is still a notable feature in the fellows' garden, which is planted with specimen and mature trees (birches, copper beech, catalpa, cherries) and shrub borders so that its layout can never be seen at one glance and the spaces must be discovered individually. Large pieces of clipped box and yew topiary, several of them in clustered cone form, appear as if out of nowhere and impart a pleasingly surreal quality. A huge blue cedar is festooned in summer with 'Paul's Himalayan Musk' rose climbing through its branches. There is an undulating lawn across the space and an island of herbaceous plants in the centre, with grasses supporting summer flowers including helenium and penstemon.

A small orchard area in the fellow's garden is associated with a secret space named Duff's Garden, which was rented from the college after 1889 by a fellow named J. D. Duff, who used it as a kind of allotment-cum-pleasure garden for his family. In 1930 it reverted to the college. In it there is a timber summer house constructed in a hawthorn hedge,

ABOVE RIGHT The giant beech hedge next to the Fellows' Bowling Green.

herbaceous borders, a weeping ash and a mulberry tree planted in memory of a college bursar.

The grass in the fellows' garden is left to grow long in some areas, with narrow paths mown through, an experiment first conducted in 1933. This led the philosopher Ludwig Wittgenstein, one of Trinity's most celebrated importations, to pen a detailed response to the college's garden committee. He disliked the way tulips and fritillaries had been mixed in the grass and felt that 'tulips of all contradicting colours filling up big stretches of the rough grass look gaudy and vulgar.' Wittgenstein – who had worked as a gardener in Austria – provided an annotated plan of the area (see page 280) in which he suggested repositioning the paths and adjusting the garden aesthetic: 'The kidney shaped bed with the dahlias in it looks very bad because of the border of Veronica round the dahlias. This fringe makes it look like a gaudy birthday cake.' Wittgenstein followed this up with a four-page letter to Prof Burnaby, chair of the garden committee:

I had a talk with our gardener about this bed a few weeks ago…I can't help thinking that it would be right to *repeat* beds again and again *with improvements*, instead of either repeating them without improvements or changing the whole plan next year (unless it's absolutely necessary)…Please forgive me these remarks, but I thought I ought to get them off my chest.

Yours very sincerely,
Ludwig Wittgenstein

PS I find that there is one more point I would like to talk about: don't the borders along the sides of New Court look extremely shabby, as though the odds and ends left over from the rest of the garden were planted there? Wouldn't it improve the appearance of this court very much if all the borders in it were entirely uniform, say with red dahlias or geraniums? This court can do with something that makes it look more quiet and dignified.

This is definitely the end.

An avenue of plane trees runs through the centre of the fellows' garden, connecting it with Burrell's Field to the west. There is a lovely quality of light in this walkway and in spring wood anemones, tulips and primulas blossom in the grass all around. Burrell's Field was open pasture,

quite marshy in places, and crossed by the Bin Brook. The college developed the land for accommodation from the 1970s, the main intervention being a series of 12 pavilions with distinctive, triangular, lead-coated steel windows added by MacCormac Jamieson & Prichard in 1995. The buildings are intended to resemble a walled town from a distance. There are pergolas, a pool and other formal garden devices inserted into the spaces between the buildings, with specimen trees including a pair of paulownias and a Wollemi pine, while the wider area still has a tranquil, field-like quality. There are six beehives and a dedicated beekeeper, with 'Burrell's Field Honey' produced each year. A central area of the development features box and yew topiaries and the rose 'Queen of Hearts', and there are 'hot borders' in front of several buildings, with dahlias, rudbeckias, cannas, tithonias and pompom dahlias. A number of existing houses in Queen Anne style and an Arts and Crafts house were also taken into college ownership, and the gardens of these are carefully maintained in period style. The gardeners' nursery area is nearby, where cut flowers are grown for the fellows' parlour.

Returning to the sublime grandeur of Great Court, the words of that great chronicler of myth and magic, James George Frazer, seem appropriate. A Trinity undergraduate and fellow, in 1898 the author of *The Golden Bough* was in his mid forties when he wrote this paean to his college:

The windows of my study look on the tranquil court of an ancient college, where the sundial marks the passage of the hours and in the long summer days the fountain plashes drowsily amid flowers and grass; where, as the evening shadows deepen, the lights come out in the blazoned windows of the Elizabethan hall and from the chapel the sweet voices of the choir, blent with the pealing music of the organ, float on the peaceful air, telling of man's eternal aspirations after truth and goodness and immortality.

TRINITY
HALL

'THE PRETTIEST CORNER OF THE world.' That is how no less a literary personage than Henry James described the fellows' garden at Trinity Hall after his visit in the late 1870s. James was not a horticultural aficionado, so his approbation must be understood as that of an interested amateur. But clearly he felt there was something special about the place, as he singled it out above the other colleges he visited on his guided excursion.

There is still something special about Trinity Hall, and its gardens do remain remarkably pretty. In recent years it has developed into one of the most impressive colleges in the university, horticulturally speaking. After the formality of its Front Court, one is released into an appealingly lopsided domain presided over by the ancient library, venerable trees, fresh flower borders and a low-key but beguilingly pleasant river frontage. The college never quite had the wherewithal to purchase land on the west side of the Cam, like its neighbours Trinity and Clare, so it does not have a bridge or a fellows' garden to discover at one remove. But the capsule-like effect of the place produces its own charms. Trinity Hall is like a little medieval hamlet, its building ranges – mainly Victorian, it is true, but antiquarian in spirit – clustered informally about a putative village green. No wonder it is one of the colleges looked upon with most affection within the university.

Founded in 1350 by the Bishop of Norwich on the site of a house and garden previously in the brief ownership of the Priory of Ely, where scholarly monks had resided, the college is one of the oldest in Cambridge. Like Peterhouse before it, the Hall of the Scholars of the Holy Trinity was not founded as a religious institution in thrall to one of the monastic orders; instead, it pursued a particular specialism in law which has endured. Yet the college does not today present an appearance that reflects its antiquity, at least initially. Its ancient Front Court was comprehensively remodelled in the 1740s in a smooth neoclassical manner, complete with a swagged cartouche

LEFT The border in front of the Old Library is a high point of the college garden, here with yellow achillea and white hollyhocks in blossom.

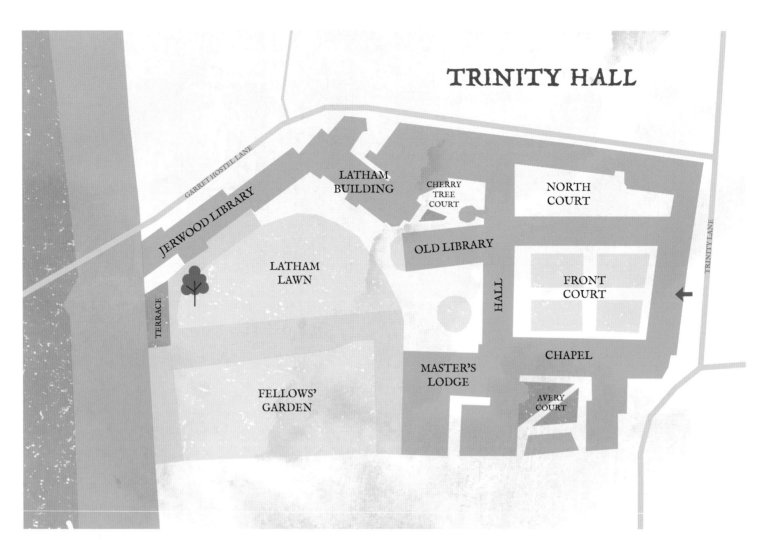

TRINITY HALL

(map labels)
GARRET HOSTEL LANE
JERWOOD LIBRARY
LATHAM BUILDING
CHERRY TREE COURT
NORTH COURT
OLD LIBRARY
TRINITY LANE
TERRACE
LATHAM LAWN
HALL
FRONT COURT
CHAPEL
FELLOWS' GARDEN
MASTER'S LODGE
AVERY COURT

in the central pediment of the west range, directly ahead as the visitor enters college.

The court's confident architectural unity exudes a sophisticated and worldly air, similar to that of Clare College, next door. But this is a facade: the clothing may be Georgian, but the heart of the college remains medieval. And this was not the original way in. Until 1852 there was a curiously old-fashioned arrangement at Trinity Hall whereby its entrance was via what is now Avery Court, opening on to Trinity Lane (then Milne Street) to the east, with the gate and porter's lodge in the south-east corner of the college. This little court had various names over time including First Court (which explains why the college's main court was known for several centuries as Principal Court), Porter's Court, South Court and Master's Lodge Court, since it also acted as a sort of front garden to the master's lodge, situated for many years in its north-western corner. In the early 18th century this entrance court was described by William Warren – a fellow (1712–45) who collated all the available historical documents about Trinity Hall – as having 'a Little Garden in it, inclosed with poles'. A plan in the college's possession dated 1731 shows a roundel that presumably contained this garden in the centre of the court. South Court went through various other architectural changes during the 19th century, when

ABOVE The gardens along the right-hand side of Loggan's 1690 engraving have all gone, but the fellows' garden (top left) remains and the old 'Backside' area to its right is now Latham Lawn.

TOP RIGHT The Georgian certainty of Front Court is a facade – the fabric of earlier buildings is hidden inside.

the central garden was replaced with a simpler design of two paths crossing grass panels.

In 2006 the court was renamed yet again – this time as Avery Court, in honour of benefactor Dennis Avery. Today it stands as an excellent example of exciting garden design in a small space: in the 1990s the garden consultant Andrew Peters, formerly head gardener at Fitzwilliam College, devised the current scheme, based on triangular box-hedged compartments with roses, poppies, aquilegias, herbs, veronicas, hibiscus, crinum lilies, bearded irises and sisyrinchium. There are various shrubs growing against the walls and in the bays of the chapel on the north side, including the lovely soft yellow rose 'Malvern Hills', curling around a doorway. (Uniquely, this court is overlooked by the windows of two college chapels, as Clare's runs across the southern side.) One particularly pleasing aspect of this court is the way the grapevine on the eastern wall, planted by Mr Peters, fruits at eye level, making for a rather luxurious ambience, harkening back to a tradition of vines in Cambridge colleges that has existed since the 14th century.

There was also at Trinity Hall another garden which caused quite a stir when it was made, in 1793, but which has since been forgotten about: a small triangular plot planted by a fellow, Joseph Jowett, in an angle next to the gatehouse on what was then Milne Street. This highly decorated little parterre, surrounded only by a low fence, was evidently viewed as pretentious by some, and for a short period became the focus of considerable interest in Cambridge. Perhaps its rather public position, on the street, invited such comment.

The main claim to posterity of 'Little Jowett', as he was nicknamed on account of his small stature, was that he composed the bell chimes of Great St Mary's Church, which are said to have inspired in turn the melody of Big Ben in London. Ackerman in his *History of the University of Cambridge* (1815) described Jowett as 'an elegant scholar, and a man of mild and amiable manners'. This gentle disposition makes the teasing that Jowett suffered seem even more unfair.

The first salvo was said to have been fired by one Archdeacon Wrangham, a colleague of Jowett's who posted up a mildly satirical verse either to 'rag' his friend, or perhaps simply to acknowledge publicly that it was he who had created the space:

This little garden little Jowett made
And fenced it with a little palisade

But then an addendum appeared, by another hand, which was rather barbed:

But little wit had little Dr Jowett
And little did this little garden show it

Other versions of the rhyme appeared, apparently commenting on Jowett's decision to simplify his maligned creation:

But when this little garden made a little talk
He changed it to a little gravel walk

Satirising Jowett's garden seems to have become quite a sport in 1790s Cambridge; it was even rendered in Latin as a mock parsing exercise (needless to say, *exiguus* and its forms means 'little'):

Exiguum hunc hortum fecit Jowettulus iste
Exiguus, vallo et muniit exiguo:
Exiguo hoc horto forsan Jowettulus iste
Exiguus mentem prodidit exiguam.

Never before or since can such an insignificant (exiguous) garden have inspired such a variety of literary production. Possibly it was sheer satirical pressure which led to 'little Jowett's little garden' being altered before it was removed altogether – apparently bullied out of existence.

Front Court has four sections of lawn, a cruciform path system of flagstones and cobbles, and narrow beds on all four sides against the ranges. The south-facing north wall has roses – including scarlet 'The Prince's Trust' and orange-white 'Ginger Syllabub' – clipped into geometric panels, while other interesting shrubs treated in this way include *Pileostegia viburnoides*, *Carpenteria californica* and, on the shadier side, *Azara microphylla* 'Variegata'. This college continues the Cambridge tradition of 'buttresses' of clipped shrubs on the walls of courts more assiduously than any other – and the Georgian architecture of Front Court is particularly suited to it. The yellow rose 'Perpetually Yours' puts on a good show each year, while clematis is allowed to grow through and around in places. Bright annuals such as zinnias and marigolds are used in the window boxes and at the base of the shrubs in the perimeter beds. Formerly there was a specimen tree in the centre of this court, in the Cambridge way. But not the usual choice of a walnut: it is recorded that a 'fir tree' (which would have been some sort of conifer) was removed in 1739, around the time the court was being modernised, which itself had been a replacement for an earlier yew tree. The fir tree can be seen on David Loggan's 1690 engraving of the college.

There are two small courts in the north of the college which have some garden interest. North Court is a shady rectangle crammed

with bicycles, and also home to the college bar. Leafy hostas and the pompom flowers of *Hydrangea* 'Annabelle' lighten the scene somewhat. Five clipped hornbeams against the north wall add a sense of dignity and a pyracantha grows in the shadiest corner. Cherry Tree Court is a 1970s development where the architects provided little opportunity for horticulture; it is a small court on several levels focused on the eponymous specimen tree.

This northern section of college was formerly (until 1879) a long rectangle given over to gardens which were established on this strip in 1545, after the college had purchased a piece of land anciently known as Henneabley (previously a neglected patch with a public road running across it). The college walled about the space to make a garden within and diverted the road, renamed Garret Hostel Lane, so that it ran across its northern edge. This walled garden is shown on Loggan's engraving of 1690, by which time it had been divided in two, formally apportioning sections to the master and fellows. The fellows' garden occupied the eastern end of the strip while the master's garden (half the size) was situated to the west. The engraving suggests that the master's garden was an orchard while the fellows' fruit garden, as it became known, consisted of a vegetable patch and a small ornamental parterre of box hedges. Fruit trees were grown on the walls and we know there

was a mulberry at each end of the fellows' section in the late 17th and 18th centuries.

As we shall find, this was not the only garden area available to the master and fellows of Trinity Hall; these gardens to the north of the site were mainly given over to produce, while the fellows' garden proper was situated in the southern part of college, on a rectangle of land that extended west from the master's lodging down to the river.

Loggan's engravings tend to repay close examination, and the Trinity Hall view contains several other telling details regarding the early history of the college. For example, some birds shown flying around a vent in the roof of a building on the southern edge of the college indicate that a pigeon-house was in use, the birds being kept for eggs and meat (the latter usually squabs, or very young pigeons of about a month old). In this case the pigeon-house was not a small wooden building located, as was usually the case, out in the garden in an isolated spot away from trees where raptors could lurk. It was instead a new use for the roof-space of the old house that had served as a hostel for the monks of Ely. Warren tells us that the near-derelict

ABOVE The garden in Avery Court (left) was redesigned in the 1990s with distinctive, triangular box-hedged compartments filled with herbaceous material. Shrubs including ceanothus (right) clothe the walls.

building was still being used for pigeons in his time, in the 1730s. This is a late date for a functioning pigeon-house – only three of them among all the colleges are shown as extant on Loggan's engravings made in the 1680s, but we know that most colleges had at least one pigeon-house or dovecote in their garden in earlier days. The ancient hostel was eventually subsumed into the refurbishment of the master's lodging by architect Anthony Salvin in 1852, and little trace of it remains. Historically, colleges have tended to be unsentimental about their old buildings.

Things start to get really interesting, from a garden point of view, when the visitor leaves Front Court by a passageway on its western side. Suddenly the college opens out, with tantalising views west towards Latham Lawn, which takes us down to the river. But first, one's attention is irresistibly drawn to the palpably ancient Old Library on the north side of this three-sided space known officially as Library Court. This characterful red-brick building is Elizabethan (built around 1590) but to most visitors probably appears even older, with its steeply pitched roof and casement windows. That impression is bolstered by the strong immediate contrast with the neoclassical complacency of Front Court, from which one has just emerged. The packed high-summer border in front of the Old Library is one of the horticultural high-points of the college. There are alliums,

irises and geraniums for earlier in the season, but the border comes into its own in July and August, with cosmos, helenium, achillea, nicotiana, heucheras, hollyhocks and salvias creating a cottage feel, backed by taller subjects such as veronicastrum and the foliage interest of macleaya. A giant *Magnolia grandiflora* in the north-east corner of this bed is one of the stand-out plants in college.

Library Court does have a formal focus of sorts in the shape of a perfect roundel of grass set in a cobbled square in the south-east corner, but its western aspect is now so open that any real sense of enclosure has been lost – which is a good thing, in the context of the landscape design at Trinity Hall. This feeling of openness was not always present. Until the mid-to-late 18th century there was a high wall across the western side of Library Court, meeting the Old Library at the point where a door can still be seen, as if suspended mid-wall, just below the line of the first-floor windows. This curiosity, which every member of Trinity Hall over several

ABOVE LEFT The roses and other shrubs and climbers in Front Court are trained on the walls to form 'buttresses', as is traditional in Cambridge colleges.

ABOVE CENTRE The middle section of the long border in the fellows' garden, with the great copper beech on Latham Lawn just over the wall.

centuries must surely have pointed out to visitors, is evidence of the master's privileged access into the library from his lodgings on the south side of the court. It has been suggested that his route was via a gallery which would have run along the east side of Library Court and then turned 90 degrees to end at the door in to the library itself. But the evidence for this is inconclusive – and in any case it was hardly the most direct route. Close perusal of Loggan's engraving suggests that a line of battlements – which can just be seen peeping over the roofline of the west side of Front Court – is in fact the top of the wall cutting straight across the court, defining its western side and running up to the 'suspended' doorway. This wall is shown on Hamond's map of Cambridge of 1592 and Loggan's city map of 1688, as well as the college's own plan made in 1731, though it had disappeared by the time of William Custance's 1798 survey. It seems most likely that an open walk along the top of this wall was the straightforward manner by which the master reached the door to the library. He would have been able to pace the battlements like some medieval king in his castle. After the wall had been taken down – possibly as part of an unrealised building project in the 1740s – it seems that some effort was made to create a sense of enclosure in Library Court; an engraving made by John Le Keux in the 1840s shows a simple post and single-rail fence running along its western side, a perfunctory way of differentiating the formal courts of the college from the garden beyond.

The rich border against the south front of the Old Library extends around the corner to the building's west-facing gable end, where *Sophora* 'Sun King' bears its bright yellow flowers in February. The herbaceous planting continues along the frontage of the Latham Building, a highly successful late-Victorian, Tudor-style building in warm red brick overlooking Latham Lawn from the north-east. The scheme here develops a more Mediterranean feel, created by strident salvias, hibiscus and wallflowers. The doorway to Staircase M is festooned with a grapevine. Latham Lawn itself undulates attractively as it slopes gently down towards the river. At its 'top', eastern end there is an old yew prefaced by pink foxgloves and box balls, and under it, ferns and forget-me-nots. Spring bulbs appear across this lawn in season – crocuses and then scillas, erythroniums, narcissus and *Anemone blanda*. A fine old copper beech stands near the centre of the lawn, its shade keeping the bulbs and corms below ground cool in the summer months.

ABOVE The gate to the fellows' garden, which is closed to all bar the master, fellows and their guests.

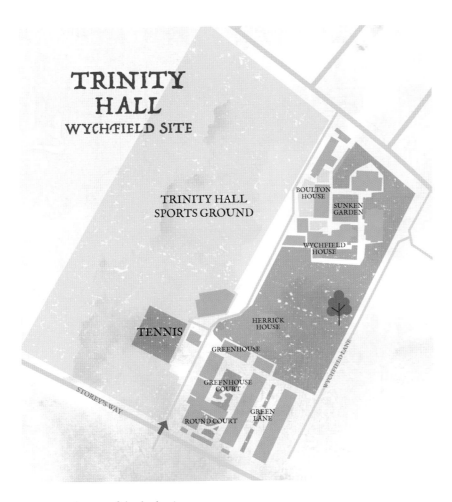

TRINITY HALL
WYCHFIELD SITE

TRINITY HALL
SPORTS GROUND

BOULTON
HOUSE

SUNKEN
GARDEN

WYCHFIELD
HOUSE

TENNIS

HERRICK
HOUSE

GREENHOUSE

WYCHFIELD LANE

GREENHOUSE
COURT

STOREY'S WAY

ROUND COURT

GREEN
LANE

TOP LEFT An area of shrub planting at the Wychfield site, with purple lupins in the foreground.

BOTTOM LEFT Green Lane at Wychfield, part of the 2007 development of the southern section of the site. Each staircase has its own putative front garden and lawn.

The college's buildings continue along the northern edge of this space, offset by cottagey plantings of *Rosa × odorata* 'Mutabilis', *Nicotiana sylvestris*, daylilies, irises and sedums galore. This is where the college really starts to feel like a quiet little village. A planting of echiums is a surprise at the western end, against the college's new library, where large clumps of *Euphorbia mellifera* and another grapevine thrive. Against the river there is a paved terrace (1957) with views to Clare College fellows' garden south, and north to Garret Hostel Bridge, a public right of way.

Latham Lawn and the buildings overlooking it now feel like the heart of the college, where students can walk and lie on the grass as they please. But this was not always the case. The north-western corner of college, by the bridge, was purchased in 1546 from Michaelhouse – the second college to be founded in Cambridge, which was just then in the process of being absorbed into the new Trinity College. (This was all part of the reorganisations north of college that also led to the creation of the master's and fellows' fruit garden.) Initially used as a service area (the college privies were poised over the water, as at most colleges, and this was the route down to them), over time the space took on a more ornamental role, though it was never referred to as a garden in its own right. By the early 18th century it was being described as the 'College Backside' – which was the usual term given by colleges to their riverside land. Compared with the 'Backs' of its neighbours, Trinity Hall's was certainly modest, but a line of lime trees was planted in an attempt to establish the feeling of a meadow with walks against the river. On the college's map of 1731 the area is labelled 'Backside' and trees with paths beneath are shown along the northern and eastern side, with a short run of four trees to the west, parallel to the river.

A 17th-century brick wall running east-west along the entire southern side of Latham Lawn divides it from the fellows' garden, which was denied to junior members in the 18th century, when they were fined sixpence for trespassing, and is still firmly off limits for undergraduates and tourists. This sequestered domain is entered through a wrought-iron gate at its eastern end, festooned with honeysuckle and seeming to promise a 'secret-garden' realm beyond (one is not to be disappointed).

The master's lodging looks directly over the fellows' garden from its eastern end, which seems a curious arrangement in a Cambridge context, where generally the college principal has his or her own garden directly adjacent to 'headquarters'. But it appears it was always

LEFT Crescent-shaped yew enclosures have been made along the length of the long border in the fellows' garden, to create semi-private teaching spaces.

the case that this area was shared by master and fellows, with the master's only private space being the small orchard garden at the northern end of college. At one time the master had a wooden gallery extending from the lodge west into the fellows' garden, with a staircase leading down into it (as also at Corpus Christi), but this garden was never his private domain. Perhaps Trinity Hall, being a legalistic sort of place where justice is taken seriously, had decided that it was only fair for the garden to be shared in this way, given that the fellows had neither bowling green nor tennis court nor archery butts to divert them, unlike most of their contemporaries at other colleges. (Even diminutive Corpus had managed to squeeze in leisure amenities for the fellows, while Queens' bought some land across the road for this purpose.)

The college's 1731 map labels this space as 'Felos Garden For Walking', apparently to differentiate it from the productive gardens then in the northern part of college, and to emphasise its role as a space for relaxation, talk and gentle perambulations. The layout of the garden as shown on this map reflects aspects of William Warren's description at this time. There are four rectangular plots, each of which is focused on an object likely to be one of the 'life-size' lead statues that Warren reports were added in 1705 and initially placed on the riverside wall: 'That with ye Book and Pen, representing Learning, That with Castle, Key and Lion, Cybele, That with Sword and Cap, Liberty, That with Sword and Blindfold, Justice'. These statues, their symbolism so suitable for this college of lawyers, appear to have been removed by the 1740s, when the garden was simplified and a broad gravel walk made down the centre.

Warren also notes that an old galleried summer house overhanging the river was taken down in 1708, which was probably when a raised terrace walk beside the river was made, reached by a central flight of steps, with seats placed at each end, against the walls. (Warren in fact refers to this garden as 'the fellows terrass garden'.) As for planting, yew hedges are mentioned in 1705, presumably to define the garden's four new compartments, and five years later a row of horse chestnuts was planted against the southern boundary wall with Clare College. These trees grew up to become a celebrated feature of the garden, until the last three survivors had to be removed in 2005.

The fellows' garden at Trinity Hall drew many plaudits in its time. Edmund Carter, writing in his history of the university of 1753, was full of praise: 'The Garden is small but well contrived and handsomely beautified with variety of Flowers; The Terras-Walk lying on the Bank of the River, affords a most agreeable Prospect.'

Henry James was most fulsome of all, writing about his visit to Cambridge in an American magazine in 1879. As was the case at other colleges, in the 1820s Trinity Hall's fellows' garden had been 'naturalised' with the addition of serpentine paths, open lawns and flower beds, and James's description reflects this:

> If I were called upon, however, to mention the prettiest corner of the world, I should draw out a thoughtful sigh and point the way to the garden of Trinity Hall. My companion…declared, as he ushered me into it, that it was, to his mind, the most beautiful *small* garden in Europe…The little garden at Trinity Hall is narrow and crooked; it leans upon the river, from which a low parapet, all muffled in ivy, divides it; it has an ancient wall adorned with a thousand matted creepers on one side, and on the other a group of extraordinary horse-chestnuts.

The horse chestnuts have been replaced by a variety of trees including an ailanthus and a liriodendron. In addition there are three *Fagus sylvatica* 'Dawyck' at the river end together with an oriental plane, while towards the master's lodging are a pair of conifers and a quince. There are so many specimen trees that this could almost be called a miniature arboretum, were they not so well placed and spaced.

The glory of the fellows' garden today is a magnificent south-facing border which runs against the entire length of its north wall, down to the riverside terrace with its jolly little greenhouse at one end. Clearly this border was not here, or at least realised at nothing like this scale, when Henry James visited. An undulating path snakes its way along the edge of the border, which is punctuated by small flowering fruit trees, magnolias and a ginkgo, helping to break up the space and create an episodic feel. The planting is classically English in style, with surging and mingling masses of daylilies, achilleas, foxgloves, poppies, peonies, white geraniums and agastache. There is alchemilla at the front of the border, while looming behind and creating structure and a foil of foliage are cardoons and macleayas. Other highlights include *Campsis radicans*, *Crambe cordifolia* and akebia. There are even cordoned pears to be discovered against the wall (a speciality of the college dining hall is pear pie). But above all, roses set the tone; for example rambling *Rosa* 'Albertine' at the east end of the border, merging with 'Albéric Barbier'. There is no overall theme, but pink is the recurring colour.

An intriguing practical innovation is a series of benches along the front of the border. These are set within little semi-enclosed spaces defined by clipped yew hedges shaped into crescent forms. The college arms features a crescent but the real reason for these spaces is to allow fellows to teach students in privacy. Before this solution was found, it was felt that the garden seemed 'occupied' if even one tutorial group was visible. Now, several fellows at a time can use the space without any sense that they are intruding on colleagues.

The riverside terrace at the end of the fellows' garden remains the most evocative spot at Trinity Hall. Self-seeded centranthus in pink and white grow directly out of the wall above the river, while two Banksian roses and rose 'Bobbie James' also cascade down towards the water. The greenhouse adds a cosily domestic air which is charming indeed. Wandering back across the lawn, one can perhaps imagine the large mahogany table that the fellows placed outside here in the 18th century so they could take their wine and dessert al fresco in the summer months. It was a strong table, clearly, for it lasted outdoors for more than 100 years, and was last recorded as being used (by the college's first-boat crew) in 1870.

A recently planted border on the southern side of the fellows' garden has a more shrubby feel, with hostas and other shade-loving subjects. The master's lodging has its own terrace and herbaceous beds which provide some privacy, with fluted earthenware pots ranged about and garrya and pittosporum growing against the wall.

The horticultural quality across the college is first rate, thanks to head gardener Samantha Hartley and her team, developing a standard set by the previous head gardener, Andrew Myson. One noteworthy recent development is Trinity Hall Gin, created in 2018 by the Cambridge Distillery in Grantchester. The distillers undertook a tour of the gardens with the head gardener and lit upon an aromatic flavouring based on rose petals ('purity and identifiability') and choisya ('extraordinary and unusual'). At £75 per bottle, one would hope this spirit is indeed fairly extraordinary.

This would usually be the end of a descriptive tour of a college garden, but in the case of Trinity Hall an exception must be made. Several other colleges have sizeable off-site properties realised almost at the collegiate scale – Corpus Christi's Leckhampton site and Gonville and Caius's Harvey Court spring to mind – but Trinity Hall's Wychfield development has sufficient horticultural interest for it to be treated in its own right.

It was in 1948 that the college bought a large late-Victorian house named Wychfield (1884), sandwiched

between Storey's Way and Huntingdon Road about a mile (1.6 kilometres) from college. The site was adjacent to a plot of land the college had owned for at least 250 years, where in 1923 it had laid out its sports pitches (the cricket pavilion of this era is an attractive adornment). Wychfield, which was previously in the hands of the Darwin family, was initially used to house a retired college master, and subsequently as accommodation for graduates. The old stables were also converted into student rooms.

There are some fine gardens set around this and other buildings in the northern and central portion of the site, but we shall begin in the south, where a porter's lodge greets visitors arriving from Storey's Way. This is part of a recent development (2007) by Cambridge architects RH Partnership. It consists of accommodation blocks which mingle the Arts and Crafts vocabulary of steeply pitched tile roofs, tile-hung walls and red bricks, with modernist details such as large plate-glass windows, stainless steel banisters and smooth limestone steps. The dormer windows in the roofs amalgamate the two apparently contrasting traditions effectively. There is also perhaps some reference to Trinity Hall's own buildings, notably the Old Library, echoed in the varied dark red-brick walls of the new buildings. Perhaps also to the ancient Ely Hostel (visible on Loggan's engraving): the shape of the new buildings is strikingly similar, as is the shape of the roof, and

even the distinctive ventilation hoods, which appear to be modelled on the pigeon-house vent so particular to the old building.

The new development consists of three 'terraces' of student staircases running parallel, north to south. The 16 staircases, housing 12 to 18 students, each has its own front door and even its own front garden area. Despite the rigour of the architectural layout, the garden spaces are deliberately varied – the architects' initial proposal to the college was entitled 'A Garden Community' – and the horticulture here equals the standard at the main college site.

The different garden areas are contained within two long rectangles formed by the accommodation blocks, the western side divided into two separate sections and the eastern side conceived as a 'green lane' running between two of the terraces. The planting was initially planned by Sarah Clayton of Cambridge Landscape Architects and was subsequently developed and maintained for a decade by former head gardener Andrew Myson and his team, and now by his successor Sam Hartley.

The western side consists of Greenhouse Court to the north and Round Court below it. Greenhouse Court features yew and box topiary as an echo of the Arts and Crafts style of Wychfield House, with a *Cercis canadensis* as a specimen tree in the centre of a generously planted 'inner garden'. The northern end of the court is closed off by

the state-of-the-art greenhouse itself, which is prefaced by a cloud-pruned box hedge with 'splashes' of golden yew. Round Court is smaller and is centred on a circular lawn with stepping stones across it, another Arts and Crafts reference. Around the edges are aralias, hebes, geraniums, and roses 'Teasing Georgia' and 'Geranium'.

Green Lane does as the name suggests, creating the sense of a thoroughfare between two of the terraces, with central panels of lawn leading up to a huge beech tree at the far north end. The 'front gardens' here contain plants such as viburnums, euphorbias, astrantias, cistus, heucheras, salvias, phlomis and plenty of roses – as ever at Trinity Hall – including 'Cardinal de Richelieu'. At one point an escallonia has been cloud-pruned against the wall.

'Behind' this new development, on the eastern perimeter of the site where it borders Fitzwilliam College, a line of whitebeams has been planted, with ferns and epimediums beneath, and sweet woodruff as ground cover. One tree was found to be growing more slowly than the rest – archaeological excavations revealed a perfectly preserved Roman road growing 1 metre/39 inches below the surface, hindering its roots.

A line of chestnuts and other mature trees running east-west divides this part of the site from the older section around Wychfield House, to the north, where Andrew Peters made major changes (for the better) as garden consultant in the mid 1990s. The 'fire road'

behind the greenhouse is perhaps an unlikely venue for horticultural hyperactivity, but there is a good border here with osteospermums, armeria, echiums, agrostemma and various grasses.

The central portion of the site is made up of lawns criss-crossed by serpentine gravel paths, with mature trees including a cedar, birches, conifers, a liriodendron, *Magnolia* 'Heaven Scent' and a big beech that is up-lit at night. The modern Herrick House (1972), built for married couples, provides another focus in this central zone, with a monumental sculpture – *Twelve* (2006) by Jonathan Clarke – positioned nearby. Here and at the fringes of the lawns are throngs of narcissus, primulas and fritillaries in spring. Later, tulips appear in abundance across the gardens, from the understated *Tulipa* 'Spring Green' to flame-coloured, lily-flowered 'Ballerina'. A huge specimen of climbing rose 'Wedding Day' smothers an old apple tree while rose 'Bobbie James' climbs through a couple of cherries. The impression overall in this older part of the site is of a mature garden with a variety of areas to discover, such as the more formal Round Garden at the centre, where echinaceas, sedum and sisyrinchium complement shrubs

ABOVE Jonathan Clarke's sculpture *Twelve* (2006), consisting of twelve aluminium pieces, is set amid the grass and spring flowers at Wychfield.

such as deutzia and weigela. It is a considerable achievement in itself that the garden team largely transcends any institutional feeling, the result of sensitive horticultural instincts.

The name of Wychfield House refers to the wych elms that were once the most prevalent tree in this part of Cambridge, though only one survives today on this site. With a little terrace and a lovely balcony, the house is framed on its south side by a series of geometric box beds filled with intensely romantic plantings of irises, foxgloves, cistus, sedum, clematis, calendula, penstemons, foxgloves, red salvias, crocosmia and self-sown nigella. The pure white rose 'Winchester Cathedral' is used as a link plant. There are echiums and osteospermums on the terrace and fine composed views across the lawns. Trinity Hall is known as a college of lawyers but one would think, given surroundings such as this, that it would be turning out romantic novelists instead.

And there is more to come. Behind Wychfield, to the north, are three modern accommodation blocks including the architecturally notable, concrete-framed Boulton House (1968) by Arup Associates. Set between them is a large sunken garden defined by yew hedges and flanked by pleached limes (*Tilia × euchlora*), with variegated ivy below, and roses along with herbaceous plantings consisting of astrantias ('Hadspen Blood'), delphiniums, hollyhocks, daylilies ('Sammy Russell') and geraniums. Specimens of cut-leaved elderberry (*Sambucus nigra* f. *laciniata*) create accents in the beds, while in spring the tulips 'Ballerina' and 'Queen of Night' steal the show, followed by *Allium stipitatum* 'Mount Everest'.

The northern and eastern perimeter of the site is woodland, where bark-mulched paths wend their way through mature yew, oak, horse chestnut and beech trees. There are hellebores, ferns, ivies and martagon lilies to enjoy, while the understorey is enlivened by shrubs and groups of small trees such as maples, photinia and euphorbia. In addition there is an apricot and apple orchard over by the sports pitches on the western side.

'The prettiest corner of the world' has gone forth and multiplied since the time of Henry James, largely thanks to several generations of skilled head gardeners and their teams, and a fellowship willing to lend its support. The result is a college that is now replete with 'pretty corners' on its two complementary sites. As the scales of justice might dictate, the ancient college of Trinity Hall and its newer Wychfield outpost happily co-exist in perfect balance.

ABOVE A perfect roundel of turf in the open-sided court south of the Old Library, with a giant *Magnolia grandiflora* in the corner.

WOLFSON COLLEGE

HERE ARE NOT MANY COLLEGES where you can find more than 60 different rose varieties, half a dozen cornus, three daphnes and any number of heucheras, but this is just the beginning at Wolfson. It's all down to the energetic horticultural experimentation of head gardener Phil Stigwood, a thoroughgoing plantsman who has arguably had more impact on college life than many an academic passing through Cambridge. The level of detail in the planting has made this into one of the most rewarding colleges to visit for the garden-minded, even if the occasional design decision seems eccentric. The soil is certainly on the gardeners' side here: unusually for Cambridge it is a deep, rich loam, further enhanced by annual doses of a 'home-brewed' mulch.

Wolfson is a modern college, founded in 1965, with an old Arts and Crafts house hidden away at its heart. Bredon House was constructed in 1914 for John Stanley Gardiner, professor of zoology, who lived there with his wife Edith and their two daughters until it was bequeathed to the university on his death in 1946. Pleasant and unpretentious – with twin gables to the front and a jaunty trio of dormer windows in the steeply pitched roof – Bredon House is faced with a mixture of deep red and pale brick, resulting in an attractive, slightly mottled appearance. Casement windows and half-timbered detailing above the central door add to the 'olde worlde' appeal. The Gardiners made a long, narrow back garden across 1.25 hectares/ 3 acres stretching south all the way from Selwyn Gardens to Barton Road. It included a large sunken rock or scree garden, well-stocked with saxifrages in its day, an orchard and kitchen garden, as well as space for rabbits, poultry and pigs. Almost all trace of that garden has now gone, but something of the site's horticultural past can still be enjoyed at Wolfson. The college was greatly expanded around Bredon House in the 1970s with little thought for its gardening possibilities, though the landscape architect Sheila Haywood was engaged as a consultant from 1974 and continued to advise into the 80s.

LEFT There is an oriental theme to Lee Court, with wisteria on the pergola and Chinese statues at the library entrance beyond.

303

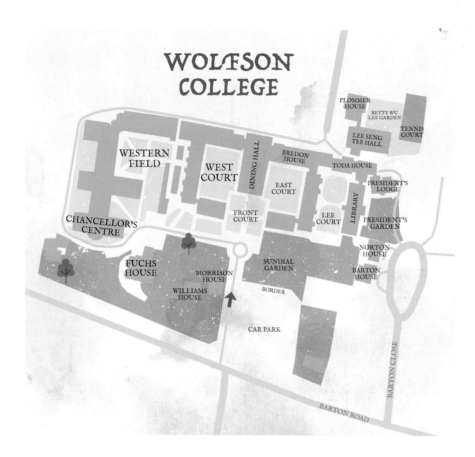

WOLFSON COLLEGE

PLOMMER HOUSE

BETTY WU LEE GARDEN

LEE SENG TEE HALL

TENNIS COURT

WESTERN FIELD

WEST COURT

DINING HALL

BREDON HOUSE

TODA HOUSE

EAST COURT

PRESIDENT'S LODGE

CHANCELLOR'S CENTRE

FRONT COURT

LEE COURT

LIBRARY

PRESIDENT'S GARDEN

NORTON HOUSE

FUCHS HOUSE

MORRISON HOUSE

SUNDIAL GARDEN

BARTON HOUSE

WILLIAMS HOUSE

BORDER

CAR PARK

BARTON CLOSE

BARTON ROAD

RIGHT The college mulberry frames a view into East Court with the casement windows of the Arts and Crafts Bredon House beyond.

The college did not start life in 1965 as Wolfson but as University College, so named because it was the first college established directly by the university. As with its sister college in Oxford, Wolfson was conceived as a graduate institution, resulting in a tangibly more relaxed, laid-back atmosphere. Its slight distance from the frenetic town centre adds to this sensation.

New buildings were obviously needed in addition to Bredon House and the college began thinking about expansion almost immediately, though it was several years before any plans could be implemented on the ground. It was able to buy land on its eastern side and in 1972 planned accommodation for 50 students following a donation from the Gulbenkian Foundation. The next year brought £2 million from the Wolfson Foundation and the change of name. More land was rapidly acquired to the west, along with several other large detached houses along Barton Road (the college today covers 4 hectares/10 acres). The firm Ferrey & Mennim of York was engaged to design two new courts around the core of Bredon House, creating an E-plan, with the long side of the E running east to west. One controversial decision was to absorb Bredon House into the East Court and to insert modern buildings around it, as opposed to retaining it as the centrepiece of the college. The result is that its Arts and Crafts architecture does not relate successfully to the surrounding modernism. It looks a little stranded. This is despite the obvious care taken by the fellows in choosing bricks sympathetic to the existing building. They even commissioned a series of low walls to be constructed in the college grounds, so they might judge which type of brick was best. This led to the interesting sight of

gowned fellows clutching glasses of sherry while wandering around these sample walls in the interval before dinner was served. The decision to keep the roofline of the adjacent buildings lower than that of Bredon House at least gives it room to breathe. This policy was extended across both courts, and as a result Wolfson has an attractively low-slung and rational feel.

The college presents a neat and orderly appearance as the visitor approaches along a dead-straight entrance drive, lined by hornbeam trees inside a yew hedge, leading due north up to Front Court and the porter's lodge. This is, quietly, one of the most effective entrances to a Cambridge college; it looks good at any time of year. The avenue was planted almost on the line of an existing row of old pink chestnuts, several of which were retained so that for a few years the entrance drive contained both hornbeam and chestnuts.

When she was contacted by Wolfson's bursar, Sheila Haywood had been advising on the landscape at Churchill College for a number of years. There, her plans had only been partially implemented, which is perhaps why she initially deflected the invitation, protesting that she was just about to retire. But she was persuaded to come and her ideas for the garden were incorporated into the earliest architectural plans. (It is noteworthy that the initiative to employ a landscape architect emanated from the college and not from the architects in this case.) In the early years Haywood's input was confined to the ground plan, paving materials and so on, as well as tree choices. Her approach was for extreme simplicity in the courts and around Bredon House, with only trees specified, and no shrubs or herbaceous material. A booklet

of postcards made of Wolfson in 1980 shows that the main college was indeed strikingly bare at that point, with the clean lines of the modern buildings meeting close-mown grass. It was only in later years that well-stocked mixed beds around the buildings became the norm. Haywood also suggested a gentle double curve to the line of the entrance drive; this would have lent a pleasing informality, but the idea was not adopted.

There was no horticultural aspect to Haywood's advice until 1977, when the time came to plant up the area south-east of the college now known as the Sundial Garden and first named the Library Garden. This was clearly conceived of as 'the college garden' and was the only space where decorative horticulture was practiced in the early years. Perhaps as a reflection of these limited ambitions, Wolfson did not invest in a head gardener but relied on an outside contractor (a gardens committee was convened only in 1981). Haywood's original plans for the Library Garden survive in the college archive and do appear to have been implemented. The main area of interest is the long east-west border which also forms a boundary screen against the adjacent car park. As at Churchill, Haywood's first scheme here was heavy – in every sense – on serviceable shrubs such as forsythia, potentilla, cotoneaster and viburnum, with the addition of sturdy 'architectural' subjects such as acanthus. Bulky and easily maintained plants had practical advantages, but it does appear that there was some slight dissatisfaction in college

with this approach, which is very much that of the landscape architect rather than the garden designer. Haywood was asked to rethink. In a letter of August 1977, in which she encloses revised plans for the garden that include colourful herbaceous material such as rudbeckia, echinacea and agapanthus, one can almost hear the gritting of teeth as she assures the bursar: 'I have tried for a "flowery" effect as far as I can.' There was a reluctance among 20th-century modernist designers to acknowledge that a 'domestic' element might be desirable in a college environment, which must of course function as a home as well as an educational establishment.

It is possible that the main border in the Library Garden was never seen as wholly satisfactory, and in 1985 it was replaced by a new border designed by Alan Bloom of the celebrated East Anglian nursery Blooms of Bressingham – but only after the gardens committee paid a visit to look at the proposed plants and assess them for scale. A memorandum in the college archive concludes: 'The intention is to travel in a minibus so that members of the Gardens Committee might take their wives if they wish.' The outcome was that the planting scheme followed Blooms' signature practice, developed in the 1970s, of utilising a palette of

ABOVE An armillary sphere is the formal centrepiece of the Sundial Garden, framed by shrubs chosen for foliage effects and a young eucalyptus.

heathers and conifers to create a largely evergreen display. It was a look blessed with originality and verve for a time, but alas it did also date rather quickly, so the border was gradually rationalised by the former head gardener and his successor. (There are still one or two surviving conifers in the border today.)

One of Haywood's most effective decisions was the choice of trees for Front Court, which was much debated at the time. The *Cercis canadensis* (Forest Pansy), to the left, is now looking extremely venerable, propped up by wooden supports, its low branches attractively covered in moss and lichen. The fine mulberry tree to the right is also contemporaneous with the new college. Mulberries disintegrate almost as soon as they are off the tree; nevertheless Wolfson's head chef picks them each year to make some form of pudding. (This can apparently be disconcerting on account of the blood-red stains the berries leave on the chef's 'whites'.) These and other trees in the college sport quite complex and colourful miniature gardens in the tree pits at their bases, more evidence of the horticultural hyperactivity which is now the college's defining visual feature.

Turning right into East Court, the friendly rear elevation of Bredon House comes into view, draped with purple wisteria and a grapevine. There are modest plantings of phormium, lavender and *Stipa tenuissima* in a bed under the central windows, before it gives way to the perimeter pathway and the lawn of the court. Arguably what this kind of

architecture really cries out for is larger-scale herbaceous planting to lend balance, context and scale, with a garden plot preferably extending across the area currently laid to lawn, all the way down to the large holm oak in the south-east corner. Ideally, in fact, such a garden would cover the whole court. It would be a radical change, in the context of a Cambridge college – but co-ed, non-hierarchical, graduates-only Wolfson is supposed to be radical, after all, and the gardener who could achieve it is in post. Mr Stigwood has created a highly effective shade planting beneath the holm oak, comprising heucheras, hostas, epimediums, liriope, variegated *Luzula* and brunnera.

Next to Bredon House, a passageway draped in climbing hydrangea and marked by a large specimen of Mount Etna broom (*Genista*) leads into Lee Court, dominated by the library on its east side. This is one of several buildings made possible through the generosity of the college's prime benefactor, Dr Lee Seng Tee of Singapore, whose daughter attended the college. (Dr Lee's first donation helped fund research into diseases of commercial pineapple crops.) The north and west sides of the court are planted with more tender subjects including cannas and a Mediterranean association of lavenders, salvias and melianthus. The

---

ABOVE A Tang dynasty sculpture (nicknamed Henry the Horse by students) stands in the centre of the Betty Wu Lee Garden.

court's south side is closed by a brick-and-timber pergola draped with Chinese and Japanese wisteria, sustaining the oriental theme which has become a leitmotif of the gardens in recent years. Indeed, the gate piers at the college entrance are now topped by Chinese guardian lions. A Beaux Arts statue of Temperance in the north-west corner of Lee Court doubles as a water fountain; the college has had the humanity to place this sculpture some distance away from the bar.

A narrow passageway leads north towards Lee Hall, a venue for events and lectures realised in the form of a Chinese-themed postmodern pavilion, which the students have unkindly nicknamed 'Pizza Hut'. Intriguing seats near the hall entrance are formed around specimens of *Acer griseum* and conifers. There is more intensive horticulture in this area, with phlox, aquilegia, fennel, *Clematis* 'Nelly Moser' and other perennials founded on a strong underlying structure of evergreen shrubs: pittosporums, choisya, elaeagnus and viburnum. On the hall's south side is a small shrubbery containing a rich mix of clipped *Osmanthus delavayi*, actinidia, *Viburnum* 'Mariesii', foxgloves, acers, brunnera, alliums and hostas, as well as a group of medlar trees, their canopies raised to allow for the underplanting. This interlude is typical of the relentless level of horticultural application at Wolfson; in most colleges, such unregarded spaces would not be deemed worthy of this sort of attention.

North of the hall is the Betty Wu Lee Garden, named after Dr Lee's wife and conceived by the donor, its detail the work of garden designer Paul Edwards in 1990. Laid to lawn, this space is dominated by a large blue cedar in one corner and features a fretwork summer house modelled after one in Singapore Botanic Gardens, and in the centre of the lawn a fine Tang dynasty sculpture of a horse. Noteworthy plants here include the China rose 'Sophie's Perpetual', tree peonies, flowering cherries in pink and white, clematis and purple-flowered abutilon. The space is not big enough to contain all the features placed in it, which imparts a slightly suburban feel. The eastern side of the garden is much more successful, closed by a white-rendered Chinese wall prefaced by decorative weathered limestone in the Chinese tradition, interplanted with conifers, bamboo and *Acer palmatum* 'Sango-kaku'. The stones are much sought-after examples sourced from the Lake Tai region in China. This arrangement means that the immaculately maintained plants stand out well as a sculptural tableau, effectively silhouetted

ABOVE LEFT Epimediums, heathers, hebes, festuca grasses and dwarf conifers are among the varied delights of the Winter Garden.
ABOVE CENTRE Typically complex plantings – including ricinus and musa – are offset by clipped evergreen shrubs in the Sundial Garden.

against the wall. A moon gate, or decorative pierced window, is an attractive and appropriate addition.

The head gardener's real playground is the Winter Garden a few steps farther east. A small space with narrow winding paths, it is jam-packed with plants, each carefully placed for maximum impact. This is a plantsman's garden, which means there may simply be too many different specimens, and too many different colour combinations in one glance, for some people's tastes. But Mr Stigwood makes no apologies about that, and his enthusiasm is certainly borne out in winter, when many of the plants come into their own: trees such as colourful *Acer* × *conspicuum* 'Phoenix' and *Tilia cordata* 'Winter Orange'; structural evergreen shrubs including corokia, pittosporum, phormium, hebe and photinia; and the berries of *Callicarpa bodinieri* var. *giraldii* 'Profusion' (purple), *Sorbus vilmorinii* (pink-red) and *Symphoricarpos* × *chenaultii* (pink). Then there are the bright stems of various cornus and rubus, golden-stemmed bamboos (*Phyllostachys*) and scented shrubs such as daphne and sarcococca. Even the much-maligned dwarf conifer range is given space here, with golden and blue subjects such as *Chamaecyparis pisifera* ''Filifera Aurea' and *Juniperus horizontalis* 'Icee Blue' mixing freely with an imaginative range of ground-cover plants including *Carex oshimensis* 'Everillo', *Libertia* 'Goldfinger' and different heucherellas used en masse. As elsewhere in college, shrubs are rarely left to grow in their own unruly fashion, but clipped into shape; here, hollies and euonymus are formed into lollipops as tiny standards. This is a mere fraction of the plant range on show, and it is not just of interest in winter, of course. For the visiting horticulturist, it's a fascinating, intense, close-range experience.

The president's lodge is south of the Winter Garden and has its own small private garden, planted up in cottage style with forget-me-nots, corydalis and masses of variegated Solomon's seal – which makes a change from the usual cranesbill geraniums used as filler. There is a small pond with yellow flag irises, and hellebores and hostas in shady parts. The college's most recent development is Barton House (2012), east of Lee Court, previously a large detached house, where the garden retains – to the delight of its users – much of its domestic feel and detail. There is a vegetable plot, shed and greenhouse, and borders rich in astrantias, wallflowers, bearded irises and pink foxgloves. The 14 rose varieties here include 'Gertrude Jekyll', 'Winchester Cathedral' and the strongly scented climber 'Red Parfum'. And there are other good

---

ABOVE Seen through the foliage of an acer in the Winter Garden, the distinctive form of the Japanese cedar, *Cryptomeria japonica* 'Sekkan-sugi' (sometimes known as 'golden curls', as the tips of the foliage change colour through the season).

shrubs and small trees: a pomegranate tree, cotinus, cornus, maples (*Acer palmatum* 'Osakazuki' and 'Dissectum') and a golden catalpa contrasting with dwarf *Cercis canadensis* 'Forest Pansy'. Golden hop grows along the fence.

Though arguably nowadays the whole college is one continuous garden experience, the Sundial Garden, focused on an attractive armillary sphere with paved surround, pots and seating, is the most popular with students. A long border along its southern edge has recently been reconceived as a late-summer extravaganza, using a range of perennials in tune with the naturalistic turn in garden style of the past 20 years or so – rudbeckia, echinacea, miscanthus, veronicastrum, salvia, helenium and so on. Interesting shrubs have been added to this mix, notably *Sambucus* 'Black Lace', *Cotinus* 'Grace' and *Physocarpus opulifolius* 'Lady in Red'. Variegated euonymus provides structure, clipped tightly into shape in the Wolfson style. Thanks to careful planning, this border performs remarkably well through late autumn and into winter, and is one of the best examples of all-season planting in the Cambridge colleges.

The western parts of the college are not as interesting horticulturally, though some large trees – lime, birch, plane, cedar, wellingtonia, sycamore, yew – are survivals from the domestic gardens on this land before Wolfson's existence. One curiosity, next to Fuchs House, is a polar-themed garden containing plants with icy connotations in their names: *Penstemon* 'Pensham Arctic Fox' and *Clematis* 'Arctic Queen', as well as *Astrantia* 'Snow Star', *Philadelphus* 'Snowbelle', *Brunnera macrophylla* 'Jack Frost' and of course *Rosa* 'Iceberg'. As might be imagined, a garden pieced together on the basis of wordplay does not hang together particularly well horticulturally. This area was until 1988 in the garden of Sir Vivian Fuchs, leader of the Commonwealth Trans-Antarctic Expedition 1955–58, which made the first land crossing of the continent – hence the polar references here. A gigantic yew topiary intended to resemble a penguin, with an egg made from euonymus, was created by the explorer in memory of his travels. It is still respectfully clipped into shape each year, though most visitors think it is supposed to be a Tyrannosaurus rex. Sir Vivian's lead husky dog is also buried in this rather eccentric corner of the garden. Near Fuchs House is a large yew beneath which snowdrops have been planted in a distinctive swirling pattern. Plain *Galanthus nivalis* is used here, though the college does have its own snowdrop variety, discovered in the garden and unfortunately named 'Mr Grumpy'.

There is nothing to be grumpy about in Wolfson's garden. The endeavours of the head gardener and his team have lent the college a distinctive character in a university context. Where else does the college bicycle shed have its own, carefully tended raised-bed border? It is apparent that the work of the gardeners is much appreciated – which is by no means always the case in hierarchy-fixated Cambridge.

LEFT A *Cercis canadensis*, or Forest Pansy, in Front Court also lights up West Court in spring and early summer.

INDEX

Readers' Note. Owing to lack of space, commonly occurring plants (e.g. dahlia) or passing mention with no species, or frequent terms (e.g. bowling greens), have not been indexed.

6a architects 37

A

abutilon 51, 146, 158, 204, 221, 238, 308
Acacia pravissima 28
acanthus 25, 46, 84, 204, *242*, 246, 269, 278
Acca sellowiana (pineapple guava) 203
Ackerman 289
actinidia 203, 308
Acton, Liz 184
Adam of Horningsea 9
Adams Road houses 230–1
aeonium 280
African hemp *see Sparrmannia africana*
agapanthus 28, 102, 306
agastache 298
agave 235
ageratum 245
agrostemma 300
ailanthus 133, 194, 298
ajuga 212
akebia 219, 204, 298
albizia (silk tree) 26, 235, 280
alchemilla 40, 62, 126, 136, 207, 219, 246, 298
alder 176, 227
All Saints' Church *143*
Allies & Morrison 66, 102, 103, 118
almond, flowering 182
Alnus glutinosa 81
Aloysia citrodora 238
alstroemeria 186, 238
alyssum 235
amaranthus 182, 238, 245
amelanchier 92
Ammi majus 269
anchusa 49, 51
Andrewes, Lancelot 224
anemone 49, 53, 195, 223, *266*, 284, 293
Angel Court 280
angelica 136
angles (college architecture) 88
Anglo-Saxon burial ground 113
Annesley, Francis 76
Arabis turrita (tower mustard) 263
aralia 300
Arbutus 23, 26, 28, 143
Archer, Michael Dan *36*
archery butts 11, 23, 204, 218–19
Aristolochia clematitis (birthwort) 144, *148*, 205
armeria 300
armillary sphere 66, *69*, *248*
Armstead, H.H. 158
Armstrong, Winifred 100
aruncus 25, 104, 183
Arundo donax 104
Arup Associates 301
Ascending Form 183, *187*
asclepia 238
Ash Court *115*, 118
asplenium 81
astilbe 84, 220, 269
aucuba 36
auditorium 99
Audley, Thomas 170, 171, 177, 178
Avenue, The 275–7
Avery, Dennis 289
Avery Court 288, 289, *291*
azalea 182
Azara microphylla 26, 62, 290

B

Babington Yew 262
Bachelor's Walk 256–7
Back Lawn 155, 156, 157
Backhouse, James 191–2
Backs 7, 10, 153, 155, 218, 251, 262, 277
Baker, Herbert 80
Ballarin, Sergio 20

Balliol College, Oxford 200
Banham, Debby 167
Banks 238
Barlow, Lady 231
Barlow, Nora and Ruth 181
Barlow, Walter 53
Barnwell Priory 8
Barton, Dave 62
Barton House 309
basil, Japanese 245
baths 13
bay laurel 44, 146, 268
Beales family 67
bear 272
Beaufort, Margaret 19, 20, 252–3, *266*, *268*
Beaumont, Charles 215
beauty bush 104
Beckwith, James 155
Bedell, William 92
beekeeping 26, *93*, 113, 132, 284
begonia 104, 126, 170, *174*, 212, 245
Benedictine Priory of St Radegund 139
Bene't College 57
Benslow House 107
Benson, A.C. 178–9
Benson Court 179
Benson Hall 179
Bentley, Richard 279–80
berberis 28, 203, 247
bergenia 114, 183, 213
Bernard, Marianne 112
Bertram, Kate 166
Betty Wu Lee Garden *307*, 308–9
Betula see birch
Bhutan pine *see Pinus wallichiana*
Big Island 66, *69*, 70
Bin Brook 228, 256, 266
birch (*Betula*): *B. alleghaniensis* (yellow birch) 81, 147
    B. utilis 186, 227
    Himalayan 245
    paperbark 66, 205
    peel-bark 104
    silver 21, 37, 40, 126, 137, 224
    weeping silver 221
bird cherry *see Prunus padus*
birthwort *see Aristolochia*
Bishop's Hostel 280
bistort 184
Björnson, Maria 231
Blomfield, Sir Arthur 234
Bloom, Alan 306–7
Blue Boar 280
bluebell 195, 263
Blundell Court 247
Bodichon, Barbara 111–12
Bodley's Court 160
bog garden 52
Boston ivy 146, *257*, 266
bothy 177
Botolph Court *58*
Boulton House 301
Bowen, Dr Anthony 143
Bradley-Hole, Christopher 69, 194
Bradley-Hole Schoenaich Landscape Architects 118, 194, *195*
Braithwaite, Margaret 165
Bramley, Robert 117
Bredon House 303, *304*, 307
bricks for buildings 15
Bridge of Sighs 251, *251*, 259, *261*, 261, *264*, *266*
Bridgeman, Charles 156
bristlecone pine *see Pinus aristata*
Brookes, John 32
broom 213
Brown, David 166, 231
Brown, Jane 114
brugmansia 221

brunnera 62, 84, 104, 307, 308, 311
Buckingham College 170
Buckingham Court 179
burial ground (Anglo-Saxon) 113
Burrell's Field *279*, 284
Bursar's Court *58*, 62
Butt Close 47, 49
Butterfield, William 199–200
buttresses 10, *11*, 16, 20, 273, 275, *277*, 290, *292*
Byron, Lord *272*

C

cacti 69, 186, 187
Caius Court 122, *123*–4, 126
calamagrostis 40, 102, 118
calendula 301
callicarpa 103, 229, 245, 309
Calocedrus 91
calochortus 161
calycanthus 158
camassia 195
Camellia sinensis 67
campanula 114, 115, 219
Campbell Court 115, 118–19
campsis 60, 62, 160, 195, 245, *277*, 298
Cantabrigia Depicta 156
Cantabrigia Illustrata 10, 14, 212, 253
Capability Brown 10, 155, 261
carex 136, 137, 186, 309
Carmefield 228
Carmelites 218
Carpenteria californica 290
Carter, Edmund 26, 60, 87, 124, *174*, 201, 259, 277
caryopteris 275
Catalpa bignonioides (Indian bean tree) 239
catmint (nepeta) 114, 118, 133, 167, 187, 201
Cave-Brown-Cave, T.R. 116
Cavendish, Lucy 165, 166
Cavendish Building 133–6
Cavendish College 130
centaurea 104, 136, 246
centranthus 118, 278, 298
Cephalanthera damasonium (helleborine) 184
cephalaria 40, 104
ceratostigma 102, 103, 105, 269
Ceres statue 167
Cereus hexagonus (torch thistle) 282
Cernuda, Luis 87
Chaderton, Laurence 92
Chaderton, William 219
Chamaecyparis pisifera 'Filifera Aurea' 309
Chamberlin Powell & Bon 181
Champneys, Basil 189, 269
Chapel Court *140*, 140, 147–8, 244, 245, 268
Chapel Lawn *114*
Chapel Yard 156–7
Chapman, Reverend 96
Chapman's Garden 93, 96
Charles, Prince of Wales 271, 272
Cheal's Nursery 264
cherry *see Prunus*
Cherry Tree Court 291
Chetwynd Court 160
Chichester elms 224
Chilean glory flower *see Eccremocarpus*
chimney, the (Jesus College) 140, *149*
chimonanthus 40, 238
Chinese garden *153*, 161, 308–9
Chinese lions 308
chionodoxa 104, 157, 238, 246, 263
chocolate vine *see Akebia*
choisya 36, 52, 117, 186, 298, 308
Chōshū Garden 186
Christ's College 10, 11, 15, **18–29**
Christ's Pieces 15
chrysanthemum 104, 114, 183, 187
Churchill, Winston 31, 40

Churchill College **30–41**
cimicifuga 246
cirsium 194
Clare Bridge *43*, 45, 47, *52*, 52, *53*
Clare College 16, **42–55**, *151*
Clare Hall 10, *16*, 46, 47
Clare House 46
Clarke, Edward Daniel 143
Clarke, Jonathan *300*, 300
Clayton, Sarah 85, 299
clematis: C. 'Arctic Queen' 311
    C. cirrhosa 20
    C. montana 45, 63
    C. 'Nelly Moser' 308
    C. 'Perle d'Azur' 51
    C. 'Polish Spirit' 183
    C. 'The President' 183
    viticella 187
cleome 238
clerodendrum 41, 266
clock tower 199
Cloister Courts 108, 114, 115, 117, 140, 142, 146, 217, *218*, 218, 219, *241*, *242*, *245*, 245, *246*, 248
cloisters 91, *92*
close *see* paddock
cloud pruning 26
Clough, Blanche Athena 191
Clough, Jemima 190
Clough Hall *189*, 191, 192
coal dust for walks 10, 23, 214, 221
Coastal Path 148
Cobb, Gerard 283
Cobb, Jo 182
cobnut 113
Codrington, John 91, 96
Coghill, Steven 158, 161
Cole of Horningsay 155
Coleridge Path 149
Coleridge, Samuel Taylor 13, 149
coleus 158
College Court 77, 80
Colletia paradoxa 102
Collis, Charlotte (Lottie) 195
Colutea orientalis 229
Colvin, Brenda 34
Commencement Ceremony 242
Cooper, Miss 96
cordyline 136, 137, *237*, 238, 275, 280
coreopsis 262
Corfield Court 269
cornflower 269
corokia 309
Coronilla valentina subsp. *glauca* 205
Corpus Christi College 11, 12, **56–63**
corydalis 268, 309
Corylus (hazel): *C. avellana* 'Purpurea' 158, *170*, 212, 220
    C. colurna (Turkish hazel) 158
cotoneaster 36, 37
cotton lavender 114
courts (*general*) 10, 15
cow parsley 133, *147*, 184, 263
Cowan Court 37
cowslip 144, 184, 195
crab apple *see Malus*
Crambe cordifolia 144, 204, 298
+ *Crataegomespilus* 'Dardarii' 91
crataegus 36
cricket pitches 84
crinum 136, 289
Cripps Building 251, 256, 264, 266, *266*
Cripps Court 176, *220*, 221, 223
Cromwell, Oliver 244
croquet lawn 63, 69, 127, 190, *200*, 204, 214, 245, 263
crouches, le 155
Crowe, Sylvia 34, 84, 264
Cryptomeria japonica 'Sekkan-sugi' *309*

Cullinan, Edward (Ted) 105, 268
cyclamen 62, 102, 136, 231, 277
cypress (*Cupressus*) 49, 91, 126
Cytisus x *praecox* 238

D
daisy 167, 252, *268*, 275
damson 184
daphne 62, 136, 143, 195, 309
Dark Planet 104, *105*
Darwin, Charles 19, *19*, 28, 65, 181, 231, 299
Darwin, Emma 100, 103–4, 182, 186
Darwin, George 65, 69, *70*
Darwin, Henrietta 104
Darwin, Jacob 76
Darwin, Margaret 76
Darwin, Maud 66, 70
Darwin College *14*, **64–73**
Darwin Garden 28
datura 186
Davidia involucrata (handkerchief tree) 25, 52, 84, 92, 144, 203, 237
Davies, Emily 108, *109*, 112
dawn redwood 40, 52, 84
de Balsham, Hugh 209
de Brasur, Walter 210
de Clare, Lady Elizabeth 46
de Koning, Philip *228*, 230
de Monchaux, Paul 119
de Windt, Harry 178
dead man's fingers *see Decaisnea fargesii*
Dean's Walk 52
Deer Park 210, 214
Decaisnea fargesii (dead man's fingers) 229
Deschampsia cespitosa 'Goldtau' 105
Descriptive Guide Through the University of Cambridge 48, 140
deutzia 247, 301
Dewey, Revd Meredith 204
Dianella tasmanica 28
Dianthus carthusianorum 167
diascia 126, 214
dicentra 102, 133, 136
dichondra 245
Dicksonia (tree fern) 26, *28*, 37, 67, *124*, 126, 220, 269, 280
Dining Group 165
Dipelta floribunda 184
DNA Double Helix 46, *51*
dogs *272*
Dokett, Andrew 218
Dominican friars 88
Dorothy Garrod Building 194
dovecotes 10, 60, 152, 155, 213, 291–2
Downing, George 74–5
Downing College **74–85**
Doyle, Arthur Conan *248*
dragon's claw willow *see Salix babylonica*
Duff, J.D. 166, 283–4
Duff's Garden 166, 283
Duns, John (Duns Scotus) 242
Dunthorne, Richard 202
Dutch elm disease 77
Dyer, George 96, 121, 140, 143, 221, 241, 246

E
eagles 252, *272*
East Court *304*, 307
East House 133
East Lodge Garden *81*, 81
Eccremocarpus 26, 158, 235
echeveria 204
echinacea 40, 105, 158, *220*, 300, 306, 311
echinops 262, 278
Edgeworth, Maria 277
Edgeworthia 158
Edward III 271
Edwards, Dr Ros 182
Edwards, Paul 308
elder *see* sambucus
eleagnus 308
Eliza Baker Court 118
Elstub, Steve 44, 53
Ely Hostel 299
Emily Davies Court 108, 112, 114–15, 117, 119
Emmanuel College 9, 11, 15, **86–97**
English Garden, The 202

Erasmus Building 220
Erasmus's Walk 219
eremurus 104, 158
erigeron 114, 220, 231
Erskine, Ralph *16*
eryngium 84, 89, 103, 117, 137, 223
Erysimum 'Bowles's Mauve' 278
erythronium 293
escallonia 28, 84, 114, 300
Essex, James 89, 96, 156, 261, 277, *280*
eucalyptus 144, 223
Eupatorium purpureum 204
eurybia 183
Evelyn, John 223
Everett, William 7

F
Fagus sylvatica 'Dawyck' 227, 268, 298
Falling Warrior 46
Fellows' Building *20*, 20–1
Fellows' Court 100, 103
Fen Garden 214
fennel 25, 308
Ferrey & Mennim 304
feverfew 167
Field Gate 156
Fiennes, Celia 259
fig 160, 215
filipendula 133
Firman, Nick 200–1, 204
First Undergraduate 105
fish ponds *see* stew ponds
Fisher Building 223
Fisher, John 252
Fitzpatrick Hall 223
Fitzwilliam College 15–16, **98–105**
fives 234
Flanagan, Barry 144, *144*, 147
flax 201
Floyer, Dr 13
football 12–13, 244, 277
Foreigner's Companion 47, 96, 214, 282
forget-me-not *124*, 126, 186, 293, 309
Fortin, John 224
Foundress Court *204*, 205–7
Fountain Court 181, 183
fountains 80, 158, 160, 175, 271, *277*, 279, *284*, 308
Four Square 31, *32*, 34, *39*
foxglove tree *see Paulownia tomentosa*
Foxley, Alice 80
foxtail lily 104
Franciscans 242
Fraxinus 31, 84
Frazer, James George 284
fremontodendron 204, 220
Frere, William and Mary 78
Friar's Gate 156, *157*
fritillary *47*, 104, 137, 195, 238, 300
Frost, Henry 252
Fuchs, Sir Vivian 311
Fuller, Guy 231
Fuller, Thomas 9, 243

G
Gallant, Paul 238
games fields 34, 37, 41, 148–9, 158, 178, 277
Garden Hostel 158, *161*
garden rooms 49, 53
gardeners 17, 23, 49, *316–18*
Gardiner, John Stanley 303
Gardiner, Walter 179
Garlick Fair 142
Garret Hostel 280
garrya 37, 205, 298
Gatehouse Court 101–2, 104
gatehouses 60, 217, 219, 227, 252
genista 307
Gerald's Bower 212
geum 104, 171, 262
Gibberd, Sir Frederick 32
Gibbs Building 10, *151*, 153, 155, 160
Gill, Eric 194
Gilpin, William Sawrey 214
Girton College **106–19**
Girton Column 119
Gisborne Court 10, 212, 212–13

Gladstone, W.E. 191
Glastonbury thorn 187
Gleditsia sinensis 158
Glutton Club 28
Godshouse 19
Golden Bough, The 284
golden rain tree *see Koelreuteria paniculata*
Gonville and Caius College 10, **120–7**
Gonville Court 121–3, 126
Gonville Hall 10, 121
Gooden, Alexander Chisholm 14
Goodwin, Andrew 257
Gormley, Antony 147
Goss, Sue 183
Grafton, Duke of 261–2
Grange, the 66
Granta, River 67
grass snakes 132
gravelled walks 23, 33, 45, 214
Gray, Ronald 91
Gray, Thomas 202
Great Court *11*, 271, 272–3, *277*, *284*
Great St Mary's Church 9
Green Lane *295*, 300
Greenhouse Court 299–300
Grim, John 8–9
Gropius, Walter 26
Grove Lodge 74
Grove, The 100, *101*, 103–4, *104*, 149, 210, *210*, 212, 213, 218, *223*, 224
Gruffydd, John St Bodfan 166, 228–9
Grumbold, Robert 24, 142
Grumbold, Thomas 47, *52*
guava, pineapple 203
guinea pigs 166
gunnera 204
Gymnocladus dioica (Kentucky coffee tree) 282

H
Ha-ha Garden 146
Haematoxylum campechianum (logwood tree) 282
Halimodendron argenteum (Siberian salt tree) 158
Hall, Nigel *41*
Hall Court 244, 245, 247
Hall of the Scholars of the Holy Trinity 287
Hallam, Arthur 275
hamamelis 40
Hancock, Tom 96
handball courts 12, 60
handkerchief tree *see Davidia involucrata*
hanging baskets 170, *174*
Happy Apple Day 187
Harber, David 104, *105*
Harraden, Richard 10, 48, 139–40, 175, 224
Harrisson, Tim 25
Hartley, Samantha 298, 299
Harvey Court *127*, 127
Hawksmoor, Nicholas 259
hawthorn 41, *194*, 195, 284
Hayhurst, Prof John 223
Haywood, Sheila 34–6, 303, 304–6
hazel *see Corylus*
heather 103, *103*, 308
hebe *34*, 40, 44, 203, 269, 300, *308*, 309
hedychium 136
helichrysum 144
heliconia 203
helleborine *see Cephalanthera damasonium*
Henneabley 291
Henning Larsen 40
Henry VI 151, 155, 217
Henry VIII 242, 271
Henry the Horse *307*
Henslow, Reverend J.S. 115
Heong Gallery 79
Hepworth, Barbara *31*, 81, 147, 183, *187*
herbs 96, 144, 167, 187, 289
Hermione 113
Hermitage, the 65, 66, 70, 181
Herrick House 300
Herring, Evelyn *146*
Heseltine, Ian 266
heuchera 62, 104, 220, 292, 300, 307
heucherella 136, 309
hibiscus 289, 293
High Walk Bridge 262

Hill, Arthur 158
Hillier, Sir Harold 148
Hobhouse, Penelope *110*, 117
Hobson's Conduit 23, 28, 93
hollyhock 144, 269, 280, *287*, 292, 301
Holmes, Sherlock *248*
Homerton Academy 129
Homerton College **128–37**
honeysuckle *see Lonicera*
Honeysuckle Walk 113, 116
Hooijenga, Tom 279
hops 155, 187, 311
Hopwood, Blasé 91
Horder, Morley 148
Hortus Sociorum 46
Hospital of St John the Evangelist 252, 269
hostels for students 10, 210
Howard buildings 85
Howell Killick Partridge & Amis 66, 84, 247
Hughes Hall *15*
Humphry, Alfred Paget 234
Huntingdon elm 224
hypericum 36
hyssop 114

I
Ibberson, Herbert 136–7
Ibberson Building 136–7
ice-skating 277
ikebana 182
In Memoriam 275
Indian bean tree *see Catalpa bignonioides*
Indigofera heterantha 203
inula 45
Isotoma axillaris 'Blue Star' *169*
itea 245
Ivor Richards Memorial Garden *179*
Ivy Court 198, *198*, 203

J
Jack, Janet 148
Jacobsen, Arne 34
James, Henry 287, 297–8
James Backhouse & Sons 191
Japanese bitter orange 278–9
Japanese gardens 40, 186, 207
jasmine 114, 221
Jasminum beesianum (red jessamine) 282
Jaye, John 70
Jekyll, Gertrude 53, 111, 112, 114–15, 192
Jellicoe, Sir Geoffrey 148
Jencks, Charles 46, *51*
jessamine, red 282
Jester 96
Jesus Close 140, *143*
Jesus College *7*, *8*, *9*, 11, 15, 16, **138–49**
Jesus Ditch *143*, 149
Jesus Grove 142–3, 149
John Bradfield Court 66, 69
Johnson, Dr 19
Johnson, Hugh 158
Jones, Emily Elizabeth Constance 113
Jowett, Joseph (Little Jowett) 289–90
jungle, the (Trinity College) 280
juniper 279
Juniperus horizontalis 'Icee Blue' 309
Jurassic Park 67

K
Kaetsu Centre *184*, 186
kalanchoe 161
Kaldor, Lord and Lady 230
kale 215
Kalendarium Hortense 223
Keble College, Oxford 199–200
Kenny Court 84–5
Kentucky coffee tree 282
Kerria japonica 'Pleniflora' *34*
Keynes Garden 161
Keynes, John Maynard 151, 158
Keynes, Yasmina 161
Keys, Dr John 15, 121–3, *124*
John Kidger, Steve 101, 104
King Edward's Tower 272
King's College 10, 16, **150–63**
King's Ditch 13–14, 149, 242, *242*, 246
King's Grove 152
King's Hall 13, 271, 278

knautia 40, 103, 104
knot gardens 10, 24, 193, 215, 278
Knox, Wilfred 166
Koelreuteria paniculata (golden rain tree) 91, 158
Kolkwitzia amabilis (beauty bush) 104
K'uei Hsing 179, *179*
Kwee Court 62

L

+ *Laburnocytisus* 'Adamii' 41, 91, 204
laburnum 51, 117, 175
Labyrinth, the 253
Lacnunga 167
lakes 33
Lamborn, Peter Spendlowe *44*, 48, 156
Lammas Land 67
Larix decidua 'Pendula' 119
Lasdun, Denys 26, 28, 99–101, 104
Latham Building 293
Latham Lawn *288*, 292, *292*, 293, 295
Laundress Yard 155
laurel, Portuguese 28, 144
lawnmowers 16, 116, 160
Lawrence, D.H. 13
Le Keux, John *28*, 48, *143*, 293
Leckhampton hostel 63
Lee Court 307
Lee Hall 308
Lee Seng Tee, Dr 307
leisure gardens 10, 11
Lennox-Boyd, Arabella 167
leucojum 107
Lever, Thomas 12
Libertia 'Goldfinger' 309
Library Court 182, 183, 292
Library Garden 81–2, 306
Library Lawn *197*, 201, 202
ligularia 40, 137, 220
lily pond *207*, 207
lime (*Tilia*): *T. cordata* 'Winter Orange' 309
    T. x *euchlora* 301
    T. mongolica 262, *264*
    T. tomentosa 53, *156*
liquidambar *36*, 66, 102, 182, 224
liriope 307
Liriodendron tulipifera (tulip tree) *29*, 62, 230
Little Island 66, 69, 70, *70*
livestock 160, 174, 266, 303
Lloyd, Christopher 237
Lobelia tupa 102
Locking Piece *129*, 132
logwood tree 282
Long, Richard 147
Longstaffe-Gowan, Todd 63
Lonicera (honeysuckle) 103, 220, 221, 245
loosestrife 184
Lucy Cavendish College **164–7**
Lupinus polyphyllus 63
Lutyens, Edwin 179, 193
Luzula 104, 307
lychnis 40, 62, 84, 103, 104
Lyne, Richard 58, 140, 152, 204, 212, 242
lysimachia 40, 104
lythrum 204
Lythrum salicaria 'Feuerkerze' 136

M

MacCormac Jamieson & Prichard 103, 104, 284
Madingley Hall 17–18
Maersk shipping line logo 40
Magdalene Bridge 14
Magdalene College 9, **168–79**
Magdalene Walks 175
'magic roundabout' 181, 182
Magnolia: *M. grandiflora* 20, 40, 63, 161, 201, 245, 273, 292, *301*
    M. 'Heaven Scent' 300
    M. kobus 36, 37, 136
    M. 'Leonard Messel' 41
    M. x *soulangeana* 28, 84, 119, 195, 230
Main Walkway 183, *187*
Maine, Dr Frank 41
Maitland Robinson Library 81
maize 'Fiesta' 187
Mallory, George 179
Mallory Court 179

Malus (crab apple): *M.* 'Evereste' 186
    M. x *floribunda* 179
    M. 'Golden Hornet' 62
    M. hupehensis (Chinese crab apple) 89
    M. 'John Downie' *110*, 117
    M. 'Red Sentinel' 62
    M. trilobata 26, *210*
malva 204
Mare's Run 119
Margaret of Anjou 217
marigold 194, 212, 290
Marquess of Queensberry 178
Marshall House 167
Mary Magdalene 176, *179*
Mason, William 202
Master's Lodge Court 288
master's paddock 140, 142
Mathematical Bridge 224, *224*
McGee, Adam 262
Meade, Gerald 212
meconopsis 52
medlar 111, 113, 133, 136, 161, 308
Melianthus major (melianthus) 103, 161, 203, 235, 275, 307
Memorial Court 45–6
memorial garden 192
Memorial Mound *189*, 192
Merton College, Oxford 279
Merton Hall 266
Metasequoia glyptostroboides 25, 96, 266
Metcalfe, Fanny 112
Michaelhouse 273, 295
Mildmay, Sir Walter 88
Milestones, le 279
Miller, Charles 261
millet *see* pennisetum
Milton, John 19, 25, *26*
Minns, Ellis 204
miscanthus 103, 105, 133, 144, 269, 311
mistletoe 133
Møller Centre 34, *37*, 40
Monarda 'Cambridge Scarlet' 104
monkey puzzle 28, 119, 133, 144
Monks' Walk 174, 175, 176
monkshood 212
Montagu, John 243
Monte Cobbeo 283
Moore, Henry 46, 63, *129*, 132, 147
Moore, John 37
Morden, Joseph 92
Morris, William 252
Mortal Man 146
muehlenbeckia 204
Muggeridge, Malcolm 166
Murray Edwards College **180–7**
Murray, Rosemary 182, 183
muscari 204
Myers, Robert 10, 45
myrtle 62
Myson, Andrew 298, 299

N

Nandina domestica 'Richmond' 202
Nash, David 147
nasturtium 238
nepeta *see* catmint
Nevile, Thomas 273
Nevile's Court 273, 277
New Cambridge Guide 45
New Garden Hostel 158
New Hall 181, 182
New Zealand daisy bush *see* Olearia
Newnham College **188–95**
Newnham Grange 65, *66*, 67
Newton, Sir Isaac *272*, 278, 280–2
Newton's Apple Tree 280
nigella 301
Nihon University 207
North Court *37*, 40, *40*, 147, 268, 290–1
North Hall 191
Norway maple 230
Nut Walk 195

O

oak *see* Quercus
observatory 191, 192
Old Divinity School 269
Old Granary 66, 67, 69

Old Labs 195
Old Library 200, *287*, 292, 293, *301*
Old Master's Lodge 199
Old Schools 123
Old Senior Common Room 100
Olearia x *haastii* (New Zealand daisy bush) 103
Oley, Barnabas 47, 152
Olisa Library *102*, 105
On the Cam 7
ophiopogon 51, 69, 238
Oratory of the Good Shepherd 165–6
Orchard Building 198, 205
Orchard Court 183, *187*
orchid 33, 41, *137*, 195
Order of the Brothers of the Sack 210
osmanthus 153, 229, 308
osteospermum 52, 215, 300, 301
Oudolf, Piet 144
Oxford University 7–8, 15

P

paddock 10, 16
Paddock, the 78, 84, *87*, 88, 91, *92*, 275, 277
pagoda tree *see* sophora
palm 204, 237, *237*
pampas grass *32*, 84, 105
Paolozzi, Eduardo 147
Paphiopedilum 'Winston Churchill' 41
Parker, Cornelia 147
Parker, Matthew 60
Parker's Piece 15
Parry, Eric 205–7
Parthenocissus tricuspidata (Boston ivy) 235, *237*
Pattern of Life, A 25
Paulownia tomentosa (foxglove tree) 37, 85, 104, 179, 213, 238, 284
pear 66, 111, 113, 117, 181, 204, 298
Pearson, John Loughborough 245
Peile Hall 192, 195
Pembroke College 11, *12*, 15, **196–207**
Pembroke Leys 76
Pennsionary 60
Pepys Library 170, 175, *175*
Perilla frutescens (Japanese basil) 245
periwinkle 113
perovskia 105, 204, 215, 278
persicaria 104, 105, 273
Peterhouse 9, 10, **208–15**
Peters, Andrew 100, 101, 104, 289, 300
Pfeiffer Arch 194
philadelphus 52, 53, 84, 175, 203, 311
phillyrea 133, 279
phlomis 117, 136, 137, 144, 203, 300
phormium 40, 51, 89, 147, 177, 213, 307, 309
photinia 62, 203, 223, 227, 266, 301, 309
Phyllostachys nigra (black bamboo) 62
physocarpus 219, 311
Picea omorika 186
Pierson, Andrew 58
Pig Club 266
pigeon-house 291–2
Pileostegia viburnoides 290
pine (*Pinus*):
    P. aristata (bristlecone pine) 144
    P. nigra (black pine) 25, 111
    P. pinaster 158
    P. strobus (Weymouth pine) 239
    P. thunbergii *153*
    P. wallichiana (Bhutan pine) 133, 136, 186
    Monterey 186
    Scots 46
    Wollemi 67, 284
pinks 114, 116, 144
Piper, John 228
Pitt the Younger, William *200*
'Pizza Hut' 308
plague 13
planetarium 201–2, *203*
plectranthus 60
plum 133, 175, 204, 223
plumbago 20, 113, 201
Plumptre, Robert 224
plunge pools 13, 45, 93, 96, 124, 203, 214
Podocarpus salignus 28
polyanthus 184
polygonum 144

pomegranate 26, 266, 311
Poncirus trifoliata (Japanese bitter orange) 278–9
Pool Garden 48, *51*, 51
poplar 166, 277
Porter's Court 288
potentilla 36, 219, 262
potting shed 144
Powell, Alfred Hoare 192, *192*
Powell & Moya 223, 264
Power, John 198–9
President's Gallery *218*, 219
president's garden 122, 221
president's house 187
president's lodge 309–10
Prideaux, Edmund 46
Principal Court 288
Priory of the Holy Trinity 88
privies *see* sewage
Procter, Chrystabel 115–16, 131
Professor's Garden 78
provost's garden *156*, 161
provost's lodge 158
Prunus (cherry): *P.* 'Asano' 207
    P. avium 'Plena' 275, *277*
    P. incisa 'Praecox' *101*, 104
    P. 'Kanzan' 105
    P. padus (bird cherry) *34*, 89
    P. serrula (Tibetan/paperbark cherry) 81, 127, 147, 221
    P. 'Shirofugen' 266
    P. 'Shirotae' 105
    P. 'Shogetsu' 201
    P. 'Tai-haku' *36*, *238*, 40, 239
    P. 'Umineko' 239
    P. x *yedoensis* 127, 246
    weeping 268, *269*
pseudopanax 67
Pterocarya x *rehderiana* 28
pulmonaria 62
pulsatilla 220
Pump Court 142, 146–7, 218, 220
Punica granatum 'Flore Pleno' 202–3
pyracantha 36, 62, 114, 291
Pyrus see pear

Q

Quadrangle, The 80, 84
Quayside 169
Queens' College 11, 16, **216–25**
Queen's Wing 133
Quercus (oak):
    Q. x *hispanica* 158
    Q. palustris 84
    Q. rubra (American red oak) 104, 147, 246
    Q. x *warburgii* (Cambridge Oak) 186
    fastigiate 186
    holm 143, 179, 238, 279, 307
    Lucombe 147
quince 113, 133, *157*, 160, 161, 298

R

Radegund Manor 140
Ramshaw, Wendy 49
Raphiolepis umbellata (Yeddo hawthorn) 245
Rath (Rats) Hall 253
Ray, John *272*, 282
Rayne Building 66, *70*
Rea, Betty 136
Red Buildings 199
Red Buildings Lawn *200*, 203
Rees, Trevor 245, 246
Renfrew, Colin 147
Renfrew, Jane 167
restharrow 184
restios 161
RH Partnership 299
rhamnus 203
rheum 40, 269
rhododendron 62, 220
Rhus typhina 36, 69, 115
Richards, Ivor 179
Ridley, Nicholas 203–4
Ridley's Walk 202, 203, 204
rills 28
River Court *170*, 177, *258*
River Garden 49
Roberts, David 118, 147

Roberts, David Wyn 264
Robinson College **225–31**
Robinson, David 230
Robinson Gillespie Kidd & Coia 228
Robinson, William 111
rock garden 204, 245, 303
Romilly, Joseph 14, 78, 266, 275
Roof-Climber's Guide to St John's 266
roof garden 223
roses:
    R. 'Abraham Derby' 136
    R. 'Albéric Barbier' 298
    R. 'Albertine' 298
    R. *banksiae* (Banksian rose) 63, 220, 298
    R. 'Blanche Double de Coubert' 137
    R. 'Bobbie James' 298, 300
    R. 'Cardinal de Richelieu' 184, 300
    R. 'Cécile Brünner' 183
    R. 'Claire Austin' 62
    R. 'Climbing Peace' 187
    R. 'Constance Spry' 51
    R. 'Crown Princess Margaret' 158
    R. 'Dublin Bay' 183, 220
    R. 'Duc de Guiche' 184
    R. 'Eden Rose 88' 263
    R. 'Ena Harkness' *113*
    R. 'Ferdinand Pichard' 184
    R. 'Francis E. Lester' 183
    R. 'François Juranville' 118, 183
    R. 'Freedom' 230
    R. *gallica* 'Versicolor' 136, 230
    R. 'Geranium' 300
    R. 'Gertrude Jekyll' 309
    R. 'Ginger Syllabub' 290
    R. 'Iceberg' 40, 194, 311
    R. 'Kew Rambler' 183
    R. 'La Sévillana' *197*, 201
    R. 'Louise Odier' 136
    R. 'Madame Alfred Carrière' 158, 220
    R. 'Madame Grégoire Staechelin' 118, 245
    R. 'Maid of Kent' 183
    R. 'Malvern Hills' 289
    R. 'Margaret Merril' 230, 269
    R. 'Meg' 220
    R. 'Mermaid' 51
    R. 'Molineux' 136
    R. 'Mousseux du Japon' 184
    R. 'Munstead Wood' 62
    R. x *odorata* 'Mutabilis' 295
    R. 'Paul's Himalayan Musk' 187, 283
    R. 'Penny Lane' 187
    R. 'Perpetually Yours' 290
    R. 'Queen of Hearts' 284
    R. 'Red Parfum' 309
    R. 'Rhapsody in Blue' 230
    R. *rugosa* 283
    R. 'Saint Swithun' 136
    R. 'Seagull' 187
    R. 'Sophie's Perpetual' 308
    R. 'Strawberry Hill' 161
    R. 'Teasing Georgia' 62, 300
    R. 'The Albrighton Rambler' 183
    R. 'The Generous Gardener' 62
    R. 'The Prince's Trust' 290
    R. 'Treasure Trove' 187
    R. 'Wedding Day' 161, 300
    R. 'Winchester Cathedral' 161, 301, 309
    Bourbon 136
    floribunda 36, 176
rosemary 20, 45, 118, 136, 144, 187
Rottenberg, Mr 231
Round Court 299, 300
Round Garden 300–1
Rowlandson, Thomas 151
Rubus thibetanus 103

S

Sackville-West, Vita 91
Sailing into the Future 228, 230
Sale, Bevis 175
Salix babylonica (dragon's claw willow) 230, 277
Salmon, Thomas 26, 47, 96, 214, 282
Salter, John 131
Salvin, Anthony 280, 292
sambucus (elder) 37, 203, 230, 238, 311
San Marco Horse 144, *144*, 147
Sandhurst 78

santolina 204
sarcococca 40, 62, 84, 103, 203, 247, 309
saxifrage 51, 212, 303
Sayers, Dorothy L. *248*
scabious 137
Sceaux tubs 184
Scholars' Garden *43*, 45, *47*
Scholar's Garden 176, 210, 214, 252, 264
Scholar's Lawn *271*, *275*, 277
Scholar's Piece *151*, 152, 155, 160
School of Pythagoras 266
scilla 175, 238, 263, 293
Scott, Alex 80
Scott, George Gilbert 200, 253, *266*, 268
Scott, Giles Gilbert 45
Seeley & Paget 133
Sellenger House 231
Selwyn, George Augustus 233
Selwyn College **232–9**
Sequoia sempervirens 204
Sequoiadendron giganteum (wellingtonia) 119, 158, 230, 262, 311
service tree, wild 111
sewage 13–14, 169, 295
Sharp, Thomas 264
Sheppard Robson & Partners 32, 33, 34
Sherwood, William 92
Shillington-Scales, Dr 231
Siberian salt tree *see Halimodendron argenteum*
Sidgwick, Henry 189–90
Sidgwick Hall 191
Sidgwick Memorial 192
Sidney, Lady Frances 241–2
Sidney Sussex College 9, **240–9**
silk tree *see* albizia
Simon, John 242
Simpson, John 213
sisyrinchium 51, 104, 221, 289, 300
skimmia 36, 53, 207, 238
Smith, B.T.D. 245
Smith, Keir 148
Solanum crispum 136, 158
solidago 49, 103, 246
Solomon's seal 70, 104, 115, 309
sophora *130*, 136, 220, 221, 229, 293
sorbus 194, 229, 268, 309
South Court 96, 137, 288–9
Sparrmannia africana (African hemp) 238
spectaculum 213
spectator's gallery 69
Spence, Basil 229
spiraea *34*, 52, 62, 104
spruce 119, 213, 230
St Catharine's College *13*
St Catherine's College, Oxford 34
St Edmund's College *17*
St John the Evangelist 252
St John's College 10, *12*, 12, 16, 165, **250–69**
St John's Ditch 256
St John's Hospital 9, 210
St John's Meadow 251, 256
St John's Walkes 256
St Mary the Less 212
St Pol, Marie de 207
St Radegund Garden 147
St Thomas's Hostel 197
stachys 49, 51, 114
Stachyurus praecox 136
Stanley, James 252
Stearn, William T. 245
Stephen, Lady 116
Stephen Hawking Building 127, *127*
Stevenson, John J. 67–9, 167
stew ponds *87*, 87, 152, 171, 174, 256
Stigwood, Phil 303, 307, 309
stipa *34*, 62, 85, 103, 104, 147, 307
strawberries 167
strawberry tree *see Arbutus*
Stretching Figure 136
Stringer, William 'Mac' 113
strobilanthes 204
Stukeley, William 278
succulents 69, 187
Sundial Garden 306, *308*, 311
sundials *109*, 136, 179, 202, 213, 272, 283, *284*
sunflower 62
swans 155, 273

sweet woodruff 300
swimming pools 13, *25*, 26, 63, 93
Sylva 223
Symphoricarpos x *chenaultii* 309

T

tagetes 268
tamarisk 279
Tang sculpture *307*, 308
Taylor, Wendy *96*
Temperance statue 308
Tennis Court Green 277
Tennyson, Alfred 26, 275
Terry, Quinlan 81, 85
tetrapanax 280
Teucrium fruticans 204
thatched buildings 91, 96, 148, 283
The Now 41
Thijsse, J.P. 228
Thoday, Ralph 264
Thomas, William Broderick 283
Thompson, George 156
Thomson, Lady 231
Thomson, Richard 133
Thorneycreek 228, *228*
thrift 51
thuja 117, 158
thyme 118
tiarella 220
Tilia see lime
Tindall, Humphrey 219
tithonia 171, 177, 195, 269, 278, 284
Tomlinson, Harold 49
torch thistle 282
torchère finial 207
tower mustard 263
trachelospermum 20, 136, 201
Trachycarpus fortunei 67, 102, 237
Tree Court 100, 101, 104, *105*, 121, *122*, 122, 124, *124*
tree fern *see Dicksonia*
Tree Form, Size and Colour 229
tree peony 308
trellis 223
Tricyrtis (toad lily) 103, 219
Trinity Bridge *12*, 277
Trinity Chapel 272
Trinity College 9, 10, *11*, 13, 16, 242, **270–85**
Trinity College Meadow 277
Trinity Hall 8, **286–301**
Trinity Hall Gin 298
Trudgill, Dr Stephen 231
tulip tree *see Liriodendron tulipifera*
Turkish hazel *see Corylus colurna*
Turnbull, William 147
Turner, Dr William 204
Twelve 300, 300
Two Forms 81
Tyrrell, Steve 223

U

Ulmus see elm
undergraduates' access to gardens 10
University College 304
University Old Schools 151

V

valerian 186
veronica 158, 289
veronicastrum 144, 292, 311
viburnum 36, 37, 103, 105, 153, 308
Victoria, Queen 271
Victorian Border *234*, *237*, 237–8
Virginia creeper 13, 32, 146, 245
    see also Parthenocissus
Vlasto, Alexis 237
von Schoenaich, Brita 69, 194

W

Wakefield Bridge 70
Walker, Revd Richard 'Frog' 282
Walnut Tree Court 220, *224*
Ward, Samuel 23
Warren, William 288, 291–2, 297
water garden 114
water meadow 224
Water-Works 201
watercourses 13–14, 228, 242, 256

Waterhouse, Alfred 108, 109, 118, 124, 146, 199–200
Waterhouse, Michael 117, 118
Waterhouse Building *148*
Watson, W.C. 193
Webb, James 78
Webb's Court 160
weigela 301
wellingtonia *see Sequoiadendron gigantea*
Welsh, Elizabeth 113
West House 137
West Lodge Garden 85
Weymouth pine *see Pinus strobus*
Whewell's Courts 280
whitebeam *122*, 183, 300
    see also sorbus
Wild Garden, The 111
Wilderness, the 252, 257–8, 261, 263
wildflower meadow 63, 105, *111*, 119, *167*
wildlife areas 49, 166
Wilkins, William 57, *76*, 76–8, 153, 157, 275
William Stone Building 214
Willmer, Nevill 49, 51, 268
Willoughby, Richard 58
Wilson Court 105
window boxes 212
wingnut 147
Winter Garden *308*, *309*, 309
wintersweet 53
witch hazel 103
Wittgenstein, Ludwig 280, 284
Wolfson College 16, **302–11**
wood rush 104
Woodlands 113
Woodlands Court 115, 116, 117–18
Woodville, Elizabeth 217
Wordsworth, William and Dorothy 262
Wordsworth Oak 262
Wrangham, Archdeacon 289
Wren, Christopher 44, 88, 199, 259, 273
Wren Library *271*, *273*, 273
Wren Bridge 262, *266*
Wren's chapel *197*, 199
Wyatt, James 78
Wyatville, Jeffry 244
Wychfield 182, *295*, 298–9, *300*, 301

X

Xanthoceras sorbifolium (yellowhorn) 158
Xiaotian Fu Garden 41
Xú Zhimó 161–3

Y

yales 252, 262, *268*, 268
Yeddo hawthorn *see Raphiolepis umbellata*
yellowhorn *see Xanthoceras sorbifolium*
Yew Walk 113
Youngman, Peter 17
yucca 103, 237

Z

zinnia 290

THE GARDENERS

CHRIST'S COLLEGE
Left to right: Martin Morris, Tania Pauley, Andy Pullin, Jenny Allwood and Sergio Ballarin (head gardener).

CHURCHILL COLLEGE
Left to right: Michael Westmore (head gardener), John Moore (head of gardens and grounds), Hayden Crane, Katherine Banarse, Kevin Hill, Stephen Farrington, Dave Hale.

CLARE COLLEGE
Left to right: Jesse Morris, Clare Milton, Steve Elstub (head gardener), Kate Hargreaves, John Mears, Josh Seaward.

CLARE HALL
Left to right: David Smith (head gardener), Andrew Graves, Paul Haynes.

CORPUS CHRISTI COLLEGE
Left to right: Dave Barton (head gardener), Verena Downes, Tim Bennett.

DARWIN COLLEGE
Left to right: Rod Ailes, Ros Keep, Dr Torsten Krude (garden steward), Andrew Burkett.

DOWNING COLLEGE
Left to right: Stacey Braybrook, Chris Light, Jason Causton, Paul Crudge, Jack Sharp (head gardener).

EMMANUEL COLLEGE
Left to right: Christoph Keate (head gardener), Oliver Macdonald, Craig Gibson, Kimberley Mcilwain, Philip Bland, Adam Whitley.

FITZWILLIAM COLLEGE
Left to right: Nick Squires, Camelia Manzoori, Steve Kidger (head gardener).

GIRTON COLLEGE
Left to right: Richard Hewitt, Steven Andrews, Pat Lambert, Colin Osborn.

GONVILLE & CAIUS COLLEGE
Left to right: Kevin Cook, Phil Brett (head gardener), Tyrone O'Rourke, Chris Ford.

HOMERTON COLLEGE
Left to right: Angus O'Brien, Helen Andre Cripps (head gardener), Jonathan Davies, Robert Day, Matt Menezes.

JESUS COLLEGE
Left to right: Paul Stearn (head gardener), George Soames, Colin Dunn, Michael Andrews, Liam Collis, Michael Morris, Duane Keedy.

KING'S COLLEGE
Left to right: Martin Larkman, Steve Coghill (head gardener), Bob Mark, Alan Evans, Julia Andersson.

LUCY CAVENDISH COLLEGE
Left to right: Rebecca Anderson, Vince Lucas (head gardener), Annette Caine, Alison Lucas.

MAGDALENE COLLEGE
Left to right: Mark R. Scott (head gardener), Lorraine M. Wright, Cairo Robb, Andy Clarke.

MURRAY EDWARDS COLLEGE
Left to right: Jo Cobb (head gardener), Zach Wright, Peter Kirkham.

NEWNHAM COLLEGE
Left to right: Paul Anderson, Hannah Heinemann, Lottie Collis (head gardener), Bee Piper, Chris Thurgood, Andy Ward.

THE GARDENERS

PEMBROKE COLLEGE
Left to right: Gary Speed, Nick Firman (head gardener), Lee Gawthrop, Sebastian Filipe.

PETERHOUSE
Left to right: Daniel Osborne, Daniel Ford (head gardener), Sally Wright.

QUEENS' COLLEGE
Left to right: Stephen Tyrrell (head gardener), Clare Watkinson, Peter Maiden, David Garlick, Ross Albon.

ROBINSON COLLEGE
Left to right: Paul Horner, Nick Ashford, Guy Fuller (head gardener), Ginny Barker, Danny Lawler.

SELWYN COLLEGE
Left to right: Alex Turner (head gardener), Emily Passmore, Laurie McPhun, Paul Baldry, Sam Weekes.

SIDNEY SUSSEX COLLEGE
Left to right: Stuart Cross, Trevor Rees (head gardener), Michael Maskell, Travis Kiddy.

ST CATHARINE'S COLLEGE
Left to right: Alan North (head gardener), Brian Phillips, Josh Bennett.

ST JOHN'S COLLEGE
Left to right: Mick Ranford, Rosanna Bailey, Adam Green (head gardener), Zoe Cullen, Shaun Mayes, David Brown, Peter Helme and Jed the dog.

TRINITY COLLEGE
Left to right: Tim Beswick, John Page, Rebecca Palmer, Sarah Claydon, Lee Froggatt, Takashi Tomura, Karen Wells, Jonathan Strauss, Tom Hooijenga (head gardener), Sarah Squires, Joy Ridgeway. Absent: Tony Harte, Andy Mead.

TRINITY HALL
Left to right: Richard Macarthy, Alicia Fordham, Graham Hale, Sam Hartley (head gardener), Chris Challis, Frances Pettitt, Louise Cook.

WOLFSON COLLEGE
Left to right: Luke Hale, Phil Stigwood (head gardener), Philip De Luca, Oscar Holgate.

CAMBRIDGE BOTANIC GARDEN
Left to right: Mark Crouch, Jessica Tyler, Alistair Godfrey, Barbara Griffith, David Austrin, Amy Spencer, Peter Michna, Sally Petitt (head of horticulture), Elizabeth Mansfield, Peter Wrapson, Louise Searle, Ciaran Bradshaw, Simon Wallis, Adrian Holmes, Alistair Cochrane, John Kapor, Paul Aston, Alexander Summers.

PHOTOGRAPHER'S ACKNOWLEDGEMENTS

The work on this project could not have had a worse start. The photographer and our friend Marcus Harpur was already ill, but had been given five years to live. I began to help him, driving-carrying in the hope he would be able to finish this book; alas this was not to be, as his advancing cancer became rapid in the extreme. On his last day of work, less than two weeks before he died, I promised Marcus I would finish his book; my contribution is to the memory of Marcus Harpur.

I deeply thank for their support Tim Richardson, and our editor Helen Griffin, who has been a champion in putting up with me and helping in every way possible.

A big thank you to Dr Michael and Gillian Nedo, and Isabelle Wiess, who so generously gave me total use of their respective homes which I could work from, making this project achievable for me.

To all the head gardeners and their teams who were utterly supportive, special thanks to Lottie Collis of Newnham College who so warmly welcomed me into my first college garden, which gave me the confidence I could complete this book for Marcus; also Steven Coghill, Steve Elstub, Tom Hooijenga, Adam Mcgee, Sally Petitt – in fact all, too many to name here.

I thank all the college porters for making me feel so at home with my early morning comings and goings over the past year. To Professor Andy Neely, Pro Vice Chancellor at the University of Cambridge. Thank you Tom Miller and Yulia Emelyanova for the help in preparing some of my pictures for publication. For Barbara who once again had to put up with my dashing off to Cambridge at a moment's notice for days at a time.

I have a passion for the college gardens and Cambridge as a whole in all its seasons and light. I photographed far more than could ever be printed, such was the immense privilege to have been able to work in all the colleges with the trust that was given to me; this will remain forever in my heart as a very special time. Thank you.

AUTHOR'S ACKNOWLEDGEMENTS

First I would like to acknowledge the contribution of Marcus Harpur, with whom I embarked on this book. Marcus continued working for as long as he possibly could, and the fact he was able to contribute as much as he did is testament to his determination as a person and his skill as a photographer. There could be no consolations after Marcus's untimely death, but it was fortunate and fitting that our friend Clive Boursnell was able to step in and continue the project in his own inimitable style. My thanks to Clive for his dedication to the task.

The head gardeners of all the colleges have been helpful and welcoming. They are all featured in the gallery on the preceding pages. My thanks to them all. In addition I would like to acknowledge those who have recently retired or moved on: Robert Bramley (Girton), Richard Thompson (Homerton), Paul Gallant (Selwyn), Andrew Myson (Trinity Hall).

I would like to thank the following college archivists, many of whom were most generous with their time: Paula Laycock (Churchill), Jude Brimmer (Clare), Lucy Hughes (Corpus Christi), Jenny Ulph (Downing), Amanda Goode (Emmanuel), Hannah Westall (Girton), S. Paterson (Homerton), Robert Athol (Jesus), Patricia McGuire (King's), Peter Monteith (King's), Tilda Watson (Magdalene, Girton), Jayne Ringrose (Pembroke), Nicholas Rogers (Sidney Sussex), Tracy Deakin (St John's), Jonathan Smith (Trinity), Adam Green (Trinity), Anna Crutchley (Trinity Hall, Jesus), Frieda Midgley (Wolfson).

College librarians have also been helpful in several cases: John Wagstaff (Christ's), Bethany Slater (Christ's), Alexander Devine (Corpus Christi), Rhona Watson (Jesus), Alan Stevens (Sidney Sussex). I would also like to acknowledge the assistance of the staff in the Rare Books Reading Room of the British Library.

Certain fellows, garden fellows and fellow archivists have also been most helpful: Geoffrey T. Martin (Christ's), Torsten Krude (Darwin), David Pratt (Downing), Alison Vinnicombe (Lucy Cavendish), Jane Hughes (Magdalene), Kanak Patel (Magdalene), Debbie Banham (Newnham), Alan Hayhurst (Queens'), Jonathan Holmes (Queens'), Stephen Trudgill (Robinson).

I would like to thank: Anthony Bowen (Jesus) for permission to reproduce in part his Latin ode to the plane tree, and for some help with Latin; Andrew Peters for information about Fitzwilliam and Trinity Hall; Roger Lovatt for help at Peterhouse, including commenting on the early history of the college; Peter Coles, for information about mulberries; and the master, fellows and scholars of Christ's College for kind permission to quote from the 'garden book'.

Thanks to the following heads of colleges for their kind co-operation: the Mistress of Girton, Susan J. Smith, and the Master of Emmanuel, Fiona Reynolds.

I would like to thank the following friends and colleagues for their assistance: Michael Hall, Jeremy Musson, Robert Myers, Marc Treib. The books by Jane Brown on Girton, Newnham and Trinity have been useful with regard to those colleges and I acknowledge Ursula Lyons's book 'A Treasure of a Garden' as the source for much material on Lucy Cavendish. Tim Rawle's *Cambridge Architecture* has been my constant companion as the best modern guide to the built fabric.

Thanks are due to Helen Griffin at White Lion for commissioning the book and Andrew Dunn of Frances Lincoln for his support of the project. I would like to thank designer Sarah Pyke and managing editor Emma Harverson for their roles. Sarah Zadoorian has been a discerning and dedicated copy-editor who improved the book considerably, just as she did with *Oxford College Gardens*.